世界遗产与可持续发展
WORLD HERITAGE AND SUSTAINABLE DEVELOPMENT

国家文物局　主编

Edited by the State Administration of Cultural Heritage
People's Republic of China

文物出版社
Cultural Relics Press

责任编辑　吴　湘　长　安

责任印制　陆　联

封面装帧　希　广

图书在版编目（CIP）数据

世界遗产与可持续发展：中文、英文／国家文物局主编．—北京：文物出版社，2012.6

ISBN 978 - 7 - 5010 - 3465 - 9

Ⅰ.①世…　Ⅱ.①国…　Ⅲ.①文化遗产 – 可持续发展 – 中国 – 文集 – 汉、英

Ⅳ.①G12 – 53

中国版本图书馆 CIP 数据核字（2012）第 103351 号

世界遗产与可持续发展

国家文物局　主编

＊

文 物 出 版 社 出 版 发 行

（北京市东城区东直门内北小街 2 号楼）

http：//www.wenwu.com

E-mail：web@wenwu.com

北京联华宏凯印刷公司印刷

新 华 书 店 经 销

889×1194　1/16　印张：20.5

2012 年 6 月第 1 版　2012 年 6 月第 1 次印刷

ISBN 978 - 7 - 5010 - 3465 - 9　定价：120.00 元

谨以此书纪念联合国教科文组织

《保护世界文化和自然遗产公约》40周年

This book is dedicated to the 40th Anniversary of UNESCO's

Convention Concerning the Protection of the World Cultural and Natural Heritage

目　录

序　言

　　1972 年，联合国教科文组织通过了《保护世界文化与自然遗产公约》，开始在全世界范围内推动对于具有突出普遍价值的文化和自然遗产的保护行动。中国于 1985 年加入该公约后，积极参与相关国际事务，在世界遗产申报、保护、管理和相关国际交流等方面做出了不懈的努力，取得了举世瞩目的成绩。至 2011 年底，中国已拥有 41 处世界遗产，其中世界文化遗产 29 处，世界文化与自然双重遗产 4 处。

　　国家文物局作为中国世界文化遗产的主管部门，一直高度重视和积极推进世界文化遗产的申报、保护、管理和研究工作。近年，国家文物局通过开展《中国世界文化遗产预备名单》更新工作，进一步加强申报项目储备，提高遗产保护和申报质量。并且组织实施了山海关长城、承德避暑山庄及周围寺庙等一批世界文化遗产重大保护工程，开展了中国世界文化遗产监测预警体系建设工作，世界文化遗产的保护、展示、监测、管理水平显著提高。

　　同时，国家文物局组织专业力量，深入开展世界文化遗产的专题研究。根据世界遗产事业发展的国际形势以及国内遗产保护管理实践活动的客观需求，在对各遗产地进行深入调查的基础上，结合国外相关理论和案例分析，全面、系统地分析现阶段中国世界文化遗产的发展状况，总结提炼出适应中国世界文化遗产特点的保护理念和方法，为充分发挥世界文化遗产的重要影响，广泛动员各利益相关群体的参与，促进遗产地经济社会的全面、协调和可持续发展提供了重要的理论和研究基础。

　　2012 年是《保护世界文化与自然遗产公约》诞生 40 周年，联合国教科文组织世界遗产委员会发起了主题为"世界遗产与可持续发展"的纪念活动，得到了世界各国的积极响应。国家文物局组织开展了一系列纪念活动，《世界遗产与可持续发展》一书的出版就是其中的重要内容。本书编选了近年来国家文物局组织相关高校、科研院所开展的世界文化遗产专题研究的部分成果，包括世界文化遗产保护与遗产地经济发展、文化景观、文化线路申报世界遗产、世界文化遗产地可持续发展模式与评估体系、世界文化遗产与社区发展等 5 个项目的研究报告中英文概要。

　　这些报告反映了中国同行对世界遗产一些重要问题的认识和理解。今后，随着世界文化遗产保护和研究工作的深入，还会有更多新的研究成果涌现出来，不断深化我们对这些问题的思考与探索。我们希望，本书的出版，能够帮助更多的人了解中国的世界文化遗产，了解相关工作的发展历程和未来走向；为各遗产地的保护、管理工作提供参考，以期进一步增强遗产地能力建设，切实提高中国世界文化遗产保护管理的理论与实践水平。

　　在此，谨以此书，隆重纪念《保护世界文化与自然遗产公约》诞生 40 周年，并向长期以来为中国世界文化遗产事业创立和发展做出卓越贡献的遗产地政府、有关部门、保护管理机构、专家学者和社会各界的朋友们，致以最诚挚的感谢和最崇高的敬意！同时，藉以此书，表达中国同行积极践行《公约》精神，全力推进世界文化遗产事业可持续发展的信心与行动。

国家文物局

Preface

The United Nations Educational, Scientific and Cultural Organization (UNESCO for short hereinafter) has launched a worldwide cause to promote the protection of cultural and natural heritage of outstanding universal value since 1972 when it adopted *the Convention Concerning the Protection of the World Cultural and Natural Heritage* (*the Convention* for short hereinafter). Ratifying *the Convention* in 1985, China has actively participated in relative international affairs and made unremitting efforts in the nomination, protection and management of the world heritage and in international exchanges in this field, making world-renowned progress. By the end of 2011, China had had 41 world heritage properties, including 29 cultural sites and 4 mixed sites.

The State Administration of Cultural Heritage (SACH for short hereinafter) is the competent authority responsible for the world cultural heritage in China and always attaches great important to and makes active efforts on the nomination, protection, management and research of the world cultural heritage. In recent years, SACH increased property reserves and strengthened heritage conservation by timely updating the China's Tentative List for World Heritage Inscription. Meanwhile, SACH has launched major protection programs for a batch of the world cultural heritage including the Shanhaiguan Pass-section of the Great Wall, the Mountain Resort and its Outlying Temples in Chengde, and started the establishment of the monitoring and pre-warning system for China's world cultural heritage sites. All such efforts have significantly improved the protection, display, monitoring and management of the world cultural heritage.

Meanwhile, SACH organized professional teams to conduct thematic studies on the world cultural heritage. Focusing on the latest development of the world heritage and the actual needs in the practical protection and management of domestic cultural heritage, these thematic studies based on in-depth investigation of heritage sites and relative theoretical analysis and case study abroad, have yielded the concept and methods of the protection and management suitable for the world cultural heritage. They presented a panoramic and systematic picture of the current status in this regard in China, provided sufficient theoretical bases for strengthening the protection and management of all new types of cultural heritage, and laid a solid theoretical foundation for giving full play to the important influence of the world cultural heritage, encouraging the wide participation of all stakeholders and promoting the all-around, coordinated and sustainable social and economic development in the heritage sites.

In Year 2012, to celebrate the 40th anniversary of *the Convention* this year, the UNESCO World Heritage Center launched the "World Heritage and Sustainable Development" campaign, and received enthusiastic response from States Parties all over the world. SACH has organized a series of activities, including the publication of *The World Heritage and Sustainable Development* as an important part. The book covers the research results of world heritage projects entrusted to some institutes, including 5 thematic study summaries on World Cultural Heritage Protection and Economic Development in the Heritage Sites, Nomination of the Cultural Route for the World Heritage, Cultural Landscape, the Sustainable Development Mode and Appraisal System in World Cultural Heritage Sites, World Cultural Heritage and the Community Development.

These thematic studies reflect Chinese professionals' knowledge and understanding on some major issues concerning the world heritage. As efforts on protecting and researching the world cultural heritage go further in future, we will reap more fruits from research and will have deepened deliberation and exploration on these issues. We hope the publication of the book will help more people know about China's world cultural heritage and about the development and the future of our projects; meanwhile, we also hope it will provide professional reference for the protection and management of the heritage sites with the view of strengthening the capability building of the heritage sites and substantially improving the capacity to manage and protect the world cultural heritage in China.

This book is hereby dedicated to the 40ᵗʰ anniversary of *the Convention concerning the Protection of the World Cultural and Natural Heritage*. Also heartfelt gratitude and best respect shall be given to governments of heritage sites, departments, protection authorities, scholars and experts and friends from all walks of life for their outstanding contribution to the initiation and development of the world cultural heritage cause in China. Besides, this book is also to convey Chinese colleagues' determination and confidence to carry out the spirit of *the Convention* and promote the sustainable development of international cultural heritage cause with all their might.

State Administration of Cultural Heritage
People's Republic of China

中国世界文化遗产保护与遗产地
经济发展研究报告摘要

清华大学

摘　要

　　截至2009年，中国参与联合国教科文组织世界文化遗产项目已有22年，在联合国教科文组织世界文化遗产名录上拥有31个文化遗产地（包括4处混合遗产）。在申遗成功给这些文化遗产带来响亮的国际声誉的同时，也对其自身以及周边城市、乡村、地区的文物保护、经济、社会和环境的发展带来了显著的影响。

　　"中国世界文化遗产保护与遗产地经济发展"课题研究基于对以上31处中国世界文化遗产地的数据收集整理，总结了中国世界文化遗产地的使用和经营状况，从经济指标、产业结构调整和旅游发展等方面分析、评价了遗产地所在城镇的经济社会发展。研究选择了5处中国世界遗产地作为重点研究对象，并另选5处国际案例作为比对。通过分析研究，本课题建议根据遗产地不同资质特点选取不同开发模式，探索未来发展的可能性。研究也尝试对文物保护对地方经济发展的影响范围、过程及其长期结果建立评价系统，评估当前的策略，并建议建立长期的数据监测结构，以支持对与文化遗产地相关城镇经济社会发展的深入了解。

　　这是中国首次在文物保护的经济方面进行学术讨论，首先研究文化旅游对遗产保护背景的影响，第一次覆盖全中国世界文化遗产地的经济案例研究，第一次从文化遗产可持续发展的视角，讨论、评价经济发展与遗产保护管理体制。以下报告是这一研究报告的缩写。

　　关键词：世界文化遗产，可持续发展，保护经济学

第一部分　课题背景·研究大纲

本部分介绍了课题背景和研究大纲。课题背景包括研究目的、基本概念界定和对研究案例选择的说明；研究大纲则包括主要研究方法的选择和技术路线的制定。由于篇幅所限，本研究节选对原有报告的国内外具体案例部分内容进行了精简和顺序调整，着重介绍研究方法和主要结论。

1　课题背景

（1）研究目的

本研究的根本目的在于：掌握中国世界文化遗产地保护和发展的总体状况及其对所在地经济社会发展的影响，包括综合效益、影响机制、现存问题等，提出改善的措施建议。本研究包括以下主要内容：1）对中国已有世界文化遗产地自身经营状况及其对当地经济社会发展的影响进行全方位的调查分析，建立对遗产地经济社会发展状况的评价指标和数据库；综合分析遗产地对地方经济发展的影响，品牌价值、知名度和美誉度的变化，以及本地居民在遗产地发展过程中受益的主要途径、份额、参与程度和满意度。

2）选择典型案例，对遗产地申报前后的长期状况进行分析，探讨遗产地对于当地经济社会发展的促进模式、产生的效益及其变化、遗产经济发展与文物保护的影响等问题。3）结合典型国外遗产地案例的分析，讨论不同模式的利弊。4）总结现状，提出完善中国世界文化遗产地保护、发展、管理机制的有效措施；提出有利于遗产地可持续发展的策略和建议。

（2）基本概念界定

世界遗产地的经济发展研究主要涉及的相关理论基础包括以下七个方面：（1）文化遗产保护理论；（2）文化经济学理论；（3）保护经济学理论；（4）公共经济学理论；（5）福利经济学理论；（6）可持续发展理论；（7）城市规划相关理论。其中"文化遗产保护理论"、"可持续发展理论"、"城市规划相关理论"是本研究的基础理论，同时研究还借鉴了"文化经济学"、"保护经济学"、"公共经济学"、"福利经济学"理论。

而保护经济学（conservation economics）作为本研究的核心理论，主要用于探讨建成文化遗产涉及的经济活动规律和影响。保护经济学为研究文化遗产提供了新的视角，使我们能够从更广泛的方面认识文化遗产的价值，提供了从经济学角度审视文化遗产相关概念和基本理论的根据，以及对文化遗产成本、效益充分认识并进行相关分析的方法。

基于保护经济学，本课题的几个重要基本观点和涉及的概念如下：

■ **文化遗产是一种特殊的"文化资本"**

保护经济学的基础在于承认文化遗产作为一种具有文化和经济双重价值的"文化资本"（cultural capital）。这里的"资本"被认为既是一种价值的储藏，也是一种长期的资产（asset），能产生一系列长周期的成本和效益，由此可以把文化遗产如普通商品一样置于生产和消费过程之中进行分析。作为一种文化资本，本研究将"文化遗产"理解为一种具有丰富构成的资源，其构成要素根据不同特点可分为自然、人造和人类资源。文化遗产在某种程度上与"固定资产"具有相似性，同样面临着"折旧"的问题，但由于文化遗产的不可再生性，则须谨慎地对待文化遗产的利用与保护之间的关系。

■ **对文化遗产效益的多重认知**

文化遗产项目的效益可从三个层次认知（Throsby，2001）。一是使用效益，即项目产生的直接产品和服务。二是非使用效益，如：遗产的内在价值；存在价值——遗产的存在、选择价值——为其他人或者后代保存对遗产消费的选择权利；遗赠价值——遗产的价值能可持续地传给后代人。三是外部效益，即对其他经济领域的连带影响。

如果对其进行更细致的划分，可以根据影响分为直接效益和间接效益。直接效益，主要指遗产利用产生的经济效益；间接效益则包括由保护项目导致的相关行业的效益和未来支出的潜在减少，以及相关社会效益等。

■ **对文化遗产地研究范围的分类界定**

保护经济学从遗产地的影响区域和影响人群的角度，界定了文化遗产地的研究范围。首先，从地理区位的角度，将研究范围分为三个层次：1）遗产地本体区域（property zone，核心区）和缓冲区（buffer zone）。2）遗产地所在地方城市，或遗产地周边城区范围。3）遗产地所在区域、城市群。本研究按照这一结构，将研究分为世界遗产地及世界遗产所在地两个层次。

世界文化遗产地是世界文化遗产赖以生存的物质空间载体，在研究中参考世界文化遗产申报文本中划定的保护区范围，主要包括核心区和缓冲区。

世界文化遗产地所在地产地及直接管理遗产地的机构或部门所属的市县级行政区划，主要包括县、县级市、直辖市或地级市的市辖区。

（3）案例选择

本研究在案例的选择上主要考虑到遗产类型、申遗时间、所属经济地理区域、列入名录的标准和申遗动机。在中国世界遗产中，本研究选择了 21 处遗产作为本课题的研究对象（详见表 1 - 1），覆盖了所有的四个经济地理区域和六种遗产类型①（图 1 - 1 及 1 - 2）。在其中又进一步对数据和资料收集情况最理想的 6 处遗产地进行详细研究，即承德避暑山庄及外八庙、丽江古城、福建土楼、敦煌莫高窟、澳门、平遥古城。本研究节选由于篇幅有限，重在方法介绍与探讨，故以总体为主，暂不包含详细个案。

表 1 - 1　本研究选取的 26 个国内遗产地案例基本情况

编号	中文名称	列入时间	所在城镇	所处经济地理分区和城镇级别
山岳型遗产地				
1	泰山	1987 年	山东省泰安市	东部沿海，地级市区
2	黄山	1990 年	安徽省黄山市区	中部地区，地级市区
3	武当山古建筑群	1994 年	湖北省十堰市丹江口市	中部地区，县级市
4	武夷山风景名胜区	1999 年	福建省南平市武夷山市	东部沿海，县级市
城镇历史中心				
5	平遥古城	1997 年	山西省晋中市平遥县	中部地区，县城
6	丽江古城	1997 年	云南省丽江市	西部地区，地级市
7	澳门历史中心	2005 年	澳门特别行政区	东部沿海，特区
民居村落				
8	皖南古村落——西递、宏村	2000 年	安徽省黄山市黟县	中部地区，县城
9	福建土楼（永定土楼）	2008 年	福建省龙岩市永定县	东部沿海，县城
10	福建土楼（南靖土楼）	2008 年	福建省漳州市南靖县	东部沿海，县城
11	福建土楼（华安土楼）	2008 年	福建省漳州市华安县	东部沿海，县城
大型历史建筑群				
12	承德避暑山庄及周围寺庙	1994 年	河北省承德市区	东部沿海，地级市区
13	曲阜孔庙孔林孔府	1994 年	山东省济宁市曲阜市	东部沿海，县级市
14	苏州园林	1997 年	江苏省苏州市区	东部沿海，地级市
15	青城山—都江堰灌溉系统	2000 年	四川省都江堰市	西部地区，县级市 *
16	明清皇家陵寝（清东陵）	2000 年	河北省唐山市遵化市	东部沿海，县级市
17	明清皇家陵寝（十三陵）	2003 年	北京市昌平区	东部沿海，直辖市区
18	明清皇家陵寝（永陵）	2004 年	辽宁省抚顺市新宾满族自治县	东北地区，自治县城

① 遗产类型主要参考 UNESCO 早期遗产申报的三个分类，包括纪念物（Monuments）、建筑群（Groups of Buildings）和遗址（Sites），并根据我国实际情况、遗产地与所在城镇的关系和遗产旅游特征略作调整。

续表

编号	中文名称	列入时间	所在城镇	所处经济地理分区和城镇级别
考古遗址				
19	秦始皇陵	1987 年	陕西省西安市临潼区	中部地区，地级市区
20	周口店"北京人"遗址	1987 年	北京市房山区	东部沿海，直辖市区
21	高句丽王城、王陵及贵族墓葬（五女山城）	2004 年	辽宁省本溪市桓仁满族自治县	东北地区，自治县城
22	高句丽王城、王陵及贵族墓葬	2004 年	吉林省通化市集安市	东北地区，县级市
23	殷墟	2006 年	河南省安阳市区	中部地区，地级市
石窟遗址				
24	敦煌莫高窟	1987 年	甘肃省敦煌市	西部地区，县级市
25	大足石刻	1999 年	重庆市大足县	西部地区，县城
26	云冈石窟	2001 年	山西省大同市	中部地区，地级市

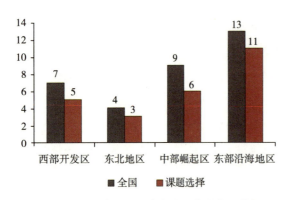

图 1-1   各经济地理区域内的文化遗产地数量

注：＊为省直辖县级市

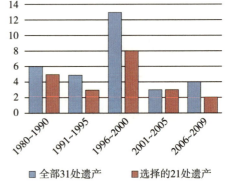

图 1-2   入遗时间分布

2   研究大纲

（1）研究方法

本课题主要从经济和社会两方面对中国世界文化遗产保护与遗产地经济发展进行研究探讨。研究思路（见图 1-3）和方法简述如下：

■   **社会学方法——考察、访谈及问卷调查等**

本研究希望打破经济学对于"地区发展"的话语垄断，尝试从更为多元化的角度思考发展的问题，建立更为全面的评价标准。社会学方法中的考察、访谈及问卷调查等研究方法不仅帮助本研究获取了大量一手资料，也有助于深入了解不同利益相关群体对遗产地之于地方发展影响的态度。

■   **经济学方法之一——成本—收益分析与影响分析**

在分析遗产地管理机构经营绩效时主要应用了成本—收益分析方法，目的在于考察遗产地的经营绩效与保护工程进展状况。用于分析遗产地自身的具体方法有财务分析、社会成本收益分析等。在分析遗产地对所在城镇的影响时，研究主要应用了影响分析方法，以此确定直接影响和间接影响和引致影响，分层次地展示遗产对于所在城镇带来的经济、社会效益。

■ **经济学方法之二——计量回归分析**

本课题采用计量回归分析的方法，用以判断具体案例中申遗事件或其他重大事件对于此后所在地旅游业发展（如游客人数增长）的影响，以及遗产地保护投入对整个地区经济和就业的引致影响。

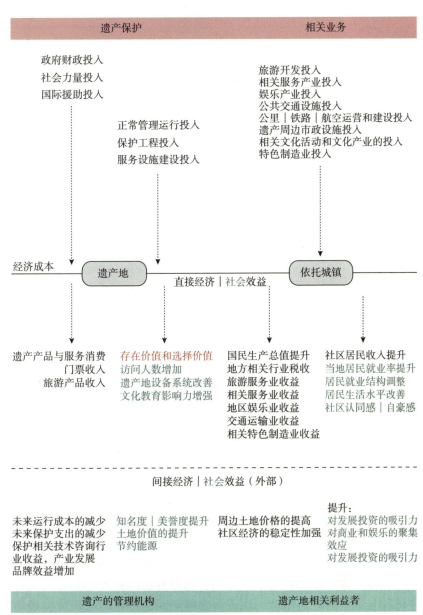

图 1-3 遗产地及其所在城镇"投入—收益"分析思路

（2）技术路线

遗产地分类及考察范围本研究总体上包括三个主要部分，一是中国世界文化遗产与所在地的保护与经济社会发展整体现状调查分析，二是重点案例详细分析，三是国外相关理论、研究的综述及相关案例研究部分。在这三部分的研究基础上，课题最后尝试建立起中国世界文化遗产与所在城镇保护与经济社会发展状况综合评价体系，并对未来遗产地的保护、管理、利用和所在城镇发展政策提出合理化建议。（见图1-4）

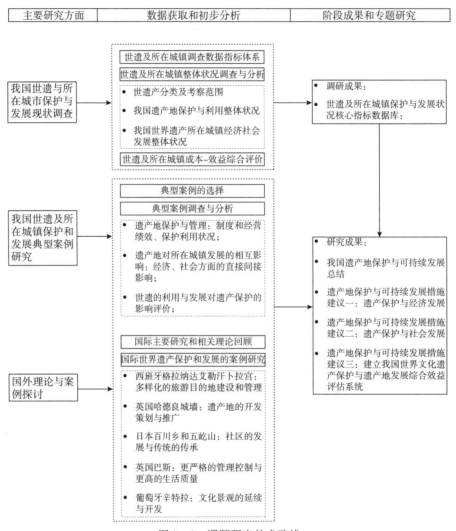

图 1-4   课题研究技术路线

第二部分   中国世界文化遗产地·利用和经营状况

本部分探讨了世界遗产地利用和可能产生的效益，总结了中国遗产地的利用和经营状况。

从利用状况看，中国遗产地产生的社会效益包括：选择价值的延续、游客的消费者剩余、工作岗位和劳务收入、增强的邻里关系、对社区教育、交流的贡献和对遗产宣传、认知的推动等；经济效益主要体现在支付价格上，主要包括门票收入和直接经营收入。

从经营状况看，中国绝大多数遗产地最为重要的收入来源是门票收入，但重要保护项目的资金来源必须依靠国家财政；对遗产地的保护仍多处于以大修为主的阶段，日常维护的投入，监测、精细管理、研究的投入尚不显著；且绝大多数遗产地在环境整治项目上的经费、时间投入都数倍于本体保护工程。

1   世界遗产地利用及产生的效益

世界遗产地与当代人的交流多种多样，其利用方式也有很多种，如，旅游休闲、公共空间、科研基地、教育基地、非物质文化遗产传承空间，甚至很多情况下是日常生活、商业活动的空间。根据不同的遗产地价值、特性和脆弱程度，其使用和保护的侧重有所不同。这里必须以保护为根本，区别对待不同遗产地，甚至某一遗产地的不同构成部分，在不对遗产地造成破坏的前提下适度地使用开发。从经济学角度来看，文化遗产是不可再生的文化资产，对文化遗产的保护和管理就意味着延续和管理我们未来共同的经济收益。

（1）中国遗产地产生的社会效益

依据《保护经济学：关于文化建成遗产的成本效益分析》（ICOMOS，1993）① 中关于文化遗产直接和间接效益的内容，结合本节探讨，可以针对中国世界遗产地的利用方式，综合归纳出其保护和利用带来的遗产地自身直接和间接效益。主要体现在如下方面：

■　**选择价值的延续**　遗产在当代的关注和参与者获得的选择价值（Option Value），即为其他人或者后代保存对遗产消费的选择权利，这包含了经济价值因素，也包含了社会价值，关系到人际公平和代际公平。

■　**游客的消费者剩余**　旅游等相关产业消费者获得的超出实际支付价格的价值，或者说是消费福利。针对文化遗产，消费者剩余跟遗产的"内在价值"有较大关联，也与门票等旅游消费定价有直接关联。近年世界遗产地登录成功后门票涨价案例较多，而如遗产"内在价值"下降则会挤压消费者剩余，影响到旅游等相关产业消费者从世界遗产地利用中获得的消费福利。

■　**工作岗位和劳务收入**　对于社区居民或其他相关人群，遗产地带来大量直接和间接的就业机会，从而为整个城镇的就业率作出了贡献。以承德市为例，在承德避暑山庄和周围寺庙管理机构就职的人员在 2008 年即超过 2000 人。除此，2006 年全市直接从事旅游业的人口达到 40,000 人，占全部从业人口比重的 15%；从事旅游业相关行业的人员达到 200,000 人，比上年增长了 8%。这一数据与避暑山庄及周围寺庙遗产地旅游的发展密切相关。这里应强调尽量雇佣社区相关居民，除专业技术要求较高职位之外，普通岗位优先照顾社区居民，而不是整体承包给承包商而大量引入外来雇工，以发挥更广泛的社会效益。

■　**邻里关系增强**　世界遗产使社区居民获得地方自豪感，增强邻里凝聚力、关系，加强邻里经济的稳定性。对于生活在世界遗产城市的居民来说，因世界遗产而产生的文化认同、城市自豪感从调查问卷中显而易见。以泰山遗产地为例，2009 年对于"因为遗产地而产生了自豪感"这一陈述表示强烈同意的居民达到 62.19%，表示同意的居民占到 34.33%；以承德为例，75% 的居民同意或强烈同意，世界遗产地的存在提高了他们的生活质量，主要表现在城市知名度上升、环境改善、就业岗位增多、公共交通改善等方面。这些数据都充分说明了遗产地在城市标志、认同感和可识别性上的作用。

■　**对社区教育、交流的贡献和对遗产宣传、认知的推动**　根据调查数据，遗产活动可加强居民间的交流和相关传统知识的教育。在承德，已有 68% 的居民表示愿意参与遗产相关的志愿者工作，而 36% 的居民表示会在工作生活中宣传自己家乡的遗产地；在平遥古城，数据也显示申遗成功后，遗产地与本地社区、居民之间的联系增强，传统文化得以延续和保持。

（2）中国遗产地产生的经济效益

遗产地运营管理机构所获得的支付价格，主要包括门票收入和直接经营收入。其中门票收入是我国遗产地经济收入的重要组成部分。门票收入一方面涉及参观人数，一方面涉及门票定价。前者一定程度上体现了遗产地社会影响的广度和承载力，后者则体现了支付意愿、遗产地价值、开放策略之间的制衡。

---

① CONSERVATION ECONOMICS: COST BENEFIT ANALYSIS FOR THE CULTURAL BUILT HERITAGE: PRINCIPLES AND PRACTICE, ICOMOS, 10th General Assembly in Colombo, Nathaniel Lichfield, William Hendon, Peter Nijkamp, Christian Ost, AlmericoRealfonzo , Pietro Rostirolla, 1993;

而直接经营收入指遗产地管理机构直接参与生产和供应的文化产品与服务的税后净收入，目前在遗产地运营管理机构获得的支付价格中占极少比例。

■ **参观人数** 综合比较中国各处遗产地的统计结果（图 2 - 1）可以看出，中国世界文化遗产地参观人数整体上呈现出较为明显的增长（除 2003 年 SARS 传染使得全国大部分遗产地参观活动受到影响）。20 世纪 90 年代入遗的遗产地，在申遗过程中，由于世界遗产宣传平台和相应活动的推广，多数遗产地参观人数有所增长，且大部分增长幅度明显高于往年。这说明"世界遗产"称号作为名誉或品牌资源，会显著影响地方吸引力。同时，早期列入的遗产地，申遗成功年份前后的参观人数变化不明显。这应是由于早期列入的遗产地本身知名度很高，而且 20 世纪 90 年代前旅游业还不发达，限制了游客的增加量。

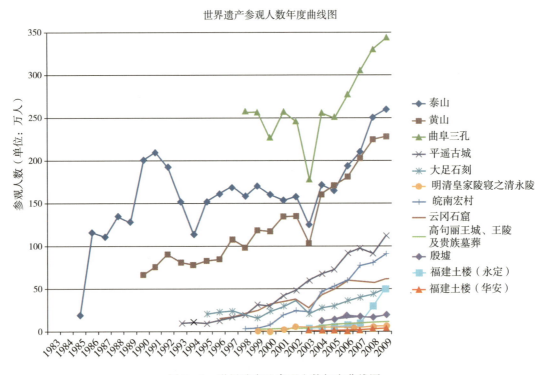

图 2 - 1　世界遗产地参观人数年度曲线图

（注：申遗年份用较大的方形在折线上进行了标注）

■ **门票收入** 20 世纪 90 年代以后申遗成功的遗产地，在成功列入后门票收入都有明显增长。而较早期申遗的遗址地申遗成功年份前后门票收入变化并不明显（图 2 - 2）。门票收入和参观人数的增长率并不能简单的归功于世界遗产带来的影响，实际上本课题研究的阶段也是中国旅游业迅速发展的时期。不过，如福建土楼（南靖、永定片区）、大足石刻等遗产地在申遗成功后的经济收益迅速增长确实表明了"世界遗产"地位带来的变化。同时，多数遗产地申遗成功后的门票收入增长幅度明显超过了参观人数的增长。如平遥自 1997 年申遗成功至今，游客数量上升为原来的 6.26 倍，门票收入上升为原来的 121.44 倍（绝对数值未考虑货币贬值等因素）。这也说明"世界遗产"称号不但带来了更多游客，同时也提高了游客的支付意愿，或者说是提高了对遗产地的价值认同。

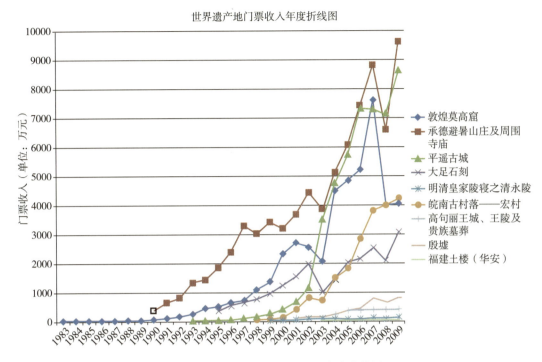

世界遗产地门票收入年度折线图

图 2 - 2 世界遗产地门票收入年度曲线图

（注：各遗产地申遗年份数据点用较大的方形在折线上进行了标注）

2 中国遗产地经营状况

（1）收入、支出的状况及构成

本节中的经济收支，是指遗产相关管理机构的收支情况，即自身运营的直接收支，不包括间接带动的相关产业效益。中国世界遗产地的主要收入来源于财政拨款、事业收入（主要为门票收入）和拨入专款；次要收入则包括经营收入、国际援助或捐款和其他收入。调查案例显示，主要收入一般占到各遗产地每年总收入的 60% ~ 95%。遗产地支出按照来源，也可分为主要与次要两部分。主要支出由基本支出和项目支出构成，其中基本支出包括人员支出和公共支出，即遗产地自身运营的成本；次要支出由经营支出、税金和其他支出构成。主要支出一般占遗产地总支出的 70% ~ 95%，且大部分情况下以基本支出为主，而次要支出占 5% ~ 30%。

■ **收入状况及构成**

虽然目前中国遗产地的总收入逐年增高，但普遍收入来源单一。与国外遗产地相比，中国世界遗产地首先很少从私立基金会筹得保护资助，其次，经营方式局限使得经营收入较低，收入严重依赖财政拨款与门票。而目前的财政拨款仅对非自收自支的事业单位有较大保障，对自收自支的单位主要划拨项目专款。如此，门票就成为绝大多数遗产地最为重要的收入来源。图 2 - 3 中 5 处遗产地，排除 2003 年 SARS 和 2008 年奥运对旅游的影响，各处遗产地门票收入占总收入的比例逐年升高。尤其是承德避暑山庄及周围寺庙，门票收入自 1997 年以来即占收入总额的 90% 左右，其他几处也基本达到 70% ~ 95% 之间。总收入过于依赖门票收入容易导致遗产地过度开发及商业化，这些遗产地应在将来发展中寻求多种收入来源。

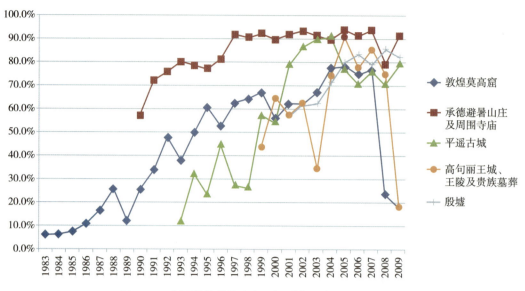

图 2-3　中国部分世界遗产地门票收入占总收入比例图

（包含莫高窟、承德避暑山庄及周围寺庙、平遥古城、高句丽、殷墟 5 处数据）

■　**支出状况及构成**

基本支出（体现遗产地运营成本）和项目支出（体现遗产地在日常维护、文物保护和环境改善等相关工程）成为遗产地主要支出。数据显示（图 2-4）：

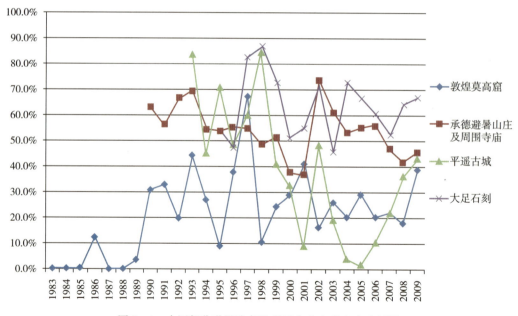

图 2-4　中国部分世界遗产地项目支出占总支出比例图

（包含敦煌莫高窟、承德避暑山庄及周围寺庙、平遥古城和大足石刻 4 处数据）

第一，维护需求相对较小或脆弱性不高的遗产地，例如承德避暑山庄和周围寺庙，经过较长时间的保护和经营，除个别有大型保护工程的年份外，其他年份支出比例较为平稳，并以基本支出为主（约为 50% ~60% 浮动）。

第二，维护需求很大或相对较为脆弱的遗产地，例如敦煌莫高窟和大足石刻，大额的项目支出需求较为频繁，折线持续呈较大波动状态。

第三，以平遥为代表的遗产地，脆弱性不高、对自身维护需求相对较低，但在加入世界遗产地之前保护状况较差，文物本体、周边环境、基础设施以及管理机构都有改善和提高的需求。因此为满足申遗提出的更高保护要求，申遗成功前后须有较长时间的项目投入，这期间项目支出成为遗产地的主要支出。而后，虽然项目支出绝对数额仍保持较高并逐年增加，但由于列入后对经营管理要求提高，在比例上，列入后项目支出比例明显较申遗前降低（平遥古城申遗前各年项目支出比例除1994年为45.3%外，各年都高于50%，1998年达到84.8%的峰值，随后历年波动都在50%以下）。

这三类遗产支出情况都反映出，中国遗产地对遗产的保护仍多处于以大修为主的阶段，遗产保存及基础设施建设、周边环境上问题较多，对大项目需求频繁，而日常维护的投入，监测、精细管理、研究的投入尚不显著。而从大部分遗产地的项目支出变化与财政拨款数额变化有明显关联的情况来看，少有遗产地的门票收入、经营收入等自身运营收入能够部分投入到相关项目之中；而项目费用来源受财政资金划拨的直接影响，项目投入多为文物主管部门及属地政府拨入的项目专款，来源渠道较为单一。此外，绝大多数遗产地在环境整治项目上的经费、时间投入都数倍于本体保护工程（如图2-5承德遗产地所示）。

综上所述，从收集的案例数据来看，一般遗产地的总体收入均在逐年上升。这一方面是受到门票收入大幅提高（部分遗产地门票收入占总收入的比例也同时提高）的带动；另一方面世界遗产地的标签带来了来自政府和民间的更多重视，财政拨款和上级补助都有所增加。归纳收入呈现明显提升趋势的世界遗产地特点，可以发现它们具有如下几方面共性：

■ **地理位置** 申遗后收入显著增加的遗产地一般地处偏远，距城市有相当的距离，而申遗期间对区域交通等必要基础设施进行了较大改善。

■ **知名度** 申遗后收入显著增加的遗产地在申遗前多不尽为人知，而"世界文化遗产"的认可和宣传平台使得其知名度大为提高，如丽江古城、福建土楼等。

■ **管理运营模式** 申遗后收入显著增加的遗产地多有较为清晰明确的旅游发展与经济促进方面的战略措施。

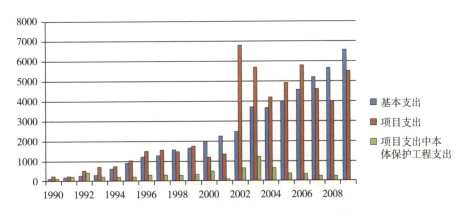

图2-5 1990~2009承德世界遗产主要支出状况（单位：万元）

资料来源：承德文物局

（2）成本收益初步分析

本研究用遗产地基本支出（运营支出）与门票收入的比值作为衡量遗产地成本—收益的重要指标。如图2-6所示，早期部分遗产地的基本支出与门票收入比值较高，至2000年前多呈下降的趋势。这是由于早期门票收入低，遗产地开放参观福利性较强；同时部分遗产地发展早期知名度较低，旅游业不发达。

而当时基本支出主要由财政拨款承担，反映出遗产地对财政依赖较大。2000 年之后大部分世界遗产地的这一比值达到了 100% 以下，说明遗产地自主获得的收入已基本可以满足自身运营成本。由此可见，大部分遗产地在目前成本投入下获得了较好的收益；不过，大部分遗产地在重要保护等项目的资金来源还必须依靠国家财政。

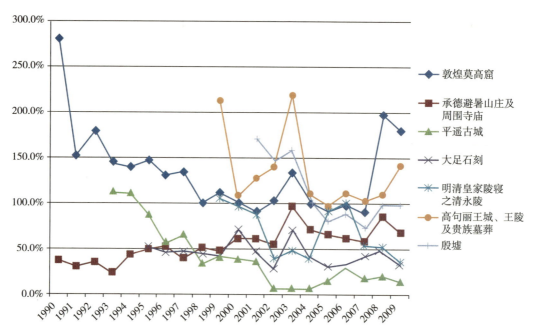

图 2－6　世界遗产地基本支出与门票收入比值年度曲线图

（注：各遗产地申遗年份用较大的方形在折线上进行了标注）

同时研究还发现，不同的遗产地类型和开放条件、参观吸引力等会导致遗产地成本收益的差异。高句丽（由于参观可达性、知名度和参观吸引力相对低）、敦煌莫高窟（由于遗产脆弱，开放条件受限）、殷墟（由于参观吸引力不足）等几处世界遗产地基本支出与门票比值相对处于较高水平。因此，国家财政的相关政策、基金支持应考虑，根据世界遗产自身特点、相关经济社会效益和成本收益进行相应统筹、调整。

第三部分　中国世界文化遗产所在城镇·社会经济发展整体状况

本部分详细阐述了中国世界文化遗产地所在城镇社会经济发展的整体状况，从四个方面展开，主要结论如下。

从遗产地与城镇的关系看，存在六类依存模式和两种不同的申遗动机。

从总体经济发展的情况看，1）多数遗产地城镇经济增速高于全国平均水平，然而在中西部和东北地区仍有不少城镇经济基础十分薄弱；2）遗产地城镇的城市化率普遍偏低，世遗身份对农村居民收入的影响积极。

从城镇产业结构的变化看，1）城镇第三产业普遍得到良好发展，并可能因入遗后知名度突增，成功招商引资促进第二产业发展；2）临近城镇中心有利于遗产地相关产业的发展；3）大多数城镇第三产业从业比重高于全国平均水平，文化产业从业者的增加则是近年遗产地城镇的发展趋势。

从城镇旅游业的发展情况看，1）旅游业在带动县级城镇经济发展的作用更为显著；2）游客量超过城镇人口 10 倍已成为多数遗产地城镇的普遍现象，但对境外游客的吸引力有限；3）人均旅游消费水平与遗产地类型也有一定的关联；4）并非所有城镇将遗产地视为旅游业的核心。

1　中国世界文化遗产与所在城镇的关系

（1）遗产地与所在城镇的依存模式

本研究主要从区位关系与文化影响两个因素入手，参考社会关联与经济贡献，将世界遗产与所在地的依存关系分为六种模式。值得注意的是，遗产作为其所在地城镇首要资源的数量占到中国目前所有世界文化遗产的一半左右，而遗产是其所在地城镇的重要资源的数量约占1/4（表3-1）。

表3-1　遗产地与所在城镇的依存模式

代号	依存模式	空间关系	文化关联	社会关联	经济贡献	遗产地案例	比重
A	城因遗产而生	近	紧密	紧密	突出	泰山、承德避暑山庄及周围寺庙、平遥古城、丽江古城、五台山	15%
B	遗产为城内首要资源	近	代表性强	一般	突出	明清皇宫（北京）、布达拉宫、曲阜孔庙孔林孔府、苏州古典园林、青城山—都江堰灌溉系统、高句丽王城王陵贵族墓葬（集安）、澳门历史中心、安阳殷墟	23%
C	遗产为城内重要资源之一	近	一般	一般	较突出	明清皇宫（沈阳）、天坛、北京皇家园林、	9%
D	遗产为城郊首要资源	远	代表性强	一般	突出	秦始皇陵、敦煌莫高窟、黄山、庐山风景名胜区、武当山古建筑群、峨眉山—乐山大佛风景名胜区、大足石刻、武夷山风景名胜区、高句丽王城王陵贵族墓葬（桓仁）、殷墟、五台山	28%
E	遗产为城郊重要资源之一	远	一般	一般	较突出	周口店"北京人"遗址、明清皇家陵寝、云冈石窟、龙门石窟、登封"天地之中"历史古迹	16%
F	遗产处于民居村落	远	代表性强	紧密	突出	皖南古村落、开平碉楼及村落、福建土楼	9%

（2）遗产地所在城镇的申遗动机

在国外已有对文化遗产效益的研究中，研究者发现世界遗产地产生的多方面效益与遗产所在城镇和所在区域的发展状况、遗产发展目标等诸多因素相关。其中，2008年英国湖区申遗可行性报告[①]认为，申遗动机是影响遗产所在地社会经济发展的重要因素，并分为四种类型："以庆祝为目的（Celebration Designation）"、"以抢救为目的（SOS Designation）"、"塑造品牌（Marketing/Quality Logo/Brand）"、"作为场所塑造的催化剂（Place Making Catalyst）"。在我国现有的世界遗产项目中，申报动机也不尽相同，并大致可分为两类：

一类是"奖励与强化保护"的目的，遗产在申报时多已具有较高知名度，旅游发展成熟稳定，申报难度不高；希望借此提升与宣传遗产地，并与国际保护行业接轨。持此类动机的地区包括大部分地级市，如北京、苏州、泰安；以及少量早期申遗的县级市，如敦煌。

另一类是"以申遗带动发展"为目的，遗产申报时自身知名度有限，旅游发展不足，地方经济水平较低；申遗过程中得到地方政府大力支持，寄期成功后利用世遗身份形成品牌富影响力，争取多方资金，改善交通条件及旅游环境，以推动旅游市场，带动地方经济发展，以县级市和县城为主。

2　遗产地所在城镇的总体经济发展

本研究主要以下列两项指标的年度变化作为判断世界遗产所处地区经济发展速度的主要指征：1）人

---

① The Economic Gain: Research and Analysis of the Socio Economic Impact Potential of UNESCO World Heritage Site Status, Lake District World Heritage Project, 2008；

均地区生产总值；2）城市化率。

（1）人均地区生产总值

比较结果显示（图3-1），研究范围内，所有城镇的人均生产总值（人均GDP）都随整个国家的平均值增长而上升，且这些城镇的人均GDP在1994年和2000年前后的拐点处①也表现出更强劲的增长势头，与全国经济发展形势相符。而从人均GDP增长曲线来看：1）大多数遗产地城镇经济总体增速要快于全国平均水平，尤其自2000年以后；2）入遗后大多数城镇的人均GDP与全国平均水平走势相符；3）个别城镇入遗后经济快速发展，人均GDP从落后于全国平均水平逐渐反超，如泰安、承德和桓仁。4）仅都江堰在2008年因地震破坏从原本领先的状态降至落后于全国平均水平的行列。

综合比较，列入世界遗产名录后，多数遗产地所在城镇的总体经济增速大于全国平均水平，少数地区出现飞跃；然而仍有一些远离城市化中心地区的遗产地所在城镇经济基础偏薄弱，这些城镇主要集中在我国中西部和东北地区的乡村。

（2）城市化率

研究对案例地区从1990年到2009年的相关统计数据进行了汇总（图3-2）。通过比较可以看出，多数遗产地所在城镇的城市化率低于全国平均水平，一定程度上表明遗产地所在地区的非农人口比重小，现代产业发展基础较薄弱，社会经济的总体发展水平有待提高。

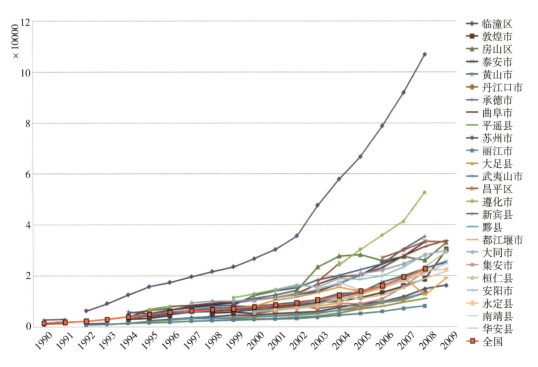

图3-1　26个遗产地所在城镇人均地区生产总值比较（单位：万元）

（注：由于澳门特别行政区数据与其他城镇差异较大，未包括在本图内）

---

① 从1985年到2008年全国人均GDP实际增长了8.17倍（按不变价格计算），此过程中有两个明显增速拐点，一是1994年外汇管理体制改革推动全国经济快速发展；一是在2002年起亚洲金融风暴的影响已完全消除，这一年起我国外贸又恢复了快速增长。

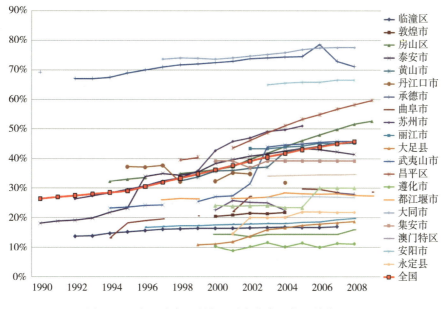

图 3-2　中国遗产地所在地城市化率比较（单位:%）

（3）居民收入状况

遗产处于城区或近郊的 18 处遗产地所在城镇中，城镇居民可支配收入高于、等于全国平均水平的仅有苏州、昌平、房山、泰安 4 处，其余均低于全国平均水平；遗产处于城市近郊或远郊乡村地区的 15 处遗产所在城镇中（图 3-3），除丹江口、大同外，多数遗产地的农村居民纯收入高于全国平均水平。这一方面反映出遗产地对农村地区居民的收入的积极影响，另一方面也说明遗产地城镇居民收入水平相对较低的现状。

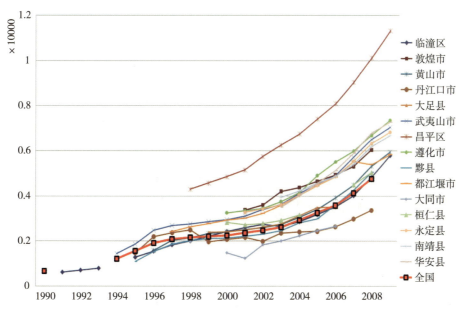

图 3-3　中国遗产地所在村镇农民人均纯收入比较（单位：万元）

3　遗产地所在城镇的产业结构变化

本研究主要以下列两项指标的年度变化作为判断遗产地所在城镇产业结构变化的主要指征：1）遗产

相关产业产值占 GDP 比重；2）遗产相关行业的从业比重。

（1）遗产相关产业产值占 GDP 比重

大量事实表明，文化遗产保护与利用将带动一系列与之相关的上下游产业（图3-4）。

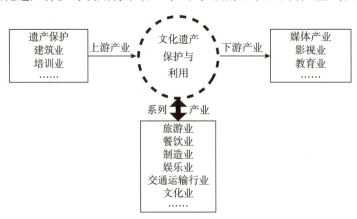

图3-4　文化遗产与地方产业的相互关系

20 世纪末，第三产业开始在中国迅速发展，这种趋势同样反映在遗产地所在城镇中。当然这并不意味着所有遗产所在城镇都将第三产业当做经济发展的支柱产业。部分遗产地所在城镇的第三产业产值虽然在入遗后呈上升趋势，但其占 GDP 的比重却有所下降，这主要是由于城镇因世界遗产身份扩大了知名度，在招商引资方面取得优势，促进了第二产业的发展。总体而言，世界遗产所在城镇第三产业的发展保持了良好的上升态势，逐年走强（如图3-5）。从世界遗产与所在地的依存关系来看，这些第三产业发展较好的都属于"遗产为城郊首要资源"或"城即遗产"类型。可见临近城镇为遗产地相关产业的发展提供了强有力的支持保障，可能体现在空间、资源、基础设施和配套服务上。

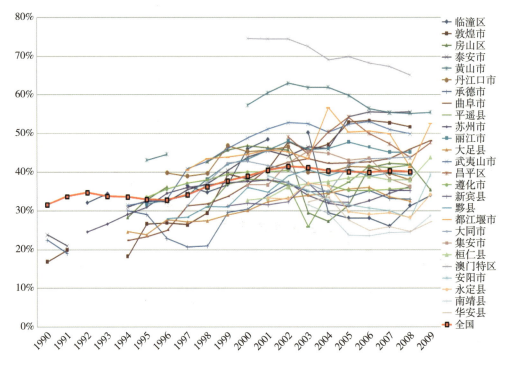

图3-5　中国遗产地所在地第三产业占 GDP 比重比较（单位:%）

（2）遗产相关行业的从业比重

在世界遗产的保护与利用过程中，相关联的产业如遗产保护业、旅游业、交通运输业等均可为所在城镇提供相应的就业岗位，包括直接就业和间接就业。由于间接就业涉及多个行业，本研究采取考察城镇第三产业的从业人员数量相关指标，以大致反映遗产地所在城镇的从业结构特点。

从遗产地所在城镇的第三产业从业人员在当地社会就业人员总数中的比重变化来看（图 3-6），案例中 19 个遗产地的比重均高于全国平均水平①，如图 2-27 所示。这说明多数遗产地所属城镇的第三产业发展水平高于全国平均水平。其中比重最高的是丽江、敦煌、遵化、澳门、黄山等地，均达到了 70% 以上（在上述分析中，这些城镇将旅游业视为支柱产业或主导产业）。在文化特征明显的曲阜、丽江等地，第三产业中的文化产业近年发展迅速，其产值占 GDP 的比重和从业人员数都有明显增长。如 2009 年曲阜市文化产业增加值占 GDP 比重已达到 4.08%。

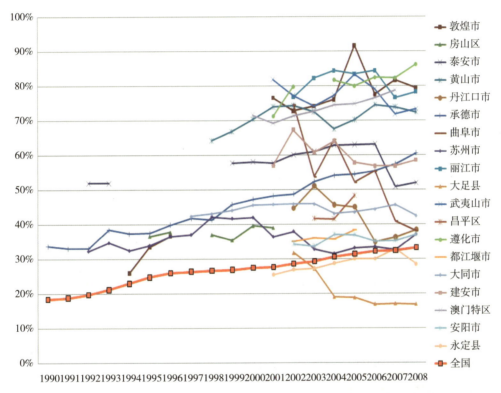

图 3-6　遗产地所在城镇三产就业人员占当地社会就业总人数的比重

（注：由于数据来源所限，本图中缺少临潼、平遥、新宾、黟县、桓仁、南靖、华安等地数据）

4　遗产地所在城镇的旅游业发展

对于拥有世界遗产的城镇来说，旅游业往往成为地方重要的产业类型，在产业结构中具有战略性地位。首先，世界遗产是旅游业发展的原动力与核心；其次，旅游业发展的成熟度也反映出世界遗产的利用水平。本研究对反映世界遗产旅游业发展的相关数据进行搜集和分析，并选出 4 个重要指标进行比较，分别是：旅游收入占城镇 GDP 的比重、游客总人数与城镇人口比重、人均旅游消费、遗产地游客人数占城镇旅游人数的比重。

---

① 根据全国各遗产地所在城镇年度统计数据，多数城镇的第三产业从业比重实为"国营单位第三产业从业比重"，因此该指标仅作为参考。

（1）旅游收入占城镇 GDP 的比重

依据旅游业收入占当地城镇 GDP 的比重，我们将所研究的遗产地城镇分为以下五种类型（图 3-7）：1）以旅游业为核心产业，旅游收入占城镇 GDP 比重高于 50%，包括丽江、黟县和武夷山。2）以旅游业为主导产业，旅游收入占城镇 GDP 比重介于 50% 至 20% 之间，高于全国平均水平，如黄山、临潼、敦煌和都江堰。3）以旅游业为重要产业，旅游收入占其城镇总 GDP 比重介于 10% 至 20% 之间，如平遥、曲阜、集安、桓仁、黟县、昌平、安阳和苏州。4）旅游业发展相对滞后，旅游收入占城镇 GDP 比重长期低于 5%，如遵化、房山等。5）旅游收入比重增速明显，虽然地处经济基础薄弱的地区，但近年在世界遗产身份的带动下旅游业快速增长，如丽江、武夷山、黟县、桓仁、黄山和都江堰等。

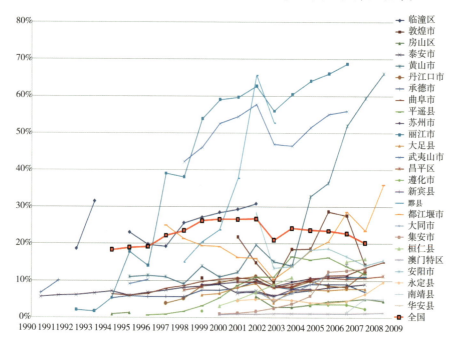

图 3-7　我国遗产地所在地旅游收入占 GDP 比重比较（单位:%）

在这些城镇中，县级市和县城的旅游收入占城镇 GDP 比重普遍偏高，最大值基本都能达到 20% 以上，可见旅游业在带动县级城镇经济发展方面起到了重要作用。

（2）游客人数与城镇人口的比值

在中国，世界遗产身份对遗产地周边城镇乃至国内外游客的吸引力是相当可观的（图 3-8a）。案例数据表明：1）游客人数最大值超过城镇人口 10 倍的地区多达 10 处，包括：澳门（极值超过 50 倍）、黟县、昌平、武夷山、黄山、都江堰、临潼、安阳、曲阜和房山；2）一些城镇的游客人数在入遗前后发生巨大变化，如黟县、平遥、桓仁、新宾、大同、集安、土楼三县、大足、承德等。同时，我们也考察了各地的境外游客人数与城镇非农人口比值，反映了城镇的国际知名度和旅游服务设施的完善程度（图 3-8b）。比较结果表明，最大值除丽江和黄山超过 4 倍，武夷山、敦煌、曲阜、集安和苏州超过 1 倍外，其余各地均不足 1 倍。可见中国大部分世界文化遗产地对境外游客的吸引力尚有较大的提升空间，可考虑通过改善区域交通条件、加强国际交流合作等措施得以实现。

（3）人均旅游消费

游客人均旅游消费从侧面反映了遗产地所在城镇的旅游设施建设、服务水平、接待能力等状况。人均旅游消费超过 1000 元的城镇，包括：澳门、苏州、丽江；二是人均旅游消费介于 500~1000 元的城镇，包括：大足、平遥、泰安、承德、敦煌、桓仁、集安、大同，以上城镇人均旅游消费高于全国平均水平。
从游客人均消费额长期变化趋势来看（图3-9），案例城镇大致分为三种情况：1）人均消费额长期高于
全国平均水平，如澳门、苏州、泰安、平遥、丽江；2）入遗后人均旅游消费额增长迅猛，如丽江、桓
仁、集安；3）人均旅游消费额长期较低，如昌平、房山、临潼等考古遗址型遗产地。可见遗产地所在城
镇人均旅游消费水平与遗产地类型也有一定的关联。

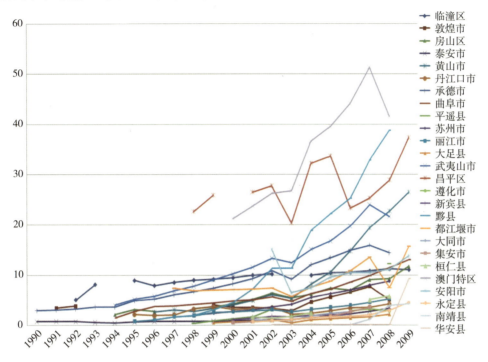

图3-8a　中国遗产地所在地游客总人数与城镇人口的比值比较

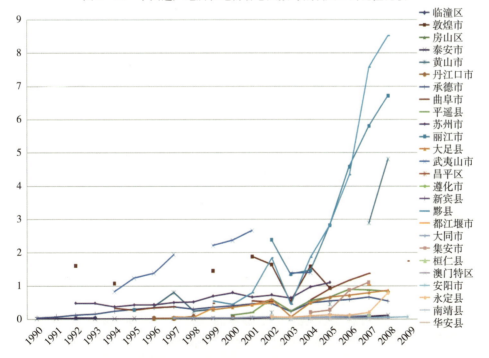

图3-8b　中国遗产地所在地境外游客总人数与城镇非农人口的比值比较

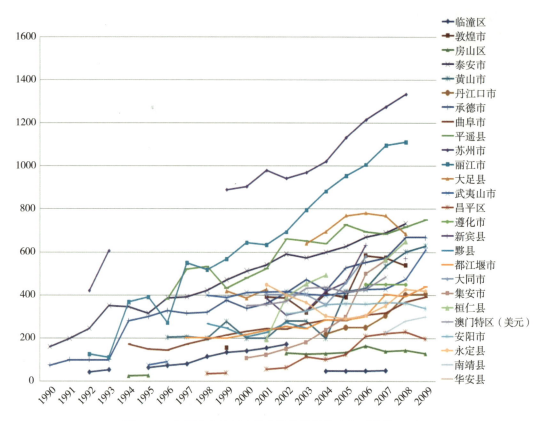

图 3-9　中国遗产地所在地人均旅游消费比较（单位：元）

（4）遗产地游客人数占城镇旅游人数的比重

由于遗产地的旅游收入难以获取，我们以"遗产地游客人数占城镇游客总人数的比重"的年度变化，来判断遗产地旅游在所在地整体旅游业发展中的地位，并可分为三类（图 3-10）。

类型一：遗产地是城镇旅游业的重要支柱　参观遗产地是游客到达城镇的主要原因，所以遗产地游客人数占城镇游客人数的比重居高不下。例如，在黄山、华安、曲阜、黟县、丹江口、丽江、昌平等 7 地，遗产地旅游人数的最大值均超过了城镇旅游人数的 50%。

类型二：遗产地带动城镇整体旅游业发展　在列入世界遗产之后的一段时期内，遗产地成为城镇旅游业的核心。随着遗产地旅游业的发展，城镇知名度和服务设施基础会随之提高和改善，地方政府积极利用优势，在遗产地开发周边发展更多旅游资源，在市域范围内形成丰富的旅游线路网和相关产业链。这样随着更大范围内的旅游业的发展，虽然遗产地本身的游客的绝对数仍在增加，但遗产地本身的旅游人数在全城镇旅游人数中所占的比重会逐渐下降。以泰山遗产地为例，在 1987 年泰山申报世界遗产成功之时，泰山旅游人数上升到了全市旅游人数的 51%，达到历史极值，并在以后的 7 年内保持了约 50% 的水平。随后，这一比重开始逐步下降，到 2008 年这一比例仅为 13.58%。

类型三：入遗后遗产地旅游占城镇旅游业比重上升　此类突出案例是华安县。该县在入遗当年随着土楼知名度上升，遗产旅游人数突增，甚至超过全县旅游人数（包含不经过县城而到访遗产地的一日游）。此外增长明显的还有永定、安阳和集安。

可见，世界遗产地并非是所有遗产地城镇旅游业的支柱。在入遗初期，遗产旅游的比重可能偏高，随着城镇旅游服务设施的完善，遗产周边旅游资源的陆续开发，遗产在城镇旅游中的份额将逐步下降。

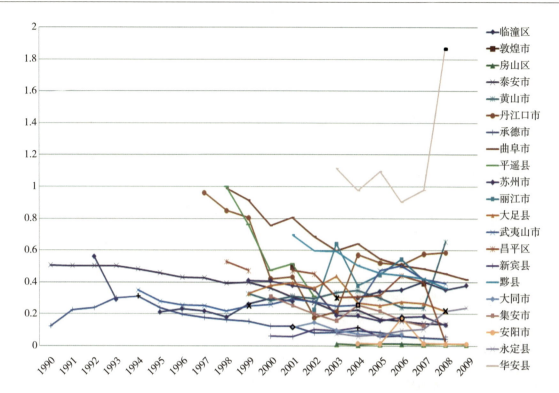

图例（从上到下）：临潼区、敦煌市、房山区、泰安市、黄山市、丹江口市、承德市、曲阜市、平遥县、苏州市、丽江市、大足县、武夷山市、昌平区、新宾县、黟县、大同市、集安市、安阳市、永定县、华安县

图 3 - 10　中国遗产地游客人数占城镇游客总人数的比重比较

（注：由于数据来源所限，缺少遵化、都江堰、桓仁、澳门、南靖等地数据，黑色标记为各地入遗时间）

第四部分　中国世界文化遗产地保护与可持续发展·评价与监测

本部分总结了中国世界文化遗产地保护与可持续发展的现状，并对遗产地—城镇监测体系的数据结构和实施方法提出建议。

评价部分从三个方面展开，主要结论如下。

遗产地保护与所在城镇的社会经济发展存在优势，反映在：1）政府对遗产保护与发展投入力度大；2）世界遗产身份吸引多方关注，交流合作和融资渠道增加；3）遗产地所在城镇在区域发展建设中占领先机；4）遗产价值推动当地文化产业发展。

大量数据计量分析结果表明：遗产地身份对所在城镇产生了社会经济引致影响，体现在：1）带动当地旅游业及整体经济发展；2）带动当地就业岗位增加；3）遗产保护的投入产出比十分可观。

基于遗产地的类型、特点与城镇的关系，本研究总结了六种不同类型遗产地保护和发展的优势和劣势，以及应注重的相应策略，并得出"并非所有遗产地城镇都适合大力发展旅游业"的结论。

最后，研究对建立和完善遗产地—城镇监测体系提出了详细的建议。

1　遗产地保护与可持续发展评价

（1）世遗身份为保护与发展带来的优势

中国入选世遗的文化遗产均为全国重点文物保护单位中最出类拔萃者，是中国文化遗产的精华；遗产地所在城镇与其他历史文化名城相比，具有更多的国际交流、合作渠道，并可能在区域发展中获取较多优待。本研究对全国 26 处遗产地所在城镇进行了遗产地（内部因素）和所在城镇（外部条件）的优势分析，总结世界遗产身份带来的社会经济优势如下：

■ 政府对遗产保护与发展投入力度大

不同于一般文物保护单位的管理，世界遗产因其重要性常常会成立专门的管理机构。这类管理机构的模式与机制多有不同，但共同点均在于级别较高，自治权利较大，统筹能力强。本研究考察了各遗产地所属城镇在列入世界遗产名录前5年至今的各类建设活动，结果显示各地在城市面貌整治、基础/服务设施建设、遗产地周边环境整治改善以及城市美化等方面，持续时间长、投入力度大（表4-1）。多数城镇也针对遗产地保护和发展制定了相应了保护规划，并在城镇层面进行总体规划编制协调、制定地方法律文件等（表4-2）。

■ 世界遗产身份吸引多方关注，交流合作、融资渠道增加

目前，中国很多世界遗产地都已经受到了包括遗产保护组织、海外媒体、境外游客以及国际友城等来自国际各个领域的关注，表现为1）遗产保护组织为遗产地提供专业技术和资金上的支持；2）各国的电视台频繁来到我国世界遗产地进行拍摄和宣传；3）遗产地境外游客人数激增；4）遗产地所在城镇与许多国外城市缔结友好关系，为城镇带来旅游、经贸以及其他领域的国际交流与合作，如表4-3所示。

同时，成为世界文化遗产之后，融资渠道也相应增加。除了从国家到地方各级政府的对口资金外，一些公募基金与专项基金也陆续成立，如孔子基金会（1984年）、敦煌石窟保护基金会（1996年）、西递宏村保护基金会（2007年）和甲骨文基金会（2009年）等。此外，中国多处遗产地城镇由政府主导，在市场经济体制下成立投资公司，这些公司具有政府公益性项目投融资功能，是遗产地及周边的开发建设活动重要的支持力量和经济后盾。

表4-1 遗产地及周边环境整治及服务设施建设

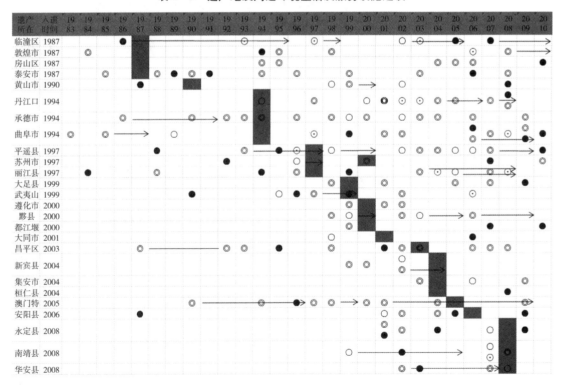

注：●表示博物馆建设，指在遗产地或周边地区设立与遗产地相关的博物馆；◎表示景区建设，主要指文物修复和基础/服务设施建设；○表示周边整治，主要指遗产地核心区及缓冲区的居民/单位搬迁、违章建筑拆除等活动；⊙表示美化开发，主要指遗产地周边的城市美化、新景区开发等建设活动。

表 4-2 遗产地所在城镇法律文件及相关规划

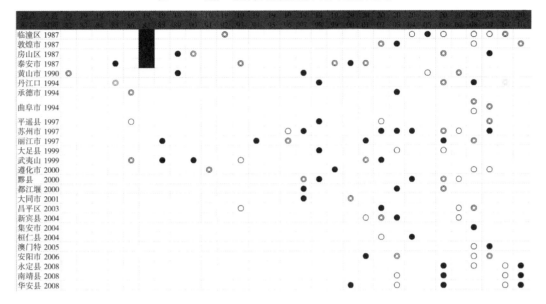

注：●表示法律文件，指各级政府制订的与遗产保护相关的法律文件；◎表示保护规划，指与遗产相关的保护规划；○指其他与遗产相关的旅游规划或城镇总体规划，以及与遗产相关的宣言。

表 4-3 遗产地及所在城镇的国际交流

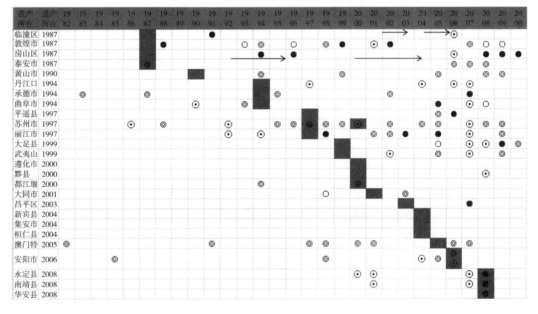

注：●表示合作保护项目，指遗产地管理部门与国际保护组织签订的遗产地合作保护项目或相关研究。◎表示友好城市，指遗产地所在城镇与国外历史文化名城签订友好城市协议。○表示国际会议，指与遗产地保护和发展相关的国际研讨会。⊙表示其他交流或合作，包括文艺演出、影视创作、捐赠物品等文化交流或纪念活动。

■ 遗产地所在城镇在区域发展建设中占领先机

充分利用世界文化遗产的品牌效应，是遗产地所在城镇奠定自身区位优势与经济地位的重要资源之一，从而建设具有区域影响的投资平台，带动区域经济发展。多数遗产地所在城镇在申遗期间，区域交通设施得到巨大改善（表 4-4），更有县级市如黄山、武夷山、丽江、敦煌、曲阜等先后开设了机场以促进旅游业的发展；也有城镇申遗成功后被纳入附近都市圈，如临潼撤县改区、大足并入重庆直辖市、丽江撤地设市等，投资环境得到改善，城镇经济发展整体加速。

表4-4   遗产地及所在城镇交通设施建设

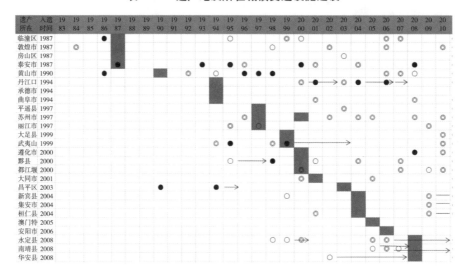

注：●表示主要指山岳型/民居型遗产地范围内的主要旅游道路建设；○主要指城镇中心区到遗产地的道路建设；◎主要指城镇对外交通设施建设，包括机场、铁路、高速公路等。

■   遗产价值推动文化产业发展

中国遗产地中不乏文化发源地或某种同源文化的代表，如曲阜为"孔子故乡"，周口店栖居"人类始祖"，敦煌孕育了"敦煌学"，殷墟是"文字发源地"，武当山则是"道教、武术发源地"，均为良好的影视、教育、艺术创作题材，培育了大量优质文学、艺术、影视作品乃至商业演出。在本研究考察的遗产地城镇中，几乎所有都举办过文化旅游相关的节庆活动（表4-5所示），并在城镇招商引资方面取得了良好的效果。此外，在中国的城镇型和村落型遗产地，如平遥古城、丽江古城和澳门历史中心等，由于规模和占地相对较大，历史建筑众多，部分居民延续传统生活方式，因而具有丰富多样的文化载体，衍生出大量非物质文化遗产，可成为发展地区文化产业的动力。

表4-5   26个世界遗产地大型文化旅游节庆活动举办情况

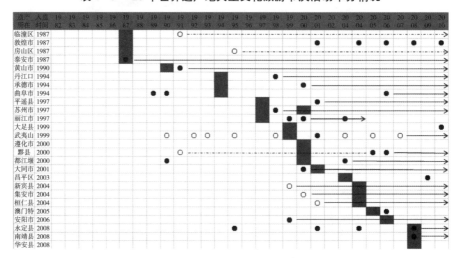

注：●代表与世界文化遗产直接相关的文化/旅游节庆；○代表与遗产不直接相关的文化/旅游节庆；→表示持续举办节庆的时间跨度。

（2）遗产地身份对城镇产生的社会经济引致影响

根据投入产出分析方法，我们计算出 2008 年中国世界遗产地对其所在城镇的经济引致影响，包括1）世界文化遗产带动当地旅游业及 GDP 发展；2）世界文化遗产带动当地新增就业岗位数；3）世界文化遗产保护的投入产出比。具体数值如表 4－6 所示。

■ **遗产带动当地旅游业及整体经济发展**

由投入产出计算结果可以看到，中国各地旅游业对世界文化遗产的依赖度从 93.67%（平遥县）到 1.43%（安阳市）不等。同时，因为各个城镇的经济基础和旅游服务设施水平各异，世界文化遗产旅游带动的旅游业产出和 GDP 也不同：其中遗产带动城镇旅游业产出最高的为泰安市、武夷山市和曲阜市，分别达到了 42.0 亿元、30.1 亿元和 27.9 亿元，相当可观；而平遥县受遗产带动的旅游业产出也高达 14.3 亿元，直追东部地区的地级市承德市（18.4 亿元）；世界文化遗产对城镇 GDP 带动率最高的为武夷山市和平遥县，分别达到了 19.81% 和 10.54% 的高水平。

■ **遗产带动当地就业岗位增加**

在带动遗产相关的就业岗位方面，泰安市、承德市、曲阜市和武夷山市十分显著，基本达到了 3 万个新增岗位的规模，说明这些地方与遗产相关的行业发展较为充分；在带动城镇其他行业就业岗位方面，则是泰安市和承德市遥遥领先，分别达到 32.5 万和 20.7 万新增岗位的规模，反映两地产业结构较为合理稳定，且旅游业在城镇发展中地位显著；第二梯队为安阳市、曲阜市和武夷山市，新增岗位数在 6 万 ~ 9 万之间，也相当可观。

■ **遗产保护的投入产出比十分可观**

由于部分遗产地 2008 年保护项目投入的数据无法取得，我们仅对其中 7 处遗产地城镇进行世界文化遗产保护的投入产出比的计算。结果显示，在安阳市、泰安市和曲阜市这三个"老牌"遗产所在城镇，由于遗产本体的维护不需要投入过多资金，而遗产地的经济引致影响（即因遗产保护和旅游产生的 GDP 增加值）因城镇长期的知名度、相关产业的繁荣发展而维持在较高水平，因此遗产保护的投入产出比都超过了 1∶100。而在平遥、黟县和新宾满族自治县等经济欠发达的乡村地区，遗产保护的投入产出比也都超过了 1∶10 的水平，从一定程度上反映了外界对乡村遗产关注的热度仍然高涨，同时也说明乡村遗产的保护力度应继续加大。

表 4－6　2008 年中国部分遗产地对其所在城镇的经济引致影响一览

	W 依赖度	带动 T	带动 G	G 带动率	相关 J	其余 J	W 投入产出比
山西平遥	93.67%	14.3	5.8	10.54%	1.3	1.3	1∶72.8
山东曲阜	45.31%	27.9	9.9	4.92%	3.2	7.2	1∶166.97
福建武夷山	44.85%	30.1	11	19.81%	2.9	6.4	——
安徽黟县	36.05%	1.8	0.7	5.31%	0.1	0.4	1∶11.3
福建永定	21.88%	2.9	1	1.11%	0.3	1.3	——
河北承德	15.20%	18.4	6.9	3.60%	3.15	20.68	1∶7
山东泰安	13.44%	42.0	14.8	2.78%	4.4	32.5	1∶244.1
辽宁新宾	5.80%	0.7	0.3	0.61%	0.1	1.1	1∶11.3
河南安阳*	1.43%	1.6	0.7	0.21%	0.1	8.8	1∶246.24

注：

W 依赖度 = 城镇旅游业对世界遗产的依赖度（%）

带动 T = 世界遗产旅游所带动的旅游业总产出（亿元）

带动 G = 世界遗产旅游所带动的 GDP（亿元）

G 带动率 = 世界遗产的带动占当年城镇 GDP 的比重（%）

相关 J = 世界遗产相关产业的发展创造的就业岗位数（万个）

其余 J = 遗产地带动的旅游业发展为其他行业创造的就业岗位数（万个）

W 投入产出比 = 世界遗产地保护投入与遗产地带动产出（包括因保护和旅游产生的 GDP 增加值）的比值，＊为 2009 年数据

（3） 六种不同类型遗产地保护和发展的策略

上文数据分析显示，游客量超过城镇人口 10 倍已成为多数遗产地城镇的普遍现象①。随着遗产地"过热"情况在全国的蔓延，有必要考察和评价世遗身份对保护和可持续发展可能造成的影响。通过大量统计数据分析和全国各地已有策略的总结，本研究认为不同类型遗产地存在不同的优势和劣势，并归纳遗产地保护和可持续发展应注重的策略如下（详见表 4 - 7）。

（4） 并非所有遗产地城镇都适合大力发展旅游业

在中国，世界遗产身份对所在城镇的旅游经济产生的影响，从遗产地在城镇旅游中的地位和旅游业在城镇产业结构中的地位上看，是相对有限的。从本研究的结论来看，具有以下特点的遗产地及城镇，不应盲目推动遗产相关的旅游业发展，而是在城镇不同层面上加以策略上的限制或补充：（1） 本体脆弱型遗产地：应限制瞬时游客量，尽量将旅游业及相关产业的发展转移到遗产地外围；（2） 对大众游客吸引力有限的遗产地：应积极开拓思路，吸引"探索型"游客到访，或在遗产地周边开发新的旅游资源以形成路线或网络；（3） 旅游供给条件尚不成熟、仍有潜力的城镇：应根据城镇规模和社会经济基础，完善旅游基础和服务设施，适当提高城镇接待游客能力；（4） 过于依赖旅游业且经济基础薄弱的城镇：可借遗产之名招商引资，适当发展第二产业，完善和优化城镇产业结构；（5） 规模过小的城镇：可借遗产申报、周年纪念活动之机吸引公共或私人投资，改善遗产地周边环境质量，吸引就业人口。

2   建立和完善遗产地—城镇监测体系

构建"世界文化遗产地保护与所在城镇社会经济监测体系"是目前中国遗产地保护工作中的一项空白。从长远角度来看，这样一个监测体系有助于对全国各遗产地及所在城镇进行长期、连续的考察。通过数据的定期更新，可以对同一遗产地及所在地在不同时期的保护与发展，不同遗产地同一时期的保护情况的变化，以及对于同一区域内、同一遗产类型、同时期入遗案例等的保护与所在地发展进行实时的分析研究，这对于国家层面以及各个地区的相关政策制定与调整具有重要意义。监测体系遵循两个原则：1） 数据处理上采用定量统计与定性分析相结合的方法；2） 监测实施中实现多层级、全方位的考察和评估。

因此本研究提出了基础数据与核心数据的概念，其中基础数据较为全面，类型上包括指标数据（定量统计）与描述数据（定性分析）两类，适用于各遗产地—城镇按年度自查、更新和完善；核心数据则在基础数据的基础上进行精简，类型上以定量统计为主，适用于在全国范围内进行汇总和比较分析。

（1） 监测体系数据结构

从监测对象来看，该体系可分为遗产地和遗产地所在城镇两个部分。每一部分的数据类型又可分为基础数据与核心数据两类。针对遗产地的监测涵盖遗产地的保护、管理、收支等方面，以统计数据和大事记为主；核心数据集中于遗产地的收入与支出情况。针对遗产地所在城镇的监测较为综合全面，涵盖城镇经济与产业发展、居民收入、人口与就业、基础/服务设施建设、文化宣传、交流合作，以及遗产地相关规划管理等方面；核心数据包括总体经济发展、居民收入和从业结构、旅游业发展、遗产地经济贡献、国际影响力等方面。监测体系数据结构如下表所示（表 4 - 8）。

---

①   参考本研究第三部分第四节"遗产地所在城镇的旅游业发展"相关内容。

表4-7 针对不同类型世界遗产地保护和可持续发展提出的策略

遗产地类型	区位类型	遗产地举例	优势	区位因素	劣势	区位因素	应注重的策略
山岳型遗产地	A	泰山、庐山风景名胜区	遗产地景区游客承载力大，游线方式达方式多样；管委会统筹管理；混合类型	遗产地周边服务设施齐全；地价、房价得以提升	景区维护成本高；索道选线及建设存在争议；文化价值易被自然价值掩盖	本地市民生活受到游客干扰；保护区范围受城市蔓延影响较大	注重城镇发展对山体、文化景观的影响；合理选择旅游项目的开发和布局，挖掘文化内涵，提高国际影响力
	D	黄山、武夷山风景名胜区等	遗产具有资源优势，对大众游客吸引力大	受城镇建成区影响较小		旅游服务设施水平较差	适当发展周边乡村游；为本地居民创造就业条件，优化产业结构
城镇历史中心	A	平遥古城、丽江古城	本体承载力较大、游线丰富；非物质文化遗产丰富，居民收入好	交通条件好；城镇为文化产业发展提供有力支撑	产权复杂，管理难度大；居民和游客需求冲突较多；居民生活质量的提高受到一定限制	本地居民居住成本上升；游客过多造成环境污染；存在消防隐患	防止博物馆化；保持一定的原住民比重；控制新老城市保持一定距离；制定本体维修的促进机制；推动文化产业多样化发展
民居村落	F	皖南古村落、开平碉楼及村落、福建土楼	非物质文化遗产丰富，文化氛围浓厚；传统延续好，保护技术及安防措施好；周边居民收入及自豪感较强	居民收入因遗产地显著提高；周边农业景观资源丰富	本体游客承载力有限；经济缺乏产业支撑；文化产业开发方式有限，居民教育程度和遗产保护技术力量有限	交通不便；旅游服务设施水平较差；市政消防等基础设施薄弱；服务设施有限，空心化趋势	适当开发周边乡村旅游资源；适当发展民俗，控制新建旅游设施的选址和规模；创造就业机会留住居民，防止博物馆化；促进非物质文化遗产保护及乡土教育
大型历史建筑群	A	承德避暑山庄及周围寺庙	知名度高，资金来源充足，多为国家级文保单位，保护技术及安防措施好；居民收入及周边居民自豪感较强	文化产业发展基础好；遗产地周边服务设施齐全；地价、房价得以提升	规模相对较小，流线较单一；本体脆弱，短时间大量踩踏；游客和市民的参观需求不易平衡	遗产地周边易产生交通问题；对周边城市建设有限制（如建筑高度、轨道交通下穿等）	改善遗产地周边交通，推动文化产业多样化发展；促进国际交流与合作，提升城市竞争力
	B	曲阜孔庙孔林孔府等					
	C	天坛、明清皇家陵寝（十三陵）等		交通便利，遗产地周边服务设施较全		对周边城镇建设有限制（如建筑高度等）	将游客引入周边其他景点，开展面向本地居民的教育活动
	D	明清皇家陵寝（清东陵）等	游客压力相对较小	受城镇发展影响不大	对大众游客吸引力较弱	交通不便，旅游服务设施水平较差	适当开发周边旅游资源，提升服务设施水平，创造居民就业条件，吸引专家学者进行科研活动

续表

遗产地类型	区位类型	遗产地举例	优势	区位因素	劣势	区位因素	应注重的策略
考古遗址	B	殷墟，高句丽遗址（集安）	多作为博物馆保护，专业性强，科普教育功能较强	交通便利，遗产地周边服务设施齐全	对大众游客吸引力相对较弱（秦始皇陵兵马俑除外）；本体具有脆弱性，可衍生的文化产业有限；可能限制周边地区第二产业的发展	受城镇建设活动影响较大	预判城镇发展对遗产地的威胁（交通设施、工业区等）；增加遗产地对市民的开放性（如建立遗产地公园，科普教育基地等）
考古遗址	D	秦始皇陵、五女山城（桓仁）					
考古遗址	E	周口店"北京人"遗址		受城镇建设活动影响较小		可达性较差，对遗产地的宣传作用有限	适当开发周边旅游资源，提升面向本地居民和游客的教育功能
石窟遗址	D	敦煌莫高窟、云冈石窟	艺术价值高，对大众游客的吸引力力强，保护力量雄厚，国际影响力相对较高	交通便利，从一定程度上推动文化、教育产业发展	本体极具脆弱性，保护难度大；游客承载力大；对更大范围的生态环境保护提出要求	周边居民受益方式有限；限制周边地区第二产业发展	城镇发展对遗产地的威胁（周边自然环境和岩土环境的破坏，如地下水位、湿度、农业灌溉方式等）；对城镇发展（如交通设施、环境污染）和规模产生极大限制；合理减少游客在遗产地内外的停留时间
石窟遗址	E	大足石刻		周边自然景观资源丰富		可达性较差，知名度对遗产地的宣传作用有限	

注：遗产地与城镇依存关系分为六类，包括 A—城因遗产而生；B—遗产为城镇内首要资源；C—遗产为城镇内重要资源之一；D—遗产为城郊首要资源，E—遗产为城郊重要资源之一；F—遗产处于民居村落。

表 4－8　遗产地—城镇监测体系数据结构

遗产地部分	基础数据	指标	两大项、五中项、十五小项
		描述	两类
	核心数据	指标	两大项、十小项
		描述	影响评价
遗产地所在城镇部分	基础数据	指标	两大项、八中项、二十五小项
		描述	五类
	核心数据	指标	三大项、六中项、十四小项
		描述	SWOT 分析；荣誉榜

（2）监测体系基础数据（年度跟踪监测）

■　遗产地部分

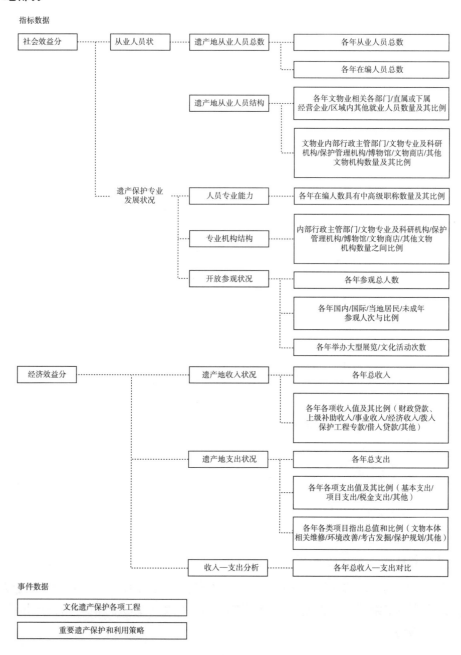

■ 遗产地所在城镇部分

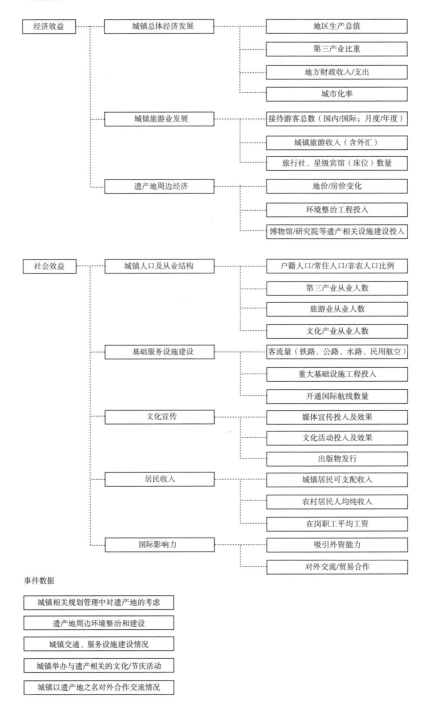

（3）监测体系核心数据（整体监测评估）

基于以上遗产地和所在城镇监测体系的基础数据，本研究在可获取度高的数据基础上选取核心数据，进行统一计算公式或消除量纲处理，以便在全国范围内建立数据库，进行横向比较和相关拓展研究。核心数据框架如表4-9所示。

表 4 - 9　遗产地—城镇监测体系核心数据

类别		遗产地保护和经营状况	遗产地在所在城镇产生的社会经济效益
定量指标	经济效益指标	总收入 各项收入值及比例 总支出 各项支出值及比例 各类项目总支出 各类项目支出比例（保护工程）	总体经济发展（总人口数、非农人口比重；人均地区生产总值；人均地方财政收入；第二、第三产业占 GDP 的比重） 旅游业发展（旅游收入与 GDP 比值、接待游客总数与城镇总人口比值、城镇旅游收入、人均旅游消费） 遗产地经济贡献（遗产地旅游人数占城镇旅游人数比重、遗产地旅游收入占城镇旅游收入比重）
	社会效益指标	遗产地从业人员总数 遗产地从业人员结构（相关人员分类比例） 专业机构结构 参观总人次（不同类别参观人员比例）	城镇从业结构（第三产业从业比重） 居民收入（城镇居民可支配收入、农村居民人均纯收入） 国际影响力（境外旅游人数比重、旅游总人数与城镇人口比值、境外旅游人数与城镇非农人口比值）
定性分析		世界遗产的利用与发展对遗产保护的影响分析	遗产地与所在城镇可持续发展 SWOT 分析；获得的相关美誉

（4）监测实施方法

基于以上数据框架，本研究建议将监测体系分为两个层次进行：

一是各遗产地独立的年度跟踪监测。以遗产地保护管理经费和城镇社会经济发展状况数据作为支撑，梳理与遗产相关的管理、建设、交流等重大活动，反映各地在每年变化的客观条件下，如何发挥优势、弥补劣势、抓住机遇、应对风险，并监测保护和可持续发展的效果。其主要内容包括：1）遗产地与所在城镇社会经济效益跟踪监测；2）遗产地利用与发展对遗产保护的影响分析；3）遗产地与所在城镇社会发展 SWOT 分析；4）遗产地与所在城镇获得的美誉。

二是全国范围内的整体监测和评估。着眼于全国世界文化遗产地及其所在城镇宏观层面的发展，通过汇总各地保护和发展数据，总结世界遗产的利用与发展对遗产保护的影响，分享遗产地所在城镇在可持续发展道路上的差异化策略，建立全国世界文化遗产地互相交流、学习的平台。其主要内容包括：1）全国遗产地保护和经营状况整体监测；2）全国遗产地在所在城镇产生的社会经济效益整体评估。

（执笔人：张杰、李建芸、卢刘颖等，清华大学建筑学院国家遗产中心）

Exccutive Summary for 'The Study of the Conservation of China's World Heritage and Economic Development at World Heritage Sites'

Tsinghua University

Abstract

Till 2009, after 22 years of participation, China has 31 cultural heritage sites inscribed on the UNESCO World Heritage List, which involve more than 40 towns and cities. World Cultural Heritage Sites inscriptions and even the application process have promoted varies effects on the sites themselves, as well as the economy, society and environment of towns and cities in their vicinity.

'The Study of the Conservation of China's World Heritage and Economic Development at World Heritage Sites', being based on data collected from these 31 world heritage sites, gives an overview of the use and commercial operation of China's world heritage cultural sites, assesses economic development of towns and cities in their vicinity, including key economic indices, changes in industry structure, and the development of tourism. The research chooses 5 world heritage sites to analyze in more depth and also 5 international cases for comparison. Then this research suggests some development models basing on different merits of the sites. The research also suggests a long term monitoring structure to be built better understand the social and economical changes related to the world heritage sites.

This research is the first academic attempt to systematically compare data, to understand and discuss the social and economical impact of world heritage status national wide in China. The following report is an executive summary for this research.

Key words: World heritage sites in China, sustainable development, conservation economics

Section 1 Background to the Study and an Outline of Research Undertaken

This section gives background information on the study and a broad outline of research undertaken. The background information including the aims of the study, definitions of basic concepts found in the study and information about the selection process for case studies used in this study. The outline of research undertaken includes the reasons for the selection of a particular research methodology as well as the technical roadmap developed for this study. Due to constraints on the length of this Executive Summary Report, Chinese and international case studies originally reported on in the full study have to be summarized and modified focusing on outlining their research methodologies and main conclusions.

1　Background to the Study

1) The aim of the Study

The fundamental aims of this study were to gain a comprehensive understanding of the conservation and development of World Heritage Sites (WHS) in China and how these sites are impacting on local social and economic development. This included the overall benefits derived from a particular site, their delivery mechanisms and outstanding issues. This study has also proposed measures that could be adopted to enhance World Heritage Sites. The main issues examined in this study included:

i. a comprehensive investigation and analysis of operations at sites in China that have already been designated as World Heritage Sites and their impact on the development of the local economy and community; the establishment of assessment criteria and the creation of a data base on the socio-economic development of sites; a comprehensive analysis of a site's impact on the development of the local economy, changes in brand value, awareness and reputation; and benefits to local residents as a site develops-primary methods, quantity, degree of participation and satisfaction.

ii. a sample of case studies representative of World Heritage Sites to analyse a long – term stuation of sites prior to and after nomination to explore the ways a site acts as a catalyst in driving socio – economic development, the derived benefits and changes, and the affects on the development of a 'heritage economy'and the site's conservation.

iii. an integrated analysis of case studies representative of sites outside China and discussed the advantages and disadvantages of the various models.

iv. a review of the current status of sites in China and an outline of effective strategies that could improve the conservation, development and management mechanisms for China's World Heritage Sites; strategies and proposals beneficial to the sustainable development of heritage sites.

2) Definitions of Basic Concepts

Research undertaken on the economic development of World Heritage Sites can be based on the following:

i. cultural heritage conservation theory

ii. cultural economics theory

iii. conservation economics theory

iv. public economics theory

v. welfare economics theory

vi. sustainable development theory

vii. theories relating to town planning.

This study is primarily based on 'Cultural Heritage Economics Theory', 'Sustainable Development Theory', and 'Theories Relating to Town Planning'. However the study also drew on theories relating to 'Cultural Economics', 'Conservation Economics', 'Public Economics'and 'Welfare Economics'.

Conservation economics was the principle theory studied to explore patterns in economic activities relating to cultural heritage and their impact on cultural heritage. Conservation economics provided a fresh perspective on research into cultural heritage and presented a much broader understanding of cultural heritage values in the context of concepts and basic theories relating to cultural heritage from an economics' perspective. This approach also allowed for a better understanding of the cost – benefit aspects of cultural heritage as well as provided a methodology for undertaking a cost – benefit analysis.

Several important perspectives and concepts in this study that have been based on conservation economics are outlined below.

Cultural Heritage as a Special Form for 'Cultural Capital'

Conservation economics is founded on the recognition of cultural heritage as a form of 'cultural capital' that has both cultural and economic value. Here 'capital' is regarded as a repository of value as well as a long – term asset, and can create a series of long cost and benefit cycles. Cultural heritage thus can be analysed just like any other commodity that is produced and consumed. By taking cultural heritage as a cultural asset, this study understands 'cultural heritage' to be a resource with a rich mixture of constituent elements composed of natural, man – made and human resources. Different categories of sites have a different mix of constituent elements. Cultural heritage is to some extent akin to a fixed asset and thus also faces the same 'depreciation' issues. However, being a non-renewable resource, great care needs to be taken in balancing use with conservation.

Recognition of the Multi – layered Nature of the Benefits of Cultural Heritage

The benefits of cultural heritage projects can be conceptualized at three levels (Throsby, 2001). The first is the use benefit, i. e. the direct products and services that emerge from the project. The second is the non – use benefit, that is the intrinsic value of heritage; the existence value-heritage's existence value and its option value-preserving the right of other people or later generations having the option to consume heritage at some future time; the bequest value-people may wish to bequeath the heritage value to further generations. The third is the external benefit, i. e. the leveraged impact for other economic sectors.

A more detailed delineation enables the separation of impacts into direct benefits and indirect benefits. Direct benefits refer to the economic benefits derived from the use of heritage. Indirect benefits are benefits that other industries or sectors may derive from conservation projects, possible reductions in future expenditure as well as social benefits.

Defining the Different Categories in the Scope of Research of this Study

Conservation economics defines the scope of research into cultural heritage sites in terms of the site's geographical locations and groups of people that are impacted. From the geographical perspective, the scope of research was divided into three levels: i. the property zone (the core zone) and the buffer zone; ii. the town or city where the heritage site is located or city or town areas in the immediate vicinity of a site; iii. the regional or city clusters where the site is located. This study used this particular structure and divided the research into two levels, World Heritage Sites and the locations of the World Heritage Sites.

World Cultural Heritage Sites

World Cultural Heritage Sites are delineated by a physical boundary. This study drew on the definition of a conservation zone used in WHS nomination documents; in this study World Cultural Heritase Sites referred to the core zone and the buffer zone.

World Cultural Heritage Site Location

The site and the municipality or county (*xian*) administrative district where the site or site management organization or department is located; this mainly refers to counties (*xian*), county – level (*xian*) cities, municipalities (under the direct jurisdiction of the central government) or prefecture – level cities.

3) Selection of Case Studies

The selection of case studies considered the different categories of heritage, the date of application for World Heritage listing, their economic regions, listing criteria and nomination motivations. This study selected 21 World Heritage Sites in China for the focus of its research (refer to Table 1. 1) thereby covering all four economic regions in China and six different categories of heritage (Figures 1. 1 & 1. 2). More detailed data and information was available on six sites and therefore regarded as suitable for undertaking more detailed investigation: i. e. the Mountain Resort and Outlying Temples in Chengde, the Old Town of Lijiang, the Fujian *Tulou* (Vernacular Houses), the

Mogao Caves in Dunhuang, the Historic Centre of Macao and the Ancient City of Pingyao. Excerpts of case studies in this executive summary focused on information and discussions about methodology and conclusions rather than specific details about individual cases.

Table 1. 1　Background Information on 26 WHS Case Studies in China in this Study

#	Name	Listed Time	Location	Economic Region & Administrative Level
			Mountains	
1	Mount Taishan	1987	Tai'an, Shandong Province	eastern seaboard, regional municipality
2	Mount Huangshan	1990	Huangshan, Anhui Province	central, regional municipality
3	Ancient Building Complex in the Wudang Mountains	1994	Danjiang, Shiyan, Hubei Province	central, county municipality
4	Mount Wuyi	1999	Wuyishan, Nanping, Fujian Province	eastern seaboard, county municipality
			Town and Historic Centres	
5	Ancient City of Pingyao	1997	Pingyao County, Jinzhong, Shanxi Province	central, county town
6	Old Town of Lijiang	1997	Lijiang, Yunnan Province	west, regional municipality
7	Historic Centre of Macao	2005	Macao SAR	eastern seaboard, SAR
			Villages	
8	Ancient Villages in Southern Anhui-Xidi and Hongcun	2000	Yi County, Huangshan, Anhui Province	central, county town
9	Fujian*Tulou* (Yongding)	2008	Yongding County, Longyan, Fujian Province	eastern seaboard, county town
10	Fujian*Tulou* (Nanjing)	2008	Nanjing County, Zhangzhou, Fujian Province	eastern seaboard, county town
11	Fujian*Tulou* (Huaan)	2008	Hua'an County, Zhangzhou, Fujian Province	eastern seaboard, county town
			Large Scale Historic Building Complexes	
12	Mountain Resort and its Outlying Temples, Chengde	1994	Chengde, Hebei Province	eastern seaboard, regional municipality
13	Temple and Cemetery of Confucius and the Kong Family Mansion in Qufu	1994	Qufu, Jining, Shandong Province	eastern seaboard, county level municipality
14	Classical Gardens of Suzhou	1997	Suzhou, Jiangsu Province	eastern seaboard, regional municipality
15	Mount Qingcheng and the Dujiangyan Irrigation System	2000	Dujiangyan, Sichuan Province	west, county level city*
16	Imperial Tombs of the Ming and Qing Dynasties (Eastern Qing Tombs)	2000	Zunhua, Tangshan, Hebei Province	eastern seaboard, county level municipality
17	Imperial Tombs of the Ming and Qing Dynasties (13 Tombs)	2003	Changping, Beijing	eastern seaboard, municipality directly under central govt.
18	Imperial Tombs of the Ming and Qing Dynasties (Yong Tomb)	2004	Xinbin Manchurian Autonomous County, Fushun, Liaoning Province	northeast, self – autonomous county town
			Archaeological Sites	
19	Mausoleum of the First Qin Emperor	1987	Lintong, Xi'an, Shaanxi Province	central, regional municipality
20	Peking Man Site at Zhoukoudian	1987	Fangshan Beijing	eastern seaboard, municipality directly under central govt.
21	Capital Cities and Tombs of the Ancient Koguryo Kingdom (Mountain Town of Wunu)	2004	Huanren Manchurian County, Benxi, Liaoning Province	northeast, self – autonomous county town
22	Capital Cities and Tombs of the Ancient Koguryo Kingdom	2004	Ji'an, Tonghua, Jilin Province	northeast, county level municipality
23	Yin Xu	2006	Anyang, Henan Province	central, regional municipality

续表

#	Name	Listed Time	Location	Economic Region & Administrative Level
Cave Sites				
24	Mogao Caves	1987	Dunhuang, Gansu Province	west, county level municipality
25	Dazu Rock Carvings	1999	Dazu County, Chongqing	west, county town
26	Yungang Grottoes	2001	Datong, Shanxi Province	central, regional municipality

NB: * County Municipality directly under Provincial Government

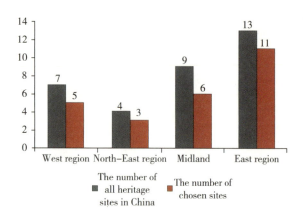

Figures 1.1 Number of Cultural Heritage Sites in each Economic Region

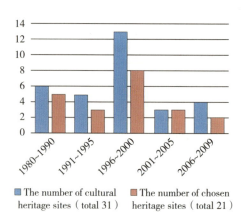

Figures 1.2 Distribution of Date of Inscription

2 Research Outline

1) Research Methodology

This study looked at the conservation of China's World Heritage Sites and the development of the economy of a heritage site from an economic and social perspective. The approaches and the methodology used in this study are briefly outlined below (Figures 1.3).

Sociology Approach-site Visits, Interviews and Questionnaires

This study aspired to break the monopoly held by the field of economics on the right to comment on "regional development". The study experimented with using a more pluralist perspective to reflect on the issue of development and to establish more comprehensive assessment criteria. The research methodology employed sociological methods during visits, interviews and questionnaires. This not only assisted in obtaining a large quantity of first hand information, but also in gaining a deeper appreciation of different stakeholders' attitudes to the impact of a heritage site on the development of the local economy.

Economics Approach I: Cost-Benefit Analysis and Impact Analysis

Analysis of the operational performance of a heritage site's management organisation used the cost – benefit analysis methodology with an aim of examining the commercial operational performance of the site in comparison with progress achieved for conservation projects. Specific methods employed included financial analysis and social cost – benefit analysis etc. An analytical method were used to assess the impact of a site on local towns and cities in order to determine direct and indirect impacts as well as induced impact. This study demonstrated the economic and social benefits achieved at several levels in the town or city where the site was located.

Economics Approach II: Quantitative Regression Analysis

This study used the quantitative regression analysis methodology to judge the impact of nomination or other major events that occurred at a site on the development of the local tourism industry (e.g. increase in visitor numbers) as well as the induced impact on the entire local economy and employment situation due to investment in conservation at a site in specific instances.

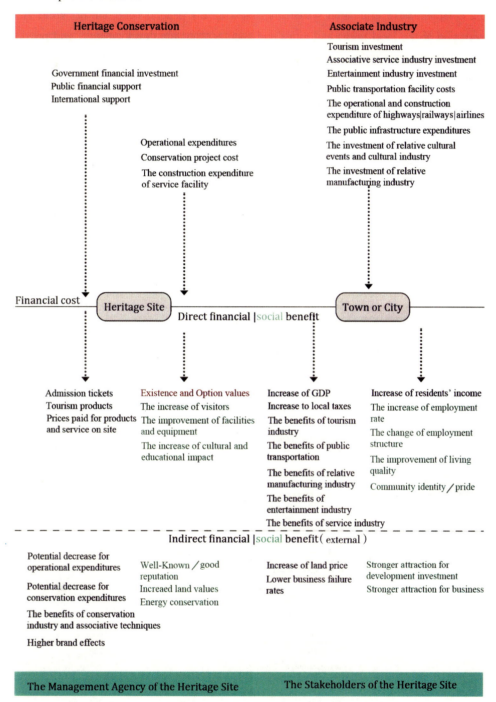

Figure 1.3   Approach to "Input-Output" Analysis for Heritage
Sites and the Towns and Cities Where They are Located

3) Technical Roadmap

This study includes three major sections: the first section comprises an investigation and analysis of the current condition and state of conservation at China's World Cultural Heritage Sites in comparison with local socio－economic developments; the second is a detailed analysis of the selected case studies and the third is a review of the most relevant theories, research and relevant case studies abroad. Based on the research in these three areas, the study developed a comprehensive evaluation system for assessing the general condition of World Heritage Sites in China, the conservation of the local towns and cities and socio – economic developments, and provided advices on future conservation, management and use of heritage sites together with the developing Strategy for the towns and cities where heritage sites are located (Figure 1.4).

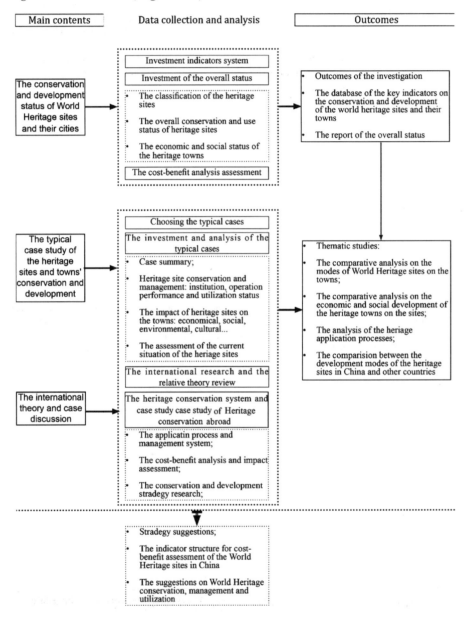

Figure 1.4   Technical Roadmap for the Study

Section 2   Overview of the Use and Commercial Operation of China's World Heritage Sites

This section explores the use of heritage sites and possible benefits derived from the sites as well as an overview of the status of use and commercial operations of China's heritage sites.

Some of the social benefits derived from China's heritage sites include: maintainance of optional value, visitor consumer surplus, creation of employment positions and labour income, engenders good neighbourhood relations, contributions to community education and community interaction as well as publicity and improved awareness of heritage. Economic benefits are generally expressed by the price paid which includes entrance ticket income and other income from commercial operations on site.

For commercial operations, the most important source of income for the majority of heritage sites in China is the sale of entrance tickets. However there is strong reliance on national government funding for major conservation projects. Major conservation projects continue to be undertaken at most heritage sites with outlays for regular maintenance, monitoring, lean management and research being insignificant. The financial and time resources spent by the majority of heritage sites on the treatment of the setting is many times greater than that spent on the conservation of the site's physical fabric.

1 Use of World Heritage Sites and Benefits Derived from Their Use

People today have a diverse range of interactions with World Heritage Sites. Similarly, sites are used in diverse ways: for tourism and recreation, public space, a facility for research or education, places for maintaining non – tangible cultural heritage. In many circumstances, a heritage site can be space where people live and engage in commercial activities. The particular emphasis given to a site's use and conservation depends on the site's values, unique characteristics and degree of fragility. The cardinal principle is that a site must be conserved; each individual heritage site needs to treated differently and in some cases various elements of the same heritage site need to be managed differently. The premise for the use and development of a site is that there should be no damage a site; use and development should be appropriate for the specific site. From the economic perspective, cultural heritage is a non – renewable cultural asset. Good conservation and management of cultural heritage assets implies their maintenance and management for the benefit of all in the future.

1) Social Benefits Derived from Heritage Sites in China

This study has drawn on a section of the paper "Conservation Economics: Cost Benefit Analysis for the Cultural Built Heritage: Principles and Practice" (ICOMOS 1993) on direct and indirect benefits derived from cultural heritage to explore the way in which World Heritage Sites in China are used. The study comprehensively summarizes the direct and indirect benefits to a site achieved through its conservation and use which are outlined below.

Maintenance of Optional Value

The present generation who care about and engage with heritage benefit from its option value; they maintain the rights of other people or future generations as heritage consumers. This includes both the economic value of heritage as well as its social value and relates to intergenerational equity and equity among individuals.

Visitors Consumers' Surplus

Consumers of tourism and other associated industries receive more value than the actual price they pay, which could be regarded as a form of consumption welfare. When this notion is applied to cultural heritage, there is a strong connection between consumers' surplus and the "intrinsic value" of heritage. That is to say that there is a direct connection between consumer surplus and tourism consumption costs, such as the price of a site's entrance ticket. There are many instances in recent years of sites raising the price of their entrance tickets after successful inscription on the World Heritage Site List. If the "intrinsic value" of heritage reduced, pressure would be put on consumer surplus. This has an impact on the consumption welfare enjoyed by consumers of tourism and other related industries who use that site.

Employment Positions and Income

Heritage sites offer the local community and other groups considerable opportunity for direct or indirect employment and contribute to the employment levels in a town or city. Chengde Municipality is a good example, with more than 2,000 people employed by site management at the Mountain Resort and Outlying Temples. In addition, in 2006 there were more than 40,000 people directly involved in the tourism industry in Chengde, accounting for 15% of the total workforce. The total number of people employed in industries related to tourism was 200,000, an increase of eight percent over the previous year. This data is closely connected with the development of tourism at the Mountain Resort and Outlying Temples in Chengde. It should be emphasised that members of the local community should be employed in positions created by the development of tourism at a heritage site and that preference be given to local members of the community when hiring for generalist positions. The only exceptions should be senior management positions that require specialized knowledge and technology. To maximize social benefits in the broadest possible manner, positions should not be contracted out to agents who employ large numbers of workers from outside the local community.

Good Neighbourhood Relations

World Heritage gives the local community a strong sense of pride and improves cohesiveness and relationships within the local community as well as making the immediate local economy more stable. For residents of towns and cities in the vicinity of World Heritage Sites, the strong sense of cultural identification and the civic pride that comes from World Heritage Listing is evident in responses to questionnaires, particularly in the example of Mount Taishan. In 2009 when respondents were asked if they agreed with the statement that "they felt a sense of pride because of the heritage site", 62.19% of respondents surveyed chose "strong affirmative". Another 34.33% of respondents chose "affirmative". Chengde also illustrates this point. 75% of local residents agreed or strongly agreed that recognition as a World Heritage Site had improved their quality of life as the city became better known, the environment improved, more employment opportunities were created and public transport was improved. This shows the positive role that a heritage site can play in becoming a symbol of the city, in creating a sense of awareness as well as a sense of identity.

Contributions to Community Education and Interaction, Promotion of Awareness and Publicity about Heritage

Data collected shows that heritage activities can improve interaction between locals and education about knowledge on traditions. In Chengde, 68% of surveyed local residents expressed a willingness to participate in heritage volunteer work; 36% stated that they talked about the heritage site in their hometown both at work and at home. In the Ancient City of Pingyao, data showed that after the site's successful inscription on the World Heritage List, the site had more contact with the local community and residents and traditional culture was maintained.

2) Economic Benefits Derived from Heritage Sites in China

Management organisations at heritage sites achieve the price paid that is mainly in the form of revenue from site entrance ticket sales and revenue that comes directly from commercial operations. Income from the sale of site entrance tickets constitutes the most significant part of a heritage site's economic revenue in China. Income from the sale of site entrance tickets depends on the number of visitors as well as the price of the ticket. The former, to some degree, reflects the extensiveness of the social impact of a site and its capacity to handle visitors. The latter reflects the checks and balances between willingness to pay, a heritage site's value and strategies for public access. Revenue directly derived from commercial operations refers to the after – tax net income of the site's management organisation from directly engaging in the production and supply of cultural products and services. The price paid achieved by site operators and managers only accounts for an extremely small proportion of the total.

Visitor Numbers

A comprehensive comparison of statistics at heritage sites around China (Figure 2.1) shows that there has been a significant overall increase in the number of visitors to World Heritage Sites (aside from 2003 when visitor numbers to most sites decreased due to the SARS epidemic). The sites that were inscribed in the 1990s saw an increase in visitor numbers mainly during the bid process due to the publicity platform that World Heritage brings and the associated promotional activities. Most sites experienced a significantly higher rate of increase in visitor numbers during this period compared to previously. Conferring World Heritage designation clearly boosts the site's reputation and brand. These two elements have a significant impact on the site's appeal to the public. Heritage sites that were initially listed as World Heritage Sites in China didn't experience significant changes in visitor numbers prior to and after WHS designation. This is because most heritage sites initially listed were already extremely well-known. In addition, the under-developed state of tourism in China prior to the 1990s restricted the increase in visitor numbers.

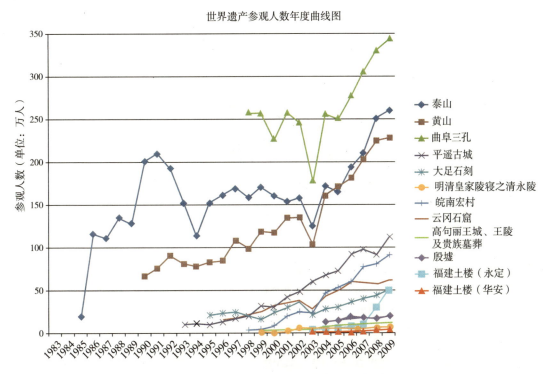

Figure 2.1　Annual Visitor Numbers to WHS

(NB: large square on broken line denotes annual data for WHS)

(Indexes from the top to the bottom are: Mountain Taishan, Mountain Huangshan, Temple and Cemetery of Confucius and the Kong Family Mansion in Qufu, Ancient City of Pingyao, Dazu Rock Carvings, Ming Qing Imperial Tombs (Qing Yong Tombs), Ancient Villages in Southern Anhui (Hong village), Yungang Grottoes, Ancient Koguryo Kingdom (Jian), Fujian tulou (Yong Ding), Fujian tulou (Hua An).)

Income from the Site Entrance Tickets

Sites that were successfully inscribed as World Heritage Sites after the 1990s experienced significant increase in income from the sale of site entrance tickets after inscription. Those sites that were initially listed did not see the same changes in income from ticket sales after inscription (Figure 2.2). The increase rate of income earned from ticket sales and visitor numbers cannot simply be attributed to the impact of conferring WHS status. This study was undertaken during a period of time when the tourism industry in China was developing rapidly. However, the rapid increase in economic benefit derived from heritage sites in cases such as the Fujian *Tulou* (Nanjing and Yongding) and the Dazu Rock Carvings after inscription clearly shows the changes resulting from World Heritage status. Nevertheless, the degree of increase in income from the sale of entrance tickets after inscription clearly exceeded the rate of increase in visitor numbers. Pingyao, for example, recorded a six fold increase in visitor numbers prior to inscription in 1997 while entrance ticket revenue increased 121. 44 fold (these figures are in absolute value terms and have not taken into consideration of factors such as currency devaluation). This shows that "World Heritage" designation results in increased visitation and also increases visitors' willingness to pay, in other words, it increases their acknowledgement of the value of a heritage site.

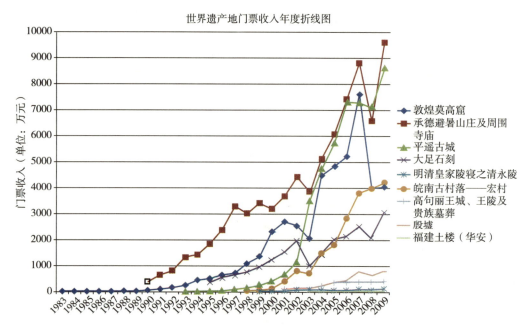

Figure 2. 2   Annual Income from Entrance Tickets at WHS

(NB: large square on broken line denotes annual data for WHS)

(Indexes from the top to the bottom are: Mogao Caves Dunhuang, Mountain Resort and Outlying Temples, Chengde, Ancient City of Pingyao, Dazu Rock Carvings, Ming Qing Imperial Tombs (Qing Yong Tombs), Ancient Villages in Southern Anhui (Hong village), Ancient Koguryo Kingdom, Yin Xu, Fujian tulou (Hua An).)

2   Operations at Heritage Sites in China

1) Review of Income and Expenditure and its Components

Economic income and expenditure discussed in this section refers to the income and expenditure of a site's management organisation and does not include benefits that other industries indirectly derive from a site. The primary source of income for China's World Heritage Sites comes from the allocation of government funding, income from the site (mainly ticket sales) and special purpose grants. Less significant sources of income include income from a site's commercial operations, international assistance, donations and other miscellaneous income. Case studies showed primary source of income accounted for between 60% – 95% of a site's total income. Site expenses can also be divided into primary and secondary expenses. Primary expenses consist of operational and project expenses. Operational expenses include the cost of personnel and public expenses, in other words, the overall cost of operating a site. Secondary expenses include commercial operational expenses, tax and other expenses. Primary expenses accounted for between 70% – 95% of a site's total expenses with operational expenditure being the largest for most sites. Secondary expenditure accounted for between 5% – 30%.

Income and its Composition

Despite the continued improvement in the overall income generated from heritage sites in China, most sites generally rely on only one source of income. Compared with heritage sites internationally, China's World Heritage Sites receive very little financial support for conservation work from private funds. Restrictions on commercial operations at sites also means that income from a site's commercial activities is quite minimal. Sites are heavily reliant on government allocations and site entrance ticket sales. Government funding is only guaranteed to those non – profit organizations that do not generate their own income and cannot cover their own expenses. Organisations that generate their income and are able to cover expenses could only receive grants for specific projects. Thus entrance tickets income has become the most important source of revenue for the majority of heritage sites in China. Figure 2. 3 shows the income increasing from entrance ticket sales as a proportion of total income at five heritage sites (excluding the impact on tourism from SARS in 2003 and the 2008 Beijing Olympic Games). This is particularly the case for the Mountain Resort and Outlying Temples in Chengde where income from entrance ticket sales since 1997 has accounted for approximately 90% of total income. For other sites it has generally reached between 70% –95% of total income. Over reliance on ticket sales income for general revenue can easily result in the over development or commercialization of a site. Heritage sites in this position should seek to diversify their sources of income in the future.

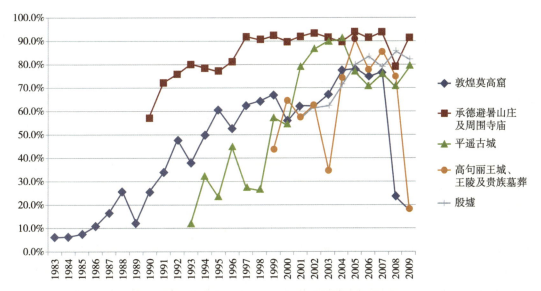

Figure 2. 3　Entrance Ticket Income Ratios at WHS in China

(Indexes from the top to the bottom are: Mogao Grottoes, Chengde Mountain Resort and Outlying Temples, Ancient City of Pingyao, Ancient Koguryo Kingdom, Yin Xu)

Expenditure and its Composition

Operational expenditure (site operating costs) and project expenditure (regular site maintenance, conservation and projects related to improving the setting) are the principal expenses at a heritage site. Figure 2. 4 shows the following data:

I. Sites that have low maintenance requirements or are not very fragile, such as the Mountain Resort and the Outlying Temples in Chengde have had both large – scale conservation and commercial operations for a long period. Aside from years when there have been large – scale conservation projects, the proportion of other annual expenditure items in the total budget have been relatively static and mainly consisted of basic expenditure items (fluctuated between approximately 50% –60%).

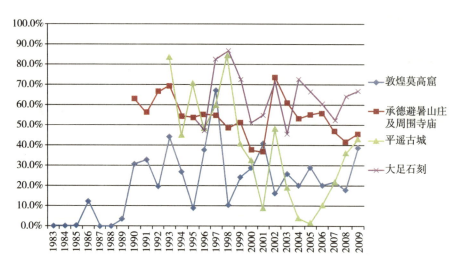

Figure 2. 4   Project Expenditure as a Percentage of Total Expenditure for China's WHS

(Indexes from the top to the bottom are: Mogao Grottoes, Chengde Mountain Resort and Outlying Temples, Ancient City of Pingyao, Dazu Rock Carvings)

II. Sites that require a large amount of maintenance or are quite fragile, such as Mogao Caves at Dunhuang or Dazu Rock Carvings, have had many large expenditure items. These large fluctuations are shown by the breaks in the lines in the Figure.

III. Pingyao is representative of another category of sites. They are not fragile and the maintenance requirements are not high. Hovever prior to being inscribed, the site had not been well conserved. The physical elements of the site, setting, infrastructure and site management were greatly in need of improvement. To meet the requirements for World Heritage Listing, considerable time and investment were needed to complete projects both before and after inscription. During this period, project expenses became the site's primary expenditure. Later on project expenses were maintained at a high level and continued to increase while operational and management costs rose after listing due to stricter operational and management requirements, as a result project expenditure as a percentage of total expenditure dropped dramatically after inscription. (Project expenditure for the Ancient City of Pingyao accounted for more than 50% of total expenditure, apart from 1994 when it was 45. 3%. In 1998 project expenditure peaked at 84. 8% and after 1998 the level of project expenditure has fluctuated below 50% of the total expenditure.)

These three different scenarios for heritage expenditure demonstrate that most heritage sites in China are still undertaking major conservation interventions. There are still many issues relating to heritage preservation, the construction of infrastructure and the immediate setting. There is still frequent demand for funding for large projects. Funding for routine maintenance, monitoring, lean management and research is still insignificant. Changes of project expenditure for the majority of heritage sites are closely linked with changes of the amount of available government funding. Only a few heritage sites are able to use operational income, that is, income from entrance ticket sales and commercial activities to fund projects. The source of project funding is directly affected by the allocation of government funds. Projects requiring large – scale investment tend to be those that receive special grants for specific projects from government departments responsible for heritage management or local government. There is in reality only one single source for project funds. The amount of funding and time spent by the majority of heritage sites on the treatment of a site's setting is much greater than the amount of funding and time spent on the conservation of a site's physical fabric (Figure 2. 5 illustrates the expenditure of Chengde) .

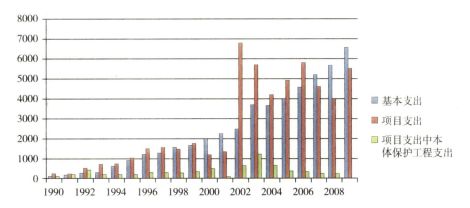

Figure 2.5   1990 ~ 2009 Chengde WHS Expenditure（unit：RMB10，000 yuan）

Source：Chengde Cultural Relics Bureau

（Indexes from the top to the bottom are：operational expenditures，project expenditures，conservation project expenditures）

Data from case studies shows that total income is generally increasing for all heritage sites resulting from a large increase in the income from site entrance ticket sales（site entrance ticket income as a percentage of total income has also risen for some sites）. However，the World Heritage Site label tends to bring increased attention from government and the public along with increased funding from central or provincial governments and financial subsidies from the local government authorities immediately responsible for the site. This trend has several commonalities that are listed below.

Geographical Location

Sites that experienced a significant increase in income after inscription are generally in remote areas far from major cities. Transport infrastructure in the region was upgraded during the bidding period.

Awareness

Sites that experienced a significant increase in income after inscription were less well - known prior to inscription. Acknowledgement as a "World Heritage Site" and the associated publicity platform have increased the public's awareness of the site，as is the case for the Old Town of Lijiang and the Fujian *Tulou*.

Management and Operation Models

Sites that experienced a significant increase in income after inscription have been mostly sites that had clear and well - defined strategies and actions for the development of tourism and the economy.

2）Preliminary Cost - Effect Analysis

This study has used the relative value of a heritage site's expenditure（operational expenditure）and site entrance ticket sales income as important criteria for measuring the cost - benefit of a heritage site. Figure 2.6 illustrates that the relative value of operational expenditure and income from sites initially is moderately high followed by a declined up until 2000. This is due to the fact that initially the cost of an entrance ticket was modest. Heritage sites that were publicly accessible then had a high degree of welfare incorporated into the price of a ticket. Some sites that were initially open to the public were also less well - known and tourism was less developed during that period. Operational expenditure was mainly provided through government allocation of funds reveals a site's high dependence on government funding. This relative value of The majority of World Heritage Sites in China had dropped to less than 100% after 2000，explaining that a site's income in most cases was sufficient to cover operating costs. It can be seen from this that most heritage sites still have a good return from current investment practices. However，most sites still have to rely on central government funding for major conservation projects.

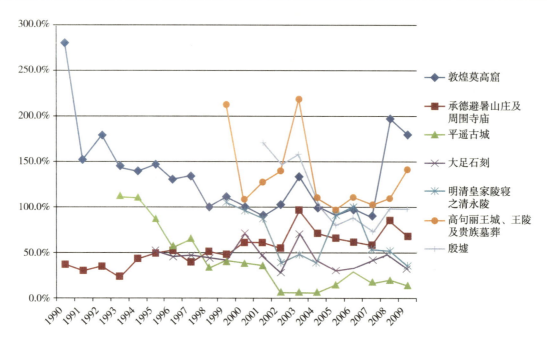

Figure 2. 6   WHS Relative Value of Basic Expenditure and Income from Site Entrance Tickets

(NB: large square on broken line signifies year applied for WHS)

(Indexes from the top to the bottom are: Mogao Grottoes, Chengde Mountain Resort and Outlying Temples, Ancient City of Pingyao, Dazu Rock Carvings, Ancient City of Pingyao, Dazu Rock Carvings, Ming Qing Imperial Tombs (Qing Yong Tombs), Ancient Koguryo Kingdom, Yin Xu)

This study also concluded that there was a difference in a site's cost – benefit depending on the type of site, its suitability to be open to the public and its ability to appeal to visitors. Several World Heritage Sites have a high level of relative value in terms of operating expenditure and income from entrance ticket sales. Sites such as the Capital Cities and Tombs of the Ancient Koguryo Kingdom (site access difficulties resulted in low awareness and low visitor appeal), the Mogao Grottoes at Dunhuang (site fragility limited public access), Yin Xu (lack of visitor appeal) are good examples. Therefore, Central government funding policies and considerations for funding support should be made with reference to the individual circumstances at each World Heritage Site. They also need to consider socio – economic benefits together with cost – benefit broadly and make funding adjustments accordingly.

Section 3   Towns and Cities in the Vicinity of China's World Heritage Sites-Review of Socio-Economic Development

This section reviews in detail the general situation of socio – economic development in the towns and cities where China's World Heritage Cultural Sites are located. The review explores this issue from four perspectives. Below is a summary of the conclusions.

The relationship between a heritage site and the town or city in its vicinity: this can be separated into six different modes of dependence and two different categories of motivation for bidding for World Heritage Listing.

Economic development: (ⅰ) the rate of economic growth in towns and cities where heritage sites are located is faster than the national average in most cases; however, there are many towns and cities in the central, western and north eastern regions of China where economic fundamentals are poor; (ⅱ) the level of urbanization is generally low in towns and cities in the vicinity of heritage sites; World Heritage labels have a positive impact on the income of rural residents.

Industry sector composition in these towns and cities: (i) the tertiary sector in these towns and cities has generally developed well. A sudden increase in public awareness after inscription may have also led to successfully attracting extra – regional investment into secondary industry; (ii) heritage sites situated close to the centre of these towns and cities have also achieved benefits from their location in developing industries associated with the site; (iii) the percentage of people working in the tertiary sector in most of these towns and cities is higher than the national average. The increase in the number of people employed in the cultural field is a recent trend emerging in towns and cities in the vicinity of heritage sites.

Development of tourism in these towns and cities: (i) tourism has played a more significant role in the development of the economies of county (*xian*) level towns and cities; (ii) for many towns and cities in the vicinity of heritage sites it is now common that the number of visitors is ten times greater than the local population, yet the appeal to international visitors is limited; (iii) there appears to be a connection between the type of heritage site and visitor consumption per capita; (iv) not all of the Hertase Sites are regarded as the center of local tourism.

1 The Relationship between China's World Heritage Sites and the Towns or Cities in Their Vicinity

1) The Dependence Models between Heritage Sites and the Towns or Cities in Their Vicinity

This study focused on an investigation of the relationship between geographic location and cultural impact, examining the connection of a site with the public and its contribution to the economy. The study found six different models to define the dependence relationship between World Heritage and its locality. It is noteworthy that currently heritage has become the primary resource for towns or cities in the vicinity of site for approximately half of the World Heritage Sites in China and that heritage has become an important resource for approximately one quarter of the towns or cities located in the vicinity of a heritage site (Figure 3. 1).

Table 3. 1 Dependence Models for Sites and Towns

No:	Dependence Model	space rel.	cul rel	soc rel	eco rel	Heritage Site Case Study	%
A	town grew out of site	close	close	close	high	Mount Taishan, Chengde Mountain Resort and Outlying Temples, Ancient City of Pingyao, Ancient Town of Lijiang, Mount Wutai	15%
B	site is primary resource for the town	close	highly rep	gen.	high	Imperial Ming and Qing Palaces (Beijing), Potala Palace, Temple, Cemetery of Confucius and Kong Family Mansion, Suzhou Classical Gardens, Mount Qing Cheng and Dujiangyan Irrigation System, Ancient Koguryo Kingdom (ji'an), Macao Historic Centre and Yin Xu in Anyang.	23%
C	site is one of the important resources for town	close	gen.	gen	comparatively high	Ming and Qing Palace (Shenyang), Temple of Heaven, Summer Palace in Beijing.	9%
D	site is primary resource in outlying district	not close	highly reps	gen.	high	First Qin Emperor Mausoleum, Mogao Caves, Mount Huangshan, Lushan National Park, Wudang Mountains, Mount Emei and Mount Leshan Buddha, Dazu Carvings, Ancient Koguryo Kingdom (Huanren), Yin Xu, Mount Wutai	28%
E	Site is one of the most important resources in outlying district	not close	gen.	gen。	comparatively high	Zhoukoudian Peking Man Site, Imperial Tombs of Ming and Qing Dynasties, Yungang Grottoes, Longmen Grottoes, Histroic Monuments of Dengfeng in 'The Centre of Heaven and Earth'	16%
F	Site is in residential village	not close	highly reps	close	high	Ancient Villages in Southern Anhui, Kaiping *Diaolou* and Villages, Fujian*Tulou*	9%

2) Motivation of Bidding for World Heritage Inscription for Sites Located in Vicinity of Towns or Cities

International research into the benefits derived from cultural heritage has revealed that there are many factors that link many benefits that a World Heritage Site brings to the development goals of a local town, city or region as well as heritage. The feasibility study prepared for England's Lakes Area inscription bid in 2008 stated an important motive for nominating the site was the positive impact this would have on local socio – economic development. The feasibility study determined that there were four different factors, being "Celebration Designation", "SOS Designation", "Marketing/Quality Logo/Brand" and "Place Making Catalyst". There have been different motivations for inscription for different World Heritage Sites in China but they can be divided into two different categories.

The first category aims to "encourage and improve conservation". This type of sites is already well – known at the time of its bidding for World Heritage Listing. Tourism at these locations was already well established and stable, thus these made it easier for these sites to prepare their bids. These sites hoped that inscription would improve the site, provide an opportunity to obtain better publicity and provide ways to connect the site with the international conservation community. Regions with this type of motivation are mainly regional cities such as Beijing, Suzhou, and Tai'an and few county (xian) level cities where sites were initially listed such as Dunhuang.

The second category of aims to "promote local development through applying for World Heritage Listing". Sites of this category were less well – known, local tourism was less developed and the local economy was under developed. During the application process sites gained the support of the local government and held high expectations that successful World Heritage inscription would create an influential brand for the site. This category of sites also sought funding from many different sources to improve transport infrastructure and the conditions for tourism to promote the development of the local tourism market and economy. This category of sites is mainly located in the vicinity of counties (xian) level municipalities and county (xian) level towns and cities.

2 General Economic Development of Towns or Cities in the Vicinity of Heritage Sites

This study examined annual changes in two criteria to judge the main indicators for the growth rate of the local economy in the vicinity of a World Heritage Site. The first criterion was per capita Gross Regional Product, the second was the degree of urbanization.

1) Per Capita Gross Regional Product

The results of the comparison are shown in Figure 3. 1. The per capita Gross Product (per capita GDP) for cities and towns in the vicinity of World Heritage Sites included in this study has increased as national per capita GDP. Per capita GDP in towns and cities before and after the two turning points of 1994 and 2000 grew even more strongly and was generally in line with national economic growth. The per capita GDP growth curve demonstrates that, (i) overall GDP growth rate in the economies of towns and cities in the vicinity of heritage sites was faster than the national average, particularly after 2000; (ii) per capital GDP stayed approximately in line with the overall national trend after inscription for most of the towns or cities; (iii) a small number of towns and cities experienced rapid economic development after inscription. Towns and cities such as Tai'an, Chengde and Huanren where per capita GDP was lower than the national average, experienced a gradual rise in per capita GDP and finally exceeded the national average; (iv) Dujiangyan was the only location where per capita GDP went from being above to below the national average due to the earthquake in 2008.

A comprehensive comparison shows that after inscription the growth rate of economies in the majority of towns and cities in the vicinity of heritage sites was greater than the national average, and in a few locations, economies grew very rapidly. However the economic fundamentals of towns or cities in the vicinity of heritage sites that were located some distance from large urbanized centres remained weak. These were mainly rural towns and cities located in the central, western or northeast regions of China.

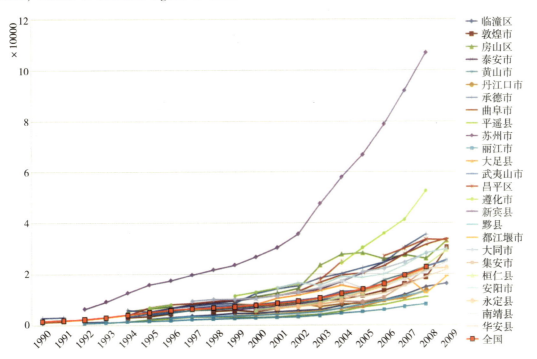

Figure 3.1   Comparison of the per Capita GDP in Towns Where 26 Heritage Sites Located

(Unit: RMB10, 000 yuan)

(NB: Macao SAR not included as circumstances quite exceptional)

(Indexes from the top to the bottom are: Lin Tong District, City of Dun Huang, District of Fang Shan, City of Tai'an, City of Mountain Huang, City of Dan Jiangkou, City of Cheng De, City of Qu Fu, Town of Ping Yao, City of Su Zhou, City of Li Jiang, Town of Da Zu, City of Mountain Wu Yi, District of Chang Ping, City of Zun Hua, Town of Xin Bin, Town of Yi, City of Du Jiangyan, City of Da Tong, City of Ji'an, Town of Heng Ren, City of An Yang, Town of Yong Ding, Town of Nan Jing, Town of Hua'an, The Country)

2) Urbanization

This study compiled data of the regions where the case studies sites are located from 1990 to 2009 (Figure 3.2). A comparison of this data showed that the degree of urbanization of most towns and cities located in the vicinity of heritage sites was lower than the national average. To some extent this showed that the non - rural percentage of the population at these localities was small and that these areas did not have a sufficient solid foundation to develop modern industry. The overall level of social and economic development in these areas needed to be addressed.

3) Overview of Local Residents' Income

Eighteen towns or cities have heritage sites located in or close to towns or cities. Of these, only Suzhou, Changping, Fangshan and Tai'an ouned the disposable income of the local residents either higher or equivalent to the national average, with all the remaining cities lower than the national average. In fifteen towns and cities where the heritage sites are located in the suburbs or rural areas, net income for rural residents in most locations was higher than the national average, with Danjiangkou and Datong being the only two exceptions. This demonstrates the positive effect of local heritage sites on the income of rural residents. However it also illustrates current low levels of income for rural residents in towns and cities in the vicinity of heritage sites.

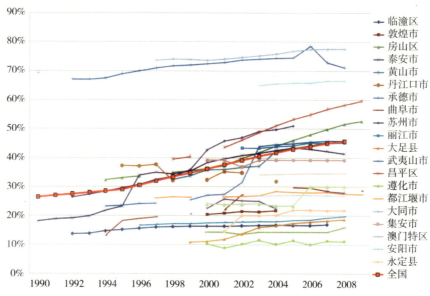

Figure 3. 2   Comparison of the Degree of Urbanization in Towns
with/in the Vicinity of Heritage Sites (Unit:%)

(Indexes from the top to the bottom are: District of Lin Tong, City of Dun Huang, District of Fang Shan, City of Tai'an, City of Mountain Huang, City of Dan Jiangkou, City of Cheng De, City of Qu Fu, City of Su Zhou, City of Li Jiang, Town of Da Zu, City of Mountain Wu Yi, District of Chang Ping, City of Zun Hua, City of Du Jiangyan, City of Da Tong, City of Ji'an, Macau, City of An Yang, Town of Yong Ding, The Country)

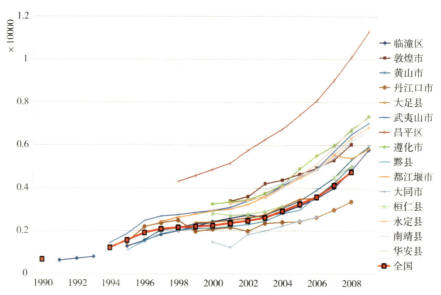

Figure 3. 3   Comparison of Net Income of Rural Residents at Towns with/in the
Vicinity of Heritage Sites (Unit: RMB10, 000 yuan)

(Indexes from the top to the bottom are: District of Lin Tong, City of Dun Huang, District of Fang Shan, City of Mountain Huang, City of Dan Jiangkou, Town of Da Zu, City of Mountain Wu Yi, District of Chang Ping, City of Zun Hua, Town of Yi, City of Du Jiangyan, City of Da Tong, Town of Heng Ren, Town of Yong Ding, Town of Nan Jing, Town of Hua'an, The Country)

3 Changes in Industry Structure in Towns and Cities in the Vicinity of Heritage Sites

This study examined the annual change in the following two criteria to judge the main indicators of structural change in industry in towns or cities in the vicinity a heritage site. The first criterion was the production value of industries associated with heritage as a percentage of local GDP; the second was the percentage of people employed in industries associated with heritage.

1) Production Value of Industry Sectors Related to Heritage as a Percentage of GDP

There is a large amount of information illustrating that the conservation and use of cultural heritage can be a catalyst in the development of associated industries both upstream and downstream (Figure 3. 4) .

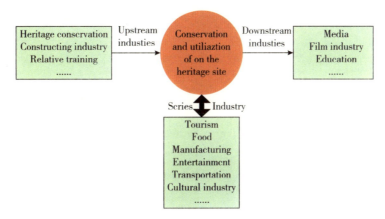

Figure 3. 4   The Relationship of Cultural Heritage and Local Industries

By the end of the twentieth century, China's tertiary sector entered a period of rapid development. This trend was similarly reflected in towns and cities in the vicinity of heritage sites. This does not imply that the tertiary sector was the principal pillar of economic development in all towns and cities near heritage sites. Total output value of the tertiary sector in some towns and cities in the locality of heritage sites rose after inscription, however in terms of a percentage of GDP it dropped in many towns and cities. Increased production value mainly occurred due to increased awareness of the town or city as a result of World Heritage Listing. Listing brings the advantage of being able to attract extra – regional capital which is the catalyst of the development of the secondary sector. The tertiary sector in towns and cities in the vicinity of a World Heritage Site generally continued to experience positive development growth (Figure 3. 5). The relationship of dependence between a World Heritage Site and its locality where the tertiary sector is developing strongly can be categorised as a locality where "the site is the most important resource for the town" or "town and heritage". This demonstrates that towns and cities in the vicinity of heritage sites provide secure and strong support for the development of industry sectors associated with the site. This is achieved through the provision of space, resources, infrastructure and related services.

2) Proportion of People Employed in Heritage Related Sectors

During the process of conserving and using World Heritage Sites, associated sectors such as heritage conservation, tourism and transport create employment in the towns and cities in the vicinity of a site through both direct and indirect employment. As indirect employment comprises many industries, this study used criteria of employment in the tertiary sector to identify the characteristics of employment in towns and cities in the vicinity of heritage sites.

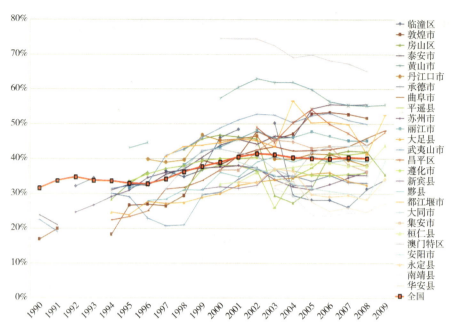

Figure 3. 5   Comparison of Tertiary Sector as % of Local GDP at Towns
with/in the Vicinity of Heritage Sites (Unit: %)

(Indexes from the top to the bottom are: District of Lin Tong, City of Dun Huang, District of Fang Shan, City of Tai'an, City of Mountain Huang, City of Dan Jiangkou, City of Cheng De, City of Qu Fu, Town of Ping Yao, City of Su Zhou, City of Li Jiang, Town of Da Zu, City of Mountain Wu Yi, District of Chang Ping, City of Zun Hua, Town of Xin Bin, Town of Yi, City of Du Jiangyan, City of Da Tong, City of Ji'an, Town of Heng Ren, Macau, City of An Yang, Town of Yong Ding, Town of Nan Jing, Town of Hua'an, The Country)

According to the changes in a town or city's tertiary sector employment ratio as a percentage of total employment (Figure 3. 6), the tertiary sector employment ratio for all 19 heritage sites used as case studies is higher than the national average. This suggests that the development level of the tertiary sector in towns and cities of most heritage sites is higher than the national average. The highest rates in this study's cases were Lijiang, Dunhuang, Zunhua, Macao and Mount Huangshan where the tertiary sector accounted for more than 70% of all employment (in the analysis above, tourism was the dominant or principal industry for the town or city) . In towns that have marked cultural identities such as Qufu and Lijiang, the fastest growing industry in the tertiary sector is the cultural industry with output value as a percentage of GDP growing significantly as well as increasingly large numbers of people are employed in this field. In 2009 the value of increased production output for the cultural industry in Qufu reached 4. 08% of local GDP.

4   Development of Tourism in Towns and Cities in the Vicinity of Heritage Sites

Tourism is often an important industry for towns or cities in the vicinity of World Heritage Sites and often develops into a strategically important industry for that town or city. The World Heritage brand becomes the driver and the central element in the development of local tourism. The highly developed nature of the tourism industry in these localities also reflects the high level of use of World Heritage. This study collected and analyzed data that illustrated the development of World Heritage tourism. Four important criteria were selected for comparison purposes: income from tourism as a percentage of the town or city's GDP; total number of visitors as a percentage of the local town or city's population; per capita tourism consumption and heritage site visitor numbers as a percentage of total visitation to a town or city.

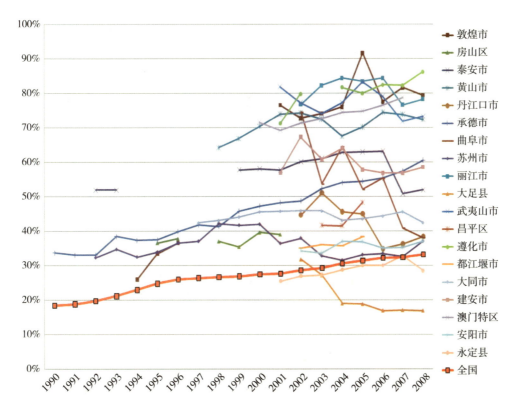

Figure 3. 6　Comparison of People Employed in Tertiary Sector as Percentage
of Total Employment at Towns with/in the Vicinity of Heritage Sites

（NB：Limited Data，Graph is Missing Data for Lintong，Pingyao，Xinbin，Yixian，Huanren，Nanjing and Hua'an）

（Indexes from the top to the bottom are：City of Dun Huang，District of Fang Shan，City of Tai'an，City of Mountain Huang，City of Dan Jiangkou，City of Cheng De，City of Qu Fu，City of Su Zhou，City of Li Jiang，Town of Da Zu，City of Mountain Wu Yi，District of Chang Ping，City of Zun Hua，City of Du Jiangyan，City of Da Tong，City of Ji'an，Macau，City of An Yang，Town of Yong Ding，The Country）

1）Income from Tourism as a Percentage of the Town or City's GDP

The towns or cities at heritage sites in this study were divided into five different categories based on income from tourism as a percentage of the town or city's GDP（Figure 3. 7）.

i. Tourism as the central industry-income from tourism accounted for more than

50% of the local town or city's GDP. This included Lijiang，Yixian and Mount Wuyi.

ii. Tourism as the dominant industry-income from tourism accounted for between

20% – 50% of local GDP，an amount higher than the national average. Mount Huangshan，Lintong，Dunhuang and Dujiangyan were included in this category.

iii. Tourism as an important industry-income from tourism accounted for between

10% – 20% of the local GDP. Pingyao，Qufu，Ji'an，Huanren，Yixian，Changping，Anyang and Suzhou were included in this category.

iv. Tourism industry as requiring development – income from tourism only accounted for less than 5% of local GDP for extended periods. This category included Zunhua and Fangshan.

vi. Rapid increase in tourism industry income ratio – although economic fundamentals continued to be weak，World Heritage Listing has stimulated the rapid growth of tourism over recent years. This category includes Lijiang，Yixian，Huanren，Mount Huangshan and Dujiangyan.

In the sampled case study towns and cities, county level municipalities and cities have a higher ratio of income from tourism as a percentage of their local GDP, the highest exceeding 20%. This illustrates that tourism plays an important role in stimulating the economic development of county level towns and cities.

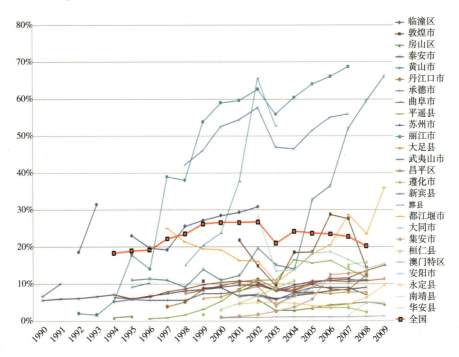

igure 3. 7   Tourism Income as % of GDP at Towns with/in the Vicinity of Sites (Unit: %)

(Indexes from the top to the bottom are: District of Lin Tong, City of Dun Huang, District of Fang Shan, City of Tai'an, City of Mountain Huang, City of Dan Jiangkou, City of Cheng De, City of Qu Fu, Town of Ping Yao, City of Su Zhou, City of Li Jiang, Town of Da Zu, City of Mountain Wu Yi, District of Chang Ping, City of Zun Hua, Town of Xin Bin, Town of Yi, City of Du Jiangyan, City of Da Tong, City of Ji'an, Town of Heng Ren, Macau, City of An Yang, Town of Yong Ding, Town of Nan Jing, Town of Hua'an, The Country)

2) Relative Value of Visitor Numbers to Town or City Population

In China, World Heritage Listing can attract large numbers of domestic and international visitors to the towns and cities in the vicinity of heritage sites (Figure 3. 8a). Statistics from the case studies in this study show:

i. Visitor numbers exceeded a local town's population by 10 times at ten sites including Macao (extremely high value where visitors exceeded local population by 50 times), Yixian, Changping, Mount Wuyi, Mount Huangshan, Dujiangyan, Lintong, Anyang, Qufu and Fangshan.

ii. Exponential changes of visitor numbers appeared in a town or city after inscription, including Yixian, Pingyao, Huanren, Xinbin, Datong, Ji'an, the three counties with *tulou*, Dazu and Chengde. The study also investigated the ratio of international visitors to the non – rural population that showed increasing overseas awareness as visitor service facilities in these towns and cities began to improve (Figure 3. 8b). A comparison of the results showed that the highest ratio for international visitors for Lijiang and Mount Huangshan was more than four times the non – rural population. At Mount Wuyi, Dunhuang, Qufu, Ji'an and Suzhou the ratio was more than double. The ratio at the remainder of sites was less than double. The majority of World Heritage Sites in China still need to improve their appeal to international visitors and should consider improving transport in the region, reinforcing interaction and cooperation with the international community.

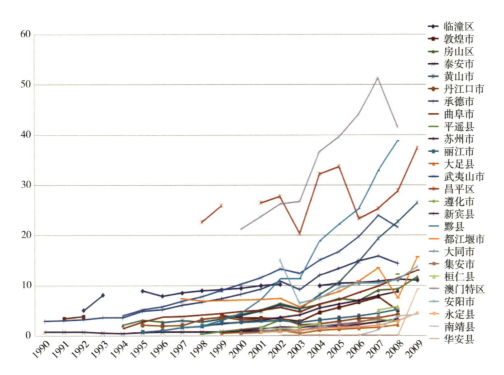

Figure 3. 8a　Comparison of Visitor Numbers and Population of Towns with/in the vicinity of Sites

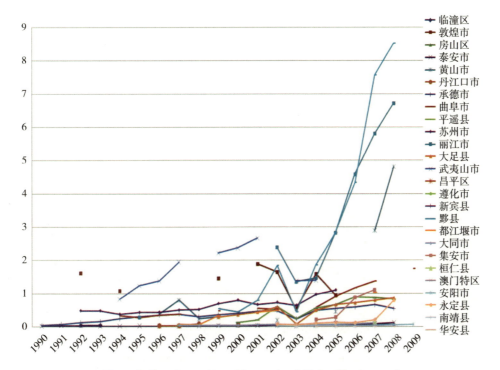

Figure 3. 8b　Comparison of International Visitor Numbers and

Non - rural Population at Towns with/in the Vicinity of Sites

（Indexes from the top to the bottom are：District of Lin Tong, City of Dun Huang, District of Fang Shan, City of Tai'an, City of Mountain Huang, City of Dan Jiangkou, City of Cheng De, City of Qu Fu, Town of Ping Yao, City of Su Zhou, City of Li Jiang, Town of Da Zu, City of Mountain Wu Yi, District of Chang Ping, City of Zun Hua, Town of Xin Bin, Town of Yi, City of Du Jiangyan, City of Da Tong, City of Ji'an, Town of Heng Ren, Macau, City of An Yang, Town of Yong Ding, Town of Nan Jing, Town of Hua'an, The Country）

3) Consumption Per Capital

Visitor per capital consumption indirectly reflects the standard of tourism infrastructure, service and the ability of a town or city to handle visitation. In Macao, Suzhou and Lijiang, visitor consumption per capita exceeded RMB1000 yuan. In Dazu, Pingyao, Tai'an, Chengde, Dunhuang, Huanren, Ji'an and Datong, visitor consumption per capita was between RMB500 yuan and RMB1000 yuan. Visitor consumption per capita in both the above two categories of towns and cities was above the national average. Long – term changes in visitor consumption per capita (Figure 3.9) in the towns and cities in the case studies can be divided into three different scenarios.

i. Consumption per capita has been higher than the national average for long periods. This includes Macao, Suzhou, Tai'an, Pingyao and Lijiang.

ii. Consumption per capita on tourism increased extremely rapidly after inscription. This includes Lijiang, Huanren and Ji'an.

iii. Per capital consumption on tourism has remained at a low level for extended periods. This includes archaeological sites such as Changping, Fangshan and Lintong.

This data clearly illustrates the connection between the level of consumption per capita on tourism in a town or city in the vicinity of a heritage site with the category of a heritage site.

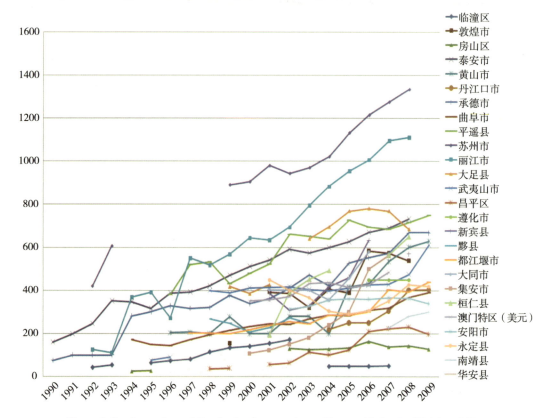

Figure 3.9　Comparison of Per Capita Consumption at Towns with/in the Vicinity of Sites

(Unit: RMB yuan)

(Indexes from the top to the bottom are: District of Lin Tong, City of Dun Huang, District of Fang Shan, City of Tai'an, City of Mountain Huang, City of Dan Jiangkou, City of Cheng De, City of Qu Fu, Town of Ping Yao, City of Su Zhou, City of Li Jiang, Town of Da Zu, City of Mountain Wu Yi, District of Chang Ping, City of Zun Hua, Town of Xin Bin, Town of Yi, City of Du Jiangyan, City of Da Tong, City of Ji'an, Town of Heng Ren, Macau, City of An Yang, Town of Yong Ding, Town of Nan Jing, Town of Hua'an, The Country)

4）Site Visitor Numbers as a Percentage of Visitor Numbers to Towns and Cities

Data on income from tourism was difficult to obtain. For the purpose of this study, annual changes in "site visitor numbers as a percentage of total visitor numbers to a town or city" were used to judge the relative position of tourism at the heritage site in total tourism numbers at that particular town or city. Three different categories were identified（Figure 3.10）.

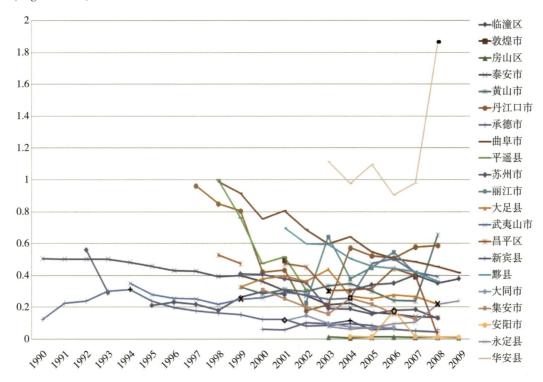

Figure 3.10　Comparison of Site Visitor Numbers with Town Visitor Numbers

（NB：Data limited, does not include data from Zunhua, Dujiangyan, Huanren, Macao and Nanjing. Black markers indicate inscription year）

（Indexes from the top to the bottom are：District of Lin Tong, City of Dun Huang, District of Fang Shan, City of Tai'an, City of Mountain Huang, City of Dan Jiangkou, City of Cheng De, City of Qu Fu, Town of Ping Yao, City of Su Zhou, City of Li Jiang, Town of Da Zu, City of Mountain Wu Yi, District of Chang Ping, City of Zun Hua, Town of Xin Bin, Town of Yi, City of Du Jiangyan, City of Da Tong, City of Ji'an, Town of Heng Ren, Macau, City of An Yang, Town of Yong Ding, Town of Nan Jing, Town of Hua'an, The Country）

Category 1：The heritage site is the principal driver for tourism in a town or city.

Visiting the heritage site is the main reason visitation to the town or city. The number of visitors to a site as a percentage of visitors to the town or city remains constantly high. Mount Huangshang, Hua'an, Qufu, Yixan, Danjiangkou, Lijiang and Changping are examples of this category. Some sites received 50% more visitors than the local town or city.

Category 2：The heritage site stimulates the development of tourism.

After World Heritage inscription, the site became the focus of tourism for a town or city. With the development of tourism at the site, the town or city became better known and service infrastructure improved. Local governments were proactive in taking advantage of this opportunity to further develop tourism resources in the vicinity of the site. This resulted in a chain of associated industries being established along tourism nodes in the vicinity of the town or city. This further development of tourism brought about an increase in total visitor numbers but visitors to the site as a percentage of total visitors to the town or city would often begin to decline. Mount Taishan is a notable example. After inscription in 1987 the number of visitors to Mount Taishan increased and accounted for 51% of all visitors to the city, an historic peak. For the next seven years the percentage of visitors to the site was maintained at around 50% until it began to gradually decline and fell to 13. 58% in 2008.

Category 3: After inscription, site visitor numbers increased as a percentage of the total number of visitors to the town or city.

The most prominent example of this scenario is Hua'an County (*xian*). Heritage visitor numbers in this county (xian) experienced a sudden surge in the year the *tulou* were inscribed as a World Heritage Site as a result of increased awareness. Visitor numbers to the site exceeded the number of visitors to the entire county (*xian*) (including day visitors who by-passed the county town when they visited the site). Yongding, Anyang and Ji'an also saw significant increases in visitor numbers.

The conclusion is that World Heritage Sites are not the principal driver of tourism for all towns and cities in their locality. A site's inscription may well result in a short-term increase in site visitation as a percentage of total visitor numbers. However, as the town or city continues to improve visitor service facilities, other tourism resources around the site will develop and the site's share of a town's or city's tourism industry will gradually decrease.

Section 4   Conservation and Sustainable Development of China's World Heritage Sites——Assessment and Monitoring

This section of the study reviews the current state of conservation and sustainable development of World Heritage Sites in China. The study also proposes establishing a monitoring system for heritage sites and the towns and cities in their locality, the categories of data required for the proposed system and the system's implementation.

The assessment section is divided into three sections. The main conclusions are outlined below. The conservation of a heritage site brings advantages to the socio – economic development of the town or city in the vicinity of a heritage site.

i. Large government investments in the conservation and development of heritage;

ii. World Heritage status attracts great interest and increases the possibilities for exchanges and cooperation as well as sources for funding;

iii. Heritage sites command an extremely important role in the future development of the region in which they are located;

iv. Heritage value promotes the development of the local cultural industry.

Measurement and analysis of a large amount of data demonstrated that World Heritage status can affect the social and economic development of the town or city where a site is located. These derived benefits are summarized below.

i. stimulated the development of the local tourism industry and the economy in general;

ii. stimulated an increase in local employment;

iii. heightened output – to – input ratio for heritage conservation.

After examining the particular circumstances of each heritage site in this study and its relationship with the town or city in the locality, this study concluded the strengths and weaknesses in conservation and development of heritage sites from six different categories, and the strategy appropriate for its particular circumstances. This study also concluded that "not all towns and cities in the locality of a heritage site are suitable for to the development of large scale tourism".

Finally, this section sets out detailed proposals on the establishment or improvement of a monitoring system for heritage sites and towns and cities.

1 Assessment of the Conservation and Sustainable Development of a Heritage Site

1) Strengths that World Heritage Status Confers on the Conservation and Development of a Heritage Site

All Chinese sites that have been selected for nomination as World Heritage Sites are National Priority Protect Sites; they are the most outstanding sites offering the quintessence of China's cultural heritage. Towns and cities in the vicinity of a heritage site have more possibilities for international exchanges and co - operation than other historic or culturally famous cities. Benefits come with inscription assist regional development. This study analysed the advantages of the site (internal factors) and the locality (external factors) of the towns and cities in the vicinity of 26 heritage sites nationally. The socio - economic advantages that World Heritage Site status brings are summarized below.

Considerable government investment in the conservation and development of a site

In contrast with ordinary protected sites, a World Heritage Site often has a dedicated management organisation due to its significance. The management model and mechanisms for these types of organisations can vary from site to site. However, what these management models have in common is their senior and autonomous position and strong capabilities in managing all aspects of a site. This study examined various construction activities undertaken at towns and cities in the vicinity of listed sites over a period of five years prior to listing to the present. The analysis showed considerable work had been undertaken to improve the city's general appearance and construction of infrastructure and service facilities. The immediate setting of the site had also been improved. These work extended over a long period of time and involved a large amount investment. (Table 4. 1). Most towns and cities had also drawn up conservation plans for the conservation and development of their heritage site and aligned these plans in line with town or city level planning documentation. Governments in these towns and cities had also enacted local legislation and regulations (Table 4. 2).

World Heritage status attracts strong interest and increases exchanges and cooperation and sources of funding

There is significant international interest in China's World Heritage Site's from people and organisations in fields including heritage conservation, international media, international visitors and international sister cities

i. heritage conservation organisations' strong support for heritage sites in the provision of specialized knowledge and technology as well as funding;

ii. international television stations frequently visit World Heritage Sites in China to make documentaries which publicize the site;

iii. dramatic increase in international visitors to heritage sites;

iv. towns and cities in the vicinity of heritage sites establish sister - city relationships with many cities overseas, bringing tourism, trade opportunities, exchanges and cooperation in other fields with other countries (Table 4. 3).

New sources of funding opens up to World Heritage Listed cultural sites following inscription. In addition to funding and grants provided by the central and local governments, public donations were channelled through specialist funds such as the Confucius Fund (1984), the Dunhuang Caves Conservation Fund (1996), the Xidi and Hongcun Conservation Fund (2007) and the Oracle Bone Inscriptions Fund (2009). With the advent of the Chinese market economy, many Chinese heritage sites in towns and cities have set up government investment corporations to provide funding solutions for public projects. These companies have now become an important form of support and economic backing for development activities at and in the immediate environments of heritage sites.

Table 4. 1   Treatment of the Setting at the Site and its Immediate Environs, Construction of Service Facilities

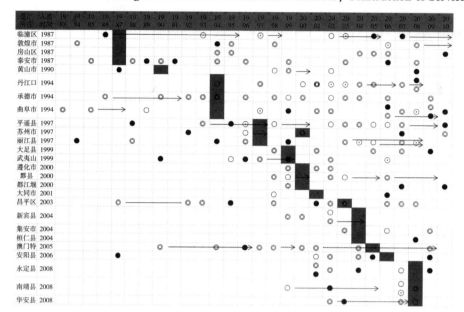

NB: ● indicates museum, refers to museums built on site or close to the site and museums related to the site;

◎ indicates scenic area, mainly refers to restoration projects and the construction of infrastructure; ○ indicates treatment of the setting, mainly relocation of local residents or staff and removal of unauthorized structures from the central areas of a site; ⊙ indicates improvements to appearance of towns close to a site and the construction of scenic zones.

(Cities from the top to the bottom are: District of Lin Tong, City of Dun Huang, District of Fang Shan, City of Tai'an, City of Mountain Huang, City of Dan Jiangkou, City of Cheng De, City of Qu Fu, Town of Ping Yao, City of Su Zhou, City of Li Jiang, Town of Da Zu, City of Mountain Wu Yi, District of Chang Ping, City of Zun Hua, Town of Yi, City of Du Jiangyan, City of Da Tong, District of Chang Ping, Town of Xin Bin, City of Ji'an, Town of Heng Ren, Macau, City of An Yang, Town of Yong Ding, Town of Nan Jing, Town of Hua'an)

Table 4. 2   Legal Documentation and Plans at Towns with Sites

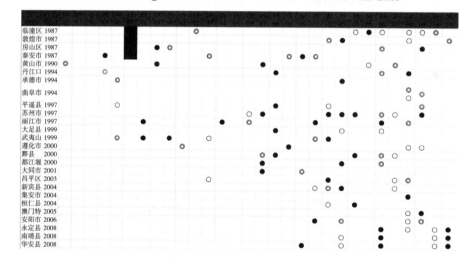

NB: ● Indicates Legal Documents (i. e. legislation and regulations), Refers to Legal Documents (i. e. legislation and regulations) Drawn up by Government of various levels relating to Site Conservation; ◎ Indicates Conservation Master Plans, Refers to Site Conservation Master Plans; ○ Refers to other Tourism Plans or Town Plans related to a Site.

(Cities from the top to the bottom are: District of Lin Tong, City of Dun Huang, District of Fang Shan, City of Tai'an, City of Mountain Huang, City of Dan Jiangkou, City of Cheng De, City of Qu Fu, Town of Ping Yao, City of Su Zhou, City of Li Jiang, Town of Da Zu, City of Mountain Wu Yi, District of Chang Ping, City of Zun Hua, Town of Yi, City of Du Jiangyan, City of Da Tong, District of Chang Ping, Town of Xin Bin, City of Ji'an, Town of Heng Ren, Macau, City of An Yang, Town of Yong Ding, Town of Nan Jing, Town of Hua'an)

Table 4.3 Sites' and Towns' International Interaction

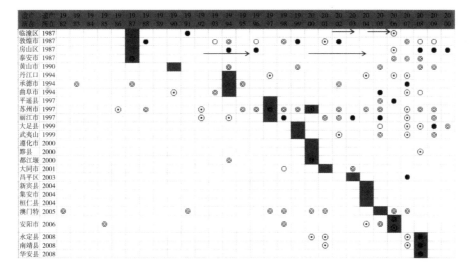

NB: ●Indicates a Conservation Project, Refers to Agreements Signed with International Conservation Organizations for Joint Conservation Projects or Joint Research. ◎Indicates Sister City Relationship, Refers to Towns with Sites Signing Sister City Agreements with International Historical and Culturally Famous Cities. ○Indicates International Conferences, Refers to International Conferences on Site Conservation and Development. ⊙Indicates Other Forms of Exchange and Cooperation, including Artistic Performances, Films and TV, Gifts and Donations and other Cultural Exchanges and Commemorative Activities.

(Cities from the top to the bottom are: District of Lin Tong, City of Dun Huang, District of Fang Shan, City of Tai'an, City of Mountain Huang, City of Dan Jiangkou, City of Cheng De, City of Qu Fu, Town of Ping Yao, City of Su Zhou, City of Li Jiang, Town of Da Zu, City of Mountain Wu Yi, District of Chang Ping, City of Zun Hua, Town of Yi, City of Du Jiangyan, City of Da Tong, District of Chang Ping, Town of Xin Bin, City of Ji'an, Town of Heng Ren, Macau, City of An Yang, Town of Yong Ding, Town of Nan Jing, Town of Hua'an)

A heritage site in the vicinity of a town or city has an important role to play in future regional development

World Heritage brand is an important economic resource giving a town or a city a regional advantage and economic standing above other regions. It is an important investment platform that can impact positively on the entire region and acts as a catalyst for general regional economic development. During the bidding period many towns and cities in the vicinity of heritage sites upgraded regional transport infrastructure extensively (Table 4.4). County (*xian*) cities such as Mount Huangshan, Mount Wuyi, Lijiang, Dunhuang and Qufu even constructed airports to promote the development of tourism. Some towns and cities were amalgamated into adjoining cities after inscription. Lintong had its administrative status raised from a county (*xian*) to a district (*qu*), Dazu became part of Chongqing – a city directly under the central government, and Lijiang became a municipality. An improved investment environment accelerated the economic development in these towns and cities.

Heritage value stimulates the development of the cultural sector

There is no lack of places in China where Chinese culture evolved as many of China's heritage sites attest. Qufu is the "hometown of Confucius"; Zhoukoudian is the place where the "first ancestors dwelt"; Dunhuang is the cradle for "Dunhuang Studies"; Yin Xu is the "birthplace of the written word"; Wudang Mountains is the "birthplace of Taoism and martial arts". Culture at all of these sites has been used by the television and film industry as the basis for major film and television productions. This culture has also been a great source of inspiration to artists, writers and educators. The cultural heritage at these sites has also has formed the basis for large – scale commercial performances. Almost all the towns and cities with heritage sites that were reviewed in this study had held cultural tourism festivals (Table 4.5). These towns and cities had also been successful in attracting investment. Heritage sites that are either towns, cities or villages such as the Ancient City of Pingyao, the Old Town of Lijiang and the

Historic Centre of Macao are extensive sites with many historic structures. Some historic buildings are still in use and part of residents continue their traditional way of life. As a result, these structures embody a rich cultural tradition and maintain a diversity of intangible cultural heritage. They are also the driver of the development of the cultural industry in these regions.

Table 4.4　Transport Infrastructure in Towns with Sites

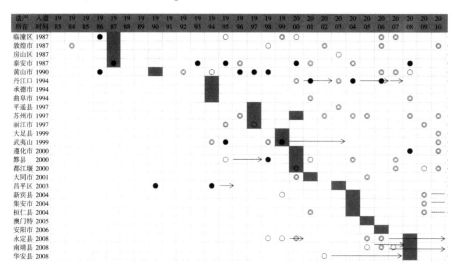

NB：●Refers to Roads Built to Cave Dwelling or Residences for Tourism；○Refers to Construction of Roads from the Town to the Site；◎Refers to Construction of Transport Infrastructure to Connect Airports, Railways and Express Ways.

(Cities from the top to the bottom are: District of Lin Tong, City of Dun Huang, District of Fang Shan, City of Tai'an, City of Mountain Huang, City of Dan Jiangkou, City of Cheng De, City of Qu Fu, Town of Ping Yao, City of Su Zhou, City of Li Jiang, Town of Da Zu, City of Mountain Wu Yi, District of Chang Ping, City of Zun Hua, Town of Yi, City of Du Jiangyan, City of Da Tong, District of Chang Ping, Town of Xin Bin, City of Ji'an, Town of Heng Ren, Macau, City of An Yang, Town of Yong Ding, Town of Nan Jing, Town of Hua'an)

Table 4.5　Large Scale Tourism or Festival Celebrations at 26 Sites

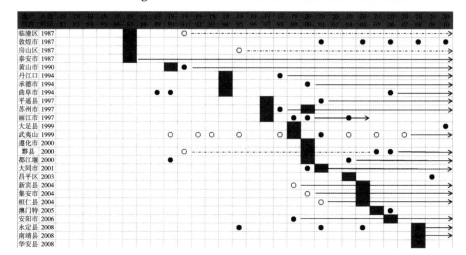

NB：●Represents WH related Celebrations；○Represents WH Non－related Celebrations；→Indicates Time Span of Celebrations.

(Cities from the top to the bottom are: District of Lin Tong, City of Dun Huang, District of Fang Shan, City of Tai'an, City of Mountain Huang, City of Dan Jiangkou, City of Cheng De, City of Qu Fu, Town of Ping Yao, City of Su Zhou, City of Li Jiang, Town of Da Zu, City of Mountain Wu Yi, District of Chang Ping, City of Zun Hua, Town of Yi, City of Du Jiangyan, City of Da Tong, District of Chang Ping, Town of Xin Bin, City of Ji'an, Town of Heng Ren, Macau, City of An Yang, Town of Yong Ding, Town of Nan Jing, Town of Hua'an)

2）World Heritage Impacts on Socio – Economic Development in Towns and Cities

Using the input – output analysis methodology we calculated the economic impact on towns and cities that flowed from World Heritage Sites in China. The results included:

i. impact on the development of local tourism and local GDP;

ii. increased local employment;

iii. the ratio of input – to – output for site conservation. (Refer to Table 4. 6 for specific values)

Heritage as a catalyst for local tourism and general economic development

Input – output calculations produced a wide range of results across sites in terms of a town or city's reliance on World Heritage Cultural Sites in the development of local tourism. Results ranged from 93. 67% for Pingyao to 1. 43% for Anyang. Different towns and cities had different economic fundamentals status and tourism service facilities so that the impact on tourism output and on GDP derived from World Heritage Cultural Sites varied from site to site. The most substantial impacts on tourism output were in Tai'an (RMB 4. 2 billion yuan), Mount Wuyi (RMB 3. 01 billion yuan) and Qufu (RMB 2. 97 billion yuan) . Pingyao's output attributed to heritage tourism reached RMB 1. 43 billion yuan. In eastern China, Chengde reached RMB 1. 84 billion yuan. The highest ratios of impact on a town or city's local GDP were at Mount Wuyi (19. 81%) and Pingyao (10. 4%) .

Heritage as a catalyst for increasing employment

Tai'an, Chengde, Qufu and Mount Wuyi are good examples where heritage site increased employment. up to 30, 000 new jobs were created in fields associated with heritage. It is clear that the heritage related sectors in these locations developed considerably. Tai'an and Chengde were significant ahead of other places with 325, 000 new positions created in Tai'an and 207, 000 in Chengde. This demonstrates the stability and appropriateness of the industry structare in those two cities, and tourism played a prominent role in the development of these two cities. Second tier cities such as Anyang, Qufu and Mount Wuyi created a large number of new positions, ranging between 60, 000 to 90, 000.

Input – output ratio for heritage conservation is high

Data was unobtainable for conservation project inputs in 2008 at some sites. Calculations were only able to be made for the input – output ratio for conservation at seven towns and cites with World Heritage Cultural Sites. The results showed that there was little need to invest in maintenance at Anyang, Tai'an and Qufu, three of the earliest listed sites, and that derived economic impact (increase in local GDP derived from heritage conservation and tourism) was maintained at a high level as these cities had been well – known for a long time with a high level of prosperity and development in associated industries. The ratio of input – to – output for heritage conservation in these cities exceeded 1: 100. In less developed rural areas such as Pingyao, Yixian and Xinbin Manchurian Autonomous County (*Xian*), the input – to – output ratio was also high at more than 1: 10. To a certain degree, this illustrates continuing support and interest in rural heritage from outside these areas. It also shows that more work should to be done in the conservation of heritage in rural China.

Table 4. 6　Brief Summary at Economic Impact of Some Sites on Towns in 2008

	W Dependence	Advance T	Advance G	G% Advance	Related J	Remainder J	WInput – output
Pingyao, Shanxi	93. 67%	14. 3	5. 8	10. 54%	1. 3	1. 3	1:72. 8
Qufu, Shandong	45. 31%	27. 9	9. 9	4. 92%	3. 2	7. 2	1:166. 97

续表

	W Dependence	Advance T	Advance G	G% Advance	Related J	Remainder J	WInput – output
Mt Wuyi, Fujian	44. 85%	30. 1	11	19. 81%	2. 9	6. 4	—
Yixian, Anhui	36. 05%	1. 8	0. 7	5. 31%	0. 1	0. 4	1∶11. 3
Yongding, Fujian	21. 88%	2. 9	1	1. 11%	0. 3	1. 3	—
Chengde, Hebei	15. 20%	18. 4	6. 9	3. 60%	3. 15	20. 68	1∶7
Tai'an, Shandong	13. 44%	42. 0	14. 8	2. 78%	4. 4	32. 5	1∶244. 1
Xinbin' Liaoning	5. 80%	0. 7	0. 3	0. 61%	0. 1	1. 1	1∶11. 3
Anyang' Henan *	1. 43%	1. 6	0. 7	0. 21%	0. 1	8. 8	1∶246. 24

NB:

W Degree of Dependence = Degree of Dependence on Word Heritage

Advances T = WHS tourism advances total tourism output (RMB 100 million yuan)

Advance G = WHS tourism advances GDP (RMB 100 million yuan)

G % Advancement = WHS advances percentage of GDP for that year (%)

Related J = Contribution of WH related industry to employment (10, 000 positions)

Remainder J = Development of WH tourism promotes employment in other industries (10, 000 positions)

W input – output ratio = Comparative value of WHS conservation inputs versus WHS promotion of output (includes increase in GDP value by tourism due to conservation)

＊ data from 2009

3) Strategies for the Conservation and Development of Six Different Categories of Heritage Sites

An analysis of the data above reveals that nowadays it is common for visitor numbers to exceed the local population of towns and cites with heritage sites by a factor greater than ten. Heritage sites have now become "too popular" throughout China so that there is a need to review and assess the possible effects of World Heritage Listing on a site's conservation and sustainable development. The results of an analysis of a large amount of information and statistics and a review of adopted strategies at various heritage sites in China reveal that there are different advantages and disadvantages for different categories of sites. Strategies that should prioritised in order to ensure effective conservation and sustainable development of heritage sites are summarized below (For details refer to Table 4. 7) .

4) Not All Heritage Sites are Suitable for Development of Large Scale Tourism

In China when assessing the impact that World Heritage Listing can have on the development of tourism and the economy in the town or city where the site is located, the role a site plays in the development of tourism and the share of tourism in the overall industry structure is somewhat limited. The conclusions of this study are that sites and towns with the characteristics outlined below should not indiscriminately promote the development of heritage related tourism but adopt strategies at different levels to either restrict or redress these developments.

i. fragile heritage sites-restrict "flash visitation" . Move tourism and other related industries off site to areas away from the site;

ii. heritage sites that have limited attraction for mass tourism – think creatively and attract visitors who have a sense of adventure to the site; consider developing new tourism resources in areas around the site so that the site becomes part of a route or network of sites;

Table 4.7　Strategies for the Conservation and Sustainable Development of Different Categories of Heritage Sites

Site Category	Location Category	Examples of Site	Advantages	Local Factors	Disadvantages	Local Factors	Prior Strategies
Mountain Sites	A	Mount. Taishan, Lushan National Park	Good visitor capacity; rich tourism resources; various ways of transportation; organization committee; a complet of tourism resources; attractiveness.	excellent Services infrastructure around site; price of land and housing rised.	Maintenance costs high; disagreement over cable car routing and construction; cultural values often disregarded for natural values.	Town residents' lives inconvenienced by visitors; site conservation zone significantly threatened by town creep.	Focus on the impact of town development on the mountain and cultural landscape; appropriate development and spread of tourism activities; focus more on the cultural side, improve international influence.
	D	Mount. Huangshan, Mount. Wuyi		Relatively unaffected by town development.		Poor tourism facilities and service levels.	Develop some tourism in the surrounding villages; optimise industry structure to create more employment opportunities.
Historic Centers in Towns and Cities	A	Ancient City of Pingyao, Old Town of Lijiang	Large site with good visitor capacity, rich in tourism resources; rich in intangible cultural heritage; local residents income quite good, strong civic pride.	Excellent transportation; town supports development of cultural sector.	Complicated ownership rights cause enormous management difficulties; residents often clash with visitors; restrictions on improving quality of life for residents.	Increase in cost of living for locals; too many visitors causing the setting to become polluted; difficulties in fighting a fire.	Prevent it becoming an open air museum; maintain a certain percentage of local residents; ensure the town's old quarter totally separated from the new quarter; establish a system to encourage maintenance; diversify cultural sector.
Living Villages	F	Ancient Villages in Southern Anhui, Kaiping *Diaolou* and Villages, Fujian *tulou*	Rich in intangible cultural heritage; strong cultural atmosphere in the area, traditions maintained, traditional clans still in existence.	Site has brought significant increase in locals' incomes; rich in rural landscapes.	Limited visitor capacity; lack of support from the industries; limited ways of development of cultural sector; level of education of locals and capabilities of unconvenient conservation technology limited	Unconvenient transportation; low quality of tourism service facilities; poor local government utilities such as fire fighting; limited tourism facilities; danger of becoming a site without content.	Appropriately develop tourism resources around the village; encourage home – stay accommodation; control new location and scale of new construction; retain locals through new employment opportunities; prevent the site from turning into an open air museum; promote education on the conservation of intangible heritage and local customs.

续表

Site Category	Location Category	Examples of Site	Advantages	Local Factors	Disadvantages	Local Factors	Prior Strategies
Large Scale Ancient Building Complex	A	Mountain Resort and Outlying Temples, Chengde	Well-known, well resourced; most Nationally Protected Sites; excellent range of local conservation technology good and security and surveillance measures are good; locals have excellent incomes and strong sense of civic pride.	Good foundation for the development of the cultural sector; land and housing prices on the increase.	Relatively small and not much room to alter visitor routings; physical fabric fragile, large numbers of visitors walk on some fabric in short periods of time; difficult to balance interests of visitors and locals.	Local traffic congestion; restrictions on local development around the site (i. e. building height, railway transportation).	Improve traffic congestion and intrusions to visual landscape; promote diversification of cultural sector; promote international interaction and cooperation; improve competitiveness of city/town.
	B	Temple and Cemetery of Confucius and the Kong Family Mansion in Qufu					
	C	Temple of Heaven, Ming and Qing Imperial Tombs (13 Tombs)		Convenient transportation, good range of local service facilities.		Development restrictions around the site (i. e. building height)	Take visitors to other places in the same area; organise educational activities for locals.
	D	Ming and Qing Imperial Tombs (Eastern Qing Tombs)	Comparatively less pressure from visitors.	Little impact from development of local towns and cities.	Lack of appeal to mass tourism vistors.	Unconvenient transportation; low level of service facilities.	Appropriate development of surrounding tourism resources; improve the quality of service facilities; create employment opportunities for locals; organize research activities for specialist academics.

续表

Site Category	Location Category	Examples of Site	Advantages	Local Factors	Disadvantages	Local Factors	Prior Strategies
Ruins	B	Yin Xu, Ancient Koguryo Kingdom (Ji'an)	Most are conserved as open air museums; managed by specialists in this field; functions well for education on general science.	Convenient transportation; good range of service facilities locally.	Lack of appeal to mass tourism visitors (Mausoleum of First Qin Emperor is an exception); fabric fragile; limited derived stimulus to cultural sector; possible restrictions to the development of the secondary sector locally.	Greatly impacted by development activities in local towns and cities.	Foreseen threat of development of local town/city to the site (transport infrastructure, industry zones); make site more accessible to locals (i.e. build archaeological parks, base for basic science education);
	D	Mausoleum of the First Qin Emperor, Mountain Town of Five Women (Huanren)					
	E	Peking Man Site, Zhoukoudian		Little impact from development of local town		Difficult to access site; limited promotion of site.	Develop surrouding tourism resources; improve site's role in educating visitors and locals.
Grotto Sites	D	Mogao Caves in Dunhuang, Yungang Grottoes	High artistic value; able to attract mass tourism; solid foundation for conservation;	Convenient transport; some promotion of local cultural and education sectors.	Physical fabric fragile, requires significant amount of conservation; small visitor carrying capacity; need to conserve the ecology in large tracts of the setting.	Limited benefits for local residents; limited development opportunities for secondary sector.	Developments threat of local town/city to the site (destruction of the natural setting and geology such as arterial water, humidity, agricultural irrigation); restriction on town/city development (transport infrastructure, environmental pollution).
	E	Dazu Rock Carvings	highly influential in conservation field internationally.	Local setting rich in landscape resources.		Site access is difficult; limited promotion and publicity about the site.	

NB: 6 types of dependency relationship between site and town: A town exists because of the site; B site is the primary resource for the town; C site is one of the main resources for the town; D site is the primary resource for the outer suburbs in a city; E site is one of the most important resources for city's outer suburbs; E site is in a living village.

iii. tourism products are not well developed but protential-town or city size and its socio – economic fundamentals needs to be considered; upgrading tourism infrastructure and service facilities to improve visitor capacity;

iv. towns and cities that are too reliant on tourism but are not sufficiently economically developed- use the brand value of a World Heritage Site to attract investment and develop an appropriate secondary sector; continue to build on and optimize the industry structure of the town or city.

v. towns or cities that are too small-by using the bid for World Heritage Listing or anniversary activities to attract public and private investment to improve the quality of the site's setting and attract more workers seeking employment to the town or city.

2   Creation and Improvement of Heritage Site-Town or City Monitoring System

The creation of a "Socio – economic Monitoring System for World Heritage Cultural Sites Conservation and the Towns and Cities in their Vicinity" is aimed at filling a void that presently exists in site conservation practice in China. This sort of monitoring system should assist all sites and their localities in China in being able to undertake long – term continuous investigations. Regular updating of data will enable research and analysis of the conservation of a site and local development over different time periods, as well as comparisons with different sites over the same time period in real – time. It will also enable the research and analysis of the conservation of sites in the same regions, of the same category and sites inscribed on the World Heritage list over the same period of time as well as local development. This information will be highly significant both nationally and regionally for the development and adjustment of policies associated with heritage. A monitoring system should observe the following two principles: i. data processing should use a method that integrates quantitative statistics with qualitative analysis. ii. the monitoring process should consist of a comprehensive set of investigations and assessments undertaken at many different levels.

For these reasons, this study has proposed the concept of baseline data and core data. Baseline data is more comprehensive and includes categories such as indicative data (quantitative statistics) and descriptive data (qualitative analysis) which sites, towns or cities would find useful for annual reviews and yearly updates of data. Core data is a synthesis of the baseline data. This type of data is mainly quantitative statistics and is suited to the compilation of data nationally and comparative analysis.

1) Data Structure for a Monitoring System

Taking in consideration the subject of this type of monitoring program, this type of monitoring system should be able to handle both heritage sites and the town or city where the site is located and therefore be divided into two sections. The type of data in each section can further be divided into baseline data and core data. Monitoring of the site should cover the site's conservation, management as well as income and expenditure. It should consist of statistical data along with a chronicle of major events. Core data should focus on a site's income and expenditure. Monitoring of the town or city where the site is located should be more comprehensive covering the development of the town or city's economy and industries, residential incomes, population and employment, infrastructure and service facilities, cultural promotion, exchanges and cooperation, along with planning and management of heritage sites. Core data should include the development of the local economy, residents' incomes, employment structure, development of tourism, contribution of the site to the local economy and international impact. Data for the monitoring system could be structured as shown in Table 4. 8.

Table 4.8 Data Structure for Monitoring System for Site and Towns

Site Section	Baseline Data	Indicative	2 major, 5 medium, 15 small
		Descriptive	2 categories
	Core Data	Indicative	2 major, 10 small
		Descriptive	Impact Assessment
Town or City Section	Baseline Data	Indicative	2 major, 8 medium, 25 small
		Descriptive	5 categories
	Core Data	Indicative	3 major, 6 medium, 14 small
		Descriptive	SWOT Analysis; Honours/awards list

2) Basic data for the Monitoring System (Annual Monitoring Assessment)

For cultural heritage site

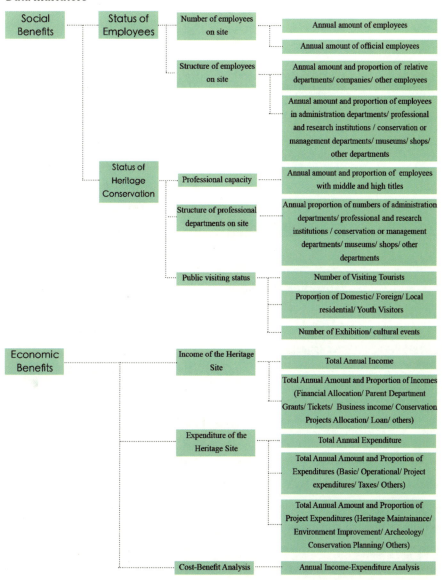

Figure 1 For Cultural Heritage Site

For the towns of the heritage site

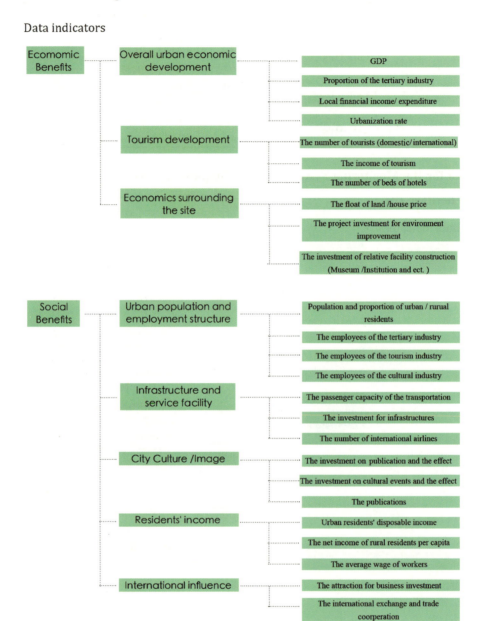

Figure 2   For The Towns of the Heritage Sites

3) Core data for the Monitoring System (Overall Monitoring Assessment)

This study collated baseline data for both heritage sites and town or cities in their vicinity that had been collected in large amounts through using the monitoring system outlined above. This data was then processed using the same calculation formula or through dimension reduction so as to create a national database which could analysis data from different sources with different dimensions. A database of this kind will enable researchers to undertake lateral comparisons between different places and research extension. Table 4. 9 gives an example of a framework for this type of core data.

Table 4. 9   Core Date for Monitoring System for Sites and Towns

Category		Site Conservation & Operations	Socio – economic Benefits that Local Towns and Cities Derive from a Site
Quantatative	economic benefits criteria	Total Income Income and Percentage（item by item） Expenditure Total Expenditure and Percentage（item by item） Total Expenditure for Projects Expenditure Percentages for Projects（Conservation Projects）	General Economic Development（total population, percentage of non – rural population, local per capita GDP, local government per capital fiscal income, secondary and tertiary sectors as a percentage of GDP Development of Tourism（tourism income as a % of local GDP, visitor numbers vs total local population, town/city income from tourism, visitor per capita consumption） Contribution of Site to Local Economy（site visitors as a% of total number of visitors to town/city, site tourism income as a % of total town/cities tourism income）.
	social benefits criteria	Number of site employees Personnel composition at site（broken down by category and percentage） management organisation structure Visitor Numbers（percentage for different categories）	Employment composition in Town/City（tertiary sector percentage） Local Residents Income（town/city residents disposable income, rural residents net income） International Influence（percentage of international visitors, total number of visitors vs total population of town or city, international visitors vs non – rural population in towns/cities）
Qualitative		Impact Analysis of the Use and Development of WHS on their Conservation	SWOT Analysis for Sustainable Development of Site and Town/city；List of Honours/Awards

4）Methodology for Undertaking Monitoring

Based on the data framework above, this study suggests that the monitoring system created could operate at two different levels.

1. Sites should independently undertake annual tracking and monitoring. Based on the data on a site's funding for conservation and management, and data from the local town or city's economic development, major activities relating to management, construction and exchanges at the site should be organized to reflect the objective conditions of the changes that occur at all sites on an annual basis. By doing this, it is possible to ensure that strengths are maximized and that weaknesses can be compensated. It allows sites to maximize their opportunities and effectively deal with risks. At the same time it allows the monitoring of a site's conservation and sustainable development. This level of monitoring should consist of the following elements：

i. tracking and monitoring the socio – economic benefits of a site and the town or city where the site is located；

ii. impact analysis of the use and development of a site on heritage conservation

iii. SWOT analysis of the social development of a site and the town or city where it located

iv. reputation achieved by a site and the town or city where it is located.

2. Comprehensive Monitoring and Assessment on a Nation Wide Basis. Through the compilation of data on conservation and development at all localities（focusing on China's World Heritage Cultural Sites and the macro – development of the towns and cities in which they are located）, produce a summary of the impact of use and development of World Heritage on heritage conservation and share different strategies of sites and local towns and cities

on their unique road to sustainable development that have set them apart, create a national World Cultural Heritage Site platform where people can interact and learn from one another. This level of monitoring should consist of the following elements:

    i. Comprehensive national monitoring of the conservation of heritage sites and their commercial operations;

    ii. Comprehensive assessment of the socio – economic benefits that a town or city derives from a heritage site.

(Written by Zhang Jie, Li Jianyun, Lu Liuying etc.)

《文化景观遗产研究报告》成果汇报

中国古迹遗址保护协会

摘　要

　　为了进一步理解文化景观遗产的类型特征、价值标准及其在真实性完整性等方面的特点，发掘中国的文化景观资源，推动文化景观遗产的管理与保护，国家文物局委托中国古迹遗址保护协会承担了《文化景观遗产研究报告》课题。

　　在系统研究世界遗产委员会及国际古迹遗址理事会（ICOMOS）等相关机构的文件报告、近年来关于文化景观的专家会议成果以及文化景观遗产申报、评估文本的基础上，结合对世界遗产领域相关专家的访谈，本课题较系统地探讨了文化景观遗产的类型特征、价值标准与真实性完整性特点，分析了中国文化景观资源的现状与潜力，并为文化景观的管理保护提出了一些建议。

　　本文认为，关于文化景观的研究、保护及利用，均应围绕其价值展开。文化景观的最大价值特征是表现了人与自然不同类型的良性互动关系。这不仅是文化景观区别于其他遗产类型的关键，也是它可以被"概念性"地分为设计类、有机演进类及关联性三大类型的基础。

　　不同的价值内涵使文化景观遗产在评估时适用不同的 OUV 标准，其中设计类景观中反映其人与自然互动价值的主要是标准四，对于有机演进类景观来说主要是标准三、四、五，标准六则是评估关联性景观互动价值最重要的标准。同时，不同类型的文化景观也具有不同的真实性完整性特点。

　　只有在深刻认识文化景观价值的基础上，才能科学合理充分地发掘中国丰富的文化景观遗产资源与理论资源，并推动文化景观保护管理工作的发展。

　　关键词：文化景观，概念，沿革，特点，分类，文化景观保护

　　1992 年，在世界遗产委员会的第十六届大会上提出了一种新的遗产类型——文化景观，反映了 1972 年《保护世界文化和自然遗产公约》（*Convention Concerning the Protection of the World Cultural and Natural Heritage*，以下简称《世界遗产公约》）问世后，遗产界在实践中对于遗产特征与价值的新认识。

　　经过逐步熟悉与了解，尤其是在国内相关部门与机构的大力推动下，近年来中国在文化景观领域取得了显著的进步。如在刚刚完成的第三次全国文物普查工作中，文化景观等新遗产类型便已被纳入视野，在 2009 年开展的第七批全国重点文物保护单位的申报工作中，国家文物局也指出对内涵丰富的文化景观类遗产应予以重视。而 2011 年 6 月，《杭州西湖文化景观》列入《世界遗产名录》，这不仅是中国第一处主动以文化景观类型申报的世界遗产，也标志着中国文化景观研究与保护的新起点。

　　在此背景下，本文将通过对国内外重要学术成果、文化景观世界遗产地评估报告的分析研究和对相关国际专家访谈的基础上，探讨文化景观遗产的类型特征、价值标准与真实性完整性特点，并对文化景观的保护管理工作提出建议。

一、文化景观的类型特征

根据世界遗产中心 2009 年底发布的《世界遗产系列丛书 26：文化景观世界遗产——保护与管理手册》（以下简称《保护与管理手册》）①，截止 2009 年，世界遗产名录上共有文化景观遗产 66 处，其中未包括我国的庐山国家公园。然而 1996 年 12 月世界遗产委员会在墨西哥梅里达举行的第 20 届大会上曾明确声明将中国庐山国家公园以文化景观列入世界名录②。因此，本课题将把包括庐山在内的 67 处文化景观世界遗产作为主要研究对象。

在《操作指南》中，文化景观被分为三类：

1. 人类有意设计和创造的景观；

2. 有机演进的景观，其中包括残迹（或化石）类景观（2a）与延续类景观（2b）；

3. 关联性文化景观。

文化景观近 20 年的实践证明，这种"概念性（conceptual）而非功能性"③ 的分类方式，既高屋建瓴又具有很大的灵活性，较准确地涵盖了文化景观的各种类型，已成为文化景观研究、申报与评估的基石之一。本文仍将以这种分类方式为基础，进一步探讨文化景观的类型特征。

（一）人类有意设计和创造的景观

按照《操作指南》的定义，这一类文化景观是"明确定义的人类有意设计和创造的景观"。经统计，这一类型的文化景观在《世界遗产名录》中共有 9 处，本文将其分为以下 3 个子类别。

1. 园林类景观（garden landscape）（1 处）：英国伦敦皇家植物园邱园（Royal Botanic Gardens, Kew）

邱园位于泰晤士河南岸的景观带中，其人与自然的互动主要体现在园内 18 至 20 世纪间一系列重要的景观设计和建筑的发展。

在邱园之外，许多学者认为像凡尔赛宫、苏州古典园林及颐和园等《世界遗产名录》上的园林亦能被看做是这一类型的文化景观。

2. 田园类景观（parkland landscape）（6 处）：葡萄牙的辛特拉文化景观（Cultural Landscape of Sintra）、捷克的莱德尼采—瓦尔季采文化景观（Lednice – Valtice Cultural Landscape）、德国的德绍—沃尔利茨园林王国（Garden Kingdom of Dessau – Wörlitz）、西班牙的阿兰胡埃斯文化景观（Aranjuez Cultural Landscape）、意大利瓦尔·迪奥西亚公园文化景观（Val d'Orcia）及横跨德国、波兰两国边境的穆斯考尔公园（Muskauer Park）

相比园林类景观，田园类文化景观具有以下一些显著特征：

1) 占地面积大，规模远远大于普通园林：如莱德尼采·瓦尔季采文化景观占地 $200km^2$，德绍—沃尔利茨园林王国占地 $145km^2$。

2) 自然、文化元素较园林类景观更为丰富：田园类文化景观均具有为数众多的园林、城堡、桥梁等人造物，并且显著地依存于各类自然要素，如山峦、森林、湖泊等。

---

① World Heritage Paper 26: World Heritage Cultural Landscapes—A Handbook for Conservation and Management, Printed at UNESCO in December 2009（以下简称 Paper 26），于 2010 年 3 月 1 日上传至世界遗产中心网站。

② http://whc. unesco. org/archive/repcom96. htm#778。关于庐山没有被列入文化景观世界遗产名录一事，本课题组曾数次致信世界遗产中心相关人员，尚未得到正式回复，但据悉遗产中心已认识到此疏漏，将在今后的工作中予以纠正。

③ World Heritage Paper 6: World Heritage Cultural Landscapes 1992 – 2002, Published in 2003 by UNESCO World Heritage Centre（以下简称 Paper 6）: P 28

3）具有活态的人文因素：这些大规模的文化景观区域中往往包含了农田、村庄甚至城镇，相较于一般的园林，人不仅只是外在于景观的参观者，更是密切融于景观之中的参与者、管理者和保护者。

由此可见，田园类景观在两个层面反映了人与自然的互动：一方面是人工建筑与自然环境的和谐共存，另一方面则是人融洽地生活于景观环境中。而这两方面又是相辅相成的。前一方面的互动为后一方面提供了舒适的人居环境，而后一方面则是前一方面得到良好利用与保护的前提。但相较而言，这类文化景观的突出普遍价值仍然体现在各类优秀的建筑杰作及其与环境的完美结合中。

3. 宗教类文化景观（2 处）：波兰的瓦利泽布日多夫斯津朝圣园（Kalwaria Zebrzydowska：the Mannerist Architectural and Park Landscape Complex and Pilgrimage Park）与意大利的皮埃蒙特及伦巴第圣山（Sacri Monti of Piedmont and Lombardy）。

这两处文化景观的突出普遍价值主要体现于宗教建筑群与其自然环境的卓越结合上。其中，和一般的圣山，如我国的泰山和日本的富士山不同，皮埃蒙特及伦巴第山本身并不具备神圣性，它被称作圣山是因为山上众多的基督教建筑。也就是说，该景观的突出普遍价值主要体现在这些宗教建筑与自然环境的结合上，而非自然环境与宗教信仰的关联上。

设计类文化景观由于涉及较多的公园与园林，不由让人联想到世界遗产领域另一个相关的术语：历史园林（historic garden）。需要指出的是，《佛罗伦萨宪章》推出的时代背景是人们更重视单体的遗产本身，因而"历史园林"仍被看做是一种文物；而设计类景观作为文化景观的一个类型，更强调人们对于遗产环境、景观整体价值以及景观中人与自然互动的重视。从"历史园林"到设计类文化景观，可以说是世界遗产理论进步的一个缩影。

（二）　有机演进的景观

按照《操作指南》的定义，这类景观产"生于最初始的一种社会、经济、行政以及宗教需要，并通过与周围自然环境的相联系或相适应而发展到目前的形态"。该类景观在所有文化景观遗产中所占比重最大，共计 47 处，其下又包含了两个子类型，下面将分别予以讨论。

1. 残迹（或化石）类景观——它代表过去某一时间内已经完成的进化过程，其中包括突发性的和渐进式的，然而，它的突出特色在于显著特点仍然存在于该实物上。

现有文化景观遗产中残迹景观共计 14 处，根据遗产地"已经完成的进化过程"所属的时代，主要分为以下两类。

1.1. 古代残迹类文化景观（共 10 处）：意大利的帕埃斯图姆和韦利亚考古遗址（Cilento and Vallo di Diano National Park with the Archeological sites of Paestum and Velia, and the Certosa di Padula）、老挝的占巴塞文化景观内的瓦普庙和相关古民居（Vat Phou and Associated Ancient Settlements within the Champasak Cultural Landscape）、阿富汗的巴米扬山谷的文化景观和考古遗迹（Cultural Landscape and Archaeological Remains of the Bamiyan Valley）、南非的马蓬古布韦文化景观（Mapungubwe Cultural Landscape）、立陶宛的克拿维考古遗址（Kernave Archaeological Site）、英国的圣基尔达岛（St Kilda）、以色列的熏香之路——内盖夫的沙漠城镇（Incense Route – Desert Cities in the Negev）、阿塞拜疆的戈布斯坦岩石艺术文化景观（Gobustan Rock Art Cultural Landscape）、加蓬的洛佩——奥坎德生态系统与文化遗迹景观（Ecosystem and Relict Cultural Landscape of Lopé – Okanda）与巴布亚新几内亚的库科早期农业遗址（Kuk Early Agricultural Site）。

此类景观主要为保存较好的大规模考古遗址，具体包括城镇、聚落、墓群、农业遗址等类型。由于生产力、技术水平等方面因素的制约，古代人的生产与生活往往要在合适的自然环境中进行，而考古遗址则往往能对此加以较完整的记录与保存。但与一般考古遗址不同的是，此类景观所记录的人类对自然的依赖与利用较为突出与明显，具有突出普遍价值。

1.2. 近现代残迹类文化景观（共 4 处）：英国的布莱纳冯工业区景观（Blaenavon Industrial Landscape）与康沃尔和西德文矿区景观（Cornwall and West Devon Mining Landscape）、古巴东南第一个咖啡种植园考古景观（Archaeological Landscape of the First Coffee Plantations in the South – East of Cuba）及日本的石见银山遗迹及其文化景观（Iwami Ginzan Silver Mine and its Cultural Landscape）

这一类景观主要见证了某种已经停止运作的产业（炼铁、采矿、咖啡种植等）的历史面貌，及其对当地景观格局和居民生活的影响，也表明了世界遗产对于近代历史的尊重。

2. 延续类景观——它在当今社会与传统生活方式的密切交融中持续扮演着一种积极的社会角色，演变过程仍在进行中，而同时，它又是历史演变发展的物证。

这一类景观突出人类与自然环境的持续性互动过程，及在其中形成和演变的生活方式和文化传统。这一类遗产在文化景观中所占的比例是最大的，共计 33 处。为了更好地理解其类型特征，根据各遗产地人与自然间互动形式的不同特点，本文将其分成四个小类：

1. 表现人类对特殊环境征服利用的延续类景观：此类景观中的自然环境往往较为特殊乃至恶劣，不适宜人类居住。但人类在漫长的生产生活实践中逐渐适应了这种环境，并顽强的在其中生存下来。如意大利的韦内雷港、五村镇以及沿海群岛（Portovenere, Cinque Terre, and the Islands）见证了当地人征服陡峭的海岸地区并长期在此定居的历史；瑞典南厄兰岛（Agricultural Landscape of Southern Öland）的南部由一片巨大的石灰石高地构成，而岛民却适应了这种恶劣的自然环境，并已经在此居住了五千年。

2. 反映特殊生产方式的延续类景观：此类景观中，人们在适应和利用环境的基础上，形成了具有突出价值和特点的生产方式。如菲律宾的科迪勒拉山的稻米梯田（Rice Terraces of the Philippine Cordilleras）是在陡峭山区进行可持续性水稻种植的典范；奥地利的哈尔施塔特 – 达特施泰因萨尔茨卡默古特文化景观（Hallstatt – Dachstein ∕ Salzkammergut Cultural Landscape）见证了当地从公元前 2000 年开始维持至今的盐矿产业。

在这一类文化景观中，尤其引人注目的是有多处葡萄园景观。它们保持了欧洲各地应对不同地理环境的各种传统葡萄种植和酿酒技术，包括法国的圣艾米伦区（Jurisdiction of Saint – Emilion）、葡萄牙的上杜罗（Alto Douro Wine Region）与皮库岛（Landscape of the Pico Island Vineyard Culture），以及匈牙利的托卡伊（Tokaj Wine Region Historic Cultural Landscape）和瑞士的拉沃葡萄园梯田（Lavaux，Vineyard Terraces）。

3. 见证多元文化传统的延续类景观：此类景观的特点在于全景式展现了世界各地不同文化族裔与自然环境的多元共存，体现了地球的文化多样性。如蒙古的鄂尔浑峡谷文化景观（Orkhon Valley Cultural Landscape）见证了保持千年之久的游牧传统；尼日利亚的宿库卢文化景观（Sukur Cultural Landscape）反映了苏库尔人政治和经济结构，等等。

4. 体现和谐栖居的延续类景观：此类景观通常具有诗情画意的美丽自然风景，长期以来，人类生活与自然环境高度融洽，成为人与自然关系的典范。如法国卢瓦尔河谷（The Loire Valley between Sully – sur – Loire and Chalonnes）沿岸分布着大量的历史名镇和村庄及雄伟的古堡，以及几个世纪以来人类开垦的耕地；而延绵 65 公里的莱茵河中上游河谷（Upper Middle Rhine Valley）与河畔的古堡、历史小城、葡萄园一起生动地描述了一段人类与变迁的自然环境相互影响的漫长历史。

需要指出的是，以上分类只是本文为了进一步认识延续类景观所包含的人与自然互动丰富形式和内涵的一种尝试，与文化景观的三大类型一样，它也是概念性而非排他性的。

（三）关联性文化景观

根据《操作指南》的定义，"这类景观以自然因素强烈的宗教、艺术或文化关联性为特征，而不是以文化物证为特征，后者对它来说是没有意义的，甚至是可以忽略的。"

此类文化景观中人与自然的互动已经从景观设计、土地利用、生活传统等方面上升到精神层面，如宗教与艺术等。如富勒所言，该类景观的推出正是为了使人们能够自由思考"理念型景观"（landscape of ideas）。[①]

到目前为止，世界遗产名录上共有 11 处关联性景观，主要具有以下几个特点：

1. 该类景观具有显著的自然元素，尤其是高山或巨石。

这一点仅从各景观的名称中便能辨认出来，如中国的庐山国家公园（Lushan National Park）、马达加斯加的安布希曼加的皇家蓝山行宫（Royal Hill of Ambohimanga）、津巴布韦的马托博山（Matobo Hills）等等。山石元素在此类景观中的突出性不是偶然的，而是和其固有的自然与文化属性密不可分的。由于山的巍峨与雄伟，在人类文明的初期，它往往被看做是神秘、永恒的，并具有沟通宇宙苍穹或神祇与祖先的神圣性，并由此衍生出历代不息的祭祀与信仰传统，成为人与自然密切关联最典型的一类例证。

2. 到目前为止，该类景观所关联的非物质价值主要体现在强烈的宗教性上。

如新西兰的汤加里罗国家公园（Tongariro National Park）与澳大利亚的乌卢鲁—卡塔曲塔国家公园（Uluru – Kata Tjuta National Park）均反映了当地原住民传统的原始宗教信仰，安布希曼加的皇家蓝山行宫与当地的宗教仪式密切相关，纪伊山地则反映了日本的神道教与佛教传统。

该类景观关联的其他非物质价值有以中国庐山为代表的国家的传统文化[②]，以及以冰岛平位利尔为代表的国家身份的象征。

3. 该类景观亦可具有价值突出的文化物证。

虽然根据关联性景观的定义，它们"不是以文化物证为特征，后者对它来说是没有意义的，甚至是可以忽略的"，而该类景观最早的两个例证，汤加里罗与乌卢鲁—卡塔曲塔也几乎没有任何物质遗迹，但此后的申报实践显示，该类遗产也可具有突出的文化物证。如在中国的庐山景观，山上分布着丰富的考古遗迹、碑文、历史建筑和中外别墅，而苏莱曼圣山也拥有大量的和祭祀相关的神坛和岩石壁画以及后期的清真寺。因此，文化物证与该类遗产的突出普遍价值并不矛盾，而是有助于证实与传达此种价值。

二、文化景观与其他遗产类型的比较研究

在工作中，文化景观容易和其他一些遗产类型，如文化自然混合遗产以及文化线路混淆起来。本节将分别就文化景观与混合遗产、文化线路及另一新兴的遗产类型——城市历史景观作比较研究，藉此进一步明确文化景观的内涵与外延。

（一）文化景观与混合遗产的比较研究

根据《操作指南》中的相关规定，可以总结出文化景观与混合遗产的两点关键不同：

1. 核心特征的不同：文化景观的核心特征是突出反映人与自然间的互动，而混合遗产的核心特征是同时具有突出的文化与自然价值，但其自然价值与文化价值间并不一定呈现出一种显著的相互影响与作用的关系；

2. 评估标准不同：文化景观的评估标准是 OUV 标准中的前六条，关键是其人与自然间的互动需要达到 OUV，而其自然属性并非一定要符合 OUV 标准；而混合遗产则需要同时采用文化与自然标准进行评估，需要最少同时满足两套标准中的各一条。

---

① Paper 6：P 58

② 在 1996 年的世界遗产委员会决议中，委员会指出，"根据标准 2，3，4 和 6，将庐山作为具有杰出美学价值和与中国精神和文化生活有着强大关联性的文化景观入选世界遗产名录"。

但是，对于混合遗产来说，由于同时具备突出的自然与文化价值，其文化与自然间难免存在某种程度的互动。而当这种互动具备突出普遍价值的时候，混合遗产可以同时被认定为是文化景观。换个角度说，如果文化景观的自然属性达到了自然价值的 OUV 标准，那么它也将被认定为是一处混合遗产。因此两者存在一定的重合关系，具体如图一所示。

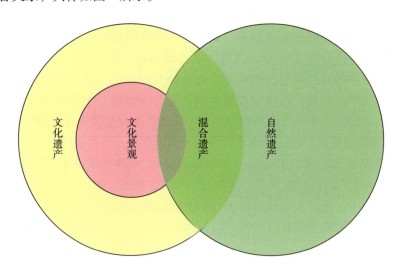

在实践中，自 1992 年文化景观类型推出以来，共有五处混合遗产没有被认定为文化景观。它们分别是：中国的峨眉山—乐山大佛与武夷山风景名胜区，南非的夸特兰巴山脉/德拉肯斯堡山公园，西班牙的伊维萨岛的生物多样性和特有文化以及瑞典的拉普人区域。其中，"伊维萨岛的生物多样性和特有文化（Ibiza, Biodiversity and Culture）"为理解混合遗产与文化景观的差别提供了较典型的例证。

在自然价值方面，该遗产由于见证了海洋与沿海生态系统的相互作用以及保持了良好的海洋生物的多样性而符合了 OUV 标准九与十。而在文化方面，岛上坚固的高城要塞对于西班牙殖民者在新大陆的防御性建筑发展具有极其深远的影响（标准二）；岛上腓尼基时代的遗址见证了腓尼基地中海西岸殖民地中的城镇化与社会生活（标准三）；该岛的上城是防御性古城的杰出范例，其城墙与城市肌理依次留下了腓尼基、阿拉伯以及文艺复兴时期的印记（标准四）。①

以上信息表明，此遗产的突出文化价值体现在人造物本身，其中没有体现出自然的作用，或人与自然的相互作用，因此不能被看做文化景观。

由此可见，文化景观与混合遗产是评估世界遗产的两种不同维度。文化景观的核心是人与自然间的互动——这种互动必须是深刻的，相互融合相互发生影响，并且伴有物质或精神的证据；而混合遗产的本质是对同时满足文化与自然标准的世界遗产的客观认定，并不关注文化与自然间的互动关系。同时，在实践中，这两种遗产的价值评估主体也有所不同。混合遗产由 ICOMOS 与 IUCN 分别评估其文化与自然价值，而文化景观中人与自然互动的价值，虽然在必要时会听取 IUCN 的建议，总的来说还是由 ICOMOS 负责进行评估的。

（二）文化景观与文化线路的比较研究

文化景观和文化线路具有紧密的联系，但又是两个不同的概念，这些不同在 2002 年 CIIC 名为"与文化景观相关的文化线路在概念上与实际上的独立性"的科学会议上有过系统阐述。会议认为将文化线路

---

① http：//whc. unesco. org/archive/repcom99. htm#417

称为"线性文化景观"是"对文化线路特征的否定，是基本概念上的错误"①，因为两者的区别十分显著：

第一，文化景观强调人与自然的联系和相互影响，但文化线路强调动态性和因迁移带来的人文交流。

第二，文化线路往往是由遗址、历史城市、建筑群、考古遗存和文化景观组成的，它不一定是一个文化景观，也不能用线性和非线性来概括其全部内容。这两类遗产不是简单的从属关系。文化景观可以是文化线路的组成元素之一，大型文化线路沿途可能会存在不同类型的文化景观。

第三，文化景观是一种社会现象，是人与自然共同作用而成的，所以必须在达到与自然和谐共处的情况下才能长期存在并自然进化；文化线路是人类因活动和交换的特殊需要创造出来的，并非总是遵从自然法则，具有很强的目的性和自主性。

第四，非物质元素在两者中的地位有所区别：文化景观中的非物质元素是随文化景观的演化而产生的，旨在反映传统生活和文化的价值，反映人和自然之间和谐的关系；而文化线路中的非物质元素是将物质元素捆绑成一个整体的纽带，它除了反映传统生活外，还反映了迁移和交换这些动态因素的影响范围和影响过程，并给予整个文化线路以价值，它的意义在某些方面甚至可以超越物质元素的意义。

由此可见，文化景观和文化线路在界定和内涵方面有着明显的区别，从不同的侧重点描述了遗产的性质和意义：文化景观作为强调人和自然、文化与自然关系的一种遗产；而文化线路则是遗产概念不断延展、内涵不断丰富的结果，它更像一种复杂的遗产组合方式，从整体上强调物质、非物质和自然元素（因素）的关联性，同时这些元素都是由于交流和动态的迁移而产生的。但是，文化景观与文化线路也绝对不是对立的，某些遗产经过不同角度的分析和价值评判，可以认定它们既是文化景观也是文化线路（如日本纪伊山朝圣线路和阿根廷的塔夫拉达·德乌玛瓦卡山谷）。

（三）文化景观与城市历史景观的比较研究

近几年来，在世界遗产领域中有一个新的概念正引起人们越来越多的关注与讨论，它便是"城市历史景观"（historic urban landscape）。作为景观类型的一种，该遗产概念与文化景观存在着密切联系，以至于在 2007 年年初俄罗斯圣彼得堡举行的关于中东欧国家"世界遗产名录中历史城市中心管理与保护"的地区性会议上，人们专门就"城市历史景观是否是一类文化景观"这个问题进行了探讨。世界遗产领域的资深专家富勒、杰瑞米·怀特汉德（Jeremy Whitehand）与布鲁诺·加比耶利（Bruno Gabrielli）先后对此进行了主旨发言，并较一致地提出，城市历史景观可以视为文化景观中的一类。②

这无疑为人们对文化景观的理解增添了新的难题——相对于《操作指南》中文化景观的三大类型，"城市历史景观"是在此之外新一类型的文化景观，还是属于对文化景观不同视角不同层面的另一种审视方式？就此问题，根据业内专家亨利·克列尔、米蒂尔德·罗斯勒和肯·泰勒的回复，本文认为：城市历史景观理论是对现有文化景观理论的发展，它将文化景观对人与自然的互动聚焦于城市之中，对城市遗产的价值认识、管理与保护都提出了新的要求与挑战。它不会对既有的文化景观类型造成冲击，但对我们理解文化景观的内涵与外延，以及进一步做好文化景观的管理与保护工作，都有着积极的意义。

三、文化景观的价值标准

根据《世界遗产公约》的规定，突出普遍价值（Outstanding Universal Value，以下简称 OUV）是遗产

① Scientific meeting of the International Committee on Cultural Routes（CIIC）on "The Conceptual and Substantive Independence of Cultural Routes in Relation to Cultural Landscapes，Madrid：Considerations and Recommendation，Madrid，Spain，2002

② http：//www. chacon. ru/about_ chair/Final%20report. htm

地列入世界遗产名录最基本也是最重要的条件。《操作指南》77条列出了评估遗产OUV的十条标准，作为文化遗产，文化景观的评估主要参照其中的前六条。本节将在吸取国际理论研究成果的基础上，结合评估实例，分析文化景观列入《世界遗产名录》的价值标准。

（一）六条标准在各类型文化景观中的应用

据统计，在所有67处文化景观遗产中，六条标准的应用情况分别是：标准一使用了4次，标准二25次，标准三41次，标准四44次，标准五32次，标准六19次，参见表一与图二。下面将针对各类型文化景观中价值标准的使用情况分别进行探讨。①

表一　各类型文化景观遗产OUV文化标准使用汇总

编号	遗产类型	遗产数量	标准一	标准二	标准三	标准四	标准五	标准六
1	设计类景观	9	2	7	1	9	1	1
1.1	园林类景观	1		1	1	1		
1.2	田园类景观	6	2	4		6	1	1
1.3	宗教类	2		2		2		
2	有机演进类景观	47	2	14	31	31	29	7
2.1	残迹类景观	14	1	4	14	10	4	2
2.1.1	古代残迹类景观	10	1	2	10	7	3	2
2.1.2	近现代残迹类景观	4		2	4	3	1	
2.2	延续类景观	33	1	10	17	21	25	5
2.2.1	对特殊环境的征服利用	11		3	1	6	11	1
2.2.2	特殊生产方式	9		1	7	7	6	1
2.2.3	多元文化传统	8		1	8	3	5	3
2.2.4	田园栖居	5	1	5	1	5	3	
3	关联性景观	11		4	9	4	2	11
	汇总	67	4	25	41	44	32	19

1. 人类有意设计和创造的景观：

在这一类型的9处遗产中，最引人注目的现象是每一处遗产均应用了标准四，标准二位居其次，被采用了7次。对于本类型文化景观而言，运用标准四需要证明它们是某一时期建筑与自然和谐相融的先锋或典范，如"18世纪是园林景观设计大发展的时期，影响巨大，德绍—沃尔利茨园林王国则是一个杰出而丰富的典范"。

标准二表现的人类价值的交流主要体现为宗教思想、哲学思想、文化传统以及科学与艺术，可以说涉及了人类精神文明

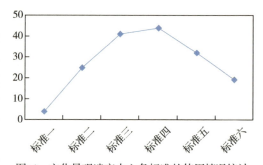

图二　文化景观遗产中六条标准的使用情况统计

的方方面面，如邱园"自18世纪以来，在植物学领域，就与全世界范围内科学和经济交流有紧密的关系"。

---

① 对作为混合遗产的文化景观使用的自然标准未纳入本文的研究对象。

2. 有机演进类文化景观：

2. 1. 残迹类景观：

与设计类文化景观相比，有机演进类的文化景观更强调作为生活者、生产者的群体的人，而非精英的、作为设计者的个体的人。标准三由此成为与此类景观关系最为紧密的一条标准，在本类型景观中所有 14 处均得到使用。此外，在本类型景观中有 10 处使用了标准四。

2. 2. 延续类景观：

在该类型 33 处文化景观遗产中，应用最多的 3 条标准依次是标准五、标准四、标准三，分别被用了 25 次、21 次与 17 次。其中：

1）表现人类对特殊环境征服与利用的延续类景观：共 11 处，均使用了标准五。

该类型景观人与自然互动的突出价值集中体现于人类对环境的显著回应和可持续利用上，标准五也由此成为其最频繁使用的一条标准，甚至有 4 处遗产地只使用了标准五（库尔斯沙嘴、新锡德尔湖与费尔特湖地区、维嘎群岛文化景观与马德留—配拉菲塔—克拉罗尔大峡谷）。

2）反映特殊生产方式的延续类景观：共 9 处，标准三与标准四均被使用了 7 次，标准五使用了 6 次。

此类型延续类景观中人与自然的互动体现在具有突出价值的生产方式上，因此其应用标准三所见证的，是拥有突出生产方式的文化传统或文明，如科迪勒拉山的稻米梯田"生动见证了一个社群可持续及公有的稻米生产体系，这一体系业已存在 2 000 多年"。

标准四则适用于人们将其特殊生产方式作用于环境而形成的人与自然和谐共处的场景，或是见证这种生产方式的相关建筑实体，如墨西哥龙舌兰景观中的"农场和酿酒厂以及相关的设备，反映了过去 250 年龙舌兰酒量的增长，是反映技术和文化融合的独特建筑综合体的杰出范例"。

而具有突出价值的生产方式也可凝结为具备 OUV 的土地利用方式（标准五），如托卡伊葡萄酒产地的"整个景观，包括葡萄园和历史悠久的居住区，生动地展示了它所代表的传统土地使用方式"。

3）见证多元文化传统的延续类景观：本类型的 8 处遗产均应用了标准三，5 处应用了标准五，3 处应用了标准六，3 处应用标准四。

此类景观中人与自然的互动关系凝结成基于对环境可持续利用和共处的生活方式或文化传统，因此标准三成为其应用最为普遍的一条标准，如泰姆格里考古景观岩刻"为从青铜器时代到如今中亚大草原地区的放牧民族的生活和信仰提供了翔实的见证"。

在此基础上，如果这种多元的生活方式与文化传统具有突出的土地使用方式，则遗产地亦符合标准五，如宿库卢文化景观；或者呈现为能够展现历史重要阶段的景观范例（标准四），并展现出人类价值的重要交流（标准二），如鄂尔浑峡谷文化景观；同时，此类景观也可能具备突出的关联性价值，如古帕玛库景观。

4）体现和谐栖居的延续类景观：共 5 处。每一处均使用了标准二与标准四。

此类遗产拥有秀美优越的自然环境，其人与自然间的相互作用主要体现为两者间持续演进着的融洽关系，并以为杰出的景观风貌为其物证（标准四），如瓦豪文化景观中的"建筑、人类居住区与农业用地都生动地展示了一个中世纪的景观随着时间有机和谐的演化"。同时，作为突出的景观范例，这些遗产地也往往见证了人类科学、艺术、文化等各种价值的重要交流（标准二），如卢瓦尔河谷"是一条主要河流旁的杰出文化景观，见证了人类价值的交流以及 2000 多年人类及其周边环境和谐的发展"。

3. 关联性景观：

在本类型 11 处文化景观中，每处均使用了标准六。该标准作为与关联性景观关系最为密切的价值标准，主要用以证明遗产地自然要素与人类宗教、文化、国家身份认同等的密切联系上。如汤加里罗国家公园"对毛利人有着重要的文化宗教意义，是当地人和自然环境之间深刻的精神联系的突出代表"。

此外，与一般的世界遗产不同，文化景观遗产被认定的关键是其所反映的人与自然环境的互动被认为是具有 OUV 的。换句话说，一个文化景观遗产可能同时满足多条价值标准，但其中至少需要有一条是用以证实其人与自然环境间互动的突出价值的。因此，除去考量各条 OUV 标准一般的使用特点，还需找出各条标准中针对文化景观的相关内容，并总结各类文化景观遗产是如何适用这些标准的。在上文对文化景观类型特征及 OUV 标准使用情况进行探讨的基础上，下面试归纳文化景观类型与相关 OUV 标准间的联系。

设计类景观人与自然环境的互动主要体现在人类建筑物与自然环境的有机融合上，并由此成为杰出的景观范例而具备了 OUV，尤其是满足标准四。也就是说，对设计类景观来说，标准四是衡量其文化景观地位成立与否的关键性标准。此外，由于设计类景观往往凝结了各种人类思想的精华，由此标准二也成为设计类景观最为普遍的衍生使用标准。

对于有机演进类的景观，不论是残迹类景观还是延续类景观，其所表现的人与自然环境的互动突出反映为人与自然间征服、利用、多元化共处或田园栖居的关系。这种种互动关系通常基于特定的人类定居或土地使用方式（标准五所包含的内容），从而形成某种特殊的景观（标准四所包含的内容），并可能见证某种与自然关系密切的文明或文化传统（标准三所含的内容）。也就是说，演进类景观与标准三、四、五都存在关系，只是各个景观与自然环境关系的特征不同，而侧重在不同的方面显示出 OUV。如表现人类与特定环境共处的景观，其 OUV 主要体现在特殊的土地利用方式上，因此标准五是其成为文化景观遗产的关键。此外，由于延续类景观也可能展示人类价值的重要交流，而某些社群在使用土地的过程中，也与环境发生了精神上的关联，标准二与标准六是此类景观使用较多的衍生标准。

关联性景观人与环境的互动主要体现在自然因素与宗教、艺术、文化等人类精神文明结晶的显著关联上，其 OUV 主要体现在自然环境与人类非物质价值的强烈联系上。因此标准六成为评估其 OUV 成立与否最关键的标准。同时，由于此类景观通常产生于某种特殊的文化传统，因此标准三成为其最主要的衍生标准。

（二）文化景观的自然价值与评估

作为"自然与人的共同作品"，虽然文化景观的自然价值不一定达到自然遗产的标准，由于其"包含了人类与其所在的自然环境之间的多种互动表现"①，各种类型的文化景观中依然呈现出丰富多样的自然品质。也正因为此，《操作指南》附件 6 的第 15 条指出，"世界自然保护联盟（IUCN）对很多文化遗产都感兴趣，特别是那些作为文化景观申报的遗产"。而在文化景观评估的实践中，虽然 ICOMOS 起着主导作用，对于自然品质尤其突出的文化景观提名地，ICOMOS 常常会与 IUCN 组成联合考察组进行实地考察。

为此，IUCN 还专门编制了一份内部文件《文化景观内自然价值的评估》（Guidelines for Reviewers of Cultural Landscapes – The Assessment of Natural Values in Cultural Landscapes）②，对文化景观自然价值的评估提出了一些建议。

在此文件中，IUCN 首先强调，起草这一文件的唯一目的是确认 IUCN 在文化景观评估中的介入程度，其正式评估仍要在六条文化标准的框架内进行，并指出，其对文化景观的密切兴趣源自许多文化景观对于自然及自然资源保护与进化的重要性，并主要集中于延续类景观中。此外，IUCN 指出，在评估文化景观申报地的过程中，其最关注的是景观自然品质的完整性与管理，及人与自然间的关系。

自 1992 年文化景观概念推出以来，根据各文化景观遗产地的评估报告，IUCN 主要参与了以下非混合遗产类文化景观的评估：科迪勒拉山的稻米梯田（1995）、奇伦托和迪亚诺河谷国家公园（1998）、夸底·夸底沙（圣谷）和神杉林（1998）、南厄兰岛的农业景观（2000）、伦敦基尤皇家植物园（2003）、维

---

① 《操作指南》附件 3 第 8 条。

② http: //cmsdata. iucn. org/downloads/guidelines_ for_ reviewers_ of_ cls. pdf

嘎群岛文化景观（2004）、平位利尔国家公园（2004）、奥孙—奥索博神树林（2005）、龙舌兰景观和特基拉的古代工业设施（2006）、康沃尔和西德文矿区景观（2006）、库科早期农业遗址（2008）、米基肯达卡亚圣林（2008）、马塔王酋长领地（2008）、莫纳山文化景观（2008）、苏莱曼圣山（2009）。

通过统计可以发现，IUCN 在文化景观评估中的参与程度近年来呈逐渐递增之势，尤其是自 2005 年以来，在成功入选世界遗产名录的十四处非混合遗产类文化景观遗产地中，IUCN 参与评估了其中的八处，比例高达 57%。这无疑体现了人们对文化景观遗产自然价值的日渐重视。而在具体的评估实践中，除了从专业角度对申报地自然价值的保护与管理作出建议，IUCN 对文化景观申报地自然品质的评估主要体现在自然价值本身以及人与自然的互动关系上。

关于文化景观的自然品质，值得我们关注的还有 OUV 标准中的第七条——"绝妙的自然现象或具有罕见自然美与审美重要性的地区"。随着文化标准与自然标准从 2005 年版的《操作指南》中被合并在一起后，人们开始日益关注文化与自然价值标准中相融相通的内容。而标准七所涉及的"美"的概念，无疑与人的主观判断密切相关，并由此具有文化内涵，成为与文化遗产，特别是文化景观遗产关系最为紧密的自然标准。

能够对此予以佐证的是，《什么是 OUV？》一文在系统回顾了六条文化标准的使用实践之外，还专门对标准七进行了论述。文章认为，"对美的判定不是科学实践，而是一个文化理解的过程，涉及不同时期人们的审美判断，因此该标准是将自然与文化联系在一起的有趣实例，并以文化、历史，以及哲学与美学为基础"。[1] 1995 年举行的亚太地区关联性文化景观专家会议也指出，该标准存在与关联性景观的潜在联系，因为对自然美与审美重要性的判断可能源自文化的关联性[2]。

目前，ICOMOS 已将自然景观（包括海景）作为文化景观的子类别之一列入其主题研究框架，因为其已注意到在许多文化景观中自然的角色是主导性的，并认为需要对此进行深入研究。而另一方面，IUCN 也不约而同的注意到了对自然美的评估带有主观因素，并指出标准七与文化景观的评估有关。

标准七与文化景观的密切联系也得到了中国学者的关注。2010 年 11 月 23 日至 24 日，"大地与水：景观美的认知"国际学术研讨会在扬州召开，国家文物局局长单霁翔、国际古迹遗址理事会副主席郭旃、中国建筑设计研究院历史研究所所长陈同滨、世界遗产资深顾问苏珊·丹耶尔、ICOMOS 景观委员会主席莫妮卡·卢恩格（Monica Luengo）等国内外专家齐聚一堂，就中外文化景观中美的认知与保护展开探讨。

自然美中的文化内涵日益得到国内外遗产界的重视，这对中国来说无疑是一个积极的信号。因为中国传统的山水美学历来重视"寄情山水"、"人景合一"、"景由心生"等审美体验，客观的自然美与人对美的主观建构在很大程度上是密不可分、合二为一的。如果能够通过挖掘中国传统美学理论的精髓，借助标准七在文化与自然美之间搭建起桥梁，不仅可以提高中国文化景观及其他相关遗产类型申报的成功几率，对于弘扬中国的传统美学理论和天人合一的世界观宇宙观，都是有着非常积极的意义的。

四、文化景观的真实性与完整性

自 2005 年版的《操作指南》开始，真实性与完整性成为 OUV 的有机组成部分，是遗产地列入《世界遗产名录》的基本条件之一。同时，《操作指南》附件三进一步指出，"选择它们（文化景观）的依据包括它们的突出普遍价值和它们在特定地理文化区域中的代表性，还包括它们体现这些地区一般和特殊文化元素的能力"。而这种代表性与能力，无疑也与真实性和完整性密切相关。本节将结合评估实例，分析文化景观列入《世界遗产名录》的真实性与完整性要求。

---

① 《什么是 OUV？》：P35

② whc. unesco. org/archive/cullan95. htm

（一）文化景观的真实性

自《世界遗产公约》推出以来，真实性成为评估文化遗产的重要标准之一。文化遗产专家尤卡·朱吉莱托认为有三种类型的真实性：创造性—艺术性的真实性、历史的—物质的真实性及社会的—文化的真实性。创造性的真实性主要指设计与技术方面，材料与实体是申报对象不同时期建筑与使用的历史证据之一，而真实性的社会与文化性主要指遗产的延续类传统与其他非物质元素。[①] 对文化景观遗产来说，由于各类型文化景观的组成要素及其 OUV 特征均各有不同，因此对其真实性评估的侧重点也有所不同。

对于设计类景观来说，由于这一类遗产地的 OUV 主要体现在人类建筑物与自然环境的巧妙结合与和谐统一，因此其真实性的重点在于朱吉莱托所提出的创造性—艺术性方面，并需具备相关的历史—物质的真实性。ICOMOS 在对此类景观进行真实性评估时，考察的重点是申报对象的原初设计格局、建筑材料与技术、整体景观的功能等要素的保存状况。一般来说，只要申报地整体上保留了历史上的景观设计格局，建筑物的位置、材料、技术等基本与历史保持一致，且景观维持了其历史性功能，那么，该设计景观即能被认定为是具有真实性的。而即使以上要素遭受了破坏，只要处于可恢复的程度以内，其真实性也能够被认定。

如邱园的真实性体现在其最初用途的保持以及园内建筑在设计、原料和功能方面的真实性，而德绍—沃尔利茨园林王国也保留了重要的景观设计作品和建筑遗迹，虽然其整体结构曾遭受过不小的损害，但可以修复其中的大部分，因此 ICOMOS 对其真实性也给予了肯定的评价。

对于残迹类景观来说，由于其进化过程已经停止，因此该类遗产的真实性主要体现在实体物理遗迹保存状况上。由于这些遗迹大多已在不同的历史时期里遭到人们的废弃，因而较少受到破坏和干扰，由此具有很高的真实性。如马蓬古布韦文化景观除了考古发掘，该地区由于已经遗弃而没有遭受任何人为干预；克拿维考古遗址也自 14 世纪末遭到遗弃，因此其文化遗址很少或仅仅受到很少的人为干预。

而延续类文化景观由于具有动态性，其真实性评估比起前两类景观要更为复杂。世界遗产专家苏珊·丹耶尔（Susan Denyer）曾专门撰文对此类文化景观的真实性特征进行讨论[②]。她指出，文化景观具有三大要素：人、环境及联系这两者的力量（主要是社会的、经济的或政治的），而延续类景观的真实性也相应包含三大要素：显著的文化回应、这些文化回应对不同利益群体的意义与价值以及形成这些回应的力量。

由此可见，延续类文化景观的真实性不能只与其物质表现相连，因为该类文化景观同时包含了物质与非物质属性的动态力量，因此其真实性也需要与非物质属性、塑造景观的力量及景观所具有的价值相联系。由于这些要素都有演进的能力，因此延续类景观的真实性也可能变化与演进。

ICOMOS 对此类文化景观真实性的评估意见表明，从物质层面来说，延续类景观的真实性主要体现在景观的外形、功能及景观对于当地历史发展轨迹的记录上，而其非物质方面的真实性主要体现在传统的生活方式与土地利用技术上的延续上。

如比利牛斯—珀杜山的真实性主要体现在其功能与景观整体面貌的延续性，韦内雷港、五村镇以及沿海群岛景观的真实性体现在其对传统生活方式的完好保留，新锡德尔湖与费尔特湖地区文化景观的真实性在于见证了自中世纪以来一直持续下来的一种土地使用方式和生活方式，等等。

与延续类景观类似，关联性景观的真实性也主要体现在物质与非物质两个方面。对 ICOMOS 关联性景观真实性评估的分析表明，对其此类景观的物质遗存来说，它们的真实性主要体现在景观的整体功能

① Jokilehto J. 2006, *Considerations on authenticity and integrity in world heritage context* . City & Time 2（1）：1.

② Susan Denyer：*Authenticity in World Heritage Cultural Landscapes：continuity and change* . New Views on Authenticity and Integrity in the World Heritage of the Americas ，Editor：Dr. F. J. L Morales，2005：P57 - 61

（如苏莱曼圣山保持了作为祭祀地的真实性）、整体格局（如庐山建筑与其周边自然环境关系保持了历史真实性）、景观元素的材质与外形等（如马托博山的岩画具有真实性）与建筑的设计（如纪伊山地与平位利尔国家公园中的传统建筑）等方面。而这类景观更为普遍与重要的则是非物质层面的真实性，即各景观中人与自然持续的精神关联。如皇家蓝山行宫一直维持了它的神圣性以及人民对它的尊重，莫纳山一直保持着其与抗争及自由精神的关联。

（二）文化景观的完整性

"完整性"最早被用于自然遗产的评估，从 2005 年版的《操作指南》开始，它被正式规定为文化遗产申报所需符合的条件之一。

朱吉莱托曾根据文化遗产各要素与特征，及其与遗产整体的关系，区分出三种类型的完整性：社会性—功能性的完整性、历史—结构的完整性以及视觉/审美的完整性。[①]

在实践中，由于完整性要求于 2005 年才正式应用于文化遗产，ICOMOS 对于完整性的评估在此前的评估报告中虽会有所涉及，但通常是包含对真实性的评估中，较少专门的评价。但对相关文化景观遗产完整性评估的分析表明，朱吉莱托对一般性文化遗产完整性的分类与分析也同样适用于文化景观。

对于设计类景观来说，其完整性主要体现在历史结构的完整性上，即要求景观能够保持设计之初及历史上的规模、布局和组成要素。而有机演进类的景观与关联性景观的完整性则主要体现在社会功能的完整性上，如各个葡萄园景观均包括了葡萄种植与葡萄酒酿造过程中相关的全部元素，巴姆城景观也完整展示了整个城市的地下水渠系统，苏莱曼圣山则完整保留了各个祭祀场所，以及连接各个祭祀地的小路。而这两类完整性也是相辅相成，密不可分的。历史结构的完整性是社会功能完整性的物质承载，功能完整性则是结构完整性的深化。而在两者的基础上，文化景观还需从视觉与审美的角度考虑整个景观的视觉完整性。

（三）文化景观的遗产区与缓冲区

遗产的真实性与完整性和遗产的范围密切相关。由于涉及活态的社会生活方式及大范围的人与自然的互动，文化景观遗产的合理划界也是其申报、管理与保护的要点之一。根据相关学术观点并结合文化景观遗产的实例，本文归纳出以下几条遗产区与缓冲区的划界原则：

1. 划界的首要原则是要保证遗产各方面的完整性。如基尤植物园的缓冲区保护了园内外重要的景致、保持了园区与和其具有很强历史联系的区域的关系并保护了植物园的特性与环境；卡瓦利泽布日多夫斯津的缓冲区也考虑了景观视线保护区的范围，以便在更广阔的范围内审视该文化遗产，因此还包括了外围的自然景观区及附近的历史村镇和建筑。

2. 对于延续类景观与关联性景观，由于景观的区划与价值和生活在当地的人们密切相关，因此划界时要认真考虑他们的传统与生活方式。如米基肯达卡亚圣林遗产区的边界就是森林的边界，大部分界线不仅在相关法律中得到认可，也被当地民众认可，该遗产没有缓冲区，森林外的公共土地由惯例法、禁忌和当地民众与遗产区间长久关联形成的习俗管理和保护着。

3. 在能充分保证遗产地 OUV 价值的基础上，划界时可适当遵照现有的管理区划或自然界线。如横跨波兰、德国两国的穆斯考尔公园的缓冲区包括遗产区的外围土地及 Bad Muskau 与 Łeknica 的城市化土地，与公园的景致联为一体，其划定考虑了波兰、德国共同的管理现状与保护要求；马篷古布韦文化景观的北边界为南非与博茨瓦纳及津巴布韦的界河 Limpopo 河。

4. 遗产的遗产区与缓冲区不是绝对的，在遗产价值能够得到保护的前提下，有时并不需要另划缓冲

---

① 什么是 OUV？：P44

区。如占巴塞遗产和文化景观的遗产区包含了大片自然景观，遗产的所有主要特点都已经包括，因此没有另设缓冲区；布莱纳冯工业区景观的遗产区代表了与其相关历史景观的全部，也没有单设缓冲区。

五、中国文化景观资源的发掘与保护利用

（一）中国的文化景观资源

到目前为止，中国在《世界遗产名录》上共有三处文化景观遗产，分别是江西的庐山国家公园、山西的五台山，以及浙江的杭州西湖文化景观。

从世界遗产中心网站上对以上文化景观遗产的描述可见，文化景观作为沟通人与自然的桥梁，与中国传统的宇宙观、世界观及审美思想等都有着很大的共通之处，客观上能够成为中国遗产价值得到表达与认定最理想的遗产类型之一。其中，于2011年6月世界遗产委员会第35届会议上被最新列入《世界遗产名录》的杭州西湖文化景观，是中国第一次主动以文化景观类型申报的世界文化遗产，开创了中国文化景观遗产研究、保护与利用的新篇章。

在此基础上，本文认为可以从以下渠道发掘我国丰富的文化景观资源，从而为今后的文化景观遗产申报和保护工作奠定更加良好的基础。

1. 中国《文化遗产预备名单》上的文化景观资源：

在2006年12月公布的《中国世界文化遗产预备名单》（以下简称《预备名单》）基础之上，时隔五年，国家文物局于2011年再次启动了《预备名单》的更新工作。目前，由于此项工作仍在进行之中，在此仅根据06年版的《预备名单》探讨相关遗产的文化景观价值。本文认为，在2006年版的《预备名单》中，目前尚未启动世界遗产申报程序，具有文化景观申报潜力的候选地主要有以下这些：瘦西湖，江南水乡古镇，牛河梁、良渚、古蜀国遗址，上林湖越窑遗址，花山岩画，西南藏、羌、苗、侗各族村寨，哈尼梯田，坎儿井等。下面将按文化景观的类型择要对相关候选地的文化景观价值进行分析：

1）设计类景观代表：瘦西湖

瘦西湖是我国湖上园林的代表，是我国古代造园思想与自然环境有机结合的杰出范例，具备设计类文化景观的价值。

2）残迹类景观代表：上林湖越窑遗址

上林湖在我国早期陶瓷史上占有重要地位，见证了我国古代制瓷业依托环境而发展兴盛的辉煌历史，具有突出的残迹类景观的价值。

3）延续类景观代表：新疆吐鲁番坎儿井

坎儿井是我国古代人民在吐鲁番盆地特殊的地理与气候环境中，经过长期实践所开发的一种可持续的水利工程，一直持续使用到今天，并仍对发展当地农业生产和满足居民生活需要等具有重要作用，属于土地使用的杰出范例。

此外，单霁翔先生在其著作中对我国西南少数民族村寨的文化景观价值进行了详细的分析①。这些村寨历史悠久，与自然和谐相处，具有浓厚的文化底蕴，均具很高的延续类景观价值。

2. 其他文化景观资源：

入选历批《全国重点文物保护单位名单》的国保单位，作为我国国家级的文化遗产，可以说是我国文化景观最直接的后备库，从在2006年5月公布的第六批《全国重点文物保护单位名单》中，便可发掘不少潜在的具备文化景观价值的遗产地，列举如下：

聚馆古贡枣园：见证了古代枣树种植技艺的发展过程，是古代农业科技发展成果的重要实物例证，

---

① 单霁翔. 走进文化景观遗产的世界［M］. 天津：天津大学出版社，2010. P156－159

具备延续类景观的价值。

杏花村汾酒作坊：见证了汾酒文化的传承和我国特有的酿酒技术。在目前的文化景观遗产中，欧洲的葡萄园种植与葡萄酒酿造景观占据了很大的比例。这一方面体现了酒对人们生活的重要性，另一方面也证明了世界其他地区酒类景观入选《世界遗产名录》的巨大空间。将我国的重要白酒作坊作为文化景观进行遗产申报，不仅对于拓展遗产类型、加强遗产保护有巨大价值，对于研究我国传统酿酒技术的科学性也有积极作用。

剑门蜀道：剑门蜀道是人类利用自然地形、鬼斧神工的杰作，其险峻历代为人所歌咏，见证了千百年来的腥风血雨，并具有较好的环境保护，该遗产具备残迹类景观的价值。

下河湾冶铁遗址：该遗址是迄今我国发现内涵最丰富、保存最完好、延续时间较长，且集采、冶、炼于一身的战国秦汉时期的官营冶铁遗址，该遗址环境优越，临近矿源、水源与森林，具备残迹类景观的价值特征。

此外，文化景观遗产的出现不仅使人们重视人与自然间的互动，也使自然中的人文价值日益受到重视。由此，一些在过去被视为是自然遗产或混合遗产的遗产地，也具备很高的文化景观价值。因此，也有必要扩大视野，从过去在理论和实践上都不属于文化遗产序列的自然遗产中，特别是《自然遗产与双遗产预备名单》及历批《国家级风景名胜区名单》中寻找潜在的文化景观资源。

（二）中国文化景观的保护利用

近年来，文化景观在我国日益受到重视，并取得了可观的成绩。理论上，以单霁翔先生《走进文化景观遗产的世界》为代表的一批优秀论著将文化景观这一兴起于西方的遗产理论与我国实践相结合，对我国的遗产类型及遗产保护和管理进行再思考，极大地推动了我国遗产事业的进步。实践中，杭州西湖文化景观成功列入《世界遗产名录》，翻开了我国文化景观及世界文化遗产工作新的一页。在此，本文对我国今后的文化景观保护利用工作提出以下一些建议，希望能藉此推动文化景观事业的发展。

1. 进一步提高对文化景观重要性的认识，增强宣传力度

文化景观作为"自然与人的共同作品"，特别是其中的大部分作为延续类或关联性的活态遗产，其对人类的环境保护、生活质量提升、可持续发展等，都具有重大意义。因此，对于文化景观，首先应将其从一种遗产类型上升为一种对待自然、对待人类生存与未来的积极的生活方式与态度。相应的，在日常的宣传普及中，遗产界也应抛开专业术语，从构建人与自然和谐关系，提升人类生活品质的角度加以介绍，从而最大程度提高人们对文化景观的认知，为文化景观的保护管理构建良好的社会氛围。

2. 深入发掘我国的文化景观遗产资源与理论资源

文化景观理论推出以来近二十年的实践证明，它具有极大的灵活性与包容性，基本涵盖了所有类型的人与自然的互动。从某种意义上来说，文化景观是一个"壳"，各国可以凭借其理论体系与遗产类型，重新认识本国的优秀传统与民族身份。而文化景观所提倡的人与自然的互动与中国传统的"天人合一"思想尤其契合，使得我国不仅是文化景观遗产资源大国，更在五千年历史的过程中积淀下关于人与自然环境和谐互动的丰富理论资源。如单霁翔先生在其著作中提出在《周易》和《尚书·禹贡》中便有关于自然地理与人文景观方面的内容，可视为文化景观理论的雏形[1]。这一看法非常有见地，并拉近了中国与文化景观的距离。这些宝贵的思想遗产急需人们加以梳理与研究，以便让其在全球化以及天人合一理念重新受到重视的今天，发挥出其应有的作用与光芒。

3. 拓展国际交流合作，在国际上推动文化景观遗产的保护和管理

文化景观，作为一个以西方声音为主导的世界遗产界的产物，其表述和世遗领域的其他概念相似，

---

① 单霁翔. 走进文化景观遗产的世界 [M]. 天津：天津大学出版社，2010. P6

带有浓重的西方思维的影子，客观上为其在中国的推广与普及带来困难。因此，在加大自身关注与研究的同时，我国也需要扩大国际交流，以便把握文化景观理论的精髓与最新动态。每年四月在无锡举办的文化遗产保护无锡论坛及 2010 年 11 月在扬州召开的"大地与水：景观美的认知"国际学术研讨会均是我国遗产界与国外同行探讨交流的良好实践。

此外，不可否认，在国际层面，对于文化景观遗产的认定，在实践上还存在不少模糊之处。如何使一处遗产以文化景观列入《世界遗产名录》？必须由缔约国以文化景观类别申报该遗产？ICOMOS 对于该处遗产文化景观价值的认定是否足够？世界遗产委员会在表决遗产是否列入《名录》时是否还需要对其文化景观地位做出决定？在《世界遗产公约》颁布四十年之际，我国可就相关问题和国际专家展开交流探讨，促进文化景观工作的进一步发展。

4. 理顺行政关系

中国现行的遗产申报与管理体制在某种程度上受到了世界遗产界过去将文化与自然相分离实践的影响，文化遗产的申报与管理由国家文物局负责，自然遗产的申报与管理由建设部负责，混合遗产的申报由建设部牵头，两部委联合进行。而文化景观遗产文化中有自然，自然中有文化的特征，使这种分工方式存在加以改进的需要。在国际层面国际古迹遗址理事会（ICOMOS）与世界自然保护联盟（IUCN）针对文化景观的合作方式，即文化景观的评估主要由负责文化遗产事务的 ICOMOS 承担，IUCN 对景观价值进行辅助性的评估与建议，在实践中卓有成效，可以为我国所参考。

此外，延续类景观与关联性景观中包含的显著的非物质的活态要素，也使人们日益认识到把物质遗产与非物质遗产结合在一起保护的必要性。而中国现行的管理体制与这种客观要求无疑还是存在差距的，需要在工作中逐步探索合理的保护方式。

5. 提高景观管理保护水平

多年的遗产申报实践使人们认识到，列入《世界遗产名录》，固然是一件十分可喜的事情，但它只是整个遗产事业中承前启后的一环。文化景观也是这样，其最大的意义不在于列入《世界遗产名录》本身，而在于通过申报和入选加深人们对于遗产价值的认识，针对文化景观特殊的突出普遍价值与活态的人文自然要素，以申报为契机改善和提高对景观的管理保护工作。

（执笔人：郑军、王毅，中国古迹遗址保护协会秘书处）

Briefing on the Cultural Landscapes Research Report

ICOMOS China

Abstract

In order to further understand the category features, value criteria, authenticity and integrity of cultural landscapes, explore China's cultural landscape resources and push forward the management and conservation of cultural landscapes, the State Administration of Cultural Heritage (SACH) entrusts ICOMOS China to write the *cultural landscapes Research Report*.

Based on a systematic study of documents and reports of ICOMOS and other relevant institutions, proceedings of professional conferences on cultural landscapes held in recent years and nomination and evaluation texts on inscription of cultural landscapes on the World Heritage List, and in combination with interviews to experts engaged in World Heritage research, the Report presents a systematic discussion on the category features, value criteria, authenticity and integrity of cultural landscapes, gives an analysis on the status quo and potential of China's cultural landscape resources and offers some suggestions on the management and conservation of cultural landscapes.

According to the Report, the study, conservation and use of cultural landscapes should be rolled out with the focus on its value. The core value of cultural landscapes features the presentation of good interactive relations of different categories between man and nature, which is not only critical in differentiating cultural landscapes from other World Heritage types but also the basis for conceptually categorizing cultural landscapes into landscape designed and created intentionally by man, organically evolved landscape and associative cultural landscape.

Different Outstanding Universal Value criteria are applicable for evaluating cultural landscapes with different value connotation. Criterion IV is the main criterion used to evaluate the man – nature interactive value for the landscape designed and created intentionally by man, Criterions III, IV and V mainly used for evaluating organically evolved landscape, and Criterion VI is the most important criterion for evaluating the interactive value of the associative cultural landscape. Also, cultural landscapes of different types have different characters on authenticity and integrity.

Only basing on a profound recognition of the value of cultural landscapes, can we realize a scientific, proper and adequate exploration of China's abundant cultural landscape resources and theoretical resources, and boost the conservation and management of cultural landscape.

Key words: Landscape; concept; history; character; category; conservation of cultural landscape

At the 16th Session of the World Heritage Committee in 1992, a new World Heritage type, cultural landscapes, were brought forward, which reflected the new understanding of the academe to the characters and value of World Heritage in the practice since the debut of *Convention Concerning the Protection of the World Cultural and Natural Heritage* (hereinafter referred as "the World Heritage Convention" or "the Convention") in 1972.

After gradual study, especially the vigorous promotion of China's relevant authorities and agencies, China has made remarkable progresses in cultural landscapes over recent years. For instance, in the just – finished 3rd Nationwide Cultural Heritage Survey, cultural landscapes and other new types of World Heritage were covered. During the nomination for the 7th Group of State Priority Protected Sites in 2009, SACH pointed out that attentions should be attached to cultural landscapes with rich connotations. And, June 2011 witnessed the inscription of the West Lake Cultural Landscape of Hangzhou on the World Heritage List, which is China's first World Heritage initiatively nominated as a cultural landscape, marking a new start of China's cultural heritage research and protection.

Against this backdrop, the Report, based on analysis and researches to important academic findings home and abroad, evaluation reports on cultural landscapes on the World Heritage List, and interviews to relevant experts, elaborates the category features, value criteria, authenticity and integrity of cultural landscapes, and offers some suggestions on the management and protection of cultural landscapes.

1. Category Features of Cultural Landscape

In accordance with *World Heritage Paper* 26: *World Heritagecultural landscapes—A Handbook for Conservation and Management*, printed at UNESCO World Heritage Center (short for "*A Handbook for Conservation and Management*" hereinafter)[①] in December 2009, a total of 66 cultural landscapes are inscribed in the World Heritage List excluding China's Lushan National Park. However, World Heritage Committee definitely announced to inscribe China's Lushan National Park into the World Heritage List as a cultural landscape at the 20th session held in Merida, Mexico in December 1996[②]. Therefore, this report will reference the 67 World Heritage cultural landscapes including Lushan Mountain as main research objects.

According to the *Operational Guidelines for the Implementation of the World Heritage Convention* (*Operational Guidelines*), cultural landscapes fall into three categories as follows:

1. Landscape designed and created intentionally by man;

2. Organically evolved landscape, including a relict (or fossil) landscape (2a) and a continuing landscape (2b); and

3. Associative cultural landscape.

The nearly 20 – year practice on cultural landscape study proves that this "conceptual instead of functional"[③]

---

① World Heritage Paper 26: World Heritage Cultural Landscapes—A Handbook for Conservation and Management, Printed at UNESCO in December 2009 (hereinafter short for "Paper 26") was uploaded to whc. unesco. org on March 1, 2010.

② http: //whc. unesco. org/archive/repcom96. htm#778. The research group has sent letters to relevant people in the World Heritage Center on the missing of Lushan Mountain as a cultural landscape on the *World Heritage List*, but hasn' t received any formal reply. It is said that the World Heritage Center has recognized the omission and will make corrections in future work.

③ World Heritage Paper 6: World Heritage cultural landscapes 1992 – 2002, Published in 2003 by UNESCO World Heritage Centre (hereinafter short for Paper 6): P 28.

categorization is both strategical and flexible, and correctly covers all types of cultural landscapes, and has become one of the cornerstones for the research, nomination and evaluation of cultural landscapes. Thus the report will further discuss the category features of cultural landscapes based on this category mode.

1. 1. Landscape Designed and Created Intentionally by Man

According to the *Operational Guidelines*, it is the "clearly defined landscape designed and created intentionally by man". Statistics indicates that nine landscapes in the World Heritage List fall into this category and can be further divided into following three sub-categories.

1. 1. 1. Garden landscape (1 site): Royal Botanic Gardens, Kew, London, the UK

Situated at the sightseeing zone along the south bank of the Thames, the Royal Botanic Gardens, Kew, expresses the interaction between man and nature through a series of important landscape design and architectural development ranging from the 18th to the 20th century.

Besides the Royal Botanic Gardens, Kew, the Chateau de Versailles, the Classical Gardens of Suzhou, the Summer Palace and other gardens inscribed in the World Heritage List may also be deemed as cultural landscape of this category.

1. 1. 2. Parkland landscape (6 sites): they are the Cultural Landscape of Sintra in Portugal, the Lednice – Valtice Cultural Landscape in Czech, the Garden Kingdom of Dessau – Wörlitz in Germany, the Aranjuez Cultural Landscape in Spain, the Val d'Orcia Park Cultural Landscape in Italy, and the Muskauer Park crossing the frontiers of Germany and Poland.

In comparison with garden landscapes, parkland landscape sites have following distinguishing features.

1) Big acreage, much bigger than ordinary gardens in size. For instance, the Lednice – Valtice Cultural Landscape covers an area of $200km^2$ and the Garden Kingdom of Dessau – Wörlitz $145 km^2$.

2) More plentiful natural and cultural elements comparing to garden landscapes. Parkland landscape sites have numerous gardens, castles, bridges and other artificial works, and noticeably depend on various natural elements like mountains, forests and lakes etc.

3) Having living humanistic factors. These large – scale cultural landscape zones often contain farmland, villages or even towns. Comparing with ordinary gardens, people are not only the visitors but also the direct participants, managers and protectors of the landscapes.

Therefore, parkland landscapes reflect the interaction between man and nature in two aspects. On one hand, it is the harmonious co – existence between artificial buildings and natural environment, on the other hand, people live in the landscape environment harmoniously. Meanwhile, these two aspects complement each other. The interactive co – existence offers an agreeable habitation environment for people. And people's harmonious habitation is the prerequisite for the healthy exploitation and conservation of the environment. But, comparatively speaking, the Outstanding Universal Value of the parkland landscapes lies in the perfect integration of excellent architectural works and the environment.

1. 1. 3. Religious cultural landscape (2 sites): they are the Kalwaria Zebrzydowska: the Mannerist Architectural and Park Landscape Complex and Pilgrimage Park in Poland and the Sacri Monti of Piedmont and Lombardy in Italy.

The Outstanding Universal Value of these two cultural landscapes is mainly showcased through the excellent combination of religious building complex and its natural environment. Different from the general sacred mountains, such as the Taishan Mountain of China and the Mount Fuji of Japan, the Sacri Monti of Piedmont and Lombardy is not a sacred symbol itself. The reason for its title Sacri Monti is due to the numerous Christian complexes on it. In other words, the Outstanding Universal Value vests in the combination of the religious complexes and the natural environment instead of the association between the natural environment and religious faith.

People often associate "landscape designed and created intentionally by man", which involves many parks and gardens, with "historic garden", another terminology in World Heritage. As we know, the *Florence Charter* was issued at a time when people attached more attention to the single site of World Heritage itself, and the "historic garden" was deemed as a monument thereby. As a category of cultural landscape, designed landscape stresses more on people's recognition to the World Heritage's setting, overall landscape value and interaction between landscape and man. The definition evolution from "historic garden" to "designed landscape" epitomizes the theoretical progress of World Heritage.

1.2. Organically Evolved Landscape

According to the *Operational Guidelines*, the organically evolved landscape "results from an initial social, economic, administrative, and/or religious imperative and has developed its present form by association with and in response to its natural environment". Such landscapes, totally 47 sites, have the largest proportion in all World Heritage cultural landscapes, and fall into two sub – categories elaborated as follows:

1.2.1. A relict (or fossil) landscape is the one in which an evolutionary process came to an end at some time in the past, either abruptly or over a period. Its significant distinguishing features are, however, still visible in the material form.

According to the era "in which an evolutionary process came to an end", the 14 extant relict landscapes fall into two classifications as below.

1.2.1.1. Ancient relict landscape (10 sites): they are the Cilento and Vallo di Diano National Park with the Archeological sites of Paestum and Velia, and the Certosa di Padula in Italy, the Vat Phou and Associated Ancient Settlements within the Champasak Cultural Landscape in Laos, the Cultural Landscape and Archaeological Remains of the Bamiyan Valley in Afghanistan, the Mapungubwe Cultural Landscape in South Africa, the Kernavė Archaeological Site in Lithuania, the St. Kilda in the UK, the Incense Route – Desert Cities in the Negev in Israel, the Gobustan Rock Art Cultural Landscape in Azerbaijan, the Ecosystem and Relict Cultural Landscape of Lopé – Okanda in Gabon, and the Kuk Early Agricultural Site in Papua New Guinea.

These landscapes are well – preserved large – scale archaeological sites in the forms of towns, communities, tombs and agricultural relics etc. Restricted by productive forces, technical levels and other factors, ancient people often required proper natural environment for production and living, which is usually completely recorded and preserved at archaeological sites. But, different from ordinary archeological sites, these landscapes boast Outstanding Universal Value thanks to their eminent and remarkable record of humankind's dependence on and development of the nature.

1.2.1.2. Modern and contemporary relict landscape (4 sites): they are the Blaenavon Industrial Landscape and the Cornwall and West Devon Mining Landscape in the UK, the Archaeological Landscape of the First Coffee Plantations in the South – East of Cuba, and the Iwami Ginzan Silver Mine and its Cultural Landscape in Japan.

These landscapes witness the history of some shutdown industrial operations (iron smelting, mining, coffee plantations etc.) and their influences to the local landscape and life. It shows the World Heritage Committee's esteem to the modern history.

1.2.2. A continuing landscape is the one which retains an active social role in contemporary society closely associated with the traditional way of life, and in which the evolutionary process is still in progress. At the same time it exhibits significant material evidence of its evolution over time.

These landscapes, with a total of 33 sites which highlight the continuing interactive process between man and natural environment, and the shaped and evolved lifestyle and cultural traditions, have the highest proportion in cultural landscapes. For a better understanding of its category features, they are further divided into four branch categories.

1.2.2.1. A continuing landscape showcases man's curb and utilization of special environment. The natural environment of these landscapes is often very rough and even severe, and not suitable for human inhabitation. However, through the longtime living and production practice, human beings have gradually adapted to the environment and survived. For instance, the Portovenere, Cinque Terre, and the Islands in Italy witnessed the local people's victory over steep coastal zones and longtime inhabitation thereby. The south of the Agricultural Landscape of Southern Öland in Sweden is a huge limestone highland. But the islanders have adapted to the atrocious natural environment and inhabited there for five thousand years.

1.2.2.2. A continuing landscape represents special production mode. As for these landscapes, people have set up a production mode with outstanding value and characteristics based on their adaptability and utilization of environment. For example, the Rice Terraces of the Philippine Cordilleras is a demonstration of sustainable rice plantation in a cliffy mountain area. The Hallstatt – Dachstein / Salzkammergut Cultural Landscape in Austria witnesses the salt mining industry evolvement from 2000B. C. to date.

In this type of cultural landscapes, there are some eye – catching vineyard landscapes, where various grape plantation and vintage techniques for distinct European geographical environments are kept, such as the Jurisdiction of Saint – Emilion in France, the Alto Douro Wine Region and Landscape of the Pico Island Vineyard Culture in Portugal, the Tokaj Wine Region Historic Cultural Landscape in Hungary, and the Lavaux Vineyard Terraces in Switzerland.

1.2.2.3. A continuing landscape witnesses diversified cultural tradition. These landscapes give a panoramic presentation of the diversified co – existence of distinct cultural legacies and natural environments in the world, representing the cultural diversification of the earth. For instance, the Orkhon Valley Cultural Landscape in Mongolia is a witness of the millenary nomadism tradition. The Sukur Cultural Landscape in Nigeria represents the political and economic structure of the Sukur people.

1.2.2.4. An idyllically continuing landscape. These landscapes often boast pastoral and picturesque natural sceneries. People have been fairly harmonious with the nature for a long time, setting a model for the relationship between human beings and nature. For example, a number of historic towns, cottages, majestic chateaus and arable land reclaimed through several centuries are scattered along the Loire Valley between Sully – sur – Loire and Chalonnes. And the 65km – long Upper Middle Rhine Valley, and the riverside castles, historic towns and vineyards together vividly describe a long story on the interrelations between human beings and the vicissitudes of natural environment.

One point to mention, the aforesaid categorization is just a sort of attempt to further identify the affluent forms and connotations of the human – nature interactions contained in continuing landscapes. Just like the three major categorizations on cultural landscapes, They are also conceptual instead of exclusive.

1.3. Associative Cultural Landscape

According to the *Operational Guidelines*, "such landscapes are justifiable by virtue of the powerful religious, artistic or cultural associations of the natural element rather than material cultural evidence, which may be insignificant or even absent. "

In these landscapes, the interactions between human beings and nature are raised from landscape design, land use and life traditions to spiritual levels, such as religions and art, etc. According to Peter Fowler, the introduction of these landscapes is to enable people to have a free reflection on "landscape of ideas". ①

So far, a total of 11 associative cultural landscapes are inscribed on the World Heritage List, and highlighted by characteristics as follows.

1) These landscapes boast remarkable natural elements, especially high mountains or huge rocks.

This point can be identified from the landscape names, such as the Mount Lushan National Park in China, the Royal Hill of Ambohimanga in Madagascar and the Matobo Hills in Zimbabwe etc. The outstanding position of mountains and rocks in these landscapes is not occasional. Instead, it is closely related with its inherent natural and cultural characters. Thanks to their loftiness and majesty, mountains had been deemed as the symbol of mystery and permanence with the sacred power to communicate with the universe, the immortals and the ancestors at the early period of human culture. Thus, continuous sacrifice and faith tradition have evolved from mountains, making them the most typical samples of the close tie between human beings and the nature.

2) Up to now, the immaterial value associated with these landscapes has mainly expressed in the intense religious aspect.

Both the Tongariro National Park in New Zealand and the Uluru – Kata Tjuta National Park in Australia reflect the primitive religious faith of the indigenous people. The Royal Hill of Ambohimanga is closely related with the local religious rituals. The Kii Mountain Range mirrors the Shintoistic and Buddhist tradition in Japan.

Other immaterial value associated with these landscapes includes the national traditional culture with China's Lushan National Park as the representative and the national identification image with the Iceland's Tingvellir National Park as the symbol.

3) These landscapes also boast cultural evidence with outstanding value.

According to the definition of associative cultural landscape, "such landscapes are ... rather than material cultural evidence, which may be insignificant or even absent. " The earliest examples of such landscapes, i. e. the Tongariro National Park and the Uluru – Kata Tjuta National Park, have nearly no material relics. However, later nomination practice proves that they may have outstanding cultural evidence. For instance, in China, Lushan Mountain are scattered abundant archeological relics, tablet inscriptions, historic complexes and Chinese and western – style villas. The Sulamain – Too Sacred Mountain also houses a number of sacrifice – related altars and rock murals and the later mosques. Therefore, the cultural evidence is not contradictory with the outstanding universal value of such landscapes. On the contrary, it helps to verify and convey this value.

2. Comparative Study on Cultural Landscape and Other Heritage Categories

In practice, cultural landscapes are inclined to be confused with other categories of heritage, such as Mixed Cultural and Natural Heritage (mixed heritage) and Cultural Routes. This chapter is to make comparative study on mixed heritage, heritage routes and Historic Urban Landscapes (an emerging category of heritage) to further define the connotation and denotation of cultural landscapes.

---

①   Paper 6: P 58.

2. 1. Comparative Study on Cultural Landscape and Mixed Heritage

In accordance with the *Operational Guideline*, there are two major differences between cultural landscapes and mixed heritage:

1) Difference in core features: for cultural landscapes, it is to reflect the interaction of man and nature, while for mixed heritage, it is to have both highlighted cultural and natural values, which, however, do not have to be related to each other by influencing and effecting on each other;

2) Difference in evaluation criteria: cultural landscapes are evaluated by the OUV criteria (i) to (vi), and require OUV for the interaction between man and nature, but not necessarily in terms of the natural qualities; mixed heritage are evaluated by both cultural and natural criteria, where at least one of each set of criteria should be met at the same time.

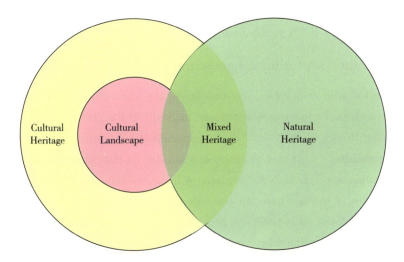

Fig. 1   Relationship among Heritage Categories

However, for mixed heritage, which have both natural and cultural values, there must be some interaction between culture and nature. Whenever such interaction shows OUV, the involved mixed heritage will be also identified as a cultural landscape. On the other hand, if a cultural landscape has natural qualities that meet the requirements of the OUV criteria for natural value, it will be identified as a mixed heritage. Therefore, cultural landscapes and mixed heritage maintain a partial coincident relationship, as shown in Figure 1.

In practice, since the inclusion of the cultural landscape category in the *Operational Guidelines* in 1992, there is a total of five mixed heritage that have not been identified as cultural landscapes. They are Mount Emei Scenic Area, including Leshan Giant Buddha Scenic Area; Mount Wuyi, China; Khahlamba/Drakensberg Park, South Africa; Ibiza, Biodiversity and Culture, Spain; The Laponian Area, Sweden. The Ibiza, Biodiversity and Culture provides a typical example for identifying the differences between cultural landscapes and mixed heritage.

In terms of natural value, the property provides an excellent example of the interaction between the marine and coastal ecosystems and supports a diversity of marine life, which meets the OUV criteria (ix) and (x). Culturally, the solid fortifications had a profound influence on the development of fortifications in the Spanish settlements of the New World (Criterion (ii)); The Phoenician ruins are exceptional evidence of urbanization and social life in the Phoenician colonies of the western Mediterranean (Criterion (iii)); The Upper Town of Ibiza is an excellent example of a fortified acropolis which preserves in an exceptional way in its walls and in its urban fabric successive imprints of the earliest Phoenicians, and the Arabs through to the Renaissance Period (Criterion (iv)) . ①

Therefore, we can see that cultural OUV of the property lies in the monuments and sites themselves, without showing notable impacts from nature or interaction between man and nature. So it was not identified as a cultural landscape.

This shows that cultural landscape and mixed heritage are two dimensions for evaluating World Heritage. The core of cultural landscapes is the interaction of man and nature, which integrate and influence each other with physical and spiritual evidences; the essence of mixed heritage is objective identification of the World Heritage that meet the cultural and natural criteria at the same time, without focusing on the interaction of culture and nature. Meanwhile, in practice, the values of these two categories of heritage are evaluated by different organizations. The cultural and natural values of mixed heritage are respectively evaluated by ICOMOS and IUCN, while, in most cases, the value of the interaction between man and nature contained in cultural landscapes is evaluated by ICOMOS, though, if necessary, suggestions of IUCN is required.

2. 2. Comparative Study on Cultural Landscape and Cultural Routes

Though closely connected with each other, cultural landscape and cultural route are two concepts different from each other. Differences between them were stated systematically at the 2002 Scientific Meeting of the International Committee on Cultural Routes (CIIC) on "The Conceptual and Substantive Independence of Cultural Routes in Relation to Cultural Landscapes". At this meeting, it was believed that the misconception to refer to cultural routes as "linear cultural landscapes" is both a "negation of their true nature and a fundamental conceptual mistake". ② These two categories of heritage have obvious differences.

First, cultural landscapes focus on connections between man and nature and the influence of them on each other, while cultural routes focus on cultural exchange that is dynamic and caused by migration.

Second, cultural routes usually include ruins, historic cities, architectural complexes, archeological relics and cultural landscapes. A cultural route is not necessarily a cultural landscape and should not be completely summarized by being "linear" or "not linear". The relationship between cultural landscapes and cultural routes is far more than a simple relation of subordination. A cultural landscape can be part of a cultural route, and a significant cultural route can have many different cultural landscapes along it.

Third, a cultural landscape is a social phenomenon that is a work of both man and nature so that it can exist for a long time and naturally evolve only under harmony with nature; a cultural route is a creation under the special needs of human for activities and exchange, and does not always follow the natural law, but is well targeted and highly independent.

Fourth, intangible elements are of different importance in these two categories of heritage: intangible elements in cultural landscapes were created in the evolution process of the cultural landscapes, reflecting the values of traditional life and culture as well as the harmonious relationship between man and nature; intangible elements in cultural routes bond all tangible elements together, reflecting not only the traditional life but also the coverage and process of the influence of dynamic elements, such as migration and exchange, and endowing the cultural routes with values

---

① http: //whc. unesco. org/archive/repcom99. htm#417

② Scientific meeting of the International Committee on Cultural Routes (CIIC) on "The Conceptual and Substantive Independence of Cultural Routes in Relation to cultural landscapes, Madrid: Considerations and Recommendation, Madrid, Spain, 2002

that, in some ways, can even surpass the significance of the tangible elements.

Therefore, cultural landscapes and cultural routes are distinctively different from each other, whether in terms of the definitions or the connotations. Each of them manifests different nature and significance of heritage: cultural landscapes focus on the relationship between man and nature as well as that between culture and nature, while cultural routes is a result of continuous concept extension and connotation enrichment, seeming like a complicated combination of different categories of heritage focusing on the associations between tangible, intangible and natural elements (factors), which are generated by communication and dynamic migration.

However, cultural landscapes and cultural routes are not in opposition to each other. Some heritage can be identified as both cultural landscape and cultural route by analysis and value evaluation from different perspectives (such as the Pilgrimage Routes in the Kii Mountain Range, Japan, and the Quebrada de Humahuaca, Argentina).

2. 3. Comparative Study on Cultural Landscape and Historic Urban Landscape

In recent years, a new concept in the World Heritage circle is attracting more and more attention of people, which is the Historic Urban Landscape. As a member of the landscapes family, it has close relationship with cultural landscapes. Therefore, at the conference on "Management and Preservation of Historic Cities inscribed on the World Heritage List" held in 2007 at St Petersburg, Russia, a special discussion was made on "Are Historic Urban Landscape a type of cultural landscape?" World Heritage experts Dr. Peter Fowler, Jeremy Whitehand and Bruno Gabrielli delivered keynote speeches at the conference, suggesting that Historic Urban Landscapes can be regarded as a type of cultural landscape. [1]

This undoubtedly brings new challenges to understanding cultural landscapes—whether Historic Urban Landscapes should be identified as a new category of cultural landscapes other than the three categories of cultural landscapes defined in the *Operational Guidelines*, or as a result of evaluation on cultural landscapes from different perspective and dimension. Concerning this question, in accordance with answers by heritage experts Dr. Henry Cleere, Mechtild Rössler and Ken Taylor, here we believed that, the theory on Historic Urban Landscapes is an extension of the existing theory on cultural landscapes, focusing on the urban interaction between man and nature. It raises new requirements and challenges for value evaluation, management and conservation of urban heritage. Instead of impacting the existing categories of cultural landscapes, it plays a positive role in helping us understand the connotation and extension of cultural landscapes and do a better job in managing and protecting cultural landscapes.

3. Value Criteria of Cultural Landscapes

In accordance with *World Heritage Convention*, Outstanding Universal Value (OUV) is the first and foremost condition that a nominated property must meet for inscription on the *World Heritage List*. Evaluation on cultural landscapes is mainly on basis of the first six criteria of the ten criteria set out in Paragraph 77 of the *Operational Guidelines* for evaluating the OUV of heritage. This section will base on the achievements from international theoretical researches and evaluation practices to make analysis on the value criteria that cultural landscapes must meet for being inscribed on the *World Heritage List*.

---

[1] http://www.chacon.ru/about_ chair/Final%20report.htm

3. 1. Use of the Six Criteria for Different Types of Cultural Landscape

Statistics show the use of the six criteria for 67 cultural landscapes: Criterion (i) for four times, Criterion (ii) for 25 times, Criterion (iii) for 41 times, Criterion (iv) for 44 times, Criterion (v) for 32 times and Criterion (vi) for 19 times (Table 1 and Figure 2) . Detailed analysis on the use of value criteria for different types of cultural landscapes is made below. ①

Table 1   Use of OUV Criteria for Different Types of Cultural Landscapes

No.	Types of Heritage	Quantity of Heritage	Criterion (i)	Criterion (ii)	Criterion (iii)	Criterion (iv)	Criterion (v)	Criterion (vi)
1	Designed	9	2	7	1	9	1	1
1. 1	Garden	1		1	1	1		
1. 2	Countryside	6	2	4		6	1	1
1. 3	Religious	2		2		2		
2	Organically evolved	47	2	14	31	31	29	7
2. 1	Relict	14	1	4	14	10	4	2
2. 1. 1	Ancient	10	1	2	10	7	3	2
2. 1. 2	Modern and contemporary	4		2	4	3	1	
2. 2	Continuing	33	1	10	17	21	25	5
2. 2. 1	Reflecting conquest and use of unique environment	11		3	1	6	11	1
2. 2. 2	Reflecting special production mode	9		1	7	7	6	1
2. 2. 3	Witnessing multicultural tradition	8		1	8	3	5	3
2. 2. 4	Idyllic landscape	5	1	5	1	5	3	
3	Associative	11		4	9	4	2	11
	Total	67	4	25	41	44	32	19

3. 1. 1. Landscape designed and created intentionally by man

Most notable, Criterion (iv) was used for each of the nine landscapes of this types. Criterion (ii) was used for seven times. For cultural landscapes of this type, Criterion (iv) is used to prove that they are pioneers or models in terms of harmony of architectures and nature during a certain period. For example, the Garden Kingdom of Dessau – Wörlitz is an exceptional example of landscape and planning of the Age of the Enlightenment of the 18th century.

Criterion (ii) is used to proves the interchange of human values in terms of religions thoughts, philosophical thinking, cultural tradition, science and technology and art, covering nearly every aspect of the spiritual civilization of human being. For example, since the 18ᵗʰ century, the Botanic Gardens of Kew have been

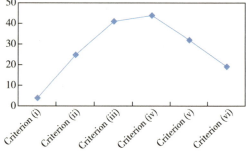

Figure 2   Statistics on use of the six criteria for different types of cultural landscapes

---

① Natural criteria used for cultural landscapes as mixed heritage are not covered by this study.

closely associated with scientific and economic exchanges established throughout the world in the field of botany.

3. 1. 2. Organically evolved landscape:

3. 1. 2. 1. Relict (or fossil) landscape

Compared with designed landscapes, organically evolved landscapes focus more on the groups of people living and working in the landscapes but not individuals as elites and designers. Therefore, Criterion (iii) has the closest relationship with this type of landscapes and it has been used for 14 times. In addition, Criterion (iv) was used for ten times.

3. 1. 2. 2. Continuing landscape:

For 33 cultural landscapes of such type, the most used criteria are Criterion (v), Criterion (iv) and Criterion (iii), respectively for 25 times, 21 times and 17 times. These landscapes include:

1) Continuing landscapes reflecting the conquest and use of unique environment: for all of 11 landscapes of such type, Criterion (v) was used.

For this types of landscapes, the OUV of interaction of man and nature is manifested by the remarkable response and sustainable use of man to environment. Therefore, Criterion (v) became the most frequently used criterion for this type of landscapes. For four landscapes (Curonian Spit, Cultural Landscape of Fertö/Neusiedlersee, the Vega Archipelago Cultural Landscape and Madriu – Perafita – Claror Valley), it was even used as the only one criterion for OUV evaluation.

2) Continuing landscapes reflecting special production mode: for nine landscapes of such type, either Criterion (iii) or Criterion (iv) was used for seven times, while Criterion (v) was used for six times.

For this type of landscapes, the interaction of man and nature is manifested by production modes with outstanding value. Therefore, what Criterion (iii) witnesses is cultural tradition or civilization with outstanding production modes, such as the Rice Terraces of the Philippines Cordilleras, which "are a dramatic testimony to a community's sustainable and primarily communal system of rice production, a system that has survived for two millennia."

Criterion (iv) is applicable for landscapes in which harmony between man and nature is established through people's acts on the environment with their special production mode, or for related buildings as testimonies to the production mode. For example, the Agave Landscape and Ancient Industrial Facilities of Tequila (Mexico), "the farm, winery and other related facilities of which reflect the increasing output of tequila in the past 250 years, and it is an outstanding example for unique architecture complex reflecting the technical and cultural integration."

Meanwhile, production mode with outstanding value can also be condensed to be land – use mode with OUV (Criterion (v)), such as Tokaj Wine Region Historic Cultural Landscape, "the entire landscape of the Tokaj wine region, including both vineyards and long established settlements, vividly illustrates the specialized form of traditional land – use that it represents."

3) Continuing landscapes witnessing multicultural tradition: for eight landscapes of such type, Criterion (v) was used for five times, Criterion (vi) and Criterion (iv) was both used for three times.

For this type of landscapes, the interaction between man and nature is based on sustainable use of the environment and common lifestyles or cultural traditions. Therefore, Criterion (iii) became the most commonly used criterion. One of the examples is Petroglyphs within the Archaeological Landscape of Tamgaly, which "provide a substantial testimony to the lives and beliefs of pastoral peoples of the central Asian steppes from the Bronze Age to the present day".

In addition, when a diversified lifestyle or cultural tradition features outstanding land – use mode, the heritage site involved should be deemed to meet Criterion (v), such as the Sukur Cultural Landscape; other landscapes meet the criteria also include those presenting as examples to show a significant historic stage (Criterion (iv)) and interchange of communication of human values (Criterion (ii)), such as Orkhon Valley Cultural Landscape; meanwhile, landscapes of such type can also feature outstanding value of associativity, such as the Koutammakou landscape.

4) Idyllic landscapes reflecting harmonious inhabitation: for each of five landscapes of such type, Criterion (ii) and Criterion (iv) were used.

Such type of heritage boasts beautiful and excellent natural environment. The interaction of man and nature is mainly reflected in the increasingly evolved harmonious relationship, with splendid landscapes as material evidences (Criterion (iv)). One of the examples is the Wachau Cultural Landscape: "The architecture, the human settlements, and the agricultural use of the land in the Wachau vividly illustrate a basically medieval landscape which has evolved organically and harmoniously over time." Meanwhile, as outstanding examples of landscapes, these landscapes also tend to witness the important communication of human values in science and technology, art and culture (Criterion (ii)), such as the Loire Valley, which "is an outstanding cultural landscape along a major river which bears witness to an interchange of human values and to a harmonious development of interactions between human beings and their environment over two millennia."

3.1.3. Associative Cultural Landscape:

For each of the eleven Cultural Landscapes of such type, Criterion (vi) was used. As the value criterion that has the closest relationship with associative cultural landscapes, it aims to show the association between the natural elements and human religion, culture and state identity of the heritage sites. One of the examples is the Tongariro National Park: "The mountains at the heart of the park have cultural and religious significance for the Maori people and symbolize the spiritual links between this community and its environment."

Moreover, unlike general categories of World Heritage, cultural landscapes are identified on basis that the interaction of man and nature reflected by the nominated properties is deemed to be with OUV. In other words, a cultural landscape may meet more than one value criteria, but at least should include one OUV criterion to justify its interaction between man and nature. Therefore, in addition to considerations on the general features of the OUV criteria, relevant content about cultural landscapes in each criterion should be identified and summarization on how these criteria are applicable to different types of cultural landscapes should be made. Based on the discussion about the features of cultural landscapes and the use of OUV criteria, the connections between the types of cultural landscapes and relevant OUV criteria are concluded as below.

The interaction of man and nature in designed landscapes is reflected in the organic integration of human – made architectures and natural environment, which made them outstanding examples with OUV, especially when Criterion (iv) is applied. That is to say, for designed landscapes, Criterion (iv) plays a critical role in deciding whether they can be identified as cultural landscapes. In addition, since designed landscapes are usually concentrated with essential thoughts of human beings, Criterion (ii) is the most commonly used derivative criterion for designed landscapes.

For organically evolved landscapes (relict landscapes or continuing landscapes alike), the interaction of man and natural environment manifests the relationships that human beings conquer and use the nature, coexist with nature under a multicultural atmosphere or keep harmonious inhabitation. Generally, all these relationships are based on specific human settlement or land – use modes (related to Criterion (v)) so that they form up certain type of landscape (related to Criterion (iv)), and may become a testimony to a cultural tradition or to a civilization which has close relationship with nature (related to Criterion (iii)). That is to say, organically evolved landscapes are associated with Criterion (iii), Criterion (iv) and Criterion (v). The relationship between each landscape and nature has its own features so that it shows OUV in a different way. For instance, the OUV of landscapes manifesting the coexistence of man and nature under unique environment is mainly reflected in specific land – use mode. In that case, Criterion (v) should be based to decide whether such type of property can be identified as a World Heritage Cultural Landscape. In addition, since continuing landscapes may also show significant interchange of human values and some communities established spiritual associations with environment in the process of land – use, Criterion (ii) and Criterion (vi) are widely used derivative criteria for such type of landscapes.

The interaction of man and nature in associative cultural landscapes is reflected in the powerful associations of the natural elements with the human spiritual civilization result such as religion, art or culture. The OUV is manifested by the intense association between natural environment and human immaterial value. Therefore, Criterion (vi) plays a critical role for assessing the OUV of such type of landscapes. Meanwhile, since such landscapes are usually from specific cultural traditions, Criterion (iii) serves as the main derivative criterion used for them.

3. 2. Natural Value of Cultural Landscape and Its Assessment

As a "combined work of nature and of man", though with natural values that may not meet the criteria for natural heritage, cultural landscapes still show many diversified natural qualities, because they "embrace a diversity of manifestations of the interaction between humankind and its natural environment". ①That's why the Paragraph 15 of Annex 6 of the *Operational Guidelines* says, "IUCN has an interest in many cultural properties, especially those nominated as cultural landscapes. For that reason, it will on occasion participate in joint field inspections to nominated cultural landscapes with ICOMOS." Although ICOMOS usually plays a leading role in evaluating cultural landscapes, for some nominated cultural landscapes with outstanding natural values, ICOMOS and IUCN usually establish joint mission to make field inspections.

For this, IUCN has prepared an internal paper, *Guidelines for Reviewers of Cultural Landscapes – The Assessment of Natural Values in Cultural Landscapes②*, which includes a number of suggestions on assessment of natural values in cultural landscapes.

In that paper, IUCN first emphasizes that, the sole purpose of the paper is to identify the extent of IUCN's interest in cultural landscapes, which should be formally inscribed only under cultural criteria i – vi. It's pointed out that, the close interest that IUCN has in cultural landscapes derives from the importance of many cultural landscapes to the conservation and evolution of nature and natural resources, and emphasis will be laid on continuing landscapes. In addition, IUCN said, in its evaluation of cultural landscapes nominated for inscription on the World Heritage List, it is mostly interested in the integrity and management of the natural qualities at a landscape level, and the relationship between man and nature.

According to the evaluation report on cultural landscapes, since 1992 when the concept of Cultural Landscapes was defined, IUCN has participated in the assessment of the following unmixed properties: Rice Terraces of the Philippine Cordilleras (1995), Cilento and Vallo di Diano National Park (1998), Uadi Qadisha (the Holy Valley) and the Forest of the Cedars of God (Horsh Arz el – Rab) (1998), Agricultural Landscape of Southern Öland (2000), The Royal Botanic Gardens, Kew (2003), the Vega Archipelago Cultural Landscape (2004), Tingvellir National Park (2004), Osun – Osogbo Sacred Grove (2005), the Agave Landscape and Ancient Industrial Facili-

---

①   Paragraph 8 of Annex 3 of the *Operational Guidelines*.

②   http: //cmsdata. iucn. org/downloads/guidelines_ for_ reviewers_ of_ cls. pdf

ties of Tequila (2006), Cornwall and West Devon Mining Landscape (2006), Kuk Early Agricultural Site (2008), Sacred Mijikenda Kaya Forests (2008), Chief Roi Mata's Domain (2008), Le Morne Cultural Landscape (2008) and Sulaiman – Too Sacred Mountain (2009) .

Statistics indicate that, IUCN is more and more involved in the assessment of cultural landscapes in recent years. Of 14 unmixed properties inscribed on the *World Heritage List* since 2005, eight (57%) were assessed with participation of IUCN. Undoubtedly, this reflects that people are paying more and more attention to the natural values in cultural landscapes. In practice, in addition to providing professional suggestions on protection and management of natural values of the nominated cultural landscapes, IUCN makes assessment on the natural qualities of the nominated cultural landscapes by focusing on both the natural values and the relationship between man and nature.

Concerning the natural qualities of cultural landscapes, OUV Criterion (vii) — "contain superlative natural phenomena or areas of exceptional natural beauty and aesthetic importance", should also be noticed. After cultural criteria and natural criteria were put together in the 2005 *Operational Guidelines*, people begin to pay more and more attention to the integration and linkage in them. The concept of "beauty and aesthetic importance" in Criterion (vii) undoubtedly has close relationship with the subjective judgment of mankind and therefore is associated with culture. As a result, it becomes the most relevant natural criteria to cultural heritage, especially cultural landscape.

This can be proved by the paper *What is OUV? Defining the Outstanding Universal Value of Cultural World Heritage Properties*, which contains specific discussion about Criterion (vii) as well as giving systematic review on the use of criteria (i) to (vi) . The paper believes that "The justification of beauty, in fact, is not a scientific exercise, but rather a cultural appreciation of the inculcation of people's aesthetic judgments over time. Criterion (vii) is an interesting case for linking nature and culture in practice, which is one of the fundamental objectives of the Convention. Whilst concerning nature and natural landscapes, the criterion nevertheless has its bases in culture and history, in philosophy and aesthetics. "[1] The Asia – Pacific Regional Workshop on Associative Cultural Landscapes held in 1995 also indicated that, this criterion has potential relationship with associative cultural landscapes, because judgment on natural beauty and aesthetic significance may be originated from cultural associations. [2]

So far, ICOMOS has made natural landscapes (including seascapes) a part of its thematic research framework as a subcategory of cultural landscapes, as it has noticed that, in many cultural landscapes, natural elements play a leading role and it believes that this deserves further research. On the other hand, IUCN has also noticed that natural beauty should be assessed with some subjective factors and pointed that Criterion (vii) should be relevant to cultural landscape assessment.

The close relationship between Criterion (vii) and cultural landscapes has also attracted the attention of the Chinese scholars. From November 23 to 24, 2010, an international academic workshop themed on "Land and Water: Perception of Beauty in Landscapes" was held in Yangzhou. It attracted a great number of Chinese and foreign experts, including, Shan Jixiang, Director of SACH, Guo Zhan, Vice President of ICOMOS, Chen Tongbin, Director of Architectural History Research Institute under China Architecture Design & Research Group, Susan Denyer, senior World Heritage advisor, and Monica Luengo, President of ICOMOS International Scientific Committee on Cultural Landscapes. The experts made thorough discussions about perception of beauty in landscapes and related conservation.

As cultural connotation in natural beauties is attracting more and more attention from the world's heritage cir-

---

① *What is OUV ?Defining the Outstanding Universal Value of Cultural World Heritage Properties* ©2008 ICOMOS-published by hendrik Bäβler Verlag. berlin: P35

② whc. unesco. org/archive/cullan95. htm

cles, this is a positive signal for China, because traditional Chinese aesthetics about landscapes have been highlighting projecting sentiments to nature, unity of man and nature as well as beauty springing out of mind, supporting that natural beauty and people's subjective construction of beauty are inseparable and united to a great extent. If a bridge between culture and natural beauty can be established by exploring the essence of the traditional Chinese aesthetic theories based on Criterion (vii), not only more Chinese cultural landscapes and other related heritage properties can be inscribed on the *World Heritage List*, but also the traditional Chinese aesthetic theories and the world view of that man is an integral part of nature can be widely promoted.

4. Authenticity and Integrity of Cultural Landscape

Since the 2005 OG, authenticity and integrity have become the integral part of OUV as one of the basic requirements for the inscription on World Heritage List. Meanwhile, the Annex 3 of OG further states that "They (cultural landscapes) should be selected on the basis both of their Outstanding Universal Value and of their representativity in terms of a clearly defined geocultural region and also for their capacity to illustrate the essential and distinct cultural elements of such regions". Such representativity and capacity are obviously closely connected with authenticity and integrity. This chapter will analyse the authenticity and integrity conditions for the inscription of cultural landscapes on the World Heritage List, on the basis of case studies.

4. 1. Authenticity of Cultural Landscape

Since the implementation of the *World Heritage Convention*, authenticity has become one of the most essential requirements for cultural heritage assessment. Jokilehto suggests three types of authenticity: creative – artistic authenticity, historical – material authenticity and social – cultural authenticity. The creative authenticity mainly refers to design and technology, material and substance act as one of the historical evidences of construction and use of the nominated property in different periods, while the social and cultural authenticity mainly refer to the continuing tradition and other intangible elements of heritage. [1] For cultural landscapes, as different types of cultural landscape features have different components and OUV characters, the emphasis for their authenticity assessment is also different.

For designed cultural landscape, as their OUV is mainly reflected in the ingenious combination and harmonious unity between human constructions and natural environment, the key of their authenticity is in the creative – artistic aspect as suggested by Jokilehto, together with related histoncal material authentiuty. When assessing the authenticity of these cultural landscapes, ICOMOS focuses on the preservation of elements such as original layout, architectural material and technology, and function of the whole landscape. Generally speaking, as long as the nominated site preserves the historical designed layout on the whole, and the location, material, technology, etc. of architectures are maintained as in history, while the landscape also keeps the historical function, the designed landscape can be considered authentic. Moreover, even if these elements are harmed, so far as they are restorable, its authenticity can be acknowledged.

For instance, the authenticity of Kew garden is embodied in the preservation of its original use, and the authentic design, material and function of the constructions inside the garden, while the Garden Kingdom of Dessau – Wörlitz also preserves important landscape design works and building remains. Though its general structure was

---

① Jokilehto J. 2006, *Considerations on authenticity and integrity in world heritage context*. City & Time 2 (1): 1.

once damaged, as the majority can be restored, ICOMOS makes positive comments on its authenticity.

For the relict landscapes, as their evolution has come to a stop, their authenticity are mainly linked with the state of preservation of the material remains. As most of these remains have been abandoned by people in the history, they have been subjected to few damage or intervention, therefore boasting high degree of authenticity. Like the Mapungubwe Cultural Landscape, besides archaeological excavation, the region has been deserted without any human intervention. The Kernavė Archaeological Site on the other hand, has also been abandoned since the end 14th century, and its remains have been subjected only to few human interventions.

Due to the dynamic character of continuing cultural landscapes, its authenticity assessment is more complicated than the previous two landscape types. Susan Denyer once discussed the authenticity features of this type of cultural landscape[①]. In her article, she points that cultural landscape has three main elements: people, environment, and the dynamism that connects the two (mainly social, economic or political) . Accordingly, the authenticity of continuing landscapes also embodies three elements: outstanding cultural responses, the meaning and value of these cultural responses for different interest groups, and the forces forming these responses.

Therefore, as continuing cultural landscapes embrace both tangible and intangible dynamic power, its authenticity is not only connected with the material expression, but also with intangible attributes, the force forming the landscape and the value embodied by the landscape. All these elements are evolving, resulting in the potential change and evolution of authenticity of continuing landscapes.

ICOMOS assessments on the authenticity of this type of cultural landscape reveal that from the tangible aspect, its authenticity is mainly reflected in the form and function of the landscape, as well as its documentation of the local historical development, while the intangible authenticity mainly exist in form of continuing traditional life style and land use technologies.

For instance, the authenticity of Pyrénées – Mont Perdu mainly reveals in the continuation of its function and overall landscape; the authenticity of Portovenere, Cinque Terre, and the Islands is manifested in the complete preservation of its traditional life style; and the authenticity of Fert / Neusiedlersee Cultural Landscape relies on the land use and life style handed down from the medieval period, etc.

Similar to continuing landscapes, the authenticity of associative landscape also embodies both tangible and intangible aspects. Study on the ICOMOS evaluations of associative landscapes manifests that in terms of material remains of such landscapes, their authenticity mainly reveals in the general function (eg. Sulaiman – Too Sacred Mountain preserves the authenticity as a sacrificial site) , overall layout (eg. the architectures on Mount Lushan maintain the historic authenticity with the natural setting) , materials and forms of landscape elements (eg. the rock paintings of Matobo Hills are authentic) , design of constructions (like the traditional constructions in the Kii Mountain Range and Tingvellir National Park) , etc. On the other hand, the intangible authenticity, i. e the continuing spiritual association between man and nature embodied in these landscapes, is more common and important. For instance, the Royal Hill of Ambohimanga always maintains its holiness and people's respect towards it, while Le Morne Cultural Landscape preserves its association with struggle and free spirit.

4. 2. Integrity of Cultural Landscape

Integrity was first used in the evaluation of natural heritage, but has been formally set as one of the require-

---

①   Susan Denyer: *Authenticity in World Heritage Cultural Landscapes : Continuity and Change , New Views on Authenticity and Integrity in the World Heritage of the Americas* , Editor: Dr. F. J. L Morales, 2005: PP. 57 – 61.

ments for cultural heritage nomination since the 2005 OG.

Based on various attributes and characters of cultural heritage, and their relationship with the integral property, Jokilehto once classified three types of integrity: social – functional integrity, historical – structural integrity and visual/aesthetic integrity[1].

In practice, as integrity was only formally applied on cultural heritage from 2005, in early years, it might be touched on by ICOMOS evaluation, but was usually contained in the authenticity assessment without much specific comments. Nonetheless, analysis of integrity assessment on relevant cultural landscapes demonstrates that Jokilehto's classification on general cultural heritage integrity is also applicable to cultural landscape.

For designed landscapes, their integrity is mainly embodied by the integrity of historical structure, i. e. the landscape shall be able to preserve its original or historical scale, layout and components. The integrity of evolving and associative landscapes on the other hand, relates to the integrity of social function. For instance, all of the vineyard landscapes embrace all elements necessary in the process of grape growing and wine brewing, the Bam landscape integrally displays the underground channel system of the whole city, while the Sulaiman – Too Sacred Mountain completely preserves various sacrificial sites, and paths linking them. These two kinds of integrity are also closely related and supplementary to each other. The integrity of historical structure is the material carrier of social function, while the functional integrity is the sublimation of structural integrity. Furthermore, on the basis of these two, the visual/aesthetic integrity also needs to be considered for cultural landscapes.

4. 3. Property Area and Buffer Zone of Cultural Landscape

The heritage authenticity and integrity is closely related to its boundary. As cultural landscapes involve dynamic social life style and large scale interaction between man and nature, the reasonable boundary demarcation is one of the keys for cultural landscape nomination, conservation and management. Based on relevant academic views and analysis of cultural landscape cases, several principles for property area and buffer zone demarcation is summarized as follows.

1) The primary principle for cultural landscape boundary demarcation is to preserve the integrity of the various aspects of heritage. For instance, the buffer zone of Kew garden preserves the important views both inside and outside the garden, maintains the relationship between the garden and areas which have strong historical links with the garden, and protects the characters and setting of the garden. The buffer zone of Kalwaria Zebrzydowska also takes into consideration the scale for visual protection, and includes the peripheral natural landscape and nearby historical villages and buildings so that the property can be enjoyed from a wider perspective.

2) For continuing and associative landscapes, as their boundary and value closely involves the local people, boundary demarcation shall carefully consider their traditions and life styles. Like the boundary of the property area of Sacred Mijikenda Kaya Forests is the boundary of the forest, most of which are not only acknowledged by relevant laws, but also by local people. The site doesn't have a buffer zone, the public land outside the forest is managed and protected by traditions and taboos formed between the local people and the property through history.

3) On the basis of sufficient protection of the OUV, boundary demarcation can take into consideration of current management demarcation or natural boundaries. Like the Muskauer Park which spans in both Poland and Germany, its buffer zone includes the peripheral area to the property, and urban land of Bad Muskau and Leknica, which integrates with the landscape of the park, and take into account the common management state and conserva-

---

① *What is OUV? Defining the Outstanding Universal Value of Cultural World Heritage Properties* P44.

tion requirements of both Poland and Germany. On the other hand, the northern boundary of the Mapungubwe Cultural Landscape is the Limpopo river, the boundary river among South Africa, Botswana and Zimbabwe.

4) The difference between property area and buffer zone is not absolute. On the premise of proper conservation of the heritage value, sometimes buffer zone may not be needed. The property area of Champasak Cultural Landscape for instance, embraces a great scale of natural landscape which offers sufficient protection of the property, therefore no buffer zone is set; the property area of Blaenavon Industrial Landscape also includes all the relevant historic landscape and there's no need for a buffer zone.

5. Exploration, Conservation and Use of China's Cultural Landscape Resources

5. 1. China's Cultural Landscape Resources

By now there are three Chinese cultural landscape heritage sites on the World Heritage List, namely the Lushan National Park in Jiangxi, Mount Wutai in Shanxi, and Hangzhou West Lake Cultural Landscape in Zhejiang.

As indicated by the description of these sites provided on the website of the World Heritage Center, cultural landscape, as a bridge between man and nature, has a lot in common with China's traditional views of the universe and the world, and aesthetic concepts, and can become one of the most ideal heritage type for the expression and identification of values of Chinese heritage sites. Among the three, Hangzhou West Lake Cultural Landscape inscribed onto the World Heritage List during the 35th session of the World Heritage Committee, is the first cultural landscape that was initiatively nominated by China as a cultural landscape, which inaugurated a new chapter for the research, protection and use of Chinese cultural landscapes.

Based on this, this report suggests that China's rich cultural landscape resources can be explored from the following channels, so as to lay better foundation for the world heritage cultural landscape nomination and conservation in the future.

5. 1. 1. Cultural landscapes from China's *World Cultural Heritage Tentative List* (hereinafter referred to as "Tentative List")

On the basis of the Tentative List announced in Dec. 2006, in 2011, SACH started the update work for the Tentative List. At the moment, this project is still under way, so the cultural landscape attributes of relevant heritage sites are discussed according to the 2006 Tentative List. It is believed that among the properties on the 2006 Tentative List, the following sites that haven' t started the world heritage nomination process possess the potential as cultural landscapes: Slender West Lake of Yangzhou, Ancient Villages in Lower Reaches of the Yangtze River, Niuheliang site, Liangzhu site, Ancient Shu Kingdom, Yue – Kiln Site at Shanglinhu, Rock Painting of Mount Huashan, Villages of Ethnic Groups of Tibet, Qiang, Miao and Dong, Hani Terraces, Karez Wells, etc. Herein a few sites are selected to discuss the different types of cultural landscape values.

1) Representative of designed landscapes: Slender West Lake

The Slender West Lake in Yangzhou is a masterpiece of Chinese lacustrine gardens. As an outstanding example of integration between ancient Chinese gardening concepts and natural environment, it possesses the value of designed landscape.

2) Representative of relict landscapes: Yue – Kiln Site at Shanglinhu

Shanglinhu enjoys an important status in early Chinese porcelain history. It witnessed the splendid history of ancient Chinese porcelain industry dependent on the environment, boasting outstanding value as a relict landscape.

3) Representative of continuing landscapes: Karez Wells in Turpan, Xinjiang

Karez Wells is a continuing water conservancy project that ancient Chinese people developed through long – term practice in the special geographic and climate conditions in the Turpan basin. It is still used today, playing an important role for the local agricultural production and daily life, and is an outstanding example of land use.

Besides, Mr. Shan Jixiang detailedly analyses the cultural landscape values of ethnic villages in southwest China[①]. These villages boast time – honored history and are harmonious with the nature. They have deep cultural connotations, and also present high value as continuing landscape.

5. 1. 2. Other cultural landscape resources:

China's *State Priority Protected Sites*, as the state level cultural heritage of China, are the most direct reserve of China's cultural landscapes. From the most recent List of 6th Group of China's State Priority Protected Sites announced in May 2006, many sites with cultural landscape values can be explored, the examples are as follows:

Ancient Chinese Dates Garden in Juguan: It witnesses the development of ancient Chinese dates planting, provides important material evidence to the ancient Chinese agricultural and scientific development, and has value as a continuing landscape.

Workshop of Fenjiu Liquor in Xinghua Village: It witnesses the transmission of Fenjiu liquor and China's special brewing technique. In the current world heritage cultural landscapes, the European vineyard landscapes take a big proportion. On the one hand, this reflects the importance of wine in people's life, on the other hand, it indicates the great potential of wine landscapes in other parts of the world for inscription on the *World Heritage List*. To nominate China's important liquor workshops as cultural landscape will not only be significant to the exploration of heritage types and strengthening of heritage conservation, but is also positive for studying the scientificity of traditional Chinese liquor brewing.

Shu Road in Jianmen: The Shu Road in Jianmen, as a masterpiece of human genius by adapting to the natural terrain, has been praised by literati through the history for its ruggedness. It is a relict landscape that has witnessed the vicissitude through more than a millennium, which also boasts quite good environmental condition.

Iron Making Site at Xiahewan: Among the similar sites found so far, this one, as an official iron making workshop used during the Warring States Period to Qin and Han dynasties, it is the richest in contents, most integrally preserved and functioned for relatively longer period. Close to mineral resources, water and forest, the site has an excellent setting, and presents value as a relict landscape.

Furthermore, the emergence of cultural landscape not only triggers people's attention to interaction between man and nature, but also results in emphasis placed on cultural values in nature. Therefore, some properties which were previously considered as natural heritage or mixed heritage sites also possess high value as cultural landscapes. So it is essential to expand our vision to look for cultural landscape resources among natural heritage sites, especially from *China's Tentative List of Natural Heritage and Mixed Heritage*, and *List of National Parks*.

5. 2. Conservation and Use of Cultural Landscape in China

In recent years, cultural landscape is attracting more and more attention in China, and considerable achievements have been made. In the theoretical aspect, a number of excellent treatises represented by Mr. Shan Jixiang's

---

① Shan Jixiang. *Journey into the World of Cultural Landscape Heritage* [M]. Tianjin: Tianjin University Press, 2010. PP. 156 – 159.

Journey into the World of Cultural Landscape Heritage combine the heritage concept of cultural landscape deriving from the west with the Chinese practice, contemplate on China's heritage types, conservation and management, and have promoted the development of China's heritage cause to a great extent. In practice, the inscription of Hangzhou West Lake Cultural Landscape on the *World Heritage List* opens a new chapter for China's cultural landscape and world cultural heritage work. Herein this report raises the following suggestions for China's cultural landscape conservation and use in the future.

5. 2. 1. To further acknowledge the importance of cultural landscape, and enhance publicity

As combined work between man and nature, cultural landscapes, especially the living properties, are highly significant to the environmental protection, improvement of living quality and sustainable development of mankind. Therefore, cultural landscape shall be elevated from merely a heritage type to an active life style and attitude towards nature and the future of man. Accordingly, during the daily awareness – raising efforts, the heritage circle shall put away the professional terminologies, and introduce cultural landscape from the perspective of construction of harmonious relationship between man and nature, and lifting the living quality of man, so that people's understanding of cultural landscape can be enhanced to the maximum, which helps to build a positive social environment for cultural landscape conservation and management.

5. 2. 2. To deeply explore China's cultural landscape resources

The twenty years' history of cultural landscape demonstrates that it is highly flexible and comprehensive, and basically embraces all types of interaction between man and nature. In some ways, cultural landscape, through its theoretical structure and heritage types, is like a shell that avails all countries to review their own excellent tradition and identity. The interaction between man and nature encouraged by cultural landscape is particularly concordant with the traditional Chinese idea of "harmony between man and nature". As a result, China is not only rich with cultural landscape resources, through the long history, it has also accumulated abundant theoretical resources concerning harmonious interaction between man and nature. As rightly pointed out by Mr. Shan Jixiang, the natural geography and humanistic landscape contents recorded in *Zhouyi* and *Shangshu · Yugong*, two ancient Chinese classics, can be seen as the rudiment of cultural landscape theory. These valuable spiritual heritages are in dire need of studying, so that they can play their full role in today's world of globalization when the idea of harmony between man and nature is cherished once again.

5. 2. 3. To enhance international communication and cooperation to promote cultural landscape conservation and management in the international realm

Cultural landscape, as a product of the world heritage circle which is overwhelmingly western oriented, has some intrinsic difficulties for its popularization in China. Therefore, while pushing forward the attention and study by its own, China also needs to expand international exchange to timely appreciate the essence and latest development of cultural landscape theory and practice. The Wuxi Forum for the Chinese Cultural Heritage Conservation held every April, and the "Earth and Water: Perception of Landscape Beauty" international workshop organized in Yangzhou in November 2010, are all good practices in this regard.

On the other hand, it's undeniable that in the international level, there are still some ambiguities concerning the identification of cultural landscape heritage. How a property can be inscribed on the *World Heritage List* as a cultural landscape? Must it be nominated as such by the State Party, or is ICOMOS' identification of its value as cultural landscape sufficient? When the World Heritage Committee decides whether to inscribe a property on the *World Heritage List*, does it need to decide whether inscribe the property as a cultural landscape? On the occasion of the 40 [th] anniversary of World Heritage Convention, China can discuss relevant issues with international experts, to further promote the development of cultural landscape.

5. 2. 4. To make the administrative structure more smooth

The current Chinese system for world heritage nomination and management is influenced by the division of cultural and natural heritage—the nomination and management of cultural heritage is under SACH, while the Ministry of Construction takes charge of the nomination and management of natural heritage, and lead the collaboration between the two departments for mixed heritage. However, the character of cultural landscape with culture and nature mixed together calls for improvement of such division of labor. The cooperation between ICOMOS and IUCN on cultural landscape in the international scale, i. e. ICOMOS is in main charge of cultural landscape evaluation, while receiving supplementary comments from IUCN, has turned out very successful in practice, and can be advisable for China.

Besides, the prominent intangible and living elements contained in continuing and associative landscapes make people realize the necessity for protecting tangible and intangible heritage together. There is an obvious gap between the current management system of China and such need, and a more sensible mechanism shall be explored.

5. 2. 5. To improve landscape management and conservation level

Years of world heritage nomination make us realize that inscription on the *World Heritage List* is only one part of the entire heritage cause. The real meaning of inscribing a cultural landscape on the *World Heritage List* is to enhance people's understanding of the heritage value, and improve the management and conservation work particularly for the special OUV and living cultural and natural elements contained in cultural landscapes.

(Written by Zheng Jun, Wang Yi)

文化线路申报世界遗产研究

清华大学

摘　要

　　本文是国家文物局重点课题《文化线路申报世界遗产研究》的开展状况及其成果报告的概述，从国际遗产保护领域中"文化线路"类型遗产的理论与实践发展过程；当前的定义阐释、价值评估及遗产认定方法；中国文化线路的基础研究、保护、管理和申报策略这三方面，对原有报告的研究过程与相关研究结论进行概括与综述，并在最后提出了课题小组对"文化线路"遗产类型保护与中国文化遗产保护事业发展的相关思考与建议。

　　关键字：文化线路，世界遗产，文化遗产保护

　　"文化线路"是20世纪90年代中期提出的一种新的遗产类型，以1995年和1998年先后登录世界遗产名录的西班牙、法国圣地亚哥·德孔波斯特拉朝圣线路①文化线路为典型。

　　随着近年来我国文化遗产保护事业的进步和国际文化遗产保护发展的新趋势，诸如丝绸之路、京杭大运河等"文化线路"或相关类型遗产也开始进入世界遗产申报的进程，相关工作日益受到重视。与此同时，对国内其他文化线路的研究与保护也逐渐成为遗产保护领域的新关注点，如蜀道、茶马古道、海上丝绸之路等。由此，与文化线路保护策略相关的问题，如基础工作方面对文化线路遗产资源进行调查、研究的迫切需要，实践方面对文化遗产资源的保护和对世界遗产申报要求的亟待了解，特别是在管理方面对进一步完善立法、行政管理体系的需求，使得当前在国内开展与"文化线路"类型遗产认定、评价和保护相关的专题研究工作变得十分紧迫。本课题也正是在这一背景下得以产生。

　　课题由国家文物局委托清华大学建筑学院吕舟教授带领的课题小组完成，期间还有来自北京清华城市规划设计研究院和中国古迹遗址保护协会的专家、学者等参与。结题报告于2011年10月完成，经国家文物局审核通过。

　　整个课题采用文献研究与案例分析结合的方式，收集、整理或翻译与"文化线路"类型直接相关的国内外文献包括近百篇相关中英文学术论文、近10篇重要国际会议文件、10项世界遗产名录和预备名录、现有"文化线路"类型遗产的案例文献、近20项欧美相关遗产案例资料以及其他研究资料，并对日本和西班牙的两项文化线路世界遗产进行了实地考察。

　　最终成果包括课题报告一份：《文化线路申报世界遗产研究》；资料汇编三份：《文化线路相关世界遗产地资料汇编》、《欧洲文化线路相关资料汇编》和《国际古迹遗址理事会文化线路委员会相关工作及文献汇编》。

　　其中，课题报告《文化线路申报世界遗产研究》对文化线路的定义阐释、概念发展、申报世界遗产的价值评估与认定、基础研究、保护管理策略、相关世界遗产案例、中国的文化线路资源和中国文化线

①　Pilgrim's Route to Santiago de Compostela

路类型项目申请世界遗产的策略等问题进行了整理和分析，提出了相应的研究结论。三份资料汇编则作为补充文件汇总了课题组收集的相关案例文件，供有需要的读者参考。

一、文化线路概念的产生背景、过程及影响

1993 年，西班牙圣地亚哥·德孔波斯特拉朝圣线路作为第一条文化线路类型的遗产登录世界遗产名录。经过近十年的探讨与发展，文化线路的概念于 2005 年正式以"遗产线路"的特殊类型进入《实施世界遗产公约操作指南》的修订文本中，并在不久之后由 2008 年国际古迹遗址理事协会提出的《文化线路宪章》得到正式确认，标志着这一概念在世界遗产保护领域的成熟。

尽管如此，对文化线路遗产或与之类似的长距离、跨文化遗产项目的研究和保护工作在此之前已在世界各国或地区得到开展，其中具有重要影响力的早期实践包括联合国教科文组织（后文简称 UNESCO）在 20 世纪 60 年代之后开展的一系列跨学科研究—活动、欧洲的文化线路项目和美国的国家公园遗产廊道体系。

1.1 背景

作为"本身具有在自然和社会科学、文化、教育与沟通领域跨学科的特点"① 的联合国教科文组织，从 20 世纪 60、70 年代开始，陆续推出了跨学科的"线路"或"道路"的研究与发展项目，范围涉及南美洲、欧亚大陆和非洲等地。

项目包括 1969 年建立的"安第斯山线路"② 的区域文化旅游项目（哥伦比亚、厄瓜多尔和秘鲁）、1972 年帮助埃塞俄比亚政府修复"历史线路"古迹的项目、1973 年在南美修复"耶稣会会士线路"部分遗存的工作计划（阿根廷、巴西、巴拉圭和乌拉圭）、1994 年开展的非洲"奴隶之路"和 1988 年至 1997 年完成的"丝绸之路——对话之路整体研究"等等。

这些项目几乎都是跨越国境、甚至贯穿大陆的大型跨文化项目，项目的侧重点根据 UNESCO 不同时期对文化多样性内涵的认识和文化政策的导向有所变化。如上世纪 60 年代末期"安第斯山线路"作为"联合国发展计划署拉丁美洲地区国家间计划"③ 的组成项目，主要关注文化旅游的开发，推动地区发展。到上世纪 70 年代，埃塞俄比亚的"历史线路"和南美"耶稣会会士线路"等项目，同样作为联合国发展计划署（后文简称 UNPD）项目，开始关注对古代遗迹的保护和修复。

直至上世纪 80、90 年代，以非洲的"奴隶线路"和欧亚大陆的"丝绸之路"为代表，真正开始进入保护"文化多样性"、推动"在当今的多元社会中进行真正文化间对话"的时代，对遗产线路所包含的"文明与文化之间延绵不断的对话中产生的丰富哲学对话和彼此交换"，及其所展现的"民族迁徙、文明和文化的动态性"给予了极大的关注。④

UNESCO 的这些"之路"项目的探索为 90 年代之后"文化线路"在遗产保护领域的正式出现奠定了强大的背景基础，也为"文化线路"概念的发展走向定下了基调。并且，在这些早期项目中，还有一些项目的影响延续至今，如"丝绸之路"和属于"安第斯山线路"范围的"印加之路"⑤ 等，在今天都已作为文化线路类型登录了世界遗产预备名录，积极筹备申请成为世界遗产。

---

① 联合国教科文组织. 临时议程项目 5.10 教科文组织《世界文化多样性宣言》十周年纪念. 36 C/51：2011

② Andean Route

③ UNDP Inter – Country Programme for Latin America

④ Federico Mayor, Director – General Of UNESCO. Preface：Integral Study of the Silk Roads, Roads of Dialogue. UNESCO. 1997

⑤ Inca Royal highway, 也被称为 QhapaqÑan 或 Main Andean Road。

除了 UNESCO 在世界范围内开展的"之路"项目之外，在国家和地区的范围内，也有早于世界遗产体系，对类似遗产类型进行保护与管理的实践，其中最有影响力的是美国国家遗产廊道①保护和欧洲文化线路②两大保护体系。他们的实践经验也在后续的国际文化线路遗产保护理论体系的建立与实践中得到了反映。

1984 年，美国议会批准通过了美国第一条遗产廊道：伊利诺伊和密歇根运河国家遗产廊道，正式开启了美国国家公园体系下的大型遗产线路保护工作的进程。而 1987 年，在欧洲理事会《保护文化线路决议》的法律框架下，西班牙圣地亚哥·德孔波斯特拉朝圣线路被列入第一批欧洲文化线路，标志着欧洲开始正式推进这项以文化线路遗产的保护推动遗产保护、多样文化交流和地区文化认同的大型文化项目。1993 年，与这条线路同名但范围有所缩小的西班牙段登录了世界遗产名录，直接推动了此后国际相关遗产概念的讨论。

美国和欧洲的文化线路遗产保护体系对文化线路作为世界遗产类型的保护实践产生了不同程度的影响。欧洲文化线路利用同主题遗产系列推动地区对话与交流、维系社会可持续发展的理念，在 90 年代逐渐与 UNESCO 将文化遗产项目作为推进对话、交流与和平的有力文化工具的理念相契合，直接推动了世界遗产委员会对这种新遗产类型的认可。而美国遗产廊道多层次、大尺度的保护规划方法则为世界遗产文化线路类型项目的管理与管理提供了有益的借鉴。UNESCO 与 UNDP 的大型地区合作项目和跨学科研究，加上欧洲与美国在本土开展的线路类型遗产保护实践，最终在 20 世纪 90 年代推动了文化线路类型遗产概念的诞生。

1.2 过程

当 1993 年西班牙的圣地亚哥·德孔波斯特拉朝圣线路被列入世界遗产名录时，西班牙政府呼吁就"文化线路"③ 这一问题进行更深入的讨论。随后，国际古迹遗址理事会（后文简称 ICOMOS）于 1994 年在马德里召开了文化线路世界遗产专家会议，这是世界遗产专业机构对文化线路从理论发展的角度召开的一次学术会议。会议最终形成了《线路作为我们文化遗产的一部分》④ 的专家报告，建构了文化线路研究的基本框架。此后，ICOMOS 和国际古迹遗址理事会文化线路学术委员会（后文简称 CIIC）于 1998 年正式成立，并组织召开了一系列会议，对"文化线路"理论框架进行了完善。这些讨论和研究大致可分为两个阶段：

第一个阶段是 1994 年至 2002 年，这是文化线路概念的提出和理论不断丰富的时期。期间召开了近十次比较重要的国际会议，讨论内容从理论研究到典型文化线路案例分析都有所涉及，基本确立了文化线路的理论研究框架和研究方法，并消除了文化线路与其他一些世界遗产概念在定义上的模糊与重叠之处。

第二个阶段则是 2002 年以后，这是文化线路理论研究的逐步完善时期。CIIC 对《操作指南》的修订给出建议，文化线路于 2005 年作为一类特殊的世界遗产，正式出现在修订后的《实施世界遗产公约操作指南》中；ICOMOS《文化线路宪章》的正式发布为文化线路建议了一个相对完善的理论研究框架。

1.3 影响

文化线路的概念产生之后，对世界遗产保护在理论和实践方面，都产生了十分深远而重要的影响。

在实践方面，自 1993 年起，前后有近 30 条具有线性特征的遗产申请列入世界遗产名录，其中具有文

---

① National Heritage Corridors
② European Cultural Routes
③ Cultural Routes
④ Route as Part of our Cultural Heritage

化线路特征或部分符合文化线路特征的遗产 10 余条，包括已被列入世界遗产名录的西班牙圣地亚哥·德孔波斯特拉朝圣路线、阿曼乳香之路、阿根廷科布拉达·德·胡迈海卡山谷、日本纪伊山朝圣线路、以色列熏香之路和内盖夫的沙漠城镇、印度高山铁路等。这些遗产项目为不同形态具有文化线路特征的遗产申报提供了可贵的实例参照。另外，经初步统计，在世界遗产预备名录中，已有近 40 处明确具有文化线路特征和可能被定为文化线路的遗产。

目前，各国正在积极研究独立或联合申报文化线路类遗产的方式和策略，若干跨国的大型文化线路的研究和申报工作，如前文提到的 UNESCO 从 20 世纪后半期就有所涉猎的跨文化项目，包括横跨欧亚大陆的"丝绸之路"，纵穿阿根廷、玻利维亚、智利、哥伦比亚、厄瓜多尔和秘鲁等国的"印加之路"，都在有条不紊地进行中，并通过多国合作和定期的国际会议对许多有争议的问题给出了建设性意见。除了这些已经被普遍关注和认同的文化线路外，其他主题的文化线路，如古罗马大道①、黄金之路、奴隶之路②等③，也在逐渐引起重视。由于各类文化线路类遗产申报实践的推动，文化线路在主题、类型和形态等各方面都日益丰富。

国际文化线路保护的发展对我国文化遗产保护事业也带来了深刻的启示。参考欧洲文化线路项目与美国国家廊道体系在各自地区与国家范围内的影响，足见文化线路项目对一个国家或地区内部的发展与促进具有超越其他类型遗产资源的多方面的力量与潜质。它不仅拓展了文化遗产保护的思路和方法，使我们有可能在遗产保护与可持续利用的同时，借助遗产资源发挥更大的社会经济效益，并在促进社会文化交流与认同方面作出贡献。通过明智的战略部署和合理规划，还能够利用文化线路具有跨文化交流和推动文化间对话的本质，提升国家的文化形象，增加文化影响力。

二、文化线路的定义阐释与价值评估

报告根据 2005 年的《世界遗产公约操作指南》和 2008 年的《文化线路宪章》及其他相关文献，结合已经成功的世界遗产案例，对文化线路概念的定义、特征、价值评估和遗产认定的方法等理论核心内容进行了总结。

2.1　文化线路定义的发展演变

"文化线路"的定义最初在 1994 年的马德里文化线路世界遗产专家会议上正式提出，当时将文化线路称为"遗产线路"④。会议报告提出：

"遗产线路是一个内涵十分丰富的概念，它提供了一个特许的工作框架，在其中兼容了相互理解、多种对待历史的方法和一种和平文化。它是基于在时间和空间上的人口迁移、冲突和对话、文化交换和相互移植而形成的；这个概念在本质上是开放的、动态的，它致力于在经济、社会、哲学及与自然环境互动等多方面提高对遗产的识别。这个概念建立在动态的迁移和交流理念基础上，在时间和空间上都具有连续性；指的是一个整体，其价值大于组成它并使它获得文化意义的各部分价值的总和；强调不同国家和地区间的对话和交流，是多维的，有着除其主要方面之外多种发展与附加的功能和价值，如宗教的、

---

① Roman Road

② Slave Route

③ United Nations Educational, Cultural And Scientific Organization (UNESCO): Convention Concerning The Protection Of The World Cultural And Natural Heritage. Report on the Expert Meeting on Routes as a Part of our Cultural Heritage (Madrid, Spain, November 1994), Paris, 1994.

④ Heritage Routes

商业的、管理的等等。"①

该定义初步确立了文化线路在之后的会议中被不断强调的几个基本内涵，即：建立在（人口）迁移或物质交换引起文化交流之上，具有动态性；应把文化线路作为一个整体来研究并进行整体性保护；文化线路是跨地域或跨国家的，具有一定的范围和尺度，这样才能形成足以对人类历史和文化产生影响的动态因素。

此外，马德里会议还提出："对遗产线路的识别需要大量收集有形遗产元素，以证明线路本身的意义……它（文化线路）首次从全球角度考虑物质、文化和精神上的交流，并将无形元素、有形元素与文化和自然结合起来。"②由此，文化线路中有形元素与无形元素二者皆必不可少的特征决定了它与其他类型遗产的不同。马德里会议取得的成果，为今后文化线路的理论研究提供了基本框架。

1994 年之后，国际古迹遗址理事会的文化线路委员会（ICOMOS – CIIC）正式启用"文化线路"（cultural routes）一词代替"遗产线路"（heritage routes）。虽然《操作指南》仍沿用"遗产线路"一词，文化线路的定义和内容却经过不断补充和扩展，为《操作指南》的修订和 ICOMOS《文化线路宪章》的形成打下了理论基础。

1998 年圣克里斯托·德·拉·拉格拉会议将文化线路保护的范围扩展到承托文化遗产的自然背景，明确提出"保护文化线路也包括保护现存的地域文化和它们完整的地理区域"。同年 9 月，特内里弗岛会议报告突出强调了文化线路总体价值和物质元素在文化线路识别中的基础性作用。③ 1999 年 5 月在伊维萨召开的关于"文化线路的方法论、定义和操作层面"的研讨会指出，依托于物质元素存在的非物质元素或无形遗产是给予文化线路整体意义的关键所在。④ 2001 年，西班牙纳瓦拉会议提出的"潘普洛那结论"进一步定义文化线路的空间形态。⑤

2002 年召开的马德里文化线路专家会议在《操作指南》修改讨论稿中，对文化线路进行了更准确和清晰的定义。⑥ 2005 年，文化线路以"遗产线路"的名称列入了《操作指南》的参考类型，与当时已有的文化景观、历史城镇与中心、及遗产运河等其他三种类型并列。

文化线路的概念经过了一系列学术会议的讨论和丰富之后，至 2008 年，它的概念在 ICOMOS – CIIC 通过的《文化线路宪章》中得到了综合反映，并以定义的形式得到了最终确认：

"无论是陆上、水上，或是其他类型都有实际的界限，并且也因其服务于一个特定而明确的目标而自身具有特殊的动态和历史的功能而呈现特点，都必须要满足以下条件：

必须来自并反映人们的互动行为，以及民众、国家、地区或大陆间在重要历史时期进行的多维、持续及互惠的货物、思想、知识和价值观的交流；

---

① United Nations Educational, Cultural And Scientific Organization (UNESCO): Convention Concerning The Protection Of The World Cultural And Natural Heritage. Report on the Expert Meeting on Routes as a Part of our Cultural Heritage (Madrid, Spain, November 1994), Paris, 1994.

② United Nations Educational, Cultural And Scientific Organization (UNESCO): Convention Concerning The Protection Of The World Cultural And Natural Heritage. Report on the Expert Meeting on Routes as a Part of our Cultural Heritage (Madrid, Spain, November 1994), Paris, 1994.

③ ICOMOS – CIIC. Tenerife Work Program, Tenerife, 1998.

④ ICOMOS – CIIC. Ibiza Declaration – Congress on Methodology, Definitions and Operative Aspects of Cultural Routes, IBIZA, Spain, May 1999, 1999.

⑤ ICOMOS – CIIC. Pamplona Conclusions – INTERNATIONAL CONGRESS OF THE ICOMOS CIIC. PAMPLONA, NAVARRA, SPAIN. JUNE, 2001, PAMPLONA, 2001.

⑥ ICOMOS. MADRID：CONSIDERATIONS AND RECOMMENDATION – ICOMOS 13th General Assembly Meetings of the International Scientific Committees. December, 2002. Madrid, Spain, Madrid, 2002.

必须要在时空上促进受影响文化间的交流，使它们在物质和非物质遗产上都反映出来；

必须要集中在一个与其存在有历史联系和有文化遗产关联的动态系统中。"①

2.2 文化线路主要特征的阐释

在文化线路概念探讨过程中所提到过的遗产地所在背景、物质与非物质内容、线路作为整体的跨文化意义、文化交流的动态性和文化线路周边的环境要素等，作为文化线路的主要特征在《文化线路宪章》中得到了确认，为考察与认定文化线路的基本指标提供了依据。②

(1) 背景

《文化线路宪章》中将"背景"阐释为："文化线路产生于自然和/或文化背景中，对其产生影响，并且作为互动过程的一部分对其进行刻画，丰富其尺度。"在这里，背景可以理解为广义上的文化线路产生的大环境，包括文化线路产生的自然和地理环境，文化线路产生和持续过程中的文化和社会背景。

因此，在分析一条文化线路的时候，首先要抓住其产生的文化、历史原因和文化线路通过的自然地理环境。文化线路的一些元素，如它的创造或设计方式、沿途节点的选择、文化习俗特征、社会特征等，都是依据自然地理环境、地形地貌特征而因地制宜或受到环境的影响而产生的。文化线路沿途自然景观与人互动关系的多样性也形成了许多重要的文化景观，有助于我们理解在这条线路上受到动态交流因素的影响，人与自然相互影响和人类社区独特的进化过程，为保护现存的传统文化以及那些已消逝文明的痕迹提供了背景资料。

从将"背景"放在文化线路定义要素的首位来看，文化线路是概念优先于实体遗产点、整体优先于部分的遗产概念。它改变了以往从遗产点到遗产集群的价值认定体系，先从遗产的产生背景入手，使得线路遗产在时间和空间上都有足够的广度，为从多角度多层面分析线路的各组成部分奠定了基础。

(2) 内容

"内容"可以被理解为最直观的组成线路的物质元素和赋予文化线路意义的非物质元素。同时，物质元素又可分为形成线路的决定性元素和维持线路的必要物质元素。

物质元素一方面包括形成文化线路的决定性元素，即与文化线路产生的原动力直接相关的物质遗产，如以宗教朝圣为目的产生的圣地亚哥－德孔波斯特拉朝圣路线和日本纪伊山朝圣线路，其决定性元素是教堂、墓碑、神社等宗教建筑和纪念物。另一方面，物质元素也包括维持文化线路的必要物质遗产，它们同样是文化线路的基础元素，如圣地亚哥—德孔波斯特拉朝圣路线沿途的旅舍、驿站等。

《文化线路宪章》中对物质元素的分析使文化线路成为世界遗产的申报项目具有可操作性。在这个层面上遴选物质遗存并将其分类，可以确保所选取的物质遗产具有代表性并可明确地指出其在文化线路总体中的地位和作用。

比起其他类型的文化遗产，文化线路的非物质元素被提升到了更重要的位置上，它包括无形遗产（非物质遗产）和人类精神层面的因素。其中非物质遗产包括城市建筑观念的特征、建筑方法和模式、不同建筑风格、风俗、政治体系和传统、宗教、传统技艺、典型的手工艺、艺术和行业、衣食住行的方式、农业耕作方法、语言等。而民族的普遍特征和气质、地域的社会风气等则是这些无形遗产诉诸人类群体精神层面的表现。

这些无形元素的重要之处在于，它们不仅能够支持文化线路的各组成部分并体现它们的意义，还可

---

① 国际古迹遗址理事会文化线路科学委员会（CIIC）. 国际古迹遗址理事会（ICOMOS）文化线路宪章［Z］. 魁北克：2008.

② 国际古迹遗址理事会文化线路科学委员会（CIIC）. 国际古迹遗址理事会（ICOMOS）文化线路宪章［Z］. 魁北克：2008.

以在实体线路缺失或遭到破坏时证明线路缺失部分曾经存在，进而得以反映出线路的整体物质形态。如沿线路分布的地方语言特征，可能蕴含着因文化线路的交流影响而汇聚其中的多元文化基因。此外，无形元素还能够重现物质遗产，如以传统工艺复原艺术品或修缮建筑物的方法，也就是说"只要特定族群的文化特征被保护并持续，人类创造的物质工具可以不断被制造"①，即只要传统和它的继承者还在，由传统衍生的物质遗产和物质元素就可以得到重现或保持。

2004 年列入世界遗产名录的日本纪伊山圣地与朝圣线路，在作为遗产要素的大量宗教建筑都已不是历史创建时的原构，但在这一过程中传承至今的宗教信仰与严格的传统建造工艺，保证了遗产地精神内涵和物质形态历史原貌的延续，使其在真实性的评估中得到了专家的认同。

（3）作为整体的跨文化意义

文化线路的重要特征之一是它作为整体的跨文化意义，且此整体意义大于组成文化线路的各部分意义之和。这一整体意义包括两方面：

一方面，从遗产的角度而言，由于文化线路具有动态特征，强调交流和民族、地域及文化间的相互影响和移植，因此不可能孤立地分析组成文化线路的某个物质遗存。同时，文化线路的内容元素拥有丰富的内涵并且相互依托，因此把有形、无形和自然元素联合起来整体理解，既是文化遗产所强调的完整性的要求，也可以在整体性提供的普遍背景上丰富和加强文化线路的意义。

另一方面，在文化线路的全球意义和现实意义上，在仍被使用的年代中，文化线路带来的不仅仅是物质交换和人群间的交流，更重要的是在物质交流的基础上联系并贯通了世界上的不同地域，如整个丝绸之路的路网即可覆盖占全球四分之一的面积。这一过程不仅在人类学的意义上对世界各民族产生了影响，包括民族间的融合、人种间的混血和优化等，而且带来了胜于物质交流的思想、知识、文化、艺术和宗教等方面的互动，产生了全球意义上的普遍价值。这也使得与文化线路相关的各类遗产得以突破国家的政治界限，成为全世界各民族的共同财产，并在和平和团结的时代背景下推动世界历史和文化的进程。

在实际操作层面，保护文化线路必然需要不同地区、国家乃至民族间的合作和沟通，因此强调文化线路的整体性也为地区、民族和国家间的合作、团结、相互尊重和欣赏、对话提供了具有普遍价值的、共同利益大于私己利益的平台，使其作为遗产的组织性价值②大大超越了以往的遗产类型。因此，可以认为，文化线路的整体既是对文化和历史的鸟瞰，又是国家和地区间共同利益的和平代表，它的整体性价值在任何角度都不可忽视。

（4）动态性

动态性是文化线路的本质特征，也是区分文化线路与其他类型世界遗产的元素之一。对文化线路动态性的理解，不应仅限于留诸物质遗存的时空中变迁痕迹，而应关注到形成动态性的原动力和维持机制的两个基本因素，以及与它们相关的重要遗存。

文化线路产生的原动力是构成动态性的本质因素。由初始意图产生的动力因素，如贸易需求、宗教传播、文化差异导致的交流需求等，是文化线路得以形成和长期持续下去的动力源泉，而原动力的变化，往往是文化线路兴衰变化的根源，决定了其动态性的基本特征。

维持动力因素的机制，包括具体路线、城镇、维持交流的基础设施，保障线路的军事设施，沿途设

---

① ICOMOS – CIIC. Pamplona Conclusions – INTERNATIONAL CONGRESS OF THE ICOMOS CIIC. PAMPLONA, NAVARRA, SPAIN. JUNE, 2001, PAMPLONA, 2001.

② 组织性价值最先由 Holden（2006）提出，并将其作为文化遗产具有的与内在元素、工具性元素并列的第三种元素。见 The Costs and Benefits of UK World Heritage Site Status: A literature review for the Department for Culture, Media and Sport, Price water house coopers, 2007, P9.

计的宗教文化的社会因素，人与自然互动的因素，途径区域的社会机制等等。是它们在适应自然及社会环境的挑战中，延续线路功能的同时，塑造了线路的多种形态特征。

原动力和维持原动力的机制组成了文化线路的整体，并且不断相互作用和变化。文化线路具体的线路改变和活动的多样性是这种动态性的结果，而更为丰富的动态性因素则广泛融入于文化线路有形及无形的基本元素，并贯穿其中。只有通过整体理解和细微观察，才能深刻理解文化线路复杂丰富的动态性特征。

西班牙和法国的圣地亚哥朝圣线路，都对促成文化线路的根本动因，机制性因素和历史上影响线路发展的其他动态因素造成的结果有清晰的反映；阿根廷的塔夫拉达·德乌玛瓦卡遗产项目，则展现了一万年以来这条商业通道由于目的和功能的转变，所形成丰富的动态变化；以色列内盖夫的香料之路，则以非常精简的遗产要素组合，展现出围绕香料贸易的根本动因，不同势力之间相互竞争的致因给这条沙漠商道带来的动态变化。这些案例，都是对文化线路中动态因素的成功阐释。

（5）背景环境

文化线路的背景环境特指与文化遗产所在的空间区域相关的环境要素。根据空间范围的层次，可以划分为地理环境、区域环境、文化景观和遗产要素周边环境四个层次。其中，地理环境指遗产地所在的地形、地质等要素，它们对文化线路的走向和变化有重要的影响；区域环境指覆盖线路段落的自然和人文地理单元，例如城市和村落的文化背景等，它们有助于对遗产价值的理解；文化景观的层面则强调了对于文化线路与环境之间的联系，它们所反映的人与自然的互动关系，从风格特点及文化多样性的角度丰富了文化线路的价值；最后，在文化线路的每个遗产要素周边，也经常分布着相关的文物古迹，是理解文化线路内涵的必要因素。

对环境要素的关注，为文化线路的保护管理提出了一系列具体可行的原则。在保护对象和范围方面，不仅强调了对地质地貌、自然景观、城市村落和相关古迹遗址的保护，也突出了人文历史、文化传统等非物质要素的保护。在遗产认定的实践操作中，环境要素对确定遗产地的保护范围和缓冲区有重要的影响。

回顾已列入世界遗产名录的文化线路案例，对环境要素的关注逐渐得到加强。从最早的圣地亚哥朝圣线路，遗产构成要素基本以沿线的建、构筑物为主，到阿根廷的塔夫拉达·德乌玛瓦卡遗产项目，关注到文化线路所在的空间环境和自然要素，突出了这些要素在文化意义上与遗产地价值联系，从而形成了空间更加宽广的遗产范围界定。

2.3 文化线路与其他相关遗产概念的辨析

文化线路的概念与很多遗产概念有密切的相关性。这些概念包括文化景观、运河遗产、美国国家遗产廊道和欧洲文化线路、线性遗产和廊道遗产等。

其中，文化景观、运河遗产作为世界遗产领域里相对较早出现的特殊类型，与文化线路在空间范围、遗产地的形成机制和是否蕴含文化交流和动态性等特征方面具有本质差别；美国国家遗产廊道和欧洲文化线路分别是美国和欧洲的地区性概念和保护体系，对我国文化线路的管理和保护可能有借鉴作用；线性遗产则是国内遗产保护界相关学者在借鉴国际遗产相关概念后，在目前对国内遗产保护和研究时所提出的概念，尚未在国际范围形成统一的准确定义。明晰这些概念之间的关系有助于文化线路类遗产的判别和认定，更准确地定位文化线路遗产的价值、保护管理和申报策略。

2.4 文化线路价值评估的方法和流程

从价值评估到遗产认定，是文化遗产保护前期研究工作中最为重要的内容，也是世界遗产申报过程中最为关键的环节。文化线路建立在众多要素组合的基础上，相比于单个或单组遗产，在主题方向、范畴和规模、要素组织筛选等方面呈现出复杂得多的可能性，为文化线路的价值评估与遗产认定增加了一定难度。

对一条文化线路形成基本认识的过程，可以概括为以下步骤。首先需要确定其时空范畴及交流内容。时空范围即对文化线路上的交流活动持续进行的起讫时间及覆盖空间的定义；交流内容则可能包括贸易、宗教、军事等活动内容。其次，需要分析这些多维度的交流内容的相互关系，分辨出哪些是线路形成的起因，哪些是由此产生的其他活动，并认定它们各自的时间与空间分布范围。之后，需要进一步考察文化线路所产生的"跨文化的整体意义"，即在其穿越的时空范围内产生的文化间交流，是否产生了不同区域或文化之间的互惠关系，以及这些互惠结果对各文化区域的影响。这是文化线路的核心价值所在。最后，需要对文化交流的动态性进行分析，即指出文化线路产生的最初动力、维持线路上的交流活动的必要条件及其历史变迁、最初动力引起的其他交流活动以及所有这些动态过程所产生的结果及其影响。

形成基本认知后，需要结合比较研究，确定遗产项目的主题和价值要点，筛选适用的世界遗产价值标准。至此，才能有的放矢地认定遗产要素，并通过真实性、完整性的评估，来检验遗产要素对遗产价值的表达是否准确和充分。

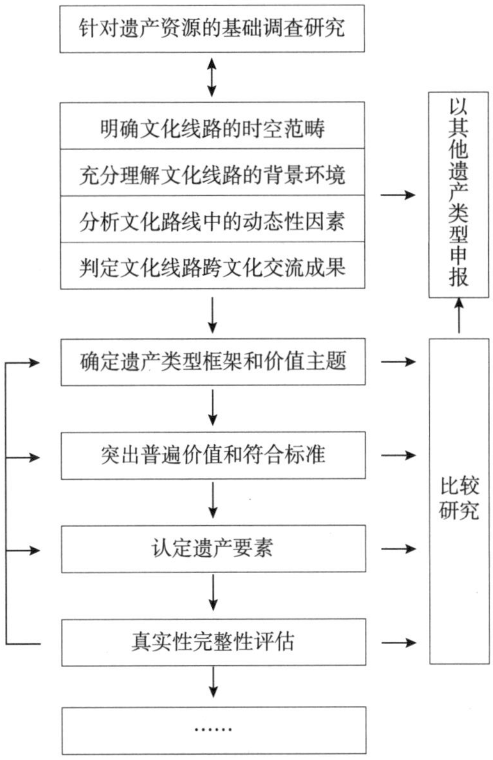

在这样一个基本的流程关系里，每个阶段工作的深入，都可能对之前工作的成果提出修正，只有经过对所有相关的遗产资源反复地认知和分析，才能对遗产地的申报项目形成系统和深刻的理解。

经过上述分析之后，可以得到整体遗产认定和突出普遍价值的基本架构（见表格 1 ）。

图 1　文化线路保护与申遗的工作流程

表格 1　遗产认定和突出普遍价值的基本架构

文化线路特征的构成要素	对遗产要素的要求	与突出普遍价值的关系
目的与功能	遗产要素应能清晰的反映线路的功能性质特征	线路形成的目的突出的反映了人类的某种文化传统，或通过极其特殊的方式实现了目的
符合延续的时间、空间定义	遗产要素连续分布在一定的历史时期和空间范围内。 如果线路本身有反映在物质层面的动态变化，则遗产要素中应有能证明这种动态变化在时间和空间上的分布，或变化的形态。	具有相当大的时空跨度规模；或处于特殊的人类文化发展阶段；或在空间上跨越特殊的地理区域
反映跨文化的整体意义	应有能够代表参与交流的文化元文化特征的遗产要素，所有遗产要素作为整体共同反映该文化线路的整体价值	文化交流的多元性；文化交流形成特别广泛或深远的影响
反映产生文化线路的最初活动、后续活动及其结果和影响	遗产要素在时空上的分布和各自特征能组成阐释文化线路的发展变化的清晰线索	表达文化线路的深远影响；或通过其复杂的历史变迁表明线路的功能与目的对人类文明的重要意义
反映维持文化线路交流活动的机制	遗产要素包括与机制运行相关的典型功能设施遗存（如管理机构、驿站、关卡、服务设施等），或能清晰反映机制运行的证据（如碑刻题记、有规律的生产、生活在环境中留下的印记等）	机制本身是某文化传统的重要内容；机制的延续和变化与相关背景环境的变化对应，使文化线路成为重要的历史主题的突出表达

2.5　世界遗产价值标准对文化线路的适用性分析

由于文化线路遗产具有遗产组合类型多样、时间和空间跨度较大、体现文化交流的动态性等特征，在申报世界遗产时对适用的标准的选择、标准的阐释上，也与其他类型遗产有所不同。世界文化遗产地六条适用标准与文化线路遗产类型在一般情况下的相关性和适用性，可参考表格 2 中的分析。

文化线路往往会以系列申报的形式进行，而根据《实施世界遗产公约操作指南》，系列申报中所有组成项目的遗产地都必须同时符合申报标准。因此，文化线路申报世界遗产时，应该关注在遗产地反映的活动内容、遗产类型、物质形态、遗产价值贡献等方面进行不同层次的组合，侧重于遗产整体价值的阐释，并同时仅选取所有遗产地都能符合的遗产价值标准作为申报标准。对于未能体现在所有构成遗产地的标准及其价值，也应当相应地做灵活调整，以达到系列申报的要求。

表格 2　世界文化遗产申报标准与文化线路遗产项目的适用性分析

标准	侧重点分析	适用性分析	建议
(i) 代表人类创造性天才的杰作。①	强调遗产物质形态对人类艺术性、技术性等创造力的体现，其中，"创造性天才"表现为突出的创造能力，而"杰作"的含义则可以指一位创造性艺术家或手工艺者最为杰出的作品，或指某项人类的杰出成就。	文化线路有多元化的构成要素，所有遗产地都达到标准一的可能性极小。如果为了达到该项标准而删减构成遗产，则又将导致难以体现文化线路本身多维度的交流内容和跨文化整体价值的境况。	一般不建议选取标准一作为"遗产线路"的申报标准。
(ii) 反映了某一文化区域内、一定时间范围内，在建筑或技术、纪念性艺术、城镇规划或景观发展方面，重要的人类价值互换。②	侧重人类价值交流在艺术和技术发展阶段方面的物质体现，其中包括建筑、技术、纪念性的艺术作品、城镇规划或景观等。符合标准的遗产地物质遗存应属于建筑或技术、纪念性艺术作品、城镇或景观的某一类型。	当文化线路的交流内容涉及上述领域，能在物质遗存上体现其中某个或若干重要发展阶段的特征，而这种特征的形成源于文化线路带来的文化间的相互影响，能在文化线路的突出普遍价值中得到体现时，就有选取该标准申遗的优势。 能够更典型和更完整地阐释人类价值交换过程和成果的文化线路，符合标准二的可能性较高。	建议文化线路申遗时，可以充分考虑选取该标准的可能性。
(iii) 是反映仍然存在或已经消逝的某一文化传统或文明的独特的或至少非凡的见证。③	突出强调遗产对文化传统或文明的见证作用，其性质既涵盖了延续至今、依然存在的文化传统或文明，也涵盖了已消逝了的传统和文明。其中文化传统可体现为宗教仪式、生活与生产方式等内容，文明也可以理解为某一特定历史时期存在过的王朝或国家等类型。	文化线路作为有时可以理解为"动态的文化景观"的遗产类型，并与文化交流相关，因此也经常能够选取标准三作为符合标准，如反映古代文明的重要商品贸易，或跨越文化区域的宗教信仰等。文化线路上文化活动的稳定的推动因素和维持机制等要素，共同构成的整体，很可能体现该标准要求的"传统"。	可以通过研究线路的功能、目的与文化传统之间的关联性；以及穿越的文化地域、时间范围与动态交流的内容，来判断是否能够反映历史上存在或仍延续至今的传统与文明，判断其能否适用标准三。

---

① represent a masterpiece of human creative genius;

② exhibit an important interchange of human values, over a span of time or within a cultural area of the world, on developments in architecture or technology, monumental arts, town - planning or landscape;

③ bear a unique or at least exceptional testimony to a cultural tradition or to a civilization which is living or which has disappeared;

续表

标准	侧重点分析	适用性分析	建议
（iv）是一类建筑或技术全体或景观的杰出典范，展现了人类历史上的重要阶段。①	该标准要求通过具体的建筑或技术类型来表达遗产所反映的时代文化特征，物质遗存在反映时代文化特征的形成与变化的典型性是该标准重要的考察要求。	所选遗产点的时代分布或线路功能比较单纯的文化线路可以较好地适应该标准，所以选取该标准时应以特定时代和建筑类型为指标对相关遗产点进行适当筛选。如时代特征，可以反映一个主要时代，如圣地亚哥朝觐线路，或同时反映多个时代，如格夫拉达·德·乌马瓦卡线路、印加之路等。	如果一条文化线路拥有较多物质遗存，且保存状况较为良好，这些遗存在类型、风格等方面彼此关联较为密切的条件下，可以考虑使用标准四。
（v）是一种传统人类聚落、土地利用或海洋利用方式的杰出典范，代表一种或多种文化，或人类与环境的互动，尤其是当这种环境在不可逆的变化影响下变得十分脆弱的时候。②	标准五要求遗产在空间分布、建筑形态或技术手段等方面体现人与自然的互动关系，或反映某种或某些文化，或反映与自然的互动关系，如文明或文化的生存方式。由于遗产需要能够反映人与自然之间挑战与应战的互动关系，符合该条标准的遗产往往具有特殊的自然环境。	当文化线路遗产选取该标准时，往往要求线路分布的环境不仅较为特殊，且人类面对自然因素挑战的应对模式较为统一。且在定义的所有时间范围内也能完全体现出这种互动关系。 因此，文化线路选取该标准申遗时，应考察线路的背景关系，即该标准反映的互动关系应在线路所属的具体历史时期内进行阐释。反映线路交流内容的遗产要素必须包括线路涉及的相关景观、环境要素，且能够体现人与自然的挑战—应对关系是维持线路的动态机制的重要组成部分。最后，还应该充分考虑周边相关环境的地质地貌等特征。	标准五对一定时期内、特殊环境下人与自然的互动关系的要求，很大程度上限制了长时间、大范围、交流内容多元的文化线路选取该标准申遗。
（vi）与具有突出普遍价值的事件、生活传统、思想或信仰、艺术和文学作品有直接或有形的关联。③	标准六强调遗存与历史、文化、精神、情感等非物质要素方面的直接联系。不仅要求遗产相关的非物质要素具有"突出普遍价值"，还要求遗产与之有直接或物质的关联。	尽管文化线路遗产的丰富内容往往可以提供大量与遗产相关的重大历史事件、历史人物、曾有或现有传统、宗教信仰、思想观念、传说故事、文学作品、艺术活动等内容，却仍需要证明这些非物质元素的突出普遍价值，并需要提供直接相关的物质遗存作为证据。这就对从内容庞杂的文化线路遗产中进行合理筛选形成了挑战。	选取标准六申遗时，仍需要从上述这些可能的非物质元素中选取最具价值、并且与文化线路的所有构成遗产地最直接相关的要素进行重点阐释。

① be an outstanding example of a type of building, architectural or technological ensemble or landscape which illustrates (a) significant stage (s) in human history;

② be an outstanding example of a traditional human settlement, land – use, or sea – use which is representative of a culture (or cultures), or human interaction with the environment especially when it has become vulnerable under the impact of irreversible change;

③ be directly or tangibly associated with events or living traditions, with ideas, or with beliefs, with artistic and literary works of outstanding universal significance.

2.6 文化线路的真实性与完整性

文化线路要作为"遗产线路"申遗时，除了需要阐述各遗产要素的真实性与完整性，还需要阐述构成申报项目的遗产要素的筛选原则与方式，以说明遴选出的遗产要素能够真实、完整地反映遗产项目的"突出普遍价值"。遗产要素之间的价值联系、遗产要素与文化线路的价值联系以及遗产要素对整体项目的价值贡献都需要得到充分阐释。

在真实性方面，遗产要素与线路的关联性的真实性可以通过考古报告、文献资料等方面的材料阐述，或通过能建立起关联性的相关非物质遗存来证明。在完整性方面，除了可从文化线路的意义与价值、遗产要素的构成等方面阐述整体项目的完整性，从遗产地本体的保存状况阐释遗产地的完整性之外，还应该从前述"文化线路的定义阐释"中对文化线路的背景、内容、跨文化的整体意义、环境、动态性等方面，对是否充分具备反映这些特征的遗产要素进行阐释。

2.7 文化线路的比较研究

比较研究作为一种研究方法，应从申报工作的前期阶段就开始应用，以确定与其他类似遗产项目的关系，明确遗产项目在意义与价值方面的定位。与其他同类遗产在物质遗存保存程度的方面进行较量，明确孰优孰劣，并不是比较研究的目的所在。因为遗产项目作为人类文化遗产，固有文化多样性的属性。只要充分挖掘遗产项目的自身特色和特殊价值，参考相关咨询机构提出的主题研究框架，合理定位遗产的时空—地域、主题和类型等特征，就能够通过比较研究找到项目的"突出普遍价值"所在，从而避免与其他同类遗产在物质遗存保存程度的各项标准方面进行简单的比较。针对一般申报世界遗产的项目，《实施世界遗产公约操作指南》中对比较研究的要求是"明确在世界遗产名录中或尚未登陆世界遗产名录的遗产项目中是否有与申报项目类似的"，和"解释申报的遗产项目在其国家的和全球语境中的重要意义"。对于系列申报，则应对系列申报中的选点进行比较研究。

具体到文化线路比较研究的展开，需要分为整体和内部两个阶段。作为整体文化线路的比较研究，可以基于构成突出普遍价值的要素，分别或综合地从三个方面进行比较分析：在同一文化主题的线路之间比较研究——如同为宗教线路、贸易线路之间的比较；或在同一文化区域的比较研究，可能会加上时间跨度上的比较；以及在同一形态类型之间进行比较研究，如铁路线路、沙漠路线、山区路线之间的比较。整体的比较研究首先应明确申报对象的突出普遍价值与上述文化主题、文化区域、形态类型等不同角度之间的关系，即突出普遍价值的阐释是否与这些要素相关，然后在相关要素的层面阐述其他比较对象的关键差别，以说明文化线路突出普遍价值的独特性。

进行文化线路内部遗产地之间的比较研究，与前面所述的真实性与完整性评估的原因类似，是由文化线路本身的多维度动态交流内容决定的。在进行比较研究时，首先需要阐明构成线路的遗产地有明确的筛选范畴，并且都经过相当详细的调查研究。比较前应尽可能全面地列出相关遗存；之后阐述明确比较筛选的原则，并针对每个遗产逐一阐明比较研究的结论。阐述应强调遗产地的价值贡献在文化线路整体突出普遍价值中不可替代的地位，并得出所有作出独特价值贡献的遗产地构成了文化遗产整体价值的结论，避免从物质遗存保存状况等单一标准进行优劣竞争的比较模式。

三、中国的文化线路遗产资源的保护与申报策略研究

通过上述研究，课题在对文化线路现有理论、实践作出分析研究之后，对中国文化线路的保护展开了进一步的研究。主要的切入点分为三方面，首先对中国应该形成的保护管理体系及保护实践提出了策略性建议，其次从现有的研究成果入手，对国内的文化线路遗产资源状况做了初步梳理，提出了中国文

化线路资源体系框架，最后针对中国的文化线路如何保护和申报世界遗产提出了综合性的建议。

3.1 文化线路保护管理的策略研究与建议

为确保当前的文化线路遗产资源得到有效的保护，并为将来申报世界遗产做好积极充分的准备，必须为文化线路的保护建立一套完整的保护管理体系。

《实施世界遗产公约操作指南》的要求和已有案例的成功经验均说明，有效的保护管理体系，需要管理的依据，管理的体制，管理的策略计划三者有机的结合。实施管理的依据，是与文化遗产保护相关的整套立法保障体系；管理的体制，包括了管理职能体系和管理制度；管理的策略计划，则包括了一系列指导保护工作实施的规划、计划，主要通过遗产地保护管理规划来体现。

立法保障体系

作为管理依据的立法保障体系主要包括四个层面，即与遗产保护和文物保护相关的法律法规、相关一般法律法规、遗产保护行业规范和准则以及相关国际公约及宪章。这些立法依据的完善度和相互的协调一致，是确保各类遗产项目得到有效管理，并能成功申报世界遗产的重要保障。

建议我国在立法保障体系方面，制定颁布针对中国文化线路保护的管理条例，将其与传统的文物保护单位区别开来，明确对文化线路遗产身份的认定、保护、管理等方面内容。同时在相关法律法规中补充对文化景观类型遗产的相应内容，以便更好的支撑文化线路内各类要素的保护，并在条件成熟时，将文化线路作为文化遗产的特殊类型，纳入《文物保护法》。针对未来被认定为国家级别的文化线路遗产项目，制定更具有针对性的保护管理条例或办法。建议在《中国文物古迹保护准则》的修订中，补充认定文化线路等新遗产类型。

考虑到文化线路多为跨省跨地区的大型综合性文化资源，建议与文化线路相关的立法体系文件和相关的总体规划，应由国务院颁布。

对于跨国文化线路，开展对相关法律法规的专题研究，总结归纳可供依据的现有法律法规，并结合国家方针政策的研究，探讨对相关法律法规进行完善的必要性。

保护管理体制

考虑到文化线路的重要价值和其规模、分布特点以及可能的对外联系，建议在国家一级认定文化线路遗产资源中的重要项目。针对已认定的国家级文化线路遗产项目的保护管理，补充完善现有的管理体系。

建议由国家文物主管部门设立针对复合性遗产资源保护的职能机构，对认定的文化线路遗产项目实施业务上的统筹指导和对核心遗产资源的垂直管理，并建立与国家其他职能部门的沟通协作渠道。在文化线路所涉及的地区，建议由省级政府联合组织各职能部门，建立文化线路保护管理委员会，在国家文物主管部门专职机构的领导下负责文化线路整体保护管理工作的部署和实施。

在经营机制方面，建议明确遗产资源经营权的界限，对于公益事业可以特许经营的方式采取市场化经营。在监督机制方面，建议由国家文物局专设的职能部门对文化线路的保护管理工作进行监督，并提倡公众参与，引入社会监督机制。在资金机制方面，建议采取分级的综合管理模式，建立多层面、多渠道、可持续的资金保障渠道。在技术保障机制方面，建议依托中国古迹遗址保护协会组建中国文化线路遗产专家委员会，负责对国内文化线路遗产保护总体的学术研究和技术支持，直接对国家文物局文化线路遗产资源的专职管理机构负责。针对具体的文化线路，应组建专门的研究机构，辅助文化线路保护管理委员会的决策制定。建议将该研究机构的组织状况和专业水平列为国家级文化线路的认定标准之一。

保护管理策划与计划

建议首先国家层面开展初步的资源调查，制定中国文化线路遗产资源总体的保护纲要，配合相关法规和行政管理体系的完善，形成中国文化线路遗产资源保护与利用的总体战略。

针对具体的文化线路遗产项目，建议参照美国遗产廊道的规划编制模式，在项目确立为国家文化线路之前首先编制规划纲要，并作为申报国家文化线路的基本条件，在得到保护身份认定后，编制完整的文化线路保护管理总体规划，并建立从总体规划到分区、分段落，甚至分主题线索的保护管理规划体系。

文化线路的保护管理规划，应以遗产价值为策略制定的核心，并体现真实性与完整性原则、可持续发展的观念、遗产保护的公益性原则，充分纳入文化线路保护的各方利益相关者，在规划中为保护管理工作的各参与方明确各自的角色、职责和任务，协调利益相关者之间的矛盾，保证线路整体保护管理的协调一致。当涉及跨国线路项目时，规划应与相关的国家方针政策密切配合，保护国家主权。

3.2 中国的资源体系

课题基于对中国的交通史、民族学、水利史、漕运史等相关学科的研究成果，分析了孕育中国文化线路的自然背景、人文背景和历史上重要对外交流活动的特点，参考世界遗产主题分类的方式，对中国文化线路的遗产资源提出了以路径形态、年代—文化地域及文化主题为背景的分类框架。基于这个框架，以全国重点文物保护单位名录（第一批至第六批已列入项目及第七批申报项目）为基础，初步整理了中国的文化线路资源名单。根据地域规模的不同特点，将中国的文化线路资源分为国际/洲际交通路线、全国性路线、国内区域性交通路线三类，并初步分析了它们与各主题的相关性。（见附录中国文化线路遗产资源概况表）

从案例呼应不同主题的统计数字来看，这些项目体现了以下特点：

（1）"运输系统形态"的各类主题分布较为平均，体现了名录代表性上的平衡，但与近代交通线路类型（铁路或公路）相关的项目仍有可以拓展的空间；

（2）"目标与功能"的各类主题中，商贸主题的代表性最为突出，体现了中国文化线路用于物质交流的普遍性特征，其他主题代表性较为平均；在进一步的研究中，对于商贸主题的细化分类（如从不同类型的商品角度）将更加有利于比较不同线路的价值和载体上的差异；

（3）在"与互动和交流相关的文化主题"部分则由于多数线路案例的文化研究成果有限，现阶段对于这些案例对这一文化主题的呼应度尚不能有准确的定论。

（4）根据现有的基本信息，多数文化线路都能呼应多个文化类主题，体现出中国文化线路的复杂性特点。

3.3 筛选标准和申报策略

在我国建立统一的文化线路资源保护体系的前提下，与文化线路主题相关的遗产申报世界遗产时，既需要考虑申报世界遗产在突出普遍价值等方面的一般标准，也要考虑现存的遗产地是否符合文化线路类型的定义和特征，以及保护管理方面的特殊要求。尽管一条可以被认定的文化线路一定有其突出的文化遗产价值，但并不是所有文化线路都有可能符合世界遗产的标准，也并不一定适合以文化线路的类型申报世界遗产。通过对照文化线路的标准和世界遗产的标准，可以为与文化线路相关的遗产资源确定大致的保护发展方向（见图2）。根据现阶段对文化线路的定义和保护管理要求，可以大致归纳出作为文化线路遗产项目的基本认定标准（见表3）。

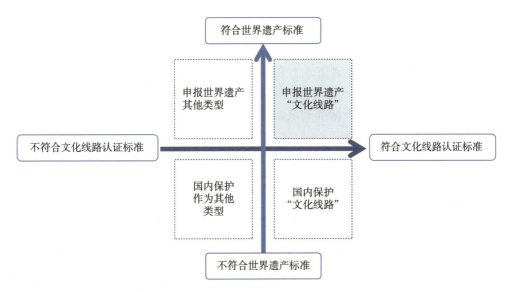

图 2   文化线路遗产资源的保护发展方向

表格 3   文化线路认证的标准

类型	细则	具体要求
遗产认定	时空定义	明确文化线路的时间起讫点及空间范围；
	背景	阐释文化线路所在的文化、地理、历史的宏观背景；
	内容	列出物质要素与非物质要素清单；
	作为整体的跨文化意义	阐述文化线路反映文化交流的整体意义；
	动态性	阐述文化线路上的活动、形态等变化过程；
	环境	明确文化线路的物质空间环境要素及分布范围，结合遗产内容明确保护范围与缓冲区；
	形态	明确文化线路在地理平面上的线路形态及其他分类结果；
管理	统一管理	确定非盈利管理机构作为统一管理机构，成立管理委员会，纳入线路覆盖区域和线路要素内容所涉及的各行政管理机构，和各主要利益相关者代表
	跨区域合作	签订跨行政区的官方合作协议等合作文件；
	保护管理规划	制定保护管理规划纲要；
	文化旅游	列出文化旅游项目机构及计划；
	经费预算	提供管理经费预算及来源说明；
研究	跨学科的研究网络	签订合作研究的协议，确定研究机构与学者的清单；
	基础研究	制定研究项目及计划，如学术活动的内容及频率、研究项目的进度等；
	基础资料	建立基础资料数据库，确定存放地点；
	经费预算	提供研究经费预算及来源说明；

当一个遗产申报项目被认为符合相关标准要求，确定以"文化线路"类型申报世界遗产时，还需要对纳入申报计划的遗产要素组合进行进一步的分析，以选择最佳的申报策略。

图 3 典型的文化线路遗产构成模式示意图说明了通常一条文化线路的遗产要素构成状况。通过初步调查统计和研究结论能够得到的若干相关遗产要素共同分布在文化线路沿线，它们与主干线的距离远近不等，规模有大小之分，类型也不尽相同，相互之间又由于分属不同的文化区域再次分为若干个较为独立的区段。每个遗产要素所承载的价值各有侧重，对文化线路整体作出的价值贡献也有所不同。选取的时空范围越广阔，遗产地之间的差异性也越明显。由于申报世界遗产时，被纳入的各构成要素必须共同符合至少一条标准的要求[1]，因此选择过大的时空范围或者过多的遗产地也会增加申报的难度。

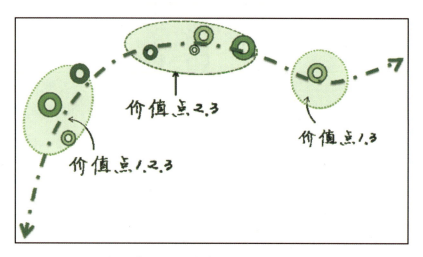

图 3　典型的文化线路遗产构成模式示意图

基于对相关案例和世界遗产申报策略的研究，课题建议文化线路申遗项目可以根据不同的情况，采用以下几种组合方式：即在最理想的条件下选取所有区段各类要素作为整体一次申报（见图 4）；选取最有完整性和真实性的典型区段单独申报（图 5），这种方式也可能由于不同段落申报条件的成熟阶段不同，而形成不同批次的系列申报；选取其中主题线索最突出的某类遗产要素构成系列申报的方法（图 6）。这些方法各有优势和劣势，需要谨慎考虑和灵活选择。

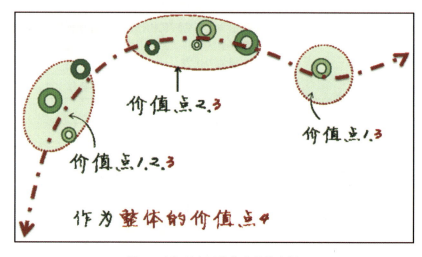

图 4　选取所有区段作为整体申报

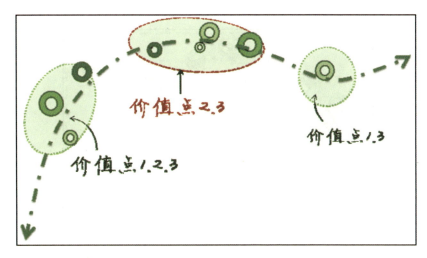

图 5 选取最有完整性和真实性的典型区段单独申报

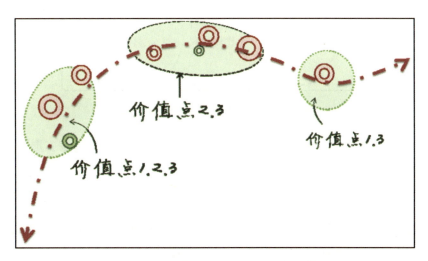

图 6 选取主题线索最突出的某类遗产要素申报

　　无论以哪种方式进行申报，都需要在对文化线路遗产地资源进行详细调查、整理和研究之后，才能够开始决策过程，以避免时间和精力的浪费。在决策过程中，则要考虑到同类遗产比较研究的结果，尽早避免可能与现有世界遗产项目重叠的策略。最后，在能够适用多种组合策略进行申报的时候，申遗的动机与目的则将成为最为关键的因素——既包括当地社区发展经济的要求，也包括当地民众对未来申遗成功以后生活方式的愿景等。而这些合理的动机与目的也都能够作为申遗文本进行阐述的理由，体现出公众参与的过程、当地社区的支持与意愿以及国家及当地政府对申遗项目的推动是深思熟虑与具有远见的结果。（见图 7 对文化线路申遗决策的影响因素）

3.4 文化线路保护与管理的技术策略建议

文化线路遗产范围和缓冲区界定

　　根据《文化线路宪章》中对文化线路环境要素的分析，在遗产范围的划定中，既要考虑线路所有遗产要素内容的分布，也需特别关注那些与线路关系密切的环境要素的空间范畴，并应将其纳入到遗产范围之中。线路整体的完整性和连续性也是划定遗产范围和缓冲区时需要考虑的重要因素。

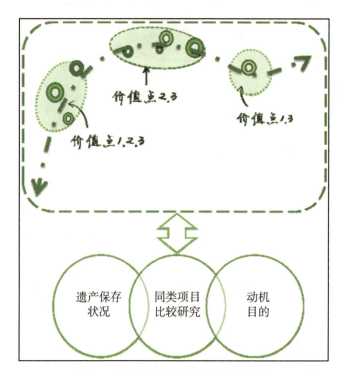

图 7　对文化线路申遗决策的影响因素

　　根据文化线路可能的构成模式，遗产范围和缓冲区的划定可能出现三种基本形态。一种是当某段线路本体比较明确，保存的延续性相对较好，可能形成沿线路的带状形态，在线路两侧有沿线遗存时将遗产范围扩展，包裹进相关遗存及其环境要素，典型的案例如法国的圣地亚哥—德孔波斯特拉朝圣之路；第二种是当线路段落周边的相关环境要素范畴巨大，形成完整包裹线路段落的文化景观体系，则遗产范围和缓冲区可能呈现整体的区域形态，典型的案例如阿根廷塔夫拉达·德·乌玛瓦卡；当道路遗存本身已经消失，仅有沿线遗存时，则遗产范围和缓冲区可围绕遗产点和其环境要素逐一划定。有些时候，当线路中的道路遗存基本延续，但不连贯时，遗产范围和缓冲区的划定可以帮助遗产的保护管理体现线路的延续性。如日本纪伊山圣地与参拜道，当保存基本完整的道路遗存出现间断，但道路经过的路由明确时，用遗产范围包围了有道路遗存的段落，在间断区域保持缓冲区的延续。

文化线路遗产保护措施的制定

　　（1）对文化线路保护措施的制定，必须建立在对遗产要素特征的充分认知和理解基础上，除了保证遗产要素自身的健康完整之外，应特别关注那些要素上最能体现其与线路联系的部分在保护上的需求；

　　（2）线路沿线针对同一类残损采取的干预性保护措施，首先应考虑对象所在的空间区域，是否有可参照的传统方式，使保护措施的实施起到对文化线路沿线的文化多样性的延续作用；当沿线区段没有可参照的传统方式，在不同对象上采用的保护措施则应尽量保证一致性，从而使保护措施成为可以体现线路整体感和延续性的积极因素；

　　（3）针对线路整体保护措施的实施计划的制定，除考虑由保存状况和价值重要性所决定的先后顺序外，还应适当考虑实施项目在线路覆盖不同区域的均衡性，以保障线路整体性的保护；

　　（4）保护措施的具体实施，应尽可能引入本地人员的参与，并鼓励加强线路涉及的不同区域的交流合作，通过保护措施的实施过程发挥文化线路的社会价值。

文化线路的风险防御体系构建

（1）由于文化线路遗产的庞大尺度，应注意可能在整体结构上影响或威胁线路完整性和连续性的因素。需要依托文化线路的保护管理机构对沿线的威胁因素建立协调统一的防御体系，并针对需要防御的对象设置相应学科专家的配置。从规范制定、相关学科研究、威胁与压力信息反馈、防御措施制定与实施多个方面来构建多渠道、多层面的工作框架。特别是对于线路中林区、水域、湿地等生态敏感区域以及沿途历史城镇等薄弱地区需要组织专门的力量进行灾害防御。

（2）避免因沿线保护措施实施水平的不均衡，形成对线路整体性的不良影响。应建立完善的保护技术管理监督机制和必要的区域间技术支援机制。同时还需设立对保护和其他相关技术的适用性检测机制，对引进和即将实施的技术，特别是环境技术，进行充分的检测，保证其长期的可行性，以维护文化线路的整体性。

（3）在对灾害威胁的评估分析中，应特别关注来自于传统的防御和应对方式，并从中汲取有效的内容加以利用，在保护遗产的同时，也起到文化传承和对传统文化的展示作用。

（4）考虑到对文化线路整体性和连续性的影响因素中，有些是目前不可控的因素，如大环境的气候变化，整个社会的发展变化等，因此应针对此类威胁产生的后果做出预案，尽可能以其他方式有效地弥补这些威胁因素造成的影响。

文化线路遗产的展示与阐释

（1）由于文化线路在价值展示和阐释上的宏大主题和丰富内容，应最终建立与其对应的大规模、多尺度的遗产与公众之间的交流平台。对文化线路各要素之间的关联性、整体的动态性要素和整体感、连续性的强调，是其展示与阐释应特别关注的重点。

（2）文化线路遗产的展示与阐释，也是为了文化多样性的传承，应成为接续文明链条和保障其延续的重要手段之一。展示与阐释应充分纳入保存、研究、认知、体验、参与的流程，以促成遗产价值传承的良性循环。

（3）同时，对文化线路遗产的展示与阐释，也是为了使利益相关者受益。创造与传承文化的主体是与此文化内涵、表象、地缘相关的人群，展示与阐释应加强遗产和人群的联系，通过促进社会和经济效益的作用，可以不同程度地激活文化线路所承载的文化传承。

（4）文化线路展示，应把文化线路放到整个历史发展的链条中进行研究，深层次发掘其内涵并予以阐释，为受众全面呈现其价值。对文化线路遗产整体内涵的展示与阐释应包含文化线路内部遗存及其外延的所有内容。

文化线路遗产的监测

（1）对文化线路监测的对象，应包括对遗产要素本身的保存状况监测，对各类威胁影响因素的监测；对线路部分或整体干预措施效果的监测；以及对沿线不同段落区域保护管理意图、保护能力状况的监测。

（2）对遗产保存状态及变化趋势的监测，除了其各个组成要素自身物质层面的保存状态和变化趋势外，还应关注要素之间、要素与线路整体之间关联关系的清晰性，以及传承至今的线路历史功能的延续状态和变化趋势，并将遗产要素自身的特征、区域性的环境特征和整个线路的文化特征之间的协调关系，作为监测的重要指标。

（3）对文化线路遗产面临的威胁因素的监测，应根据风险评估建立完整的系统的威胁和影响因素清单，特别是那些可能影响线路整体完整性和连续性的因素，将其纳入监测对象。

（4）对保护干预效果的监测，在周期性的监测过程中，需要对上期的保护与干预效果进行整体的评价，同时对具体的实施过程以及实施后果进行及时的分析，对保护过程中不当的影响进行及时的纠正，并要求保留书面的报告进行备案。

保护与管理文化线路的能力建设

（1）应建立系统的跨学科研究机构，为文化线路遗产的保护管理提供知识的维护和更新，并由该机构承担在遗产研究和保护方面的对外交流，通过交流合作促进该文化线路保护能力的提升。

（2）在管理机制中加大保护与管理人员的培训机制，并关注线路中技术水平相对落后的区域，避免能力的差距给文化线路的整体性保护带来严重的影响。

（3）可以尝试在整个文化线路的保护管理系统内建立知识管理系统。在管理系统内形成信息知识和能力技能的积累和沟通，并传递给利益相关者。

矛盾与冲突的调节与管理

文化线路遗产，往往跨越不同的文化区域，涉及的相关利益方面复杂，可能遇到多文化区域的文化认同冲突及文化抵触，经济利益矛盾，合作过程中的责权矛盾等问题。需要考虑建立对矛盾与冲突的调解管理机制的必要性，来促进其遗产的有效管理。

（1）应在确立遗产项目时对各种可能的矛盾进行充分的预估和评价，分析其形成原因和威胁后果；

（2）通过在保护管理机构的组织建立中纳入必要的利益相关者，并借助宣传、教育和沟通，在协作群体中建立对遗产地价值和保护目标的统一认识，并在保护管理的工作执行中时刻保持这种统一认识；

（3）通过立法、规划、制度颁布等为预估的可能发生的矛盾冲突提供必要的解决依据；

（4）在涉及文化线路的任何保护管理工作中，特别是在涉及有文化和发展差异区域的合作事务上，各方应贯彻相互尊重、理解的基本原则。

四、结论

最后，报告对中国文化线路资源的现状和申报世界遗产面临的形势进行了分析，并总结概括前面章节的研究分析结论，对中国文化线路申报世界遗产提出总体的策略建议。

4.1　中国文化线路资源申报世界遗产总体形势

我国的文化线路资源面对当前世界遗产的申报要求，既有优势，也有劣势。优势在于已发现的资源较丰富、类型多样。中国作为多民族国家，地域广阔，区域环境差异大，文化线路资源潜力较大。文化线路跨文化的整体意义也比较突出，很多文化线路联系到其他国家和地区。劣势在于我国的相关基础研究总体上较为薄弱。一方面，基础性研究尚未建立完善；另一方面，针对具体线路的相关研究，也大都处于起步阶段，一时难以形成完善的研究成果。对大部分文化线路来说，全线相关遗产资源的调查和记录工作都存在巨大的空缺。文化线路的保存状况不够理想，目前的遗产保护管理系统对文化线路的保障不足。此外，国内对文化线路概念的认知理解尚不深入，申报策略和技术体系发展不成熟。

面对日渐引起重视的世界遗产文化线路类型项目申报，我国同样面临机遇和挑战。一方面，有部分文化线路具有极高的世界知名度、认可度和关注度，如丝绸之路是这方面的典型代表。而文化线路是世界遗产名录中亟待充实的类型。在我国和周边很多国家尚没有，或仅有很少的同类世界遗产。此外，国家强有力的行政力度，可能对文化线路的保护和申报提供特殊的支持。

另一方面，国际上大量的文化线路资源正准备申报世界遗产，可能有较多的竞争对手，对我国申报世界遗产形成了挑战。加上国际遗产保护领域对中国文化的了解仍有很多局限，中国对外交往关系的复杂变化，也可能从其他方面影响跨国文化线路的申报进程。中国已有的世界遗产数量，和近年来持续的快速增长，可能导致对中国申报项目的评估更加严格，增大申报的难度。国内经济发展的压力也有可能对因为不合理的开发与利用为遗产资源带来破坏，构成对文化线路保护和申报的威胁。

4.2　资源保护与申报策略建议

为保障我国文化线路遗产资源，发挥其遗产价值，促成有优势的项目成功申报世界遗产，课题提出以下总体策略建议。

加强基础研究

首先应从基础研究做起，组织对文化线路遗产资源的发现、评估、认定以及保护有支持作用的相关学科研究，并强调学科间的沟通与互动。在宏观层面，基础研究应为文化线路遗产资源，以及国内各类文化遗产资源的梳理和评估建立起清晰、详细的年代、地域框架和系统的文化主题框架，并对中国文化线路的遗产资源进行总体的发掘与整理。在具体项目层面，基础研究工作应落实到对文化线路历史文化背景的清晰梳理，线路准确的时空分布，完整的现存遗产要素清单，和各要素完整的档案记录等方面，为线路遗产价值的挖掘与论述，保护策略和措施的制定提供准确的依据。

这方面的具体措施应包括：成立各级学术研究机构，组建学术资源网络（包括现有研究成果的汇总和研究力量的汇集），设立相关学术研究课题，积累和发布研究成果等。

促进社会认知

加强对文化线路概念理论的推广，并关注三个层面对文化线路价值与意义的认知。一是使专业人员正确理解，科学把握文化线路的概念和保护管理方面的原则与技术要点；二是使社会公众对文化线路有广泛的认知，通过了解逐步理解，进而关注，并形成参与；三是使领导决策部门深入理解其重要性，特别是国家高层的领导决策部门，通过认知和理解，认同文化线路的保护与利用对国家和社会的重大意义。

这方面的具体措施应包括：将研究成果转化为适应各个层面推广的材料，通过出版、新闻、媒体宣传、网络等多种途径向推广对象传递信息。同时应关注推动行动对各个对象形成的影响效果，进而不断调整具体策略。

纳入国家战略

将文化线路遗产资源的保护工作和申报计划与国家大政方针接轨，纳入国家战略体系，获得最高层次的支持，为建立文化线路的保护管理体系，推动相关项目申报世界遗产提供保障。

这方面的具体措施可能包括：与中央相关决策部门联合设立研究专题，探讨文化线路的保护与利用和国家战略的关系，确立重点项目和总体的战略体系，制定相关战略规划，并为每一个文化线路的申报项目明确国家层面的根本动机。

另外，也需要针对跨国文化线路的保护与申报可能带来的对国家与国际的影响进行预先的评估分析，制定相应的预案，以保障对国家主权的维护，或准备有效的策略与措施，应对由于特殊原因对文化线路申报带来的策略转变可能引起的社会反响。

完善保护管理

针对国内重要文化线路资源的保护，设立国家级别的文化线路认定和保护管理体系，逐步形成对文化线路类型遗产有效的、可持续的保护和利用，并使被认定的文化线路资源成为未来申报世界遗产的项目储备，在申报时以良好的保存状态和保护管理水平获得国际认可。

这方面的具体措施包括：制定必要的法律法规，设立文化线路遗产类型的保护身份，成立相关管理机构，设立国家级别文化线路的申报标准和认定程序，建立各级保护管理制度，执行对文化线路保护、管理和利用的监督。更具体的策略建议，可参考第七章的相关内容。

规范申报程序

根据世界遗产申报的要求，充分考虑文化线路的特点，为国内文化线路申报世界遗产制定申报程序，并由官方编制文化线路申报世界遗产操作指南，设立相应的咨询机构，帮助有条件的文化线路以科学的流程，有效的方式开展申报工作。避免因技术缓解的失误给相关的项目带来时间上、物质上、经济上的损失，避免盲目申报给国家、社会、民众带来的负面影响，甚至对遗产本身造成伤害。有关申报程序的建议，可参考第四章和第九章的相关内容。

增进国际合作

加强国际交流合作。一方面应结合国内的基础研究，加强与国外相关学科的合作，为相关的资源梳理和研究提供基础。另一方面，应将国内的相关研究成果，及时的推广给世界遗产的相关权威机构，如补充完善 ICOMOS 各主题框架里中国部分的内容，丰富 CIIC 在文化线路专题研究上的成果，展现中国文化线路资源的丰富性和特点，使其中具有重大意义的文化线路资源获得更多的国际认可。在具体申报项目的推进中，也应重视国际交流与合作，并在交流对象的选择上充分考虑其在文化线路和世界遗产相关领域内的权威性。

引导社会参与

对文化线路这类大型的文化遗产，其保护、管理和利用，必须重视社会公众的积极参与。通过公众参与，一方面使公众成为遗产价值传播和延续的媒介，使文化线路的遗产价值获得更广泛的理解和认知，相关的文化传统得以在代际间得到传承，另一方面使公众成为遗产保护的力量，为文化线路遗产的保护提供更广泛的人力、物力、财力及智力方面的支持。同时，社会的积极参与，特别是参与以文化线路主题意义为线索的相关活动，使文化线路成为社会纽带，起到增进相互理解，促进沟通的作用，这本身，也是发挥文化线路所具有的独特的组织价值的重要手段。具体的策略建议可参考第七章的相关内容。

以上七个方面的策略是相互联系，相互支撑的整体策略体系，每一个策略相关措施的有效执行，效果的充分发挥，能够帮助复杂的文化线路的保护与申报工作在坚实的基础上有效的进行，并得到世界遗产的认可。

（执笔人：魏清，清华大学建筑设计研究院；徐知兰，清华大学建筑学院）

附表：中国文化线路资源概况表

地域规模	命名	遗存现状	保护和研究现状	地理位置	延续时间	结构特点（直线的，环形的、十字形的，合或其它国际网状的或网状的。）	自然环境（陆地、水上、混合或放射物理环境。）	民间（国家）官驿道	（国家）运河	自然水路网络	（国家）古代陆道	草原通道	（国家）近代铁路	（国家）使节交流路线	军事（关、卡）	朝圣	明货漕运	商贸	宗教信仰	技术/科学知识	文学/艺术	音乐/舞蹈/运动	社会跟系系统	语言/口头传统神话
国际/洲际交通路线	建议以地名+主题（命名）：1，包含关系：以整体价值考虑，确定申报遗产范围。例如金牛道遗产VS秦蜀古道，也可分段申遗。2，以遗存状况作第一……																							
丝绸之路 崤函古道等/x大运河		沿线性分布的相关遗存	世界遗产预备名录	河南-陕西-甘肃（其它国家）	西汉-明	方向性网状	陆路				●			●	●				●	●	●			●
中蒙俄茶叶之路 /欧亚商道/x草原丝路		茶叶之路起点处古道、街区、码头遗存清晰，其余不详	茶叶之路起点处申报第七批国保	羊楼洞-汉口-社旗-呼和浩特-恰克图-莫斯科/圣彼得堡	明末至民国	线性	水陆混合	●										●					●
茶马古道 滇藏道、贡茶道、买马道等/x南方丝路		1，部分遗路保存较好；2，沿线分布多处相关设施遗存	部分遗产点已列入国保、大遗址或申报第七批国保	云南、四川、贵州、西藏省	唐代至今	网状	陆路	●		●	●					●		●	●	●			
中日交流线路 鉴真路、商品路/x中国登岸后从山东走陆路进或在江南沿运河运河内地		可移动文物，其他不详	非文保单位	日本-高雄-登州/日本-扬州/日本-明州（宁波）	（主要）唐-明	线性	海洋水路							●				●	●	●	●		
中印交流线路 五尺道、灵关道、博南道/南方陆上丝绸之路、蜀身毒道等/x唐可与海上丝路相连		博南段遗存清晰	其中博南古道段申报第七批国保	成都-西昌-印度或缅甸/成都-腾冲-缅印	（主要）汉-清	方向性网状	山岭陆路				●					●			●		●			
吐蕃尼泊尔交流线路 蕃尼古道、吐蕃尼婆罗道/x唐番古道		考古发掘出大唐使节碑	非文保单位	拉萨-喜马拉雅山-加德满都-印度	公元7世纪-15世纪	跨线不清晰	山岭陆路							●		●			●					
中国与南洋交流线路 /海上丝绸之路、唐广州通海夷道等/x岭南道？and大运河		不详	非文保单位	广州或泉州-真腊-天竺……	（主要）汉-清	线性	海洋水路	●										●	●	●			
南海贸易交流线路之路 陶瓷之路、唐广州通海夷道？/x海上丝绸之路		县石山文化遗址、头礁遗址等沿线各类有文化联系的各类考古遗址	非文保单位	上海-福建-菲律宾群岛-印尼-所罗门群岛-斐济-大溪地	约50000年前开始	线性	海洋水路											●		●			
中韩交流线路 唐入渤海、高丽道等/x中国登岸后从山东走陆路进后江南沿运河运河进内地		沿线分布有相关遗存、寨堡等）以及可移动文物	非文保单位	高丽-胶东半岛-登州/高丽-扬州或泉州	（主要）隋-宋	线性	海洋水路								●				●	●			
中东铁路 /东清铁路、满洲铁路、中东铁路		铁路沿线相关遗存凯建筑精清、部分车站保存完好；沿线村落各具特色鲜明	部分列入国保单位、沿线近代建筑申报第七批国保	以哈尔滨为中心，西至满洲里、东至绥芬河，南至大连	清末至今	线性	陆路						●		●					●				
滇越铁路 ///		米轨铁路、不同国家的铁路工程技施遗存、法式风格的站舍、沿线村寨；独特的自然环境		北段自河口至云南省南昆明、南段自南昆明至越南海防老街	清末至今	线性	陆路						●		●			●				●	

地域规模	命名	包含线路/其它名称/x交叉关系	遗存现状	保护和研究现状	基本情况		运输系统形态					目标和功能			与互动和交流相关的文化主题				
全国性路线	滇越铁路	///	米轨铁路，不同国家的铁路工程设施遗存、法式风格的站舍，沿线村寨、独特的自然环境		北段自河口至云南昆明、南段南至越南海防至老街	线性								●	●		●	●	●
	大运河	通济渠、永济渠、邗沟、江南运河等/隋唐大运河and京杭大运河/x海丝and陆丝	1、交通设施；2、线性分布的相关遗存	第六批国保、世界遗产预备名录	北京-扬州-杭州/长安-洛阳-扬州/杭州-扬州-杭州	（主要为线性）隋-清	水路，局部陆路	●				●	●	●	●	●	●	●	●
	长江水运	川鹽軌道/etc	不详	非文保单位	长江沿线	鱼骨型 先秦-清	水路			●		●	●	●	●	●	●	●	●
	西北走廊（费孝通）	《中国北方草原通道（王三今）、阿尔泰民族走廊（李星星）and陆丝	岩画等遗迹	非文保单位	阴山-河套地区（东经75-120，北纬42-50）	网状 史前-先秦	草原		●		●		●	●	●	●	●	●	●
	藏彝走廊	（纵向）阴平道、松潘道、青藏道、金川道等，（横向）川藏道、滇藏道等/x南方路上丝路、茶马古道	有部分考古发掘出的可移动文物及/其它不详	非文保单位	北起甘肃，南到豫陕晋、洛阳，实际是一条东北-西南向的线条	约始于13世纪	陆路	●						●	●	●		●
	南岭走廊	/壮傣走廊（李星星）/	不详	非文保单位	大致东经104—116°，北纬23—26°之间的	网状（话跃期）唐宋	陆路水路交叉				●	●		●	●	●	●	●	●
	中国南北海上道路	/海洋之路/x大运河and中日韩的海道	有部分考古发掘出的文物/其他不详	非文保单位	沿中国东部的海岸线	线性 先秦-清	海洋水路		●					●	●	●	●	●	●
国内区域性交通路线	秦蜀道	/x秦北边道	1、部分道路遗存；2、线性分布的相关文物（佛教石窟等）	第六批国保	陕西甘肃林兆九原一军事重镇九原	直线型 （部分）清	陆路						●					●	●
	唐蕃古道	/丝绸南路/x潘尼古道	1、古驿道遗存；2、相关设施遗存、城池、其他不详	非文保单位	西安-天水-临洮-临夏-河州北古城-乐都-拉萨	线性 唐-今	陆路			●								●	●
	东向南蜀道（秦陇蜀）	褒斜道/金牛道/褒江水道	1、道路及设施，沿线线性分布的相关遗存	其中剑门蜀道为第六批国保	陕西、四川、甘肃	多方向性网状 战国-今	陆地为主，也有水上				●						●	●	●
	灵渠	/湘桂运河、兴安运河/x潘江Land湘江	1、河道遗存；2、水利设施遗存	第三批国保、世界遗产预备名录	大榕江-湘江门，东向南穿越仙山峡	线性 秦-今	水道	●									●	●	●
	江西入岭南道	/红浦运河、浙闽管江/x海上丝绸	1、古驿道存较好；2、部分古道遗存、其他不详	申报第七批国保	赣江-大庾岭-浈水-北江-广州	水道为主，同陆路	水路为主，同陆路									●	●	●	●
	仙霞古道	/江浦驿道、浙闽管江/x海上丝绸	1、古驿道存较好；2、沿线古建筑遗址等遗存较好	第七批国保	北起江山市大南门、南至福建省浦城县等	线性 唐代-民国	陆路						●				●	●	●
	井径古驿道	///	遗存保存较好的驿道2000米	第六批国保	井径县	线性 明清	陆路											●	●
	川盐古道	秦枝道、褒斜道、三尺道、五尺道、和茅道等/x丝绸	1、分码头、驿站等相关设施遗存	其中川鄂陕农架段申报第七批国保	川东向全国范围内辐射	网状 战国-近代	陆路水路混合											●	●
	古驿道独松关段	///	遗存200余米的卵石驿道以及土群4幢	第六批国保	浙江省安吉县	线性 宋至清	陆路						●					●	●
总计			26				6	8	2	4	5	3	1	7	7	4	6	4	21

Study on the Nomination for Inclusion of Cultural Routes on the World Heritage List

Tsinghua University

Abstract

This paper is an overview of the efforts and results of the *Study on the Application for Inclusion of Cultural Routes on the World Heritage List* , a priority research project launched by the State Administration of Cultural Heritage. By going into the three aspects of, firstly, international theories and practices of cultural route heritages protection; secondly, the applied definition, interpretation, evaluation and verification of such type of heritage; and, thirdly, China's research, protection, management of cultural routes and application with the UNESCO, the paper summarizes and reviews the comments on the process and conclusions of the original study. The research task team's thoughts and suggestions on the protection of heritage cultural routes and China's protection of cultural heritages are expressed as a conclusion.

Key words: Cultural route, world heritage, cultural heritage protection

The term "cultural route", coined in the mid – 1990s, refers to a new category of heritage, good examples of which are Spain and Santiago de Compostela-France's pilgrim's route①, included in the world heritage list in 1995 and 1998 respectively.

The recent years great progress has been seen in China's protection of cultural heritage amidst the emerging of new tendency at the world scale in this aspect, which is demonstrated by China's ongoing application of such heritages of cultural routes as the Silk Road and the Grand Canal for world heritage status. It is now on higher agenda of China. Meanwhile, other cultural routes, such as Sichuan Passage, Delamu, Marine Silk Road, have come into highlight of heritage research and protection. In consequence, related issues, including necessity of the investigation and research, efficient comprehension of protection practices and requirements for such application, especially of legislative and administrative enhancement, add emergency to the study of the verification, assessment and protection. In this context this research project was launched.

The research project was a teamwork headed by Lv Zhou, an architecture professor of Tsinghua University, with members of experts and scholars from Beijing Tsinghua Urban Planning & Design Institute and the International Council on Monuments and Sites China (ICOMOS China) . The project was concluded in October, 2001 with the approval of the State Administration of Cultural Heritage.

The researchers adopted both archival research and case studies. They colleeted, analysed or translated nearly

---

① Pilgrim's Route to Santiago de Compostela

a hundred of academic essays related to Cultural Routes in either Chinese or English, 10 international conference documents, 10 cultural routes included in the World Heritage List, 20 cases in Europe and the US and other materals. In addition, the team also paid field visit to two enlisted routes in Japan and Spain respectively.

Results includes *Study on the Application for Inclusion of Cultural Routes on the World Heritage List* ; *Compilation of Cultural Heritage Routes in the World* ; *Compilation of Cultural Routes in Europe* ; *and Compilation of Works and Paper Materials of International Committee on Cultural Routes (CIIC) under the International Council on Monuments and Sites (ICOMOS)*.

The *Study on the Application for Inclusion of Cultural Routes on the World Heritage List* covers definition, interpretation, concepts, evaluation and verification on the application, fundamental research, protection and management, parallel cases in the world, resources of cultural routes in China, strategies for China in the application, and conclusions. For readers' reference, the studied cases are available in the three compilations as mentioned above.

I. Background, Development and Influence of the Concept

In 1993, the pilgrimage route of Santiago de Compostela in Spain was inscribed on the World Heritage List as the first Cultural Route. After nearly a decade of investigation and development, in 2005, the concept of 'cultural route' formally entered the revised text of *Operational Guidelines for the implementation of the World heritage Convention* as a new category of world heritage, and was soon in 2008 officially justified by the *The ICOMOS Charter on Cultural Routes*, marking the establishment of the concept in the domain of World Heritage conservation.

In fact, study and protection of the cultural heritage routes or similar ones that are long – distance and cross – cultural had been undergoing in various countries or regions. Among them the most prominent efforts are the interdisciplinary study undertaken by the UNESCO, the European Cultural Route and the National Park Heritage Corridor in the United States since 1960s.

1.1   Background

As an international organization integrating natural and social sciences, culture, education and interchange①, the UNESCO, since 1960s, launched research and development of the routes from an interdisciplinary perspective, involving South America, Eurasia and Africa.

Examples are the 1996 "Andean Route"② of regional cultural tourism (Colombia, Ecuador and Peru), the 1972 restoration of "Historic Route" in Ethiopia, the 1973 restoration of Jesuit Route (Argentina, Brazil, Paraguay and Uruguay), the 1994 African "Slave Route" and the "Research on the Silk Road" from 1988 to 1997. All the above projects are trans – boundary or even trans – continent, with their focuses varied with the comprehension of cultural diversity and cultural policies in different times. For example, the "Andean Route" project, a part of the UNDP Inter – Country Programme for Latin America③, focused on the development of cultural tourism as a means to drive the local economy. In 1970s, the Ethiopian "Historic Route" and the South American "Jesuit Route", both UNDP projects, are the efforts to protect and restore historic sites.

---

① UNESCO. Temporary Agenda Item 5. 10, *Universal Declaration on Cultural Diversity*, 10th anniversary. 36 C/51: 2011

② Andean Route

③ UNDP Inter – Country Programme for Latin America

The African "Slave Route" and the Eurasia "Silk Road" project in the 1980s and 1990s signified the arrival of a time when "cultural diversity" was effectively protected and "cross – cultural dialogues in this pluralistic society" were promoted. Great attention were turned to the "profound philosophical dialogue and exchanges generated out of the everlasting cross – cultural dialogues", as well as the "national migration and cultural and civilization dynamism" from those routes ①.

These "Route" projects have laid a solid foundation for the emergence of the concept of "Cultural Route" in the post – 1990s era and set the tone. Those early projects, some still exert their influence today, such as "Silk Road", "Inca Royal Highway" of "Andean Route"②, are all included in the Tentative List, waiting for the final approval of the application as world cultural heritage routes.

Besides, in precedence, some countries and regions had adopted measures for the protection and management of similar heritages, the most influential of which are the National Heritage Corridors③ and the European Cultural Routes④. These experiences were incorporated into the theoretical system for the protection of international cultural routes.

In 1984, the US Congress passed its first heritage corridor – Illinois and Michigan canal, a milestone in systematic protection of the National Heritage Corridors. In 1987, the European Council, according to its *Resolution on Cultural Routes Protection*, included the pilgrimage route of Santiago de Compostela in Spain into the list of its first European Cultural Itinerary, marking the launch of a grand cultural campaign to protect cultural routes, promote interchange and recognition among different cultures. In 1993, a section of the Spanish pilgrimage route with identical name was inscribed on the world heritage list, a direct force to the international discussion on this category of heritage.

The US and Europe has different impact on the worldwide protection of cultural routes. Europe take cultural routes of same theme as a means to promote regional interchange and maintain social development echoed in 1990s with the UNESCO's ideal of using cultural heritage projects to promote dialogue and peace, which accelerated the recognition of this new type of heritage. Meanwhile, the US's more varied and powerful approach in heritage protection serves as valuable references for the management of cultural routes in other countries. With the combined efforts of UNESCO, UNDP, the US and Europe, the concept of cultural heritage routes was born in 1990s finally.

1.2　Process

As the pilgrimage route of Santiago de Compostela in Spain was the first of its kind inscribed on the World Heritage List in 1993, the Spanish government called on a deeper discussion on "cultural routes"⑤. In consequence, ICOMOS opened a meeting of world heritage experts on cultural route in Madrid in 1994, an academic conference on such topic by a professional international organization. The meeting was concluded with an expert report on *Route as Part of our Cultural Heritage*, which instituted the framework for research on cultural routes. Later, ICOMOS and CIIC (ICOMOS International Scientific Committee on Cultural Routes) were established in 1998, followed by a series of conferences to improve the theoretical framework of cultural routes. The discussions and resear-

---

① Federico Mayor, Director – General Of UNESCO. *Preface: Integral Study of the Silk Roads, Roads of Dialogue*. UNESCO. 1997
② Inca Royal highway, also Qhapaq Ñan or Main Andean Road
③ National Heritage Corridors
④ European Cultural Routes
⑤ Cultural Routes

ches fall into two stages.

First stage from 1994 to 2002, the concept was proposed and improved. Ten international conferences were held to discuss from theoretical research to typical cases, which helped to lay out the research framework and methods, as well as to resolve confusion of understanding cultural routes with other heritages.

The second stage started after 2002, this is a period of gradual improvement in theoretical research. CIIC forwarded recommendations to the revision of the *Operational Guidelines*, leading to the inclusion of the cultural routes as a new category of heritage in the revised *Operational Guidelines for the Implementation of the World Heritage Convention* in 2005. The release of the *Cultural Route Charter* by ICOMOS recommended a sound framework for theoretical research.

1.3 Influences

The birth of cultural route concept is a significant event to the protection of world heritage, theoretically and practically.

Practically, since 1993, 30 linear heritages were filed for world heritage status, among which more than ten exhibit all or part of cultural routes characteristics, including those already in the World Heritage List: pilgrimage route of Santiago de Compostela in Spain, Frankincense Trail in Oman, Quebra da de Humahuaca in Argentina, Pilgrimage Routes in the Kii Mountain Range in Japan, Incense Road in Israel, Desert Cities in Negev, Mountain Railways in India. They set examples for application of cultural routes of different characteristics. Besides, data show that in the tentative list, there are 40 heritages likely to be categorized as cultural heritage routes.

At present, every country is working on the approaches and strategies for the individual or collective application for their cultural routes. Many trans – boundary routes, such as the cross – cultural projects since the second half of the 20th century by UNESCO, including the "Silk Road" across Europe and Asia, Inca Royal Highway spanning Argentina, Bolivia, Chile, Colombia, Ecuador and Peru, were objects of research and application. Constructive suggestions were given to settle disputes through cooperation between countries and international conferences held on a regular basis. In addition, those less – known cultural routes such as Roman Road, Golden Route, Slave Route, etc. [1], are attracting more attention. Driven by the application of varied cultural routes, more themes, styles are explored.

International experience in protecting cultural routes can be good lessons to China. The cases in Europe and the US have far reaching influence in their countries and regions, which demonstrate the potential and power of such heritage can have in promoting the country's development. It brazes new trails of thinking and method for the protection, enabling us to protect, sustain resources, while serving the economic benefit of the society and facilitate the exchanges and recognition among different cultures. Given a sound strategic planning and the nature of cultural exchanges, a country's image can be polished and its cultural influence can be extended.

II Definition and Evaluation of Cultural Routes

According to the 2005 *Operational Guidelines for the Implementation of the World Heritage Convention* and the

---

[1] United Nations Educational, Cultural And Scientific Organization (UNESCO): Convention Concerning The Protection Of The World Cultural And Natural Heritage. Report on the Expert Meeting on Routes as a Part of our Cultural Heritage (Madrid, Spain, November 1994), Paris, 1994.

2008 *Charter on Cultural Routes*, and taking into consideration of the enlisted world heritages, definition, characteristics, evaluation and identification of cultural routes were given.

2.1 Evolvement of the Definition

The term "Cultural Routes" was originally defined at the Expert Meeting on "Routes as a Part of Our Cultural Heritage" in Madrid in 1994, when it was mentioned as "Heritage Routes". The meeting report stated:

> *The concept of heritage routes is shown to be a rich and fertile one, offering a privileged framework in which mutual understanding, a plural approach to history and a culture of peace can all operate. It is based on population movement, encounters and dialogue, cultural exchanges and cross – fertilization, taking place both in space and time. The nature of the concept is open, dynamic and evocative, bringing together the conclusions of the global strategic study striving to improve the recognition within Heritage "of the economic, social, symbolic and philosophical dimensions and constant and countless interactions with the natural environment in all its diversity". The concept of cultural routes: is based on the dynamics of movement and the idea of exchanges, with continuity in space and time; refers to a whole, where the route has a worth over and above the sum of the elements making it up and through which it gains it cultural SIGNIFICANCE; highlights exchange and dialogue between countries or between regions; is multi – dimensional, with different aspects developing and adding to its prime purpose which religious, commercial, administrative or otherwise* ①.

The above definition outlined the key factors of cultural routes that were frequently mentioned in subsequent meetings i. e., based on the (population) movement and exchange of materials, Cultural routes are dynamic; they should be studied and protected as a whole. Cultural routes are trans – regional or trans – nationals in certain scale and extent before it can be a dynamic factor of impacting human history and culture.

Besides, the meeting had also made it clear that: *the identification of a heritage route is based on a collection of strength and tangible elements, testimony to the significance of the route itself···These initiatives fall within the scope of a global vision of exchanges, which includes material, cultural and spiritual ones, combining tangible and intangible elements, culture and nature* ② Hence, the combination of intangible and tangible elements in cultural route makes it unique. The accomplishments achieved at the Madrid meeting helped to lay down the framework for later theoretical research on cultural routes.

Since 1994, the term "cultural routes" was officially adopted by ICOMOS – CIIC to replace "heritage routes". Though "heritage routes" was still in use in the *Operational Guidelines*, the definition and contents of cultural routes were further developed, which laid a theoretical foundation for the revision of the *Operational Guidelines* and the formation of the *Charter on Cultural Routes.*

The 1998 San Cristóbal de La Laguna Conference stated that, " protection of cultural itineraries or routes im-

---

① United Nations Educational, Cultural And Scientific Organization (UNESCO): Convention Concerning The Protection Of The World Cultural And Natural Heritage. Report on the Expert Meeting on Routes as a Part of our Cultural Heritage (Madrid, Spain, November 1994), Paris, 1994.

② United Nations Educational, Cultural And Scientific Organization (UNESCO): Convention Concerning The Protection Of The World Cultural And Natural Heritage. Report on the Expert Meeting on Routes as a Part of our Cultural Heritage (Madrid, Spain, November 1994), Paris, 1994.

plicitly includes protection of the regional or local cultures currently existing and integrated into their respective geographic areas". In September 1998, the Tenerife conference highlighted the value of cultural routes and the fundamental role of tangible elements in the identification of cultural routes①. In the May 1999, Ibiza Congress on "Methodology, Definitions and Operative Aspects of Cultural Routes", declared that the intangible elements or assets that rely on tangible elements are key to the comprehensive meaning of cultural routes②. In 2001, the Navarra conference in Spain put forward the "Pamplona Conclusions" in which a further spatial definition of cultural routes was stipulated. ③

At the 2002 Madrid expert meeting, in the tentative *Operational Guidelines* revision, a more accurate and specific definition of cultural routes was decided. ④In 2005, cultural routes, named "heritage routes" were enlisted in the *Operational Guidelines* as a reference category, in parallel with the already existing three categories of cultural landscape, historical towns and centers, and heritage canals.

After extensive discussions and enhancement in a wide variety of academic conferences, in 2008, it was fully described in the *Charter on Cultural Routes*, adopted by the ICOMOS – CIIC, and its definition was finally justified as follows:

> Any route of communication, be it land, water, or some other type, which is physically delimited and is also characterized by having its own specific dynamic and historic functionality to serve a specific and a well – determined purpose, which must fulfill the following conditions:
>
> a) it must arise from and reflect interactive movements of people as well as multi – dimensional, continuous and reciprocal exchanges of goods, ideas, knowledge and values between peoples, countries, regions or continents over significant periods of time;
>
> b) it must have thereby promote a cross – fertilization of the affected cultures in space and time, as reflected both in their tangible and intangible heritage;
>
> c) it must have integrated into a dynamic system the historic relations and cultural properties associated with its existence. ⑤

2.2   Interpretation of the Main Characteristics of Cultural Routes

Defining elements of Cultural Routes including context, tangible and intangible content, cross – cultural significance as a whole, dynamic character, and setting, were confirmed in the *Charter on Cultural Routes*, which serve as criteria in investigation and justification of cultural routes. ⑥

(1) Context

The *Charter on Cultural Routes* interpreted "context" as follows:

---

① ICOMOS – CIIC. Tenerife Work Program, Tenerife, 1998.

② ICOMOS – CIIC. Ibiza Declaration – Congress on Methodology, Definitions and Operative Aspects of Cultural Routes, IBIZA, Spain, May 1999, 1999.

③ ICOMOS – CIIC. Pamplona Conclusions – INTERNATIONAL CONGRESS OF THE ICOMOS CIIC. PAMPLONA, NAVARRA, SPAIN. JUNE, 2001, PAMPLONA, 2001.

④ ICOMOS. MADRID: CONSIDERATIONS AND RECOMMENDATION – ICOMOS 13th General Assembly Meetings of the International Scientific Committees. December, 2002. Madrid, Spain, Madrid, 2002.

⑤ ICOMOS – CIIC Charter on Cultural Routes, Quebec, 2008

⑥ ICOMOS – CIIC Charter on Cultural Routes, Quebec, 2008

Cultural Routes occur in a natural and /or cultural context upon which they exert an influence and which they help to characterize and enrich with new dimensions as part of an interactive process.

Hereby, the context can be understood in a more macro way, involving the natural and geographic setting, cultural and social background, as the results of cultural routes existence.

Thus, in studying a cultural route, priority shall be given to what cultural and historical factors give birth the route and in what natural geographical setting the route exists. The elements of cultural routes, such as its innovation or design, cultural sites along the route, customs, social nature, are all the outcome of natural factors. The diversified interaction between the natural landscape and people gives rise to many prominent cultural landscape, which are conducive to our comprehension of the impacts imposed by dynamic exchanges on the route, the interaction between human and nature, and the unique evolution of human society. They offer background information on the protection of existing traditional cultures and the disappeared civilizations in human history.

As "context" is the paramount factor in defining cultural routes, we come to the conclusion that its concept is of greater value than tangible heritage, and the whole is greater than the parts. Rather than starting evaluation from heritage site to heritage cluster as before, this type of heritage is approached first by its background, which gives sufficient space and time to accommodate multi – dimensional research into all parts of the route.

(2) Content

"Content" can be understood as the tangible elements that bear witness to its cultural heritage and provide a physical confirmation of its existence, and the intangible elements serves to give sense and meaning to the various elements that make up the whole. Meanwhile, the tangible elements can be further categorized into indispensable elements and substantive elements

Tangible elements includes the indispensable elements, i. e. , the tangible heritage that determines the existence of a Cultural Route, such as the pilgrimage route of Santiago de Compostela of Spain, Pilgrimage Routes in the Kii Mountain Range of Japan, whose indispensable elements are such religious architectures and monuments as church, gravestone and shrine. Tangible elements also involve the substantive tangible heritage related to its functionality as a cultural route, which function equally as the fundamental factors of the routes, such as inns, staging posts along the pilgrimage route of Santiago de Compostela of Spain.

The analysis of tangible elements offered in the *Charter on Cultural Routes* makes possible the application for inclusion of cultural routes on the world heritage list. Based on this, the selection and categorization of the tangible traces ensure that the chosen tangible heritage is typical and its role and influence in the whole routes can be recognized.

Comparing to other cultural heritages, the intangible aspect of cultural routes are given more significance in terms of the intangible and spiritual factors. Specifically, the intangible heritage (non – material heritage) involves characteristics of urban architecture design, architectural techniques and model, architecture styles, custom, political systems and traditions, religions, traditional skills, certain typical crafts, arts and industries, way of dressing, eating, housing and traveling, farming, languages etc.

These intangible elements are important. Not only can they support and embody the integral parts of the route, but also act as testimony to the existence of the already lost or destroyed tangible part so as to reflect the tangible existence of the route as a whole. For example, linguistic features along the routes may accommodate multi – cultural factors as a result of the communication among different cultures brought by the route. Besides, intangible elements can bring back the tangible heritage, such as the restoration of artworks or renovation of architectures with traditional craftsmanship, which means, given that "a particular community's culture is protected and sustained, the material properties may continue to be produced"[1] . So long as its tradition and successor exist, the corresponding tangible heritage and elements can be reproduced or maintained.

Today's Pilgrimage Routes in the Kii Mountain Range of Japan, enlisted as a world heritage site in 2004, is not original in terms of its massive religious architecture. Still, the religious faith and the exquisite architectural arts that have been passed on guarantee the continuity of both its intangible and tangible context, which are key to gaining the recognition of the experts in evaluation.

(3) Cross – Cultural Significance as a Whole

The concept of Cultural Route implies a value as a whole which is greater than the sum of its parts and gives the Route its meaning. The whole value comes from two parts:

On one hand, cultural routes are dynamic, defined by the mutual influence between communication and nation, region and culture. Thus, the tangible parts of the route shall not be approached separately. Meaning of element of the route is rich and inter – dependent. Therefore, a comprehension of the tangible, intangible and natural elements integrated, as is necessary, can enrich and enlarge the implications of cultural routes against the whole context.

On the other, the usage of cultural route, when it was used, brought about the communication of goods and people, and more importantly, on that basis, connected and channeled different regions of the world. For example, the whole network of the Silk Road covered a quarter of the world. This process had exerted influences on each nation of the world in the sense of anthropology, including integration of nations, inter – marriage and genetic improvement. More than that, it had also gone beyond tangible communication to ideological, intellectual, cultural, artistic and religious interaction, which generated universal values.

In practice, protection of cultural routes calls for cooperation and communication among regions, states and nations. Therefore, it serves well as a universally accepted platform on which different regions, nations and states could cooperate, unite, mutually respect and appreciate, and talk in the spirit that the mutual benefit outweigh the individual, which makes its organizational values standing out over other heritages. In this sense, the integrity of cultural routes is an overview of culture and history, and can serve as peace envoy to balance interest among regions and countries. From any perspective, we cannot afford to neglect its comprehensive values.

(4) Dynamic Character

Cultural Routes include a dynamic factor, which differentiate them from other types of heritage. The understanding of a Cultural Route as a set of dynamic elements should not be limited to its cultural traits changed over time and space. Attention shall be given to the driving force and continuation, the two fundamental factors, and related significant traces of the route.

The driving force to the cultural route is the defining element of its dynamic character The force, generated by initial motivation, such as trade, religion dissemination, cultural exchange arising from differences, is the source driving the formation and continuity of the route. Changes in this driving force are the root cause of the ups and downs of the route and, in consequence, define its dynamic character

The factor that maintain its continuity is composed of infrastructure of a particular itinerary, town or city,

---

[1] ICOMOS – CIIC. Pamplona Conclusions – INTERNATIONAL CONGRESS OF THE ICOMOS CIIC. PAMPLONA, NAVARRA, SPAIN. JUNE, 2001, PAMPLONA, 2001.

found a mental military facilities along the route, social factors behind the religious culture, interaction between human and nature, social mechanisms of the areas where the route passes by. It was these factors that fostered the multi – facet of the route in their response to natural and social challenges for the continuation.

The driving force and continuity build up the whole of cultural route, in constant interaction and change. Any alteration of the itinerary and diversity of activities are the result of this dynamic factor, while more dynamic factors melt into the fundamental elements, tangible or intangible, and stay throughout the whole existence of the route.

The Pilgrim's Route to Santiago stretching into both France and Spain has clearly manifested the results caused by the fundamental motivation and mechanism of the route as well as other dynamic elements. The enlisted heritage of Quebrada de Humahuaca in Argentina demonstrates the dynamic and diversified changes caused by the motivational and functional alteration of this commerce passage over the past 10, 000 years, while the Incense Road of the Negev (Israel) with its simple combination of heritage elements, illustrate the motivation of trading frankincense and the dynamic changes brought by competitions among different interest groups to this desert commerce passage. All the above cases are good interpretations of the dynamic elements of cultural routes.

(5) Setting

The setting for cultural routes refers specially to the environmental factors in the space where the route is located. By the standard of spatial dimension, it can be geographical, regional, cultural landscape and environment of heritage elements. Among them, the geographical setting refers to the topology and geological conditions of the area where the heritage is located, which exerts significant influence on the development or change of the route. Regional setting is the natural and human geography, such as the culture of cities and villages along the route, which are helpful in the understanding of heritage values. The cultural landscape is mainly on the linkage between the route and its environment, or the interaction between human and nature, enriching the value of the route in the perspectives of style and cultural diversity. Besides, alongside the routes there are usually some related cultural relics and historic sites that are necessary in the comprehension of the meaning of the route.

The protection and management of the Cultural Routes requires a close attention on its setting. Accordingly, equally emphasis are given to the protection of tangible heritage including geological condition, landform, natural landscape, cities, villages and historic sites, as well as the intangible ones including its history with the human, cultural and traditional elements. The surrounding of a culture route is crucial to determine its protection area and buffer zone in practise.

In reviewing the cultural routes enlisted in the World Heritage List, we can see that more attention has been turned to their setting. In the case of the Pilgrim's Route to Santiago, the pioneering one, heritage was limited to the architectures along the route. Then, in the case of Quebrada de Humahuaca heritage in Argentina, people had turned their attention to its spatial environment and natural elements, of which the cultural meaning was stressed in connection with the value of the heritage site. In this way, definition of heritage is more profound by spatial boundaries.

2.3   Comparison Between Cultural Route and Other Heritages

Cultural route is closely correlated with such other heritages as cultural landscape, canal heritage, the US National Heritage Corridor and European Cultural Itinerary, lineal heritage and corridor heritage.

Cultural landscape and canal heritage are earlier types of heritages, which are fundamentally different from cultural routes in spatial extent, formation of heritage site and whether or not being featured by cultural exchange and dynamic character. The American and European cases are regional and protection – oriented, from which China can draw a lesson in its own management and protection. Lineal heritage it a concept proposed by Chinese scholars of heritage protection who have combined international experience with China's protection of and research on heritage. The concept has not been widely recognized in the international community. A good understanding of the relation between these concepts helps identify and determine the cultural routes, to more precisely position the values, protection and management of cultural route and the nomination strategies.

2. 4   Methods and Process of Evaluation

Evaluation and identification are the vital during preparatory research on the protection, also key to the nomination process. A cultural route is an integration of diverse elements, therefore, comparing to other types, it shows much more complex possibilities in terms of orientation, scale and categorization, selection of elements, which makes the assessment and identification more difficult.

A systematic comprehension of a cultural route can be generalized into the following steps: First, determine its spatial – temporal aspect and the interchange content. The former refers to the temporal start and end of the related activities and the identification of spatial coverage. The later involves trade, religion and military activities. Second, analyze the inter – relationship of the multi – dimensions of the interchange content, telling one from each other the cause and other activities as the results, and identifying the spatial and temporal reach of each of the dimensions. Third, further assess the cross – cultural significance as a whole, or whether the cultural exchanges had generated "reciprocal relation among different regions and cultures" and the influence had exerted on each culture. This is where the core value of cultural route lies. Last, analyze the dynamism of cultural exchange, i. e. , to identify the original driving force giving birth to the route, necessary conditions for these activities along the route and change of conditions over time, oth-

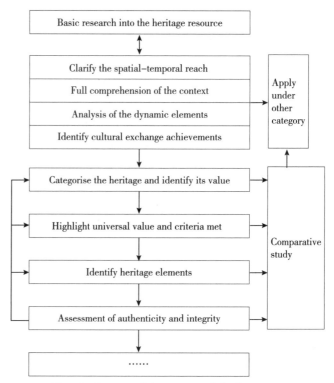

Chart 1   Process of Protection and Application

er cultural exchanges provoked by the original driving force, and the results and implications from the dynamic process.

After getting a general idea, we shall then use comparative study to identify the theme and value of the heritage, adopt applicable criteria in judging the value of world heritage. On this basis, it can be possible to determine elements of the heritage through authentic and integral assessment, and judge whether the elements are accurate and sufficient in expressing the value of the heritage.

In this process, what we have achieved is always subject to modification as the work goes further. Only after repeated analysis of related resources can we be able to acquire a systematic and deep understanding of the nomination.

On the basis of the above analysis, a framework of identifying the heritage as a whole with emphasis on the universal value can be built up (Chart 1) .

Form 1   Framework of Identifying the Heritage as a Whole with Emphasis on Universal Value

Elements of the defining features	Requirements for heritage elements	Relation with outstanding universal values
Purpose and function	clearly reflect the functions of the route	The motivation behind the formation of the route is good testimony to some human cultural tradition, or the motivation was fulfilled in a special way.
Fit the definition of continuous space and time	Extend across in space and time coutinuously. In case of dynamic change in tangible dimension, proofs of such change or the status of change shall be provided.	Spans significant time and space, or at certain stage of cultural development, or crosses certain geographical region.
Cross – cultural significance as a whole	Represented by cultural factors involved in the exchange, and reflect the value of the route as a whole.	Cultural exchange is multi – dimensional, or exerts profound or far – reaching influence.
Initial activities, following activities and their results and influence	Distribution in space and time and their respective features combined to perform as a clue to the development and change of the route.	Express the profound influence of the cultural route, or manifest the significance of the route's function and purpose to civilization by sophisticated historic changes
Mechanism to sustained exchanges	Include remains of typical facilities related to the operation of the mechanism, such as administrative organization, staging posts, gateway, service facilities, or strong evidence to the function (tablet inscription, regular production, traces of human living)	The mechanism itself functions as an integral part of some cultural tradition. The continuity and changes of the mechanism echo to the change of the context, which enable the cultural route to eloquently express significant historic themes.

2.5   Study on the Applicability of World Heritage Evaluation Criteria on Cultural Routes

As cultural route is diversified in combination of heritage, far – reaching in time and space, dynamic in cultural exchange, it is different from other types of heritages in choosing the applicable criteria and interpretation of the criteria. For correlation and applicability of the six criteria on cultural routes, please refer to the analysis in Form 2.

Cultural route is usually nominated in a series. According to the *Operational Guideline*, each of the component heritage sites shall comply with the criteria. Therefore, in the application, attention shall be given to the combination in different dimensions of such facts as activities, heritage type, tangible status, contribution of the heritage site, with priority on the interpretation of its value as a whole, while guarantee that all the chosen heritage sites meet the standards of world heritage in terms of its value. Those that fail to meet the standards shall be adjusted to meet the requirements for nomination.

Form 2   Study on the Applicability of World Heritage Evaluation Criteria on Cultural Routes

Criteria	Analysis on emphasis	Analysis on applicability	Suggestion
(i) Represent a masterpiece of human creative genius	Represent of the artistic and technical innovation of human in the tangible form, among which the genius is creation – maker and the masterpiece can be the best works of an innovative artist or craftsman, or an outstanding achievement of human	The possibility of making all component parts of the route meet standard (i) is very low. Deleting of any part will disable the representation of the multi – dimensional exchange and the value in whole.	It is not advisable to adopt standard (i).

续表

Criteria	Analysis on emphasis	Analysis on applicability	Suggestion
(ii) Exhibit an important interchange of human values, over a span of time or within a cultural area of the world, on development in architecture or technology, monumental arts, town – planning or landscape design	Representation of interchange of human values in artistic and technological development, involving architecture, technology, monumental arts, town – planning or landscape design, the tangible residue of one of which shall meet the standard.	When the interchange, involving the above fields, can represent the features of (a) significant development period (s) in tangible way, and the features, coming from the interaction of different cultures caused by the route, can be demonstrated in its universal value, it is in advantageous position to aim at such standard. It is more likely to meet standard two when the route can be more typical and comprehensive in expressing the process and achievements of the interchange of human values.	Take into consideration the standard.
(iii) Bear a unique or at least exceptional testimony to a cultural tradition or to a civilization which is living or which has disappeared	Testimony to the heritage of a cultural tradition or to a civilization which is living or which has disappeared. The cultural tradition can be in the form of religious ritual, way of living and production. Civilization can be an empire or a state having disappeared in history.	Cultural route can be categorized under dynamic cultural landscape, and relates to cultural interchange. Therefore, standard (iii) is applicable in case of goods trade that can represent the significance of ancient civilization, or religious faith that crossed cultural areas. The stable driving force and maintenance made of the whole, which can be what the "tradition" in the standard means.	Through the route's function, purpose and its correlation with cultural tradition, as well as the cultural areas, span of time and content of the dynamic interchange, judge whether it can reflect the living or disappeared tradition and civilization and consequently whether it comply with standard (iii)
(iv) Be an outstanding example of a type of building, architectural or technological ensemble or landscape which illustrates (a) significant stage (s) in human history	Requirement for expressing typical formation and change of cultural features of the heritage by a type of building or technology.	The routes that are simple in time span or function are more likely to meet the standard. So, heritage components shall be selected by the time they belong to and the style in which they were built. In case of temporal feature, it can be representation of an significant era, such as the pilgrim's route of Santiago. or several eras, such as the route of Quebrada de Humahuaca and the Inca Royal highway.	This standard is applicable when a route embraces large quantity of tangible residues in good shape and different parts of the residue closely related in type and style.
(v) Be an outstanding example of a traditional human settlement, land – use, or sea – use which is representative of a culture (or cultures), or human interaction with the environment, especially when it has become vulnerable under the impact of irreversible changes.	Criteria (v) requires for the representation of the interaction between human and the environment in time span, building or technological means, or in the means of existence of civilization and culture. As human is the challenge – taker and nature is the challenge – maker, heritages meet this standard shall be located in a special natural environment.	When this standard is adopted, not only is the route in a special environment, but the way human confronting the challenges shall be unified. Besides, such interaction shall be clearly reflected in the defined time span. Thus, the interaction as defined by the standard shall be interpreted against the background time of the route. The heritage elements related to the interchange, including landscape, environment, and the relationship of challenger – make – and – taker, are crucial to the dynamic mechanism. Furthermore, other factors such as the surrounding geological condition shall be taken into consideration.	Standard (v) 's requirement on the interaction between human in certain time span and special environment extensively excluded cultural routes that span long time, have grand coverage and involve multi – dimensional exchanges.

Criteria	Analysis on emphasis	Analysis on applicability	Suggestion
(ⅵ) Be directly or tangibly associated with events or living traditions, with ideas, or with beliefs, with artistic and literary works of outstanding universal significance.	Emphasis on direct association with intangible elements including history, culture, emotion, spirit, that have outstanding universal value, which are directly and tangibly linked with the heritage.	Though its diverse content can afford a whole lot of significant historic events, historic figures, living or disappeared tradition, religious faith, ideas, concepts, tales, literary works, artistic activities, it is still necessary to justify its outstanding universal values and provide the related tangible residues as evidence, which pose great challenge to the selection of heritage involving such diversity.	When this standard is applied, the most valued element shall be selected from such diversified mass and the selected shall be directly associated with the heritage and be interpreted extensively.

2.6　Authenticity and Integrity

When a cultural route is nominated as "cultural route", besides the authenticity and integrity of all elements, it is also necessary to state the selection methods and principle for the composing elements, so as to testify that the selected elements can reflect the authenticity and integrity of the nominated cultural route's outstanding universal values. Factors also needed to be made clear are the value relationship among elements, between the elements and the route, and the value contribution of the elements to the whole project.

The authenticity of the correlation between the elements and the routes can be testified by archeological reports, documents, or by intangible relics that can establish the correlation with the routes. Integrity can be verified by the meaning and values of the routes, the composition of elements, the protection of the heritage, as well as the elements that can represent such mentioned characters of the heritage as context, content, cross – cultural meaning as a whole, setting and dynamic character.

2.7　Comparative Analysis

Comparative analysis shall be adopted in the early stage of nomination to determine correlation with other heritage type and clarify the positioning of the heritage in terms of its meaning and values. The research purpose is not to outweight other heritage of same types by comparing the extent to which the heritage is reserved. As cultural heritage, it is endowed with diversity. If we can fully tap its characters and special values, work under the thematic research framework set by consultative agency, properly position its span of time and space, theme and category, we can locate its "outstanding universal values" to avoid indulging in comparing to other similar heritages in terms of the extent to which the they are preserved. According to the *Operational Guidelines*, the requirement for comparative analysis is: *A comparative analysis of the property in relation to similar properties, whether or not on the World Heritage List, both at the national and international levels, shall also be provided; The comparative analysis shall explain the importance of the nominated property in its national and international context.* In case of nomination in a series, comparative analysis shall be done on the selected sites.

The comparative analysis shall be executed in two stages: whole and parts. In the comparative analysis on the whole route, on the basis of the elements contributing to its outstanding universal value, efforts shall be directed into three aspects: among routes of the same cultural theme, such as religion and trade; in the same cultural area with consideration of time span; and within those of the same style, such as railway routes, desert routes, and mountain routes. The prerequisite for comparative analysis is a clear correlation between the nominated route's outstanding universal values and the above research perspectives of cultural theme, cultural area and cultural style, or whether the interpretation of its outstanding universal values is related to these elements. On the basis of which the vital differences to other compared objects are stated, the uniqueness of its outstanding universal values could be testified.

The comparative analysis on the parts of the routes is for the same reason as in the assessment of the authenticity and integrity, which is defined by its multi-dimensional and dynamic interchange. In the analysis, it shall be clearly stated that the composing heritage sites were selected with strict standard and prudent investigation and research. Before the comparison, related site remains shall be listed as complete as possible; then principles for the selection shall be stated and conclusion of each heritage site shall be given. Emphasis shall be given to the irreplaceable role of each heritage site's contribution to the outstanding universal values of the cultural route as a whole. This is to avoid the irrational comparison method of judging solely by one standard such as the preservation of the tangible heritage.

III. Analysis on Heritage Resource Protection of Cultural Route and Nomination Strategies

Based on the above study on the existing theories and practice related to cultural routes, efforts shall be put in the protection of cultural routes in China in three aspects: first, give strategic suggestions to the establishment of protection, managements and practice; second, according to the research results, straighten out the status quo of heritage resources of cultural routes in China, and set the framework; and third, offer suggestions to the overall protection of cultural routes in China and the nomination work.

3.1 Study on the Strategy of the Protection and Management of Cultural Routes and Suggestions

To ensure efficient protection of the heritage resources and prepare for the future nomination, it is necessary to establish a whole protection and management system for the routes.

The requirements stipulated in the *Operational Guidelines* and the successful nominations testify that an efficient protection and management system is an integration of its three aspects, respectively the basis, institution and strategic planning. The basis for management is the related legislative system; the institution is composed of function and regulations; the strategy planning refers to the planning, management and protection of the heritage sites.

Supportive Legislative System

The legislative system as the basis of the management covers four levels: laws and regulations on heritage and cultural relic protection; commonly applicably law and regulation; industry standards and norm; and international conventions and charters. The maturity and inter-coordination of these legislative basis is a cornerstone for the efficient management of all heritages and the success of the nomination.

To establish a supportive legislative system, management regulations on protection of cultural routes in China shall be worked out to differ them for traditional heritage protection and make it clear how to identify, protect and manage the cultural routes. Meanwhile, the heritage type of cultural landscape shall be included into related laws and regulations, to uphold the protection of all its elements and incorporate cultural route into *Law on Protection of Cultural Relics*. As for those cultural routes to be identified as state – level, special regulations and measures shall be put in place. It is advised that the revision of *Principles for the Conservation of Heritage Sites in China* shall be updated with the justification of new types of heritage including cultural routes.

As cultural routes may cross provinces or regions, it is recommended that related legislation and master planning shall be promulgated by the State Council.

As for those transnational routes, efforts shall be made to conduct research on formulation of laws and regulations, sort out applicable laws and regulations, and seek alternatives in updating the existing laws and regulation on the basis of research on related state policies.

Protection and Management System

Considering the significant value and scale, distribution and possible connection with the external environment, it is recommended to identify key projects of heritage routes at state level. Management of the already nationally justified routes shall be enhanced.

It is recommended that the State Administration of Cultural Heritage establish special organization to manage heritage of diverse contents that can guide and coordinate works on the justified cultural routes and implement a direct control over the core resources, and coordinate with other related government departments. It is suggested that involved provinces shall integrate the functions of related departments to establish an administrative committee, working on the execution and allocation of duties of overall protection and management under the special organization at the state level.

In terms of operation, it is recommended to clarify the boundary of management right. In cases involving charity, it can be market – oriented with franchised rights. In supervision, it is suggested to be undertaken by the special organization of the State Administration of Cultural Heritage which may promote public participation and introduce social supervision. In terms of funding, a system should be in place to ensure funding from different sources in a continuous manner under a multi – level management model. In terms of technical support, it is advised that the ICOMOS China establish China CIIC to be responsible for technical support and academic research on the protection of cultural routes as a whole in China, directly under the special organization of the State Administration of Cultural Heritage. Special research institutions shall be launched for each cultural route to provide assistance to the administrative committee. It is recommended that the organizational and professional capacities be one of the criterion for the identification of the route at state level.

Designing and Planning of the Protection and Management

First, it is recommended that the state shall conduct preliminary research, formulate guidelines on protection, assist to improve legislative and administrative system, and finally work out the master strategy.

In each project, it is advised to refer to the American experience in drawing up the plan on the national corridor. Work out guidelines on planning prior to the route being identified at state level as a prerequisite for the nomination to the state; when identified, compile a whole set of master planning on the protection and management, and establish a system to manage and protect the route both as a whole and in parts or even under different themes.

The planning shall strategically center on the heritage's values and embody authenticity and integrity, sustainability, public interest. All stakeholders shall be incorporated. The participants involved in the protection and management whose roles, duties and tasks shall be made clear, and whose interests shall be balanced, so as to ensure coordinated and unified protection and management. When it involves other country or countries, international cooperation is necessary in the planning to avoid disputes over sovereignty.

3. 2　Heritage Resources in China

In this research study, on the basis of academic achievement in such fields as ethnology, history of transportation, water conservancy and water transportation, analysis was made on such features as the natural environment, cultural background and historic foreign exchanges that gave birth to the cultural route. With reference to the categorization of heritages in the world, the methodical framework was offered for categorizing China's cultural routes by shape, temporal – cultural domain, and cultural theme. Under this framework, the enlisted key heritage sites of China (including the past 6 batches and the 7th batch under nomination) will give a general idea about cultural routes resources in China. Judging by the spatial span, cultural routes fall into three types: international or inter – continental routes, national routes, and local routes. The correlation between their themes was also studied. (see appendix – Cultural Routes in China)

The statistics of echoing between each case and its theme reveal such features of the cultural routes as follows:

(1) "Transportation" routes are more evenly distributed, which shows the balance of representativeness. Still there remains great potential for cultural routes of the modern transportation types (railway or road);

(2) "Purpose and function" routes are extraordinarily represented under the theme of business and trade, illustrating the widespread feature of China's cultural routes being used for tangible interchanges, while other themes are evenly distributed. Further analysis on more detailed categorization e. g. , from the perspective of goods category, will be helpful in comparing values and cultural embodiment of different routes;

(3) As there is limited advances in the research on the "interaction and interchanges" of the routes, there is not yet accurate judgment of the echoing between cases and such themes;

(4) According to the acquired information, in most cases, the cultural routes echo multiple cultural themes, which endows the routes with complexity.

3. 3　Selection Criteria and Strategies for Nomination

Under the premise that China has established a nationwide coordinated protection system of cultural routes, the nomination for world heritage asks for the consideration of not only the criteria of outstanding universal values, but also the compliance of the existing heritage sites with the definition and features of cultural routes and its special requirements for protection and management. Any routes possibly identified as cultural routes ought to have its outstanding universal value as cultural heritage, not necessarily in line with the criteria of world heritage however, neither applicable for nomination as cultural routes. Comparison between criteria for cultural routes and for world heritage can set orientation for protection of the heritage resources related to the cultural routes (see Chart 2) . According to the definition and requirements for protection and management of cultural routes, justification for cultural routes can be as generalized as in Table 3.

Given that the nomination meeting the criteria and requirements under the category of cultural route, further analysis shall be made on the heritage elements of the nominated routes to determine the best strategy for nomination.

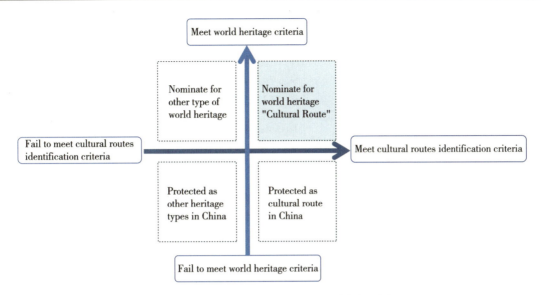

Chart 2 Protection of Heritage Resources of Cultural Routes

Table 3 Identification Criteria for Cultural Routes

Aspects	Elements	Concrete requirements
Heritage identification	Definition of time and space	Clarify start and end times and spatial reach
	Context	State the cultural, geographical and historical context
	Content	List tangible and intangible elements
	Cross – cultural significance as a whole	State the cultural route representing cross – cultural significance as a whole
	Dynamic character	State changes of activities and pattern along the route
	Setting	Identify tangible and spatial elements and their distribution, preservation area and buffer zone with consideration to the heritage content
	Pattern	Clarify the route's pattern on the ground and that of other categories
Management	Integrated management	Ensure the management organization is nonprofit, and that an administrative committee is established, with the participation of all government bodies in regions related to the route and its elements, as well as major interest parties
	Cross – regional cooperation	Reach official agreement among different administrative regions on cooperation
	Planning of protection and management	Work out guidelines for planning of protection and management
	Cultural tourism	List management organization and planning of cultural tourism
	Budget	Provide source of budgetary fund

Aspects	Elements	Concrete requirements
Analysis	Inter – disciplinary analysis network	Sign cooperation agreement on research and study, determine participating research institutions and scholars
	Primary research	Formulate research project and planning, such as content of academic activities, frequency, advancement of project
	Elementary data	Establish database, fix the place where to save
	Budget	Provide source of budgetary fund

Chart 3 illustrates the common composition of a cultural route. The heritage elements, discovered through investigation and research, scattered along the route, are different in the distance to the trunk route, scale, type, and areas they belong to, which divide the cultural area into comparatively independent sections. Each heritage site or element bears the values with its own emphasis and contributes to different extent to the value of the route as a whole. The wider the ranges of the chosen time and space are, the more differentiated the heritage sites are from another. As is required that the incorporated element shall all meet at least one common criterion, the nomination would be less likely to be approved when it involves great coverage of time, space and number of heritage sites.

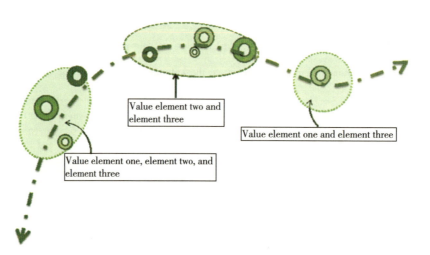

Value element two and element three

Value element one and element three

Value element one, element two, and element three

Chart 3   Composing Model of a Typical Cultural Route

After analysis on other cases and nomination strategies, the research team suggests the following ways of combining heritage components to a whole route for nomination. Ideally, choose all the elements and sections to be nominated as a whole (see Chart 4); or select the typical sections that demonstrate authenticity and integrity to the largest extent (see Chart 5). In this way, as sections may be not unified in development levels, nomination might be done in different batches; or select one heritage element with the most outstanding theme to be nominated (see Chart 6). Each of the above approaches has its own merits and demerits, which asks for prudence and flexibility in making choice.

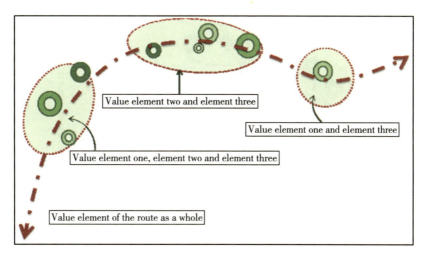

Chart 4   Select All the Sections for Nomination as a Whole

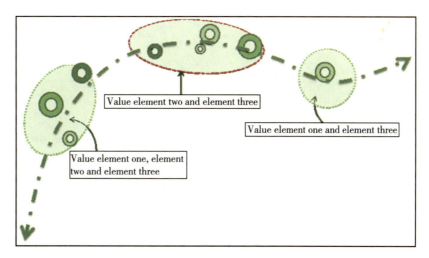

Chart 5   Select the Typical Sections that Demonstrate Authenticity and Integrity to the Largest Extent

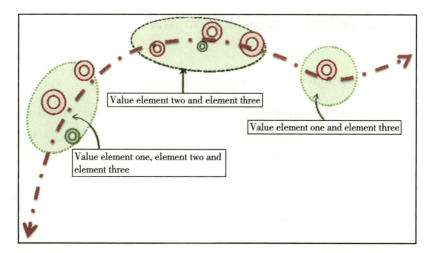

Chart 6   Select one Heritage Element with the most Outstanding Theme to be Nominated

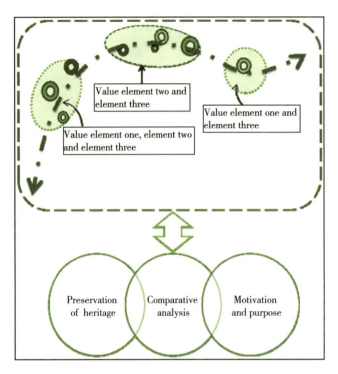

Value element two and element three

Value element one, element two and element three

Value element one and element three

Preservation of heritage

Comparative analysis

Motivation and purpose

Chart 7   Defining Factors to the Decision of Nomination

Any nomination choice requires thorough investigation and study into the heritage site to avoid waste of time and efforts. In the process of decision – making, research results of other comparative heritages shall be taken into consideration, to avoid at the earliest the possible overlapping of nomination of the already listed heritage. Finally, given that the combination of strategies has been mastered, purpose and motivation of the nomination become the key factor, including economic development motivation, expectation of the local people for their life after the approval of the nomination. The purpose and motivation can be stated in written to support the nomination, which is a testimony to the participation by the public, the support and common aspiration of local communities, and that the nomination is a result of prudent and far – sighted decision by the state and local government. (See Chart 7)

3. 4   Strategic and Technical Suggestions to Management and Protection of Cultural Routes

Definition of Boundary and Buffer Zone of Cultural Heritage Routes

According to stipulation of setting in the *Charter on Cultural Routes* , in the definition of heritage boundary, consideration shall be given to both the distribution of all heritage elements, especially the spatial span related to its setting that shall be incorporated into the heritage. Integrity and continuity of the route as a whole are also crucial in considering heritage boundary and buffer zone.

Determined by possible composing model of cultural routes, the definition of heritage boundary and buffer zone may subject to three patterns. One, when the route's main body is clear and well preserved in continuity and may be assembled into a belt along the route, the heritage traces alongside will extend the heritage boundary to include other related traces and environmental elements, as in the case of the pilgrim's route to Santiago. Second, when sections of the routes are submerged in extensive environmental elements to form many cultural landscapes surrounding the section, the heritage boundary and buffer zone might take the shape of an integral region as a whole, as is in the case of Quebradade Humahuaca in Argentina. Third, when the route has disappeared except the remains along, the heritage boundary and buffer zone can be defined one by one according to heritage sites and their background elements. In some cases, when the route is preserved but not in continuity, the definition can be conducive to the realization of continuity of the route by protection and management. As in the example of pilgrim's route of Kii Mountain Range in Japan, when the preserved route is disrupted while the direction of the route is clarified, buffer zone can still be maintained in continuity in the disrupted areas that is within the heritage boundary.

Formulation of Measures on the Protection of Cultural Route Heritage

(1) Formulation of the measures shall be founded on thorough understanding on the features of heritage elements. Aside from the soundness and integrity of the elements, special attention shall be given to the demand for protection of the section that can best represent the correlation between the elements and the route.

(2) In taking measures to counter the damages of the same kind along the route, consideration shall first be given to the location of the object, whether there is any tradition that can act as reference, to give the protection measures the play in continuing the cultural diversity along the route. When there isn't any tradition for reference, protection measures on different targets shall to the best be unified, so that the measures can have positive impact on the representation of the continuity and integrity of the route;

(3) As for the formulation of protection measures for the route as a whole, attentions shall be given not only on the sequence determined by the preservation status and importance of value, but also the balance of coverage of the route in different regions, to ensure the protection of the route as a whole;

(4) The execution of the protection measures shall involve the participation of local people, and efforts shall be made to encourage the cooperation among different regions along the route, so that the social values of the route can be fully explored by the execution of the measures.

Establish Risk Prevention System for Cultural Routes

(1) Because of the wide involvement of cultural route, attention shall be given to elements that may affect the structural integrity and continuity. The protection and administration organizations are in the position to establish a coordinated risk prevention system for cultural routes, and put in place professionals and experts. A multi – channeled and multi – dimensional framework shall be established to set forth standards, research on related disciplines, feedback on the threats and pressure, formulate and execute protection measures. A special effort shall be made to mobilize resources in disaster prevention in ecologically sensitive areas such as forest, water and wetland, and in ancient towns where the heritage is vulnerable.

(2) Negative impact on the route as a whole caused by the imbalance in protection along the route shall be avoided. A sound supervision system of protection and management as well as technical support system among regions shall be established. Meanwhile, a system to test the compatibility of protection technologies shall be also launched. Technologies introduced or to be introduced, especially environmental protection technology, shall be tested thoroughly to safeguard its longterm applicability and the integrity of the cultural route.

(3) In assessment of disasters threats, special attention shall be turned to traditional disaster prevention and countermeasures, from which good lessons can be drawn, so that, in protecting the heritage, culture and cultural inheritance can be demonstrated to the public.

(4) Considering that some of the factors that affecting the integrity and continuity of the cultural routes are still not controllable, such as climate change, the societal development and change, emergency plan shall be made to tackle the aftermath of such threats, so as to make up for the negative impact by other effective means.

Illustration and Interpretation of Cultural Route Heritage

(1) As the value represented by cultural routes and its interpretation are of different themes and contents, a platform for large – scale and multi – dimensional interaction between the public and heritage shall be established. Emphasis of the presentation and interpretation shall be correlated among all the elements of the route, dynamism and integrity, continuity.

(2) The illustration and interpretation are aimed at the inheritance of cultural diversity and function as an effective means to link civilization and guarantee its continuity. Preservation, research, cognition, experience and participation shall be integrated to create virtuous cycle of passing on the values of heritages.

(3) The illustration and interpretation are also in the benefit of interest parties. The subject of creation and inheritance of culture are groups related to the culture's meaning, presentation and geographical location. Thus, attention shall be turned to strengthening the interaction between the heritage and people. Boosting social and economic benefits is an enabler of the cultural inheritance.

(4) Illustration of the cultural route shall focus on its meaning which can be acquired through research on the route against the background of whole history, so that visitors can have a sense of its whole values. Remains and traces of the route and contents extended from the route shall be included in the illustration and interpretation.

Monitoring of Cultural Route Heritage

(1) Monitoring shall target at preservation of heritage elements, threatening factors, effects of intervening measures into the whole or part of the route, and intention and capability of management and protection of different sections of the cultural route.

(2) Monitoring of preservation and tendency shall extend from tangible dimension of composing elements, to what extent elements and the whole route are correlated within or one to another, to preservation and tendency of the still living routes. Such factors as features of heritage elements and regional environment, and coordination correlation of different cultural features shall be taken as significant indicators for monitoring.

(3) In monitoring of the threats, a complete list of threats and impacts shall be made according to risk assessment, especially those factors that have bearing on the route's integrity and continuity.

(4) In monitoring the effects of intervening measures, in the process of periodical monitoring, comprehensive assessment of the effects of most recent intervening measures shall be made. Meanwhile, prompt analysis on the execution and results shall be done, as the basis for eliminating negative impact, of which the written report shall be archived.

Capacity – building in Protection and Management for Cultural Routes

(1) Organizations of systematic and interdisciplinary research shall be established, to provide and update know – how on the protection and management, and undertake exchanges and cooperation with external parties which can be conducive to the capacity – building in protection and management for cultural routes.

(2) Enhance training to staff for the protection and management, with emphasis in areas where it is technically lagging behind, to prevent negative impact to the cultural route as a whole inflicted by the weak links.

（3）Information management system covering the whole route may be established on a trial basis, in which information and skills can be accumulated and passed on to stakeholders.

Reconciliation and Management of Disputes and Conflicts

Cultural routes usually cross different cultural areas, involving complicated relationship among stakeholders, which might giver rise to cultural clash and conflict, economic disputes, and the issue of responsibility and rights. Attention shall be given to establish reconciliation and management system of disputes and conflict, as an efficient way of managing the heritage.

（1）Forecast and assess possible conflicts and disputes during the launch of the project, and analyze the cause and impact;

（2）Engage into administrative organization the necessary stakeholders, by promotion, education and exchange of opinions to reach unified understanding of the values and purpose of heritage protection among partners who shall stick to the understanding in the execution of protection and management;

（3）Provide basis for the settlement of possible conflicts and disputes by working on the legislation, planning and regulations.

（4）In cooperation with culturally economically less – developed areas, follow the principle of mutual respect and understanding.

IV. Conclusion

In conclusion, the report provides analysis on cultural routes in China and nomination for world heritage, summarization of previous research results, and finally strategic suggestions to China's nomination of cultural routes to world heritage list.

4. 1　Overall Situation of China's Nomination of Cultural Routes to World Heritage List.

From the perspective of requirements for world heritage, cultural routes inChina embrace both advantages and disadvantages. Advantages are based on the abundance and diversity of discovered routes. China is home to multiple ethnic groups in a vast territory, the differences among which endow China with a host of potential cultural routes. The cross – cultural significance as a whole is outstanding, as can be seen that many routes extending beyond home territory to other countries. Disadvantages are located at the weak research in general. On the one hand, basic research yet needs to be enhanced, on the other, research on specific route is still in starting stage far from significant achievements. In most cases, survey and recording of heritage resources are still a far cry from being complete. Preservation of the routes is not satisfactory and the protection and administrative system fails to give sufficient support to the security of the routes. Besides, China has yet to deepen its understanding of the concept of cultural routes and improve its nomination strategies and technical support system.

The fact that nomination of cultural routes that has drawn greater attention in the world brings China both challenges and opportunities. On the one hand, some routes have drawn worldwide reputation, recognition and attention, typical example of which is the Silk Road. Against the backdrop that the category of cultural routes in the world heritage list is in urgent need to be enriched. There are few or even no such heritage in China or neighboring countries. Still, the strong administrative support from China government can be specially helpful to the protection and nomination of cultural routes.

On the other, there are many candidate routes in the world, which impose challenge on China's nomination. To make it more challenging, there are limited international understandings of Chinese culture. China's foreign relation is intricate and volatile. In recent years, the world has seen accelerated approval of China's nomination, which might in turn impose stricter assessment on other China's nominated heritages. Irrational development of heritages for economic benefits causes damages to the heritages, a negative impact on the protection and nomination.

4. 2　Strategic Suggestions to Protection and Nomination

To preserve our cultural routes, give play it its values, and promote successful nomination, the research team offers the following suggestions:

Enhance Primary Research

Efforts shall be started by primary research to discover, assess, identify and protect cultural heritage routes, with emphasis on the interdisciplinary interchange and interaction. In general, primary research shall be aimed at establishing cultural theme framework that defines clearly spatial and temporal span for the assortment and assessment of all cultural heritages including cultural routes, as well as the exploring and planning of the cultural routes as a whole. In detail, primary research shall go as far as to the historic and cultural background, accurate temporal and spatial reach, list of living heritages, complete recording of all elements, as a solid foundation of the discovering and description of heritage values and formulation of protection strategies and measures.

Concrete measures may include: establish academic institutions at different levels, set up academic network (covering existing achievements and strength), launch related academic research projects, accumulate experience and announce research results.

Promote Social Awareness

The concept of cultural routes shall be promoted with emphasis on the recognition of its values and significance in three dimensions. First, enable professionals to understand and master the concept and protection and management measures. Second, promote awareness among the public on cultural routes, understanding, attention and finally participation. Third, make efforts to let policy makers, especially the state level regulators, to understand the significance of the protection and use of cultural routes to the country.

Concrete measures shall include: spread research achievement to different levels in a proper way, release the information via a variety of means – publication, news, mass media, internet. Attention shall also be given to the effects of such measures so as to adjust tactics accordingly.

Incorporate Cultural Routes into State Strategies

Protection and nomination shall be put in line with state strategies and policies to gain support from the high level, which is a guarantee for the management and nomination. Concrete measures may include: launch research project in cooperation with state regulators to discuss on the relation between the cultural routes and state strategies; launch key projects and set strategies accordingly; make planning; and identify state motivation behind each nomination.

In addition, assessment and analysis of possible impact at home and abroad brought on by the protection and nomination of trans – boundary routes in advance. Efforts shall be made to map out correspondent emergence plan to safeguard state sovereignty; or put in place effective measures to respond to social reactions rising from change of nomination strategies for special reasons.

Enhance Protection and Management

In protection of priority cultural routes, state – level management system for identification and management shall be established for effective and sustainable protection and exploration of cultural routes as new type of heritage. Maintain the identified routes in good preservation and management for future nomination, which may earn credit for international recognition.

Concrete measures include: work out laws and regulations; institute the new type of heritage; establish administrative organizations; draw up state – level nomination and identification procedures; put in place protection and mechanism at local levels to supervise protection, management and use of cultural routes. For more details, please refer to chapter seven.

Standardize Nomination Procedures

According to requirement for nomination for world heritage and features of cultural routes, efforts shall be made to: set forth nomination procedures for nomination of cultural routes in China as world heritage; compile operational guideline by the government; establish consultation agencies to assist in the nomination of candidate routes in a scientific and effective manner. Great attention shall be taken to avoid, first, technical mistakes that might result in loss of time and money, and second, irrational nomination that might bring negative impact to the state, society and public, or in the worst case significant damage to the heritage. For suggestions on nomination procedures, please refer to chapter four and chapter nine.

Beef up International Cooperation

International cooperation, on the one hand, shall involve primary research in China and international academic cooperation to provide basis for research on related resources. On the other, ask for acknowledgement from international authoritative organizations on the research advances in China, so as to make up and update information of China under ICOMOS framework, enrich CIIC's achievement in cultural routes and demonstrate the abundance and diversity of cultural routes in China. This would be helpful for cultural routes of significant values in China to gain international recognition. In the proceeding of specific cases, emphasis shall be put on international exchanges and cooperation. Consideration shall be given to authoritativeness of the foreign counterpart in the field of heritage especially cultural routes.

Elicit Public Participation

The protection, management and use of cultural routes, a type of profound heritage, shall involve active participation by the public. The public will act as the medium of spreading and continuing the heritage values among the society and between generations. On the other side, the public contributes their effort, intellectual, financial support to the protection of cultural routes. Meanwhile, public participation, especially in cultural route – themed activities, will bring people closer in better understanding and interchange, which is a major means for cultural routes to embody their comprehensive values. See chapter seven for detailed suggestions.

The above – mentioned seven suggestions are inter – connected and interdependent as a whole. Effective application of the suggestions will be conducive to protection and success of nomination.

(Written by Wei Qing, Xu Zhilan)

Appendix : Cultural Routes in China

Category	Item	Silk Road	China–Mongolia–Russia Tea Road	Delamu
Cultural themes	Population movement	●		●
	Language/verbal tradition/myth	●		●
	Social system	●		●
	Music/dancing/sports	●	●	
	Arts/literature	●		
	Technology/science	●		
	Religious faith	●	●	●
Purpose and Function	Business and trade	●		
	Grain transportation by water			
	tribute			
	pilgrimage			
	Military (pass)	●		
	(government) route taken by diplomatic envoys	●		
Type of Transportation System	(government) Modern railway			
	Grassland		●	
	(government) Ancient international land transportation	●	●	●
	maritime			
	Natural River network		●	
	(government) Canal			
	(government) Post station			●
	civil		●	●
Basics	Natural setting (land, water, mix, or others)	land	land and water	land
	Structural features (lineal, circular, cross, radiated in all directions, or network)	Directioned network	lineal	network
	Time span	West Han Dynasty – Ming Dynasty	End of Ming Dynasty to the Republic of China	Since Tang Dynasty
	Geographic location	Henan–Shaanxi–Gansu–/Qinhai–Sinkiang–(foreign counties)–	Yangloudong–Hankou–Sheqi–Hohhot–Moscow/St.Petersburg	Yunnan, Sichuan, Guizhou, Tibet
Preservation & Research		In tentative list	The starting section nominated for the seventh batch under national protection	Some heritage sites have been listed at national level, and large numbers of remains are being nominated for the seventh batch under national protection
Traces		Lineal distribution along the route	Ancient road, street, ferry quay well–reserved at the start of the Road, others not identified	1, partially well–preserved; 2, many traces of facilities along the line
Sections/other name(s)/connection with other routes		Xiaohan Ancient Path/x Grand Canal	/Europe–Asia Trade Route/ x Grassland Silk Road	Yunnan–Tibet Road, Tibute Tea Road, Yunnan–Burma Road, Horse–Buying Road etc// x South All–Land Silk Road
Naming (Suggestion: named after location and theme (1, inclusion relation, identify heritage coverage by its values as a whole, eg., Jinniu Road vs Qin Shu Road; or nominate in sections; 2, select one by the situation of traces))		Silk Road	China–Mongolia–Russia Tea Road	Delamu

International/inter-continental

China–Japan Exchange Route	Silla Road, South Island Road, Grand Sea Road/ x from Shandong or inland rivers to hinterland	Movable heritages; others not identified	Not protected as cultural heritage	Japan–Korea–Dengzhou/Japan–Yanzhou/Japan–Mingzhou(Ningbo)	Mostly from Sui Dynasty to Song Dynasty	lineal	maritime
China–India Exchange Route	Wuchi Path, Lingguan Path, Bonan Path/ South All-LandSilk Road, Shu–India Path etc/ the south end connects with Maritime Silk Road	Bonan sectionwell preserved	Bonan section nominated for the seventh batch under national protection	Chengdu–Xichang–India or Burma/ Chengdu–Tengchong–Burma and India	Mostly from Han Dynasty to Qing Dynasty	Directioned network	Mountainou uslandroad
Tibet–Nepal Exchange Route	/Tibet–Nepal Ancient Path, Tibet–Nipoluo Path/ Tang Tibet Path	Tang Envoy Cupexcavated	Notprotecteda sheritagesite	Lasha–Himalayas–Katmandu–India	7th–15th century	Not clearly identified	Mountainou slandroad
China–Southeast Asia Exchange Route	/Maritime Silk Road, Ceramics Road, Tang Guangzhou to the Sea Path/ Lingnan Road and Grand Canal	Not identified	Not protecte dasheritagesite	Guangzhou or Quanzhou –Siem Reap–India...	Mostly from Han Dynasty to Qing Dynasty	lineal	Maritime route
Austronesian Origin-tracing Route	/// Maritime Silk Road	Tanshishan Cultural Relics, Pingtankejiutou Cultural Relics and others along the route	Not protected asheritagesite	Shanghai–Fujian–Philippines–Indonesia–Solomon Islands–Fiji–Tahiti	Since 50000 years ago	lineal	Maritime waterway
China–ROK Exchange Route	Stretch to Bohai Sea and Korea in Tang Dynasty// land in Shandong and stretch to hinterland by land or waters	Traces scattered along the route (Korea Pavilion, tombs), and moveable cultural relics	Not protecte dasheritage site	Korea–Shandong Peninsula–Dengzhou/ Korea–Yangzhou or Chuzhou	Mostly from Sui Dynasty to Song Dynasty	Lineal	Maritime waterway
Mideast Railway	/DongQin Railway, Dongsheng Railway, Manchu Railway/	Well-preserved Russian and Japanese styles of architectures, some railway stations in	Some heritage sites have been listed at national level, and large	From Haerbin at the center stretch to Manzhouli in the west, Suifenhe in the east, and Dalian in the south	Since the end of Qing Dynasty	lineal	land

Category	Name	Representative routes / components	Material remains / features	Value	Protection status	Spatial range	Period	Spatial form	Type
national	Yunnan–Vietnam Railway	///	Migui Railway, remains of facilities of different countries, French style stations, villages along the line, unique in natural environment	good maintenance, unique in cities developed on the basis of the transportation hub	number of remains are being nominated for the seventh batch under national protection	The north section stretches from Hekou to Kunming of Yunnan, the south section goes from coast of Vietnam to Laojie	Since the end of Qing Dynasty	lineal	land
	Grand Canal	Tongji Dyke, Yongji Dyke, Han River, South China Canal etc/ Sui–Tang Canal and Beijing–Hangzhou Canal/ Maritime Silk Road and Land Silk Road	1 Transportation facilities; 2,tracesinlineal distribution		Included in the sixth batch of national heritage, and the tentative list of world heritage	Beijing–Yangzhou–Hangzhou/ Changan–Luoyang–Bianzhou–Yangzhou–Hangzhou	Mostly from Sui Dynasty to Qing Dynasty	Mostly lineal	Waterway and partially on land
	Yangtze–River Transportation	ChuanGan Shu Way/	unidentified		Not protected asheritagesite	Alongthe YangtzeRiver	Pre–Qin Dynasty–Qing Dynasty	Fishbone–shaped	waterway
	Northwest Corridor (advocated by FeiHsiao–Tung)	/North China Grassland Passage (proposed by Wang Zijing), Altai Ethnic Group Corridor (Li Xingxing)/	Frescoeson stones		Not protected asheritagesite	Ying Mountain–Hetao Area (42'–50' N, 75'–120' E)	Pre–historic time to pre–Qin Dynasty	network	grassland
	Tibet–YiCorridor	(vertical)Yingping Road, Qinhai–Tibet Road, Songpan Road, Jinpan Road etc, (horizontal) Si–chuan–Tibet	Some excavated moveable cultural relics/others not identified		Not protected asheritagesite	Start from Ganshu in the north, to Chayuand and Luoyu in the south, stretching from northeast to	Since about 13thcentury	network	landway

Route	Alias	Remains	Protection	Range	Time	Shape	Type
Nanling Corridor	Passage, Yunnan–Tibet Passage,etc// South All–Land–Silk Road, Dela–mu, etc /Zhuang–Dong Corridor (proposed by Li Xing xing/	Not identified	Not protected as heritage site	southwest	Active in Tang and Song Dynasties	Complicated lineal shape	Maritime and land
China South–north Maritime Passage	/Maritime Passage/ Grand Canal and Maritime Passage between China, Japan and Korea	Some excavated moveable cultural relics	Not protected as heritage site	Along the east coastline of China	Pre–Qin Dynasty to Qing Dynasty	lineal	Maritime
Qin Straight Passage	//Qin NorthPassage	1traceson part of the passage; 2tracesinlineal distribution (BuddistGrottoetc)	Listed in the sixth batch of national heritage	Shaanxi Ganquan Lingguang Palace– Military Pass Jiuyuan	Qin Dynasty–(some) Qing Dynasty	lineal	Landway
Tang/Tibet Ancient Road	//Silk Roadsouth section//Tibet–NepalAncient Path	Traces of post stations, walled cities, cottages and ancient temple in lineal distribution	Not protected as national heritage	Xi'an–Tianshui–Linzhao–Linxia–Minhechaaigoubei Ancient City–Le–dou–Lasha	Since Tang Dynasty	lineal	Landway
Shaanxi–Gansu–SichuanRoute	BaoxiePath/ JinniuPath/ JialingjiangWaterway/etc	1 road and facili–ties; 2 traces in lineal distribution	Jianmenshu Path, a section of the route, is list ed in the sixth batch of national heritage	Shaanxi, Sichuan, Gansu	Since Warring States time	Directioned network	Mostly land–way and par–tially water–way
Ling Dyke	/Xianggui Canal, Xing'an Canal/ Lijiang River and Xiangjiang River	1 traces of water–way; 2 traces of water conservan–cy facilities	Listed in the third batch of na–tional heritage, the tentative list of world heritage	Darong River–Xiangjiang River (Xing'an, Guangxi)	Since Qin Dy–nasty	lineal	waterway
Jiangxi–Dayuling Route	Includes Gan River,	1 traces of an–cient	Meiguan Ancient	Gan River–Dayuli	Qin Dynasty	lineal	Mostly waterw

Name	Other names	Preservation	Heritage status	Location	Period	Form	Type	Count
	Dayuling Path, Gong River, Bei River/ Dayuling Path or Meiling Path/ Maritime Silk Road, Yangtze River	post stations; 2 traces of related facilities, others not identified	Post Path, a section of the route, was listed in the sixth batch of national heritage	Gan River–Dayuling Path–Zhen River–Bei River–Guangzhou	to Qing Dynasty		...ay, partially landway	
Xianxia Ancient Route	/Jiangpu Post Path, Zhejiang–Fujian Official Road/ Maritime Silk Road	1 traces of ancient post path well preserved; 2 traces of ancient architectures well preserved	Nominated for the seventh batch of national heritage	From Jiangshan City Dananmen in the north, end in Fujian Province Pucheng County Guanqian in the south, through Xianxia Mountain Ranges in east–south direction	Tang Dynasty–the Republic of China	lineal	landway	
Jingxing Ancient Post Route	///	2,000m of post path well preserved	Listed in the sixth batch of national heritage	Jingxing County	Ming and Qing Dynasties	lineal	landway	
Sichuan Ancient Salt Route		1 traces on of part of the route; 2 traces of some ferry quays, post stations facilities	Shennongjia Section of Sichuan–Hubei Ancient Salt Path nominated for the seventh batch of national heritage	Across the whole country from East Sichuan	Warring States time to moder times	network	Waterway and landway	
Ancient Post Route Dusongguan Section	///	Traces of 1,200 m pebble post path and 4 ancient bridges	Listed in the sixth batch of national heritage	Anji County of Zhejiang Province	Song Dynasty to Qing Dynasty	lineal	landway	
total	26							

世界文化遗产地可持续发展模式与评估体系研究

北京大学

摘 要

本课题主要以研究中国世界文化遗产为重点，着力从世界文化遗产地可持续发展的总体要求出发，通过分析中国经济、居民消费结构及水平的发展变化，评价中国政府相关政策法规，来证明中国对世界文化遗产保护的供给能力；通过梳理世界文化遗产地保护、经营、管理现状，总结世界文化遗产地的总体年度需求；建立若干评估指标，分析中国世界文化遗产地对遗产所在区域的综合贡献，最终得出中国世界文化遗产地可持续发展模式与评价体系。

关键词：世界文化遗产，需求与供给，可持续发展，模式，评估体系

一、导论

（一）研究对象、背景、意义及目的

1. 研究对象

本课题的研究对象为，截至 2011 年 6 月第 35 届世界遗产委员会会议为止，被列入世界遗产清单的中国的世界文化遗产、文化和自然双重遗产，共 33 处。根据文化遗产的本体特性及形式的不同，中国世界文化遗产可以分为古文化遗址、古建筑群、园林、古墓葬、石窟寺、历史文化名城村镇、山岳等七大类别，主要分布在黄河及长江流域的中下游人口分布密集地区。

2. 研究背景

中国的世界文化遗产目前分布在 21 个省市，将来还会更多分布更广泛，中国将成为保护世界级文化遗产最多的国家。这种态势说明世界文化遗产的总体保护应该成为国家的战略责任。而此课题对"世界文化遗产地可持续发展模式及评估体系"的研究，将对这种态势的可持续发展机制做出分析和对策。

3. 课题研究的意义与作用

（1）从政府（国家文物局）角度：通过对遗产地运营、管理及模式的分析，设置评估指标体系，提炼中国世界文化遗产经营模式，将为政府制定可持续政策、编制发展规划、确定资金额度、监测和把握发展方向提供科学依据。

（2）从遗产所在区域的主管机构角度：分析发展环境、研究持续发展模式、探讨文化遗产地对当地经济社会的促进作用等，对于促进区域经济社会文化的协调发展具有现实的指导作用。

（3）从文化遗产地管理运营机构的角度：分析遗产地运营机构的保护措施，明确遗产保护方向和开发运营的关键点，选择最佳运营模式，建立持续保护和利用的机制，对于运营机构承担保护责任具有现实意义。

（4）从世界文化遗产研究者角度：将为遗产地研究提供发展模式和指标体系方面的成果，并可利用经济与管理方面的指标体系作为平台，做进一步的监测和发展模式研究。

4. 本课题研究解决的主要问题

采取什么样的办法和机制，能够在保证世界遗产价值有效保护的前提下，使世界文化遗产地持续发展、永续保存。

（二）研究概念界定

1. 世界文化遗产的概念

世界文化遗产是与当代社会发展、社会价值和社会需求相关的过程的产物，在联合国《保护世界文化和自然遗产公约》中被定义为以下几点：

（1）文物：从历史、艺术或科学角度看具有突出的普遍价值的建筑物、碑雕和碑画、具有考古性质成分或结构、铭文、窟洞以及联合体；

（2）建筑群：从历史、艺术或科学角度看在建筑式样、分布均匀或与环境景色结合方面具有突出的普遍价值的单立或连接的建筑群；

（3）遗址：从历史、审美、人种学或人类学角度看具有突出的普遍价值的人类工程或自然与人联合工程以及考古地址等地方。（联合国教育、科学及文化组织，1972 年）

世界文化遗产地是指世界文化遗产赖以生存的物质空间载体，本课题在研究中参考了世界文化遗产申报文本中划定的保护区范围，主要包括核心区和缓冲区。

2. 可持续发展的概念

世界环境与发展委员会对可持续发展的定义为："既满足当代人的需求，又不损害子孙后代满足其需求能力的发展"（WCED，1987）。该可持续发展体现了以下原则：

（1）公平性原则：公平性原则包括代内公平、代际公平和公平分配有限资源；

（2）持续性原则：持续性原则表示人类的经济和社会发展不能超越资源和环境的承载能力；

（3）共同性原则：共同性原则是指由于地球的整体性和相互依存性，某个国家不可能独立实现其本国的可持续发展，可持续发展是全球发展的总目标。

可持续发展的核心是发展，即要做到经济、社会、环境的共同发展，但发展不是无所节制的，而是有条件的，即要做到发展方式的可持续性。

世界文化遗产作为人类的共同财富，其发展需要强调"代际均等性"，即后代有权利享受与当代同样的真实完整的遗产，因此当代就有责任完好地把遗产保存下去。对于当代人来说，上至国家及相关管理部门，下至地方政府，在保护好这些珍贵的遗产资源的同时，必须协调好遗产地的保护与开发，以及与涉及遗产地各方利益之间的关系，不得以牺牲一方权利（尤其是遗产地居民的利益）换取一方或多方的效益，违背"代内均等性"原则。

（三）研究思路及方法

1. 技术路线

本课题研究，首先进行界定问题，在此基础上搜集相关的文献资料，设定研究思路和研究大纲，通过深入研究得出世界文化遗产可持续发展的评估体系及模式总结。然后，通过实地调研及案例验证分析，组织相关专家对该体系进行论证，最终得出可操作、实用的评估体系，完成研究。

2. 研究方法

根据课题基本要求，本报告采取宏观与微观相结合、典型调查与综合论证相结合、国内实证与国际对比相结合、定性与定量相结合的方法进行研究。获取数据并进行分析的方式主要是通过实地调研与评估、监测系统来进行。调研的对象主要由遗产属地主管领导、遗产保护管理机构负责人、游客、当地居民、研究机构人员等。

（四）主要创新点

1. 新的分析框架

本课题研究从世界文化遗产可持续发展的总体要求出发，通过调研、考察遗产地的保护、发展现状，结合中国国情和地方特点，总结出了有针对性的遗产地可持续发展需求和特征，涵盖资源、管理、人才、资金以及基础设施能力等，建立了完整的系统分析框架和模型，对世界文化遗产的保护和开发提供理论分析基础。

2. 使用新的监测数据

本课题研究吸纳了已有的关于中国世界文化遗产监测研究和实践的成果，充分利用先进的技术手段对遗产地及所在区域相关数据进行定性、定量分析，这将是在此类分析上首次使用第一手数据成果来完善课题的数据分析基础，为课题研究搭建了坚实的信息和专业基础。

3. 采用创新的评估指标体系

本课题在遗产地模型和数据分析成果的基础上，就遗产地可持续发展的来源、基量、投入比例、增长幅度、连续性、综合成效等方面设计了较为完备的综合指标体系，既满足了世界文化遗产保护和发展的要求，又体现了中国社会、经济、文化的特殊发展需求以及各级经营、管理组织的工作需要，具有较强的创新性和实用性。

（五）整体课题结构描述

本课题将针对世界文化遗产地经营、管理及与政府的关系，遗产地对遗产所在区域经济拉动作用及贡献，文化遗产地及其所在区域两者的互动关系对文化遗产保护的影响等三个主要方面，通过分析中国经济的飞速增长、居民消费的增长及消费结构的变化来证明中国对世界遗产保护的供给能力，以及对国家出台的相关政策的评价。通过对于中国遗产地管理、经营、开发等状况的分析，总结世界遗产地的总体年度需求。最终得出中国世界文化遗产地可持续发展模式与评价体系。

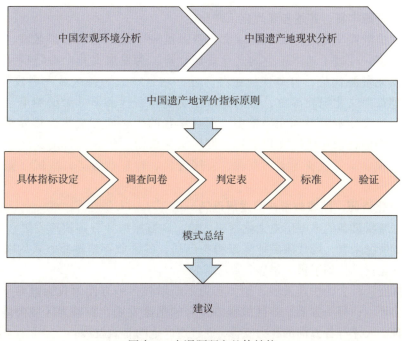

图表1 本课题研究整体结构

二、中国世界文化遗产地所在区域可持续发展环境

（一）中国世界文化遗产地所在区域经济发展状况分析

"十一五"期间，我国经济和社会发展取得巨大成就。国内生产总值达到397983亿元，扣除价格因素，比2005年增长69.9%，年均实际增长11.2%，远高于同期世界经济年均增速，成为仅次于美国的世界第二大经济体。经过课题组统计分析，中国世界文化遗产所在区域的27个地区（含县级市）经济发展迅速，其中25个地区的GDP年增速高于全国平均水平，占遗产地所在区域的92.59%。为区域世界文化遗产的保护与发展营造了良好的经济环境。同时，各个遗产所在区域财政一般性预算收入在逐年增长，说明各区域政府有足够能力从根本上满足区域世界文化遗产保护发展的客观需求。

另外，从我国世界文化遗产所在区域的经济发展结构来看，有12个地区（占44.44%）工业产业发达，传统支柱性产业能够为区域遗产发展提供有效的经济供给；有11个地区，（占40.74%）三大产业呈均衡状态发展，不仅工业基础较好，而且服务业也相对发达，形成良性循环；4个地区（占14.81）第三产业服务业发展较为突出，区域遗产的发展具备良好的产业服务环境。这说明中国世界文化遗产地所在区域的产业结构趋于优化，能够为遗产的可持续发展提供均衡的条件。

（二）中国世界文化遗产地所在区域消费能力分析

根据图表3显示，中国世界文化遗产所在区域消费能力呈现两种趋势。一种是遗产地处在省市一级城市，其城镇化率相对较高，区域消费能力较强，能够有效地供给遗产的可持续发展，也从一定程度上说明地区经济社会发展对于世界遗产的"依赖性"较弱；另一种是遗产地处在三线及三线以下城市，其城镇化率大部分偏低，区域消费能力相对有限，世界文化遗产吸引力对于区域经济社会发展的贡献作用较大，对地方经济社会发展的带动效力显著。

（三）中国世界文化遗产地所在区域文化资源与旅游产业分析

1. 区域传统文化资源丰富，并逐步现代化、产业化

从总体上看，我国世界文化遗产所在区域文化资源蕴藏丰富，各种古都名城、园林、不可移动文物、博物馆等内容丰富，成就了地方特色的文化资源优势，为发展文化产业特别是旅游产业提供了天然土壤。依托传统文化资源优势，打造现代旅游产业，越来越成为各区域发展现代文化的共同举措。以西安为例，历史悠久而文化积淀厚重，但又是一座历史与现代和谐共融的城市。在现代文化产业发展中，西安不仅使历史文化资源得到充分挖掘，而且年轻的生态旅游文化也是异军突起，观光旅游文化异军突起。以重庆为例，依托巴渝文化资源，发展文化旅游；依托浓郁的民间歌舞文化资源，发展演出业；依托民间传说、文学故事等文化资源，发展音像、影视业等等，重庆已完全将丰富的传统文化现代化、产业化。

2. 依托丰厚的文化资源，区域旅游产业发展迅速

依托遗产所在区域所具备的丰厚历史文化资源优势，区域旅游业普遍快速发展。从2011年遗产所在区域旅游产业发展的情况来看，现代旅游业发展势头迅猛，各区域年旅游总收入均以10%以上的速度迅速增长，区域旅游文化资源得到了极大彰显。

综上所述，中国经济社会的快速发展，整体实力不断增强，一方面为我国世界文化遗产可持续营造了良好的经济、社会环境；另一方面，各区域经济社会的迅速发展，能够为区域内世界文化遗产的健康发展提供资金、管理、人才等各方面的有力支撑，促进遗产地的有效发展。

图表2　"十一五"期间中国世界文化遗产地所在区域经济、社会及环境发展情况

"十一五"期间

序号	遗产地名称	城市名称	经济发展						社会民生				资源环境	
			区域生产总值		区域财政一般预算收入		期末社会消费品零售总额（亿元）	三大产业结构	城镇及农村居民收入情况				森林覆盖率（%）	城市绿地率（%）/人均面积（m²）
			期末总值（亿元）	年增速（%）	期末收入（亿元）	年增速（%）			城镇可支配收入（元）	年增速（%）	农村纯收入（元）	年增速（%）		
1	周口店遗址													
2	颐和园													
3	天坛	北京	13777.9	11.4	2353.9		4470	0.9:24.1:75	29073	9.2	13262	9	37	45
4	明清皇宫（北京故宫）													
5	长城（以北京段为主）													
6	明清皇家陵寝（北京十三陵）													
7	秦始皇陵及兵马俑坑	西安	3241.49	14.5	241.8	27	1611	4.3:43.5:52.2	22244	17.3	7750	23.5	45	31.97
8	大足石刻	重庆	7800	14.9	1018.39	30	2880.1	8.7:55.2:36.1	17532	11.3	5200	13.1	37	39.80/11.69 m²
9	西湖	杭州	5945.82	12.4	671.34	21.8	2146.08	3.5:47.8:48.7	30035	12.6	13186	11.5	64.56	
10	苏州古典园林	苏州	9168.9	13.9	900.55	20.9		1.7:57.7:40.6	29219	12.4	14657	11.8	23.5	
11	河南登封天地之中历史建筑群	郑州	4000	13	386.8	28.1	1678	3.1:56.7:40.2	18897	10.4	9225	13.6	25.68	10.5 m²
12	龙门石窟	洛阳	2321.2	14.6	142	18.1	808.8	8.1:60.1:31.8	17639		5680		45	
13	曲阜孔府、孔庙、孔林	曲阜	235.29	13.4	10.77	13.1	92.23	10.3:40.5:49.2	14011		7402			24.2
14	布达拉宫（大昭寺、罗布林卡）	拉萨	182	16	15	36	88.8	4.9:30.3:64.8	16323	11.61	5000	15.79	18.3	
15	开平碉楼与古村落	江门	1570.42	13	104.29	24	655.86	7.5:55.5:37	21153	10.4	8589	9.98		11 m²
16	庐山	九江	1032	13.7	116.7	24	284.1	9.5:56.2:34.3	15764	12.6	5588	11.3	54.7	
17	泰山	泰安	2000	14.5	116.9	23.5	687.4	9.5:53.5:37	19800	13.9	7592	13	36.9	

续表

序号	遗产地名称	城市名称	经济发展						社会民生				资源环境	
			区域生产总值		区域财政一般预算收入		期末社会消费品零售总额（亿元）	三大产业结构	城镇及农村居民收入情况				森林覆盖率（%）	城市绿地率（%）/人均面积（㎡）
			期末总值（亿元）	年增速（%）	期末收入（亿元）	年增速（%）			城镇可支配收入（元）	年增速（%）	农村纯收入（元）	年增速（%）		
18	承德避暑山庄及周围寺庙	承德	880.5	14	54.84			15.8:51.0:33.2	13212	12.2	4382	11.2	55.8	42.6
19	云冈石窟	大同	694.3	10	2.0615	8.1	303.02	5.1:48.8:46.1	16103		4063		20.11	37.46/7.72 ㎡
20	安阳殷墟	安阳	1311.3	14.3	65	17.5	345.3	12.1:61.7:26.2	16394	13.2	6359	14.6	29.1	
21	敦煌莫高窟	酒泉	405	14.6	16.68	30.9	87.6	13.4:51.9:34.7	5852	10	2715	10	30.24	10.3 ㎡
22	武当山古建筑群	十堰	630	12.5	30	21	375	12.1:46.2:41.7	12400	12.1	3400	11.3	53	
23	丽江古城	丽江	143.59	13.6	16.46	32.3	45.5	18.1:38.3:43.6	15521	8.6	3410	13.3	66.2	
24	平遥古城	晋中	636.8	12	64.8	27.5		8.5:54.9:36.6	14628		5194		37.98	9.84 ㎡
25	五台山	忻州	435.4	13.2	42.34	26.2	169.8	10.8:44.8:44.4	13683	14.3	3445.7	12.3	14.3	
26	皖南古村落（西递宏村为代表）	黄山												
27	黄山	黄山	309.3	11.8	43.3	28.5	126	12.7:44.1:43.2	15834	13.2	6710	16.3	77.4	
28	都江堰—青城山	都江堰	143.5	11.3	55.6	40.8		12.1:34.7:53.2	14000				57.23	
29	高句丽王城、王陵及贵族墓葬	集安	72	28.2	5.3	29.4	22	8.7:52.8:38.5			6095	14	78.3	
30	福建土楼	龙岩	991.5	14.6	66.75	22.8		13:53.3:33.7		11.7		10.9	77.9	
31	武夷山	南平	728.73	13.3	38.58	20.7	254.08	21.9:41.9:36.2	17332	11.9	6759	10.7	75.7	93.1
32	峨眉山—乐山	乐山	743.92	15.2	45.77	27.8		13.4:59.5:27.1	15237	15.2	5613	11.6	54.4	9.3 ㎡
33	澳门历史城区	澳门特区	1870.04				437.71		305621.5					

注：本表中涉及跨区域世界文化遗产"明清皇宫"、"长城""明清皇家陵寝"均以北京为主；另外，澳门特区GDP统计按照2010年底的汇率82.65进行折算。

图表3 "十一五"期间中国世界文化遗产地所在区域人口规模及消费情况

序号	遗产地名称	所在区域	人口因素					消费指数			
			常住人口（万人）	城镇人口		农村人口		城镇人均消费支出		农村人均消费支出	
				数量（万人）	占比（%）	数量（万人）	占比（%）	支出（元）	同比增长（%）	支出（元）	同比增长（%）
1	周口店遗址	北京	1961.2	1685.9	86	275.3	14	21984	10.3	11078	
2	颐和园										
3	天坛										
4	明清皇宫（北京故宫）										
5	长城（以北京段为主）										
6	明清皇家陵寝（北京十三陵）										
7	秦始皇陵及兵马俑坑	西安	851.34	596.79	70.1	254.55	29.9			6705	19
8	大足石刻	重庆	2919	1605.96	55.02	1313.04	44.98	14974.49	12.3	4502.06	24.2
9	西湖	杭州	870.04	637.27	73.25	232.77	26.75	18，595	11.2	14995	20.7
10	苏州古典园林	苏州	1046.6					21046	17.7		
11	河南登封天地之中历史建筑群	郑州	862.65	551	63.87	311.65	36.13	14605.48	16		
12	龙门石窟	洛阳	654.95					13884	1815 元		
13	曲阜孔府、孔庙、孔林	曲阜	64.05								
14	布达拉宫（大昭寺、罗布林卡）	拉萨	55.94					14500	5.8		
15	开平碉楼与古村落	江门	446.55	280.43	62.8	166.12	37.2	15561	15.5		
16	庐山	九江	472.88	201.05	42.52	271.83	57.48	10823	15.5		
17	泰山	秦安	551.4	283.5	51.41	267.9	48.59	14888	10.9	4855	13.6
18	承德避暑山庄及周围寺庙	承德	347.32					10902.6	14.9	4984	35.7
19	云冈石窟	大同	333.97	188.66	56.49	145.31	43.51	12243	20.7	3740	51.3

续表

序号	遗产地名称	所在区域	人口因素					消费指数			
			常住人口（万人）	城镇人口 数量（万人）	占比（%）	农村人口 数量（万人）	占比（%）	城镇人均消费支出 支出（元）	同比增长（%）	农村人均消费支出 支出（元）	同比增长（%）
20	安阳殷墟	安阳	515	208.52	40.49	306.48	59.51	11863	12.4	4304	15.5
21	敦煌莫高窟	酒泉	110.07	56.23	51.09	53.84	48.91	14238	17.3	6462.48	14.04
22	武当山古建筑群	十堰	334.08	136.97	41	197.12	59	3674.2	17.8		
23	丽江古城	丽江	124.48					5056	8.9		
24	平遥古城	晋中	327	149.57	45.74	177.43	54.26	11207	10.9	5351.8	40.8
25	五台山	忻州	308.5	122.8	39.8	185.7	60.2	9064.9	1.8	3793	24.72
26	皖南古村落（西递宏村为代表）	黄山									
27	黄山		148.05	36.38	24.57	111.67	75.43	11069	0.6	4163	2.9
28	都江堰—青城山	都江堰	60.95	17.27	28.33	43.68	71.67	9715	18.6		
29	高句丽王城、王陵及贵族墓葬	集安	23.24	10.92	47	12.31	53	3844	9.3		
30	福建土楼	龙岩	255.95	115.22	45.02	140.73	54.98	14483	9.2	4815	7.3
31	武夷山	南平	313.9	134.23	50.74	130.32	49.26	11284	9.3	4991	9.3
32	峨眉山—乐山	乐山	323.58	127.73	39.48	195.84	60.52	4394	3.7		
33	澳门历史城区	澳门特区	552，503								

注：本表中涉及跨区域世界文化遗产"明清皇宫"、"长城"、"明清皇家陵寝"均以北京为主；另外，澳门特区GDP统计按照2010年底的汇率82.65进行折算。

我国世界文化遗产所在区域旅游业发展收入增速占比

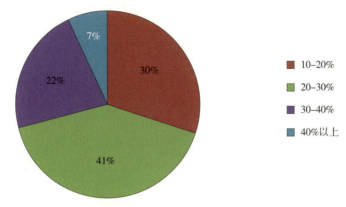

图表4　中国世界文化遗产地所在区域2011年旅游业发展总收入增速占比分析

三、中国世界文化遗产地现状分析

（一）中国世界文化遗产地保护政策

改革开放三十年来，尤其是"十一五"以来，我国文化遗产事业发展取得了阶段性的显著成果。特别是针对世界文化遗产的保护，国家在加大对世界遗产保护与开发经济投入的同时，不断制定与完善保护世界遗产的相关政策法规，从中央到地方的文化遗产体系法规建设方面取得了很大成绩。

"十一五"期间，我国不断加大对世界文化遗产保护管理的法规建设，文物法制建设进程进一步加快，文化遗产保护的各项制度进一步完善。根据《文物保护法》和《世界遗产公约》，国家先后制定颁布了一系列世界文化遗产保护的专项法规、规章和规范性文件，如《长城保护条例》、《历史文化名城名镇名村保护条例》、《世界文化遗产保护管理办法》、《中国世界文化遗产监测巡视管理办法》、《中国世界文化遗产专家咨询管理办法》、《文物进出境审核管理办法》、《文物认定管理暂行办法》等行政法规和部门规章，以及《田野考古工作规程》、《国家考古遗址公园管理办法（试行）》、《文物入境展览管理暂行规定》、《世界文化遗产申报项目审核管理规定》等重要的规范性文件；与此同时，地方各级人大常委会和政府也不断加大对世界文化遗产保护管理的法规建设，结合本地实际制定并修订了一系列保护管理条例或办法，如《江西省三清山风景名胜区管理条例》（2006年）、《郑州市嵩山历史建筑群保护管理条例》（2007年）、《阿坝藏族羌族自治州实施〈阿坝藏族羌族自治州实施四川省世界自然遗产保护条例的条例〉的办法》（2008年）、《杭州西湖文化景观保护管理办法》（2008年）、《福建省"中国丹霞"自然遗产保护办法》（2009年）、《布达拉宫保护管理办法》（2009年修订）等等。再者，与文化遗产事业有着密切联系的《博物馆条例》、《自然遗产保护法》、《非物质文化遗产法》及《旅游法》等也呼之欲出。这些法律、法规和规范性文件使我国文化遗产事业在管理体制、经营机制、监督机制等方面的规则日益完备，使文化遗产事业的管理有法可依，日常工作能更加规范地进行。

（二）中国世界文化遗产地管理体制

1. 中央政府管理

我国加入世界遗产公约以后，对世界遗产资源的管理逐步完善。我国《世界文化遗产保护管理办法》第四条明确规定，"国家文物局主管全国世界文化遗产工作，协调、解决世界文化遗产保护和管理中的重大问题，监督、检查世界文化遗产所在地的世界文化遗产工作。县级以上地方人民政府及其文物主管部门依照本办法的规定：制定管理制度，落实工作措施，负责本行政区域内的世界文化遗产工作。"从中央来看，我国世界文化遗产主要由国家文物局整体统一管理，由文物局专门设立的文物保护与考古司（世界文化遗产司）具体负责管理、指导世界文化遗产（含世界文化和自然混合遗产中的文化遗产部分，以下同）的申报和保护、保护规划与修缮、年度项目及经费预算等工作，但建设、文化、旅游、林业、环保甚至水利等很多国家部门在遗产地有其管理范围，如世界文化遗产多是5A级景区，在受国家文物局管理的同时，又受国家旅游局管辖。2011年10月下旬，国家旅游局对全国5A级景区（包括世界文化遗产）组织实施暗访工作就是一个实例。

图表5　我国文化遗产管理体制结构图

2. 地方政府管理

我国世界文化遗产大多实行属地化管理，遗产所在区域政府一般采取直接管理和指导相应的事业单位管理等形式，在管理体制方面具有多样性的特点。大体上有三种管理模式，第一种是事业单位管理体制，建立一级地方政府的管理体制。这类文化遗产地往往辖区面积较大，不但有古建筑群、宗教活动场所、自然景观，甚至还有村镇居民。第二种是当地政府设立具有政府职能管理局或管委会，对辖区内事务实行统一管理，协调与周边的关系。如，杭州市为西湖遗产专门设立了西湖风景区管理委员会，用行政管理的机制保护及开发西湖遗产。泰安市政府成立了泰山管委会，作为其派出机构，对泰山文化自然遗产实行统一管理。都江堰市青城山风景名胜区内有一个行政乡镇，管理局和镇政府基本上是一套机构，管理局长同时任镇长。这类机构管理和保护工作基本是有序的。第三种是交由公司进行企业化经营管理。少数地方把世界文化遗产全部或其中一部分作为资产交由公司经营，如黄山，将遗产地的部分开发功能交给黄山旅游发展股份有限公司负责——景区开发管理、酒店、索道、旅行社等旅游领域的经营管理。

图表6　中国世界文化遗产地行政归属及运营管理概况

序号	名称	所在地区	行政归属	管理及运营机构
1	周口店北京猿人遗址	北京	房山区政府	周口店北京人遗址管理处
2	长城	北京	八达岭延庆县政府	八达岭特区办事处
		甘肃	嘉峪关市文化广播电视局	嘉峪关文物景区管理委员会
		河北	山海关秦皇岛市政府	山海关文物局
			金山岭滦平县政府	金山岭长城管理处

序号	名称	所在地区	行政归属	管理及运营机构
3	颐和园	北京	北京公园管理中心	北京市园林局颐和园管理处
4	天坛	北京	北京公园管理中心	北京市天坛公园管理处
5	明清皇宫（北京故宫、沈阳故宫）	北京	文化部（北京故宫）	故宫博物院
		辽宁省沈阳市	沈阳市文化局（沈阳文物局）	沈阳故宫博物院
6	敦煌莫高窟	敦煌市	甘肃省政府	敦煌研究院
7	秦始皇陵及兵马俑坑	陕西省西安市东临潼区	西安市文物局	秦始皇帝陵博物院
8	承德避暑山庄及周围寺庙	河北省承德市	承德市文物局	承德市文物园林管理局
9	曲阜孔府、孔庙、孔林	山东（曲阜市）	曲阜市政府	曲阜市文物管理局
10	武当山古建筑群	湖北省十堰市	十堰市政府	武当山旅游经济特区工委管委会
11	布达拉宫（大昭寺、罗布林卡）	西藏（拉萨市）	西藏自治区文物局	布达拉宫管理处
				大昭寺管理委员会
				罗布林卡管理处
12	丽江古城	云南（丽江市）	云南省丽江纳西族自治县文化局	丽江古城保护管理局
13	平遥古城	山西（古陶镇）	平遥县人民政府	平遥古城保护管理委员会
14	云冈石窟	山西（大同市）	大同市人民政府	云冈石窟研究院
15	五台山	山西（繁峙县，五台县）	五台山风景区人民政府	山西五台山管理局
16	苏州古典园林	江苏（苏州市）	苏州市人民政府	苏州园林局
17	大足石刻	重庆（大足县）	重庆大足县人民政府	重庆大足石刻艺术博物馆
18	皖南古村落（西递宏村为代表）	安徽（黟县境内的黄山风景区）	景区由市直辖	
19	龙门石窟	河南（洛阳市）	洛阳市政府	龙门石窟园区管委会
20	安阳殷墟	河南（安阳小屯村及其周围）	安阳市人民政府	殷墟博物苑
21	河南登封天地之中历史建筑群	河南（郑州登封市）	河南省文物局	登封市文物局
			登封市	
22	都江堰—青城山	四川（都江堰市）	都江堰市人民政府	青城山—都江堰旅游景区管理局
23	中国高句丽王城、王陵及贵族墓葬	吉林（集安市太王乡）	集安市人民政府	集安市文物局
24	澳门历史城区	澳门	澳门特区政府	澳门文化局
25	开平碉楼与古村落	广东（江门市下辖开平市境内）	开平市人民政府	开平市文物局
26	福建土楼	福建	永定县文化体育局	申报项目所在的乡（镇）分别成立土楼保护管理所
27	庐山	江西（九江市）	九江市庐山区规划局	江西省庐山风景名胜区管理局
28	西湖	浙江（杭州市）	杭州市园林文物局	杭州西湖风景名胜区管理委员会

续表

序号	名称	所在地区	行政归属	管理及运营机构
29	明清皇家陵寝			
	明显陵	湖北（钟祥县城北）	钟祥县文化局	显陵管理处
	清东陵	河北（唐山市遵化市）	遵化市人民政府	清东陵文物管理处
	清西陵	河北（易县城西）	易县人民政府	清西陵文物管理处
	明孝陵	江苏（南京市）	南京市人民政府	南京中山陵园管理局
	十三陵	北京（昌平区）	昌平区人民政府	十三陵特区办事处
	盛京三陵	辽宁（沈阳市、抚顺市新宾县）	福陵、昭陵沈阳市人民政府	福陵、昭陵沈阳市城建局
			永陵新宾满族自治县政府	永陵文物管理所
30	泰山	山东（泰安市）	泰安市规划局	泰山风景名胜区管理委员会
31	黄山	安徽（黄山市境内）	黄山市人民政府	黄山风景区管委会
32	峨眉山—乐山	四川（峨眉山市）	峨眉山市人民政府	峨眉山管理委员会
33	武夷山	福建（中国福建省的西北部，江西省东部，位于福建与江西的交界处）	武夷山市政府	武夷山风景名胜区管理委员会

资料来源：本课题组调研数据。

3. 遗产地内部管理

我国世界文化遗产种类丰富而复杂，如，故宫、敦煌莫高窟、大昭寺、苏州园林等都是全国重点文物保护单位，其构成主体相对封闭，边界较为清晰。另一部分遗产地涉及了社区管理，所以遗产地管理内容不尽相同。从整体上看，大部分遗产地采取政府直接管理或事业单位编制的管理机制，内部设置配备相应的管理机构。管理机构一般依照遗产地自身特点设置不同的职能管理部门，并根据相关的遗产管理法规，分类分级管理遗产地的监测、保护、开发、综合治理等主要事务。从功能上来看，遗产地管理机构主要可以分为遗产保护和遗产开发两大类。

以苏州园林为例，苏州园林的主体是由苏州市园林和绿化管理局统一负责管理，下设拙政园管理处、狮子林管理处、留园管理处、网师园管理处、东园管理处及世界文化遗产古典园林保护监管中心等专业机构。各机构分别下设相应的主要功能科室，其中履行保护功能的部门除了世界文化遗产古典园林保护监管中心之外，还包括园管科、园博科、安保科、档案业务科；履行开发功能的职能部门主要是综合业务科——负责经营工作、票务营销、基建管理，实施对检票、导游、服务、综合维修组的管理。

4. 人力资源管理

世界文化遗产可持续发展的关键在于人才的培养与开发。根据课题组对我国世界文化遗产地调研的总体情况来看，遗产专业技术人员的引进与培养开始引起遗产地管理机构的重视，各个遗产地开始着重吸纳、配备与自身遗产特点相关的专业资格技术人员，具有丰富的经验和专业知识的职工队伍在不断壮大，同时各个遗产地还建立世界遗产的培训与研究机构，主动与高校、科研单位开展广泛合作，不断加大对本遗产地人员进行培训与提升。以敦煌为例，2006～2011 年敦煌研究院主动引进了一大批具有专业知识的硕士、博士以及博士后，极大地满足了敦煌遗产保护、利用、管理与研究等各类工作的需求，知识分子干部占敦煌研究院职工总人数的 70%，同时敦煌研究院不断加强对所有员工的专业技能培训，一支具有综合遗产保护与管理能力、并具有丰富经验和专业知识的职工队伍已基本建成。

（三）中国世界文化遗产地保护措施

世界文化遗产是一种不可再生的珍贵资源，是人类宝贵的文化财富。随着近年来一些世界文化遗产地申报成功之后知名度大增，经济效益和社会效益显著，我国出现了空前的"遗产热"，地方政府积极参与其中，遗产保护工作也引起了中央和地方政府的高度重视。特别是申遗成功以后，围绕世界文化遗产的保护性政策、措施得到了进一步的继承和加强，据统计，目前33个世界文化遗产地均为配合国家对遗产地的监测力度，设立相应的监测机构，配备专业监测人员，利用并开发先进的科技监测手段及工具，并设立相应的专项保护监测资金，文化遗产保护工作得到了前所未有的重视。

以西湖为例，西湖申遗用了十多年的时间，在申遗过程中体现保护原则，将申遗过程视作保护过程，完全符合世界文化遗产的保护理念。从2002年起实施的西湖综合保护工程和2008年起开展的西湖文化景观重点整治工程是新中国成立以来规模最大的西湖保护工程，极大地改善了西湖的保护状况。申遗成功后，杭州西湖坚持"六个不"：一是"还湖于民"目标不改变；二是门票不涨价；三是博物馆不收费；四是土地不出让；五是文物不破坏；六是公共资源不侵占。建立健全西湖风景名胜区资源保护管理制度，实现公共资源利用效益的最大化、最优化；在遗产社区中所有新建项目都要通过文化遗产环境影响评估，防止城市发展对西湖景观区域的渗透。为了配合国家对世界文化遗产的监测保护工作，杭州西湖于2011年7月15日正式挂牌成立"杭州西湖世界文化遗产监测管理中心"，下设西湖景观实时管理监测中心和世界文化遗产监测管理中心，建设和实施西湖文化景观遗产的监测和预警体系，始终保障西湖文化景观良好的保护状况。

（四）中国世界文化遗产地需求与供给

维系一个世界文化遗产地正常运转的需求，一般涵盖保护维修费用、人员费用、行政开支、研究开发费用以及重大项目支出等。遗产地保护资金需求能否及时保证是衡量遗产地可持续发展的根本性前提。目前，我国世界文化遗产地保护资金的来源主要依靠遗产地门票收入、开发（经营性）收入、政府资金支持三个主要方面。根据遗产地经营状况的不同，三种资金来源所占遗产地保护需求的比例不同。经统计，目前90%的遗产地自身收入都足够满足遗产地保护的资金需求。

综上所述，我国世界文化遗产的可持续发展既面对良好的机遇，又面临着困境与挑战。一方面，从国内经济形势来看，当前我国经济发展依然强劲，国内居民可支配性收入不断增高，国内旅游消费水平不断提升，为遗产地门票收入增加提供了可能；从遗产保护政策来看，目前中央及地方政府高度重视对世界文化遗产的保护，各类政策、措施、资金的投入不断加大，为遗产地的可持续发展奠定了扎实基础。另一方面，从遗产地内在来看，目前我国世界文化遗产仍然存在诸如遗产软性开发程度较低，管理体制不清晰等方面不利情况；从外在来看，国内旅游消费热也可能给遗产地本身保护带来较大的压力，这些情况均不利于我国世界文化遗产地的可持续发展。总之，若要实现遗产地的可持续发展，必须综合考虑并衡量以上两个方面的影响因素，所以制定出衡量遗产地可持续发展的参考标准，通过评测推动遗产地可持续、健康的发展，势在必行。

四、中国世界文化遗产地可持续发展评估体系

中国在世界文化遗产拥有数量上，排列世界第三位。中国土地面积广阔，人口众多，并且拥有很长的历史跨度，不同文化在一个国家内出现，融合并且互相影响。在这种大环境下，世界遗产，特别是世界文化遗产的特点更是呈现多元化。从史前的古人类北京人到中国文化声名远扬的唐宋时期，再到康乾盛世的幅员辽阔经济强大，时间的跨度已远远超过了2500年。从北到南，从东到西，在中国的960万平

方公里的大地上，矗立的一座座世界文化遗产，无论是价值、文化、以及复杂程度，远远不是西班牙、意大利这样的欧洲国家可以比拟的。因此在审视中国世界文化遗产的可持续发展问题上，不能直接套用世界上通行的可持续发展理论。课题组认为，在思考并研究世界文化遗产可持续发展评估体系的过程中，应立足中国本国的自身情况，结合中国目前的社会状况、自然状况、经济水平、文化程度等多方面因素，借鉴世界其他国家世界文化遗产保护的成功经验，制定出有中国特色的世界文化遗产可持续发展的评估体系。

通过前面对中国综合环境与遗产地现状的描述和分析，本章将主要进行中国文化遗产可持续发展评估体系的搭建和说明。本课题的评估体系原则是定性为主，定量为辅来架构整个体系。评估体系主要依靠的是等级判定方法来进行遗产地的评价和分级，为可持续发展的评估体系建立框架模型。

整个评估体系由三大价值主体、四级信息架构组成，其中，三大价值主体包括遗产地基准价值、保护能力和发展水平等，将遗产地可持续发展的整体特征由内而外地分解为遗产地价值的基础条件、遗产地价值的维护和保持以及遗产地价值的创新和拓展等三个层次，全面覆盖与遗产地相关各级组织以及社会公众对其保护和发展的需求和愿望。

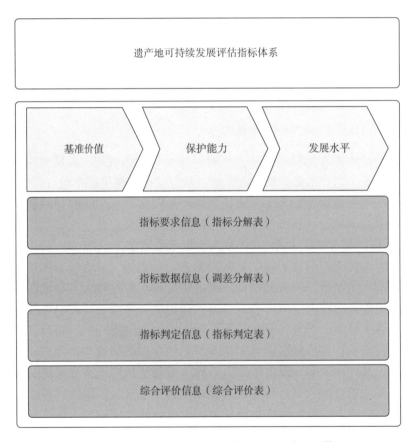

图表7　中国世界文化遗产地可持续发展评估指标体系

同时，为了更有效、全面地对各类遗产地本地和运营组织进行评估、管理和指南，确保遗产地可持续发展工作保持正确的方向，评估体系又从实施角度将价值主体自上而下地映射为四级信息架构，包括指标要求信息、指标数据信息、指标判定信息和综合评价信息等四部分，涵盖整个评估工作流程从目标制定、信息采集到信息分析和处理等各个环节，其具体信息规格分别对应于等四类信息表格。在具体的信息规格方面，四级信息架构分别对应于指标分解表、调查问卷表、指标判定表、综合评价表等四类表格，即由指标分解表明确具体的指标要求，并以调查问卷表的方式按对应指标分项获取评估对象的数据信息，然后根据所采集的数据信息进行整理、分析，并结合文件评估、现场审核等方法得出初步的评价意见，最后在综合各类信息的基础上对遗产地的可持续发展水平作出整体的综合评价。

（一）评价体系的设定

1. 指标分解表

指标分解表出于本课题是为了研究世界遗产地的可持续发展，按照遗产地基本信息、遗产地保护能力、遗产地发展状况三方面，将整个遗产地分解成单元。这些单元显示了遗产地的性质、特性及综合信息。第一部分内容主要包括三个模块的内容，分别是基本信息、价值类型以及遗产所在区域环境。通过这些信息的汇集，描述出了遗产地现实的基本情况。第二部分，保护能力指标通过组织机构、管理文件、技术保障、研究开发、资金保障这五个模块描述了遗产地内部情况。这部分内容主要是考察遗产地自身保护的能力。第三部分内容由游客数量，产品形态，组织机构，开发管理，开发投入、收入、结余等模块构成，用来考察遗产地在保护的基础上进行开发情况及持续发展能力。

指标分解表作为说明性文件，包括指标类别、评价指标对象、指标选择说明。完整构成了遗产地内外部以及所在区域情况，为帮助本课题进行信息收集、调查问卷表的设定打下基础，并为指标的判定及评价提供依据。

2. 调查问卷表

调查问卷是信息搜集的基础性文件，由各遗产地运营机构填写，上报给国家文物局主管部门，用于对遗产地可持续发展评价的基本依据及课题研究者验证评价体系。由于篇幅关系，调研问卷作为附件提供。

3. 指标判定表

指标判定表是世界遗产地评价体系的第一步工作，是根据遗产地调研表的书面填报内容及专家现场观察结合使用。具体执行由政府指定的第三方专业机构进行。判定记录是指对调查表中与判定相关的关键事实的分析、描述信息。判定依据是对相关标准、制度、规范和法律文件的引用信息。判定结论是针对所判定指标、参照判定记录和相关标准等得出的定性判定结论，根据评判标准分别填写 A、B、C 等级。

4. 综合评价表

综合评价表是考量遗产地是否可持续发展的最终评价表。具体执行由政府出面组织的专家委员会及委员会主任负责。通过政府组织的世界遗产地监测及定期调研出来的数据，用综合评价表的标准来判定世界遗产地可持续发展等级。

（二）评价体系的案例分析

课题组在评价体系建立的基础上，对部分遗产地进行了指标验证。课题组通过对苏州古典园林，周口店北京猿人遗址，曲阜孔府、孔庙、孔林，平遥古城，杭州西湖文化景观的调研、核实、分析，来验证指标体系的合理性及完整性，考量世界文化遗产可持续发展评价体系等级划分的科学性。由于篇幅有限，现将五处世界文化遗产的特点进行简要概述。

苏州古典园林作为坐落在经济活力较强的二线城市苏州的世界遗产地，拥有较高水平的管理模式，在设备配套运营方面较其他遗产地来说占有一定优势。同时，苏州园林有较强的观赏娱乐价值，因此仅仅是门票收入就足以支撑苏州古典园林的保护需求。加之政府在政策和资金上面的扶持，苏州古典园林作为世界遗产地在可持续发展方面有很大优势和能力。

周口店北京人遗址作为远古时期人类发源地之一，拥有较强的考古和研究价值，但是由于遗址出现的年代过于久远，在功能性的业务开发方面受到了一定限制。所以周口店北京人遗址在门票收入上并不具备像苏州园林那样有优势，门票等直接业务收入规模不是很高，因此不能采用业务收入再分配的形式来支撑日常维护和管理，更多需要各级政府出资来进行遗产地日常的维护和管理。

图表 8　中国世界文化遗产地可持续发展评估指标分列表

指标类别	指标名称	指标要素	指标说明	指标作用	数据来源
一、遗产地信息	1. 基本信息	遗产地名称	官方确认的遗产地正式称谓	确认遗产的统一、公平正式名称，并以此为基础，确保与遗产地相关各系统间的统一性和一致性	世界遗产官网
		遗产地类型	参照国家文物保护法类型进行划分，按遗产本体特征类型进行划分，如古墓葬、古建筑群等	将遗产地按不同属性特征进行分类，便于比较研究其属性值规律，便于制定适用评价标准和发展策略	国家文物保护法
		入选世界文化遗产名录时间	世界文化遗产申报及入选时间	遗产正式列入世界文化遗产后，文化遗产人特别保护范围，相应的保护、发展要求将作为实际工作的参照和基准	世界遗产官网
		遗产地面积	世界文化遗产申报时所指明的范围，包括本区和缓冲区在内	遗产地面积对相应的保护措施、保护成本以及参与保护的人员规模具有一定的影响	遗产地提供
		遗产地所在区域	遗产地直接隶属并具有财政关系的行政区域，如省、市、县等。	遗产地所处区域的城市规模、社会经济发展水平等对遗产地可持续发展具有一定的支撑和相互影响作用	
		运营机构名称	直接具体负责遗产地日常运营的机构	确认遗产地的直接日常运营机构，是判定和评价遗产地管理运营水平的重要基础	中国遗产地网站
		运营机构类型	运营机构的单位性质，如行政机构、事业单位、企业单位、社会团体等	有助于了解遗产地日常运营管理的基本工作性质和特点以及对遗产地可持续发展的重要基础	
		运营机构归属关系	运营机构的直接上级行政归属部门	有助于了解遗产地相关的管理体系和管理模式以及对遗产地可持续发展的影响	
	2. 价值类型	文化价值	遗产地所承载的内在文化、情感或精神价值，包括：年代、传统、延续性、性、传说、奇迹、精神、宗教、纪念、象征、政治、爱国主义、民族等	遗产地内在文化价值会对当地文化生活、社会公益等产生一定的影响力，同时也决定了遗产地保护在内容层面的重要性以及发展潜力等	
		专业价值	遗产地外在形式上所体现的技术性或专业性价值，包括在设计、技术、结构、功能、工艺等方面的重要性以及与类型、风格、建造者、时期、社区等相关的稀有性、代表性和独特性等	遗产地外在专业价值对于遗产保护和发展具有经济、技术等方面的影响	中国遗产地网站 世界遗产官网
		文物保护级别	遗产地本体内所含文物等级、类型、种类、数量等	遗产地内含的文物等级、数量与将采取的保护程度，投入相关。可以作为一个重要衡量来考察遗产地保护工作量	中国遗产地网站

续表

指标类别	指标名称	指标要素	指标说明	指标作用	数据来源
一、遗产地信息	3. 区域环境	自然环境	区域内的绿植覆盖率	绿植覆盖率会影响当地环境，也是影响遗产保护的因素之一	遗产地所在区域园林局
			区域内的年降雨量	降雨量会影响当地空气的湿度以及因为雨水所产生的自然灾害，例如泥石流、洪水等	遗产地所在区域气象局
			区域内水系状况，如河流、湖泊、瀑布、沿海等	水系存在也会对空气有一定影响，当降雨量过高的时候可能会出现洪灾	遗产地所在区域水利局
			区域内环境质量状况，包括空气、水环境质量等	污染将严重影响遗产地的变化，涉及保护因素分析	遗产地所在区域环保局
			区域内不可抗力影响因素，比如地震、洪灾、风暴、传染病等灾害发生情况	灾害产生会影响遗产保护的因素	中华人民共和国环境保护部
		旅游环境	区域内的酒店数量	酒店数量可以反映当地经济发展状况及接待能力。酒店的档次反映与当地经济消费有关	统计年鉴
			区域内的餐饮店数量	餐饮店数量可以代表当地特色饮食的丰富程度，作为其中一项旅游资源可以吸引更多游客。而中、高级饭店比较多，则说明旅游团队较多，餐饮的规模接待能力比较强	
			区域内其他景点数量	级别高的景点较多地吸引游客。如果周边能多高级别景点比较多，可能会相应减少世界遗产地的吸引力，同时也会减小游客过多的接待压力	
			区域内交通设施状况	交通条件首接影响游客的访问数量。交通条件说明该文化遗产景点是否容易到达	遗产地所在区域的旅游局
		社会经济	区域内国民生产总值（五年）	经济总量，可与不同遗产地进行比较整体经济发展水平	统计年鉴
			区域内的人口数量，包含户籍人口人数、外来人口人数等，常驻人口人数	人口规模既决定了遗产地保护的人员和社会环境基础，也决定遗产地发展的空间和潜力	
			区域内财政收入（五年）	体现地方政府可支配资金对遗产地保护、发展的支撑能力，反映当地财政对于遗产地保护和履职能力	

续表

指标类别	指标名称	指标要素	指标说明	指标作用	数据来源
一、遗产地信息	3. 区域环境	社会经济	区域内第三产业产值（五年）	可据此计算出第三产业产值占 GDP 的百分比，直接反映当地国民经济对第三产业的依赖程度，主要包括金融、运输、旅游、文化等	统计年鉴
			区域内旅游业产值（五年）	可据此计算出旅游业产值占第三产业的百分比，间接反映当地旅游服务业对遗产地的依赖程度	
			区域内居民可支配收入（五年），包括城镇和农村居民在内	反映当地居民的生活水平、消费水平，是考察遗产地发展潜力的基础指标之一	
			区域内居民恩格尔系数（五年）	恩格尔系统与区域内居民富裕程度具有一定相关性，同时也决定了该区域内文化类消费的潜在需求水平，是考察遗产地发展潜力的基础指标之一	
			遗产地周边城市建筑及商业设施开发情况	考察城市建设和商业地产开发对遗产地保护和发展的影响	遗产地运营机构提供
		遗产聚集	区域内其他相关遗产聚集数量	了解在同一个遗产地所在区域内相关遗产的数量，有助于分析不同遗产之间的相互影响	遗产地运营机构提供
二、保护能力指标	1. 组织机构	内部组织架构及人员配置	指与遗产地日常运营、维护相关的内部部门设置及人员配置，一般应涵盖旅客管理、环境保护、安全防护、监测监控、维护修缮以及后勤保障等运营管理职能，需具体说明部门名称、部门职能以及配备人数等	组织机构设置及人力资源配备情况直接反映了遗产地保护的管理水平和能力，以及与遗产地保护需求的匹配程度	
		外部相关管理机构	与遗产地保护和发展相关的行政和专业管理机构、部门配置情况，包括机构名称、级别、管理职责和内容等	与遗产地保护相关的政府管理机构、行业组织及相关机构的配置情况不仅反映出遗产地的整体管理模式和管理效率，也反映出整体支撑水平	
		外部合作机构	与遗产地保护相关的外部合作机构情况，包括机构名称、机构性质、机构职能、合作内容等	合作机构和遗产地运营机构在资源和能力等方面具有一定的互补性，因而可以整体提升遗产地保护的质量和水平	遗产地年度报告
	2. 管理文件	文件制定	与遗产地日常运营维护工作相关的指导和管理类文件的编制和配备情况，一般应涵盖规划计划、规章制度、标准规范以及管理记录等类文件和文档，同时也应考虑与日常管理职能、岗位的匹配性	管理文件是用于规范、控制和统一协调遗产地日常运营维护的重要保证，是决定遗产地保护质量的重要基础	遗产地运营机构提供

续表

指标类别	指标名称	指标要素	指标说明	指标作用	数据来源
二、保护能力指标	2. 管理文件	文件管理	与管理文件发布、传递以及版本更新等相关的管理状况，包括管理要求、分发数量、完好情况以及更新次数等	管理文件本体的完好性，适用性和有效性是保证相关管理要求切实有效执行的前提条件	
		文件执行	指相关管理文件的执行情况，包括监督措施、检查情况、执行情况等	贯彻执行是制定管理文件要求的最终目的，有效的监督管理措施是运营管理质量的重要保证	
	3. 技术保障	系统或设备配置	包括安全防护、监控监测，维修维护、环境管理，等相关设备或系统的配置情况，包括类别、规格说明和配置数量、使用周期或使用年限等	遗产地保护是一项专业性较强的系统工程，需要有专业化的系统和系统的配备，专业设备和系统的配置、管理能力是遗产地可持续发展的技术基础	
		系统或设备管理	相关设备和系统的维护保养以及完好情况等		
	4. 研究开发	研发能力	包括研发部门设置、研发人员数量、研发人员构成以及研发设备配置等		
		研发计划	包括研发项目计划、研究预算以及保障措施等	有计划、有保障的遗产地保护技术研发以及创新应用将为可持续性发展提供切实的基础保障	遗产地年度报告遗产地运营机构提供
		研发实施	包括每年研发经费投入、研发项目应用情况等，其中应考察重要或关键项目名称及其影响		
	5. 社会宣传	宣传活动或项目	遗产地保护相关的社会宣传、教育活动正常开展的资金或项目	考察遗产地运营机构在遗产地保护宣传、提高社会公众保护意识方面的工作	
	6. 资金保障	运营成本（需求）	保证遗产地日常运营维护工作正常开展所需的资金以及研究开发工作所需的资金数量（五年），一般涵盖开发费用、人员费用、行政开支，研究开发费用以及重大项目支出等，按科目分别列举及汇总支出项目名称、类别、金额、用途等	分析遗产地年来所有用于维护保持遗产地运转和文物保护的资金需求数量、变化趋势，落实情况以及财务结构特点，从财务角度分析遗产地运营能力水平和运营状况	
		资金来源（供给）	运营所需资金的落实情况（五年），企业捐（赠）助、收入再分配各类资金渠道，按类型分别列举名称、金额以及用途等，一般涵盖财政拨款、行政拨款等		

续表

指标类别	指标名称	指标要素	指标说明	指标作用	数据来源
三、发展性指标	1. 游客数量	区域内游客数量	包括（五年内）遗产地所在区域内游客总点数以及本地、外埠（含国内、国外）游客数量的统计数据	掌握遗产地所在区域的客流情况，构成比例及变化趋势，分析遗产地开发的潜力和重点	地区旅游统计年鉴
		遗产地游客数量	包括（五年内）遗产地本身游客总数以及本地、外埠（含国内、国外）游客数量的统计数据	掌握遗产地本身的客流情况，构成比例及变化趋势，分析遗产地发展的规律以及与当地旅游业发展的相关性	遗产地年度报告
	2. 产品形态	直接产品	以遗产地本体作为产品提供的直接服务，一般包括参观、游览及其他附属服务等	以旅游为主的直接产品是遗产地的主要收入来源，为遗产地提供基本收入保证，是评估遗产地的自身经营能力的重要指标	
		衍生产品	以遗产地本体价值或内容为蓝本开发的其他形态产品和服务，一般包括纪念品、内容产品（音像、图书、影视）等	衍生利授权产品的开发代表遗产地运营机构对于遗产地附加价值的增值开发、创新利用能力	
		授权产品	以遗产地品牌、形象或相关元素为基础的授权权服务产品，包括专利权、商标权、著作权以及其他相关无形资产授权		
		配套服务	包括博物馆、餐饮服务、场地租用（一次性、长期）、零售服务等与遗产地主体业务项目或相配套的其他服务收入	配套服务一般用于衡量遗产地对于内外部资源的整合或挖掘利用能力，但同时也应考虑对于遗产地本体家孩子及环境的影响程度	
		项目开发	为服务社会、文化传承需要开展的其他类服务项目或主题活动等，包括科教类项目、文化类项目和公益类项目等		
		新建设施	在遗产地内部开发建立新的建筑或服务设施等，对原有本地进行功能性补充，进而产生附加的产品或服务收入	代表遗产地本身对社会文化或精神文明的贡献程度，是本体价值上可以拓展遗产地价值的延伸和发展	
				作为遗产地本体的必要补充和或自然延展，新建设施在一定程度上可以拓展遗产地价值的覆盖范围或提升其功能性，但也会因过度开发削弱遗产地本体价值甚至造成一定的破坏风险	遗产地年度报告 遗产地运营机构提供
	3. 组织机构	部门设置及人员配备	指与遗产地产品开发、宣传推广、销售服务等职能相关的部门设置及人员配备情况，包括部门名称、部门职能以及配备人数等		
	4. 开发管理	经营计划	指产品开发、宣传推广、产品销售和客户服务等与开发经营工作相关计划及执行保证措施的制定情况 相关计划的实施、完成情况以及所产生的影响或或效果等	考察遗产地运营机构对产品开发以及市场经营的重视程度以及实际的执行能力	
			与遗产地相关知识产权的保护情况，包括产权名称、产权类型、保护措施以及登记、保护状况等		

续表

指标类别	指标名称	指标要素	指标说明	指标作用	数据来源
三、发展性指标	5. 开发投入	产权保护类支出	与知识产权或无形资产保护相关的各项支出	遗产地运营机构用于产品开发和经营的实际投入，用于判定其对开发的投入程度规模和机构成比例，	
		产品开发类支出	与新产品开发和维护相关的各项支出，包括人工费用，设备费用，场地费用和行政费用等		
		宣传推广类支出	与产品和服务宣传推广相关的各项支出		
		产品销售类支出	在产品销售和客户服务过程中所发生的经营成本和各项支出，包括人工费用，行政费用等		
		其他经营性支出	与经营性收入直接相关的税金以及其他管理、服务等支出费用等		
	6. 收入	事业收入	包括：门票收入，其他附加收入（讲解，游览车船）	考察遗产地运营机构产品和市场开发，运营的实际效果以及构成，从一个侧面反映其价值转化能力，发展模式以及开发经营水平	
		经营收入	包括：衍生产品收入，授权产品收入，配套服务收入，项目开发收入		
		财政收入	指当地财政提供的事业单位的正常经费		
		财政补助收入	指中央政府及地方政府提供的专项经费，重大专项经费		
		上级补助收入	指预算外资金来源		
		其他收入	指对外投资，利息，出租，其他单位补助，杂项收入，及经过等措施制得到的相关国际组织及国内企业，慈善机构等民间组织给予的资助等		
	7. 结余	事业结余	在一定期间除经营支出以外的各项经常收支相抵后的余额 事业结余＝财政补助收入＋事业收入＋附属单位缴款＋其他收入－事业支出－对附属单位补助－拨出经费－结转自筹基建－上缴上级支出－销售税金	考察遗产地运营机构的综合盈利能力和经营管理水平	
		经营结余	在一定期间各项经营收入与支出相抵后的余额。经营结余＝经营收入－经营支出－经营税金		
	8. 社会效益	遗产地对所在区域的社会贡献	遗产地的可持续发展对所在区域的社会，经济，文化，生活等方面影响和影响状况及程度	考察遗产地对当地社会，经济，文化，生活的带动作用和贡献能力	遗产地年度报告 遗产地运营机构提供

图表 9　中国世界文化遗产地可持续发展评估指标判定表

指标类别	指标名称	指标要素	判定结论	判定记录（问卷、现场）	评定标准
一、遗产地信息（基准）	1. 基本信息	遗产地名称			□准确 □基本准确 □不准确
		遗产地类型			□单体 □集中 □分散
		入选世界文化遗产名录时间			A 成熟运营 B 初步运营 C 运营准备
		遗产地面积			保护范围：A 大 B 中 C 小
		遗产地所在区域			城市规模：A 大 B 中 B 小
		遗产地运营机构			A 标准型 B 受限型 C 制约型
	2. 价值类型	文化价值			A 综合价值 B 实体价值 C 精神价值
		专业价值			
		文物保护级别			A 高 B 中 C 低
	3. 区域环境	自然环境			A 正面影响 B 没有影响 C 负面影响
		旅游环境			A 条件较好 B 条件一般 C 条件较差
		社会经济			A 高速发展 B 稳定发展 C 发展迟缓 A 消费旺盛 B 消费一般 C 消费不足 A 结构合理 B 结构均衡 C 结构失衡
		周边地产开发			A 适度开发 B 较少开发 C 过度开发
		遗产聚集			A 丰富 B 较少 C 没有
	总体特征				A 基础较好 B 基础一般 C 基础薄弱
二、保护能力指标（保值）	1. 组织机构	内部组织架构及人员配置			A 组织健全 B 满足需求 C 配置不足
		外部相关管理机构			A 统一管理 B 分头管理 C 多头管理
		外部合作机构			A 紧密合作 B 松散合作 C 没有合作
	2. 管理文件	文件制定			A 文件完备 B 满足需求 C 类别缺失
		文件管理			A 管理完善 B 管理尚可 C 管理不足
		文件执行			A 执行较好 B 基本执行 C 执行较差
	3. 技术保障	系统或设备配置			A 配置较好 B 满足需求 C 配置不足
		系统或设备管理			A 管理完善 B 管理尚可 C 管理不足
	4. 研究开发	研发能力			A 能力较强 B 能力一般 C 能力较差
		研发计划			A 计划较好 B 计划一般 C 计划较差
		研发实施			A 实施较好 B 基本实施 C 实施较差
	5、社会宣传	宣传活动或项目			A 组织较好 B 偶尔组织 C 没有组织
	6、资金保障	运营成本（需求）			A 结构合理 B 满足要求 C 浪费严重
		资金来源（供给）			A 资金充裕 B 基本满足 C 资金不足
	总体特征				A 保护较好 B 满足需求 C 保护较差或过度保护

指标类别	指标名称	指标要素	判定结论	判定记录（问卷、现场）	评定标准
三、发展性指标（增值）	1. 游客数量	区域内游客数量			□数量递增 □数量稳定 □数量递降 □本地为主 □外埠为主 □内外均衡
		遗产地游客数量			A 数量递增 B 数量稳定 C 数量递降 □本地为主 □外埠为主 □内外均衡
	2. 产品形态	直接产品			A 产品丰富 B 产品单一 C 开发不足或过度开发
		衍生产品			
		授权产品			
		配套服务			
		项目开发			
		新建设施			
	3. 组织机构	部门设置及人员配备			A 配置较好 B 满足需求 C 配置不足
	4. 开发管理	经营计划			A 计划较好 B 计划一般 C 计划较差
		实施情况			A 实施较好 B 基本实施 C 实施较差
		知识产权保护			A 保护较好 B 部分保护 C 保护较差
	5. 开发投入	产权保护类支出			A 投入充足 B 投入一般 C 投入不足
		产品开发类支出			
		宣传推广类支出			
		产品销售类支出			
		其他经营性支出			
	6. 收入	事业收入			A 开发依赖 B 资源依赖 C 政府依赖
		经营收入			
		财政收入			
		财政补助收入			
		上级补助收入			
		其他收入			
	7. 结余	事业结余			A 盈利 B 持平 C 亏损
		经营结余			
	8. 社会效益	遗产地对所在区域的社会贡献			A 贡献较大 B 贡献一般 C 较少贡献
	总体特征				A 发展较好 B 发展一般 C 发展不足或过度发展

图表10 中国世界文化遗产地可持续发展评估综合评价表

评分项目			评分记录	A	B	C
基础条件	遗产地本体以及环境的特征（非考核项）			基础较好	基础一般	基础较差
运维能力	运维组织	组织机构设置		组织机构完整，职能界限清晰	具备基本组织机构或相关职能分工	缺少关键组织环节
		人员配备		岗位齐备，人员配置充足	人员配置基本满足要求	关键环节人员配置不足
		管理文件		管理文件齐全，系统性较强	具备必要的基本管理文件	缺少关键管理文件（如记录文件等）
		技术保障		技术手段齐全，管理完善	具备基本的技术保障能力	支撑性技术手段欠缺或不能满足要求
		创新开发		具备完善的创新开发能力，每年具有一定的开发投入	具备一定开发能力，但开发投入一般	不具备开发能力
	合作机构（选项）			具有合作关系，且具有双向的协作关系	具有一定的合作关系	
	经营组织	组织机构设置		组织机构完整，职能界限清晰	基本组织机构健全	缺少关键组织环节
		人员配备		岗位齐备，人员配置充足	人员配置基本满足要求	关键环节人员配置不足
	发展规划及管理措施			规划及管理措施文件齐备，实施记录完整	具备基本的规划和管理措施	缺少规划或计划，尚未制定有效的管理措施
	综合能力等级			所有选项等级评分均达到A，则为能力满足要求，评为A	所有选项中出现一项以上B等级评分，则为能力基本满足要求，评为B	必选项中出现一项C等级评分，则为能力不满足要求，评为C
资金保障	成本结构			结构合理，重点突出	结构满足日常支出需要	结构不合理，浪费严重
	资金渠道			资金来源较为均衡（没有资金缺口）	资金来源基本满足运维开支要求（资金缺口小于10%）	资金来源不能满足开支要求（资金缺口大于10%）
发展水平	游客数量			游客增长	游客稳定	游客数量递减
	经营开发			类型丰富，重点突出，系统性强	类型单一，基本依赖旅游服务	没有核心产品，业务或过度开发
	收入构成			收入来源较为均衡（非财政和直接业务占比30%以上）	直接业务为主（大于50%）	财政补贴为主（大于50%）
	社会效益			对当地社会、经济、文化、生活具有很强拉动作用	对当地社会、经济、文化、生活具有一定拉动作用	对当地社会、经济、文化、生活的贡献较少
总评分				均为A	一项以上为B	一项以上为C
评价结论				可持续发展	基本可持续发展	不可持续发展

曲阜孔府、孔庙、孔林作为儒家孔子学派的起源地，在遗产特点上对当代具有重大的教育意义和纪念意义。然而孔府、孔庙、孔林坐落在经济方面有所欠缺的三线城市，曲阜的经济实力也相对单薄，三产结构有待调整。因此由孔府、孔庙、孔林所带来的旅游收入对曲阜的经济贡献较大。同时，孔府、孔庙、孔林既有古墓葬群，也有森林名木，在维护管理方面难度较高，对高科技设备的要求也比较广泛。因此在保护方面需要较高的资金投入。

平遥古城由于城市本体就是世界文化遗产，因此该遗产为开放式管理，并没有专业的管理队伍进行整座城市的管理和维护。因此，平遥古城的破坏情况较严重，出现城墙裂缝等情况，严重威胁了古城的价值，使得平遥古城作为世界文化遗产在可持续发展方面面临困难。

杭州西湖文化景观作为新加入世界文化遗产的文化景观，在各方面都有较为成熟的发展规划。有系统的管理制度还有合理的保护资金供给结构。因此杭州西湖景区具有较好的可持续发展能力。

总之，通过对不同类型的遗产地进行分析、调查和研究后，课题组发现中国遗产地类型复杂，各具特色。遗产地的多样性，对于遗产地管理要求高。本课题旨在在不同中寻找共性，将不同遗产地的运营发展模式进行总结归类，得出国内遗产地可持续发展的一般规律及相应发展模式，为指导遗产地管理者的有效决策奠定基础。

五、中国世界文化遗产地可持续发展模式

由于受经济、社会影响力、品牌、管理与开发能力等多种关联要素在不同程度上的影响与作用，世界文化遗产地的可持续发展呈现出不同的特征。本课题着眼于遗产地本体经营运作的角度进行研究，发现我国世界文化遗产地的发展可以归纳为资源依赖型、政府支撑型及开发补充型等三种重要模式。

需要说明的是，本课题研究发现，有些世界文化遗产的发展呈现出多种特点，可能兼备两种以上的不同模式，针对这种情况，课题组主要是根据某种模式所起的的作用程度，来评断遗产地具有何种发展倾向。如果门票收益比例大，则可判定其倾向于资源依赖性；如果政府支撑比例大，则可判定其倾向于政府支撑型，等等。这些不同模式之间的相互作用与影响，共同构成了遗产地整体的可持续发展。

（一）资源依赖型

该模式突出"遗产经济"的特点，遗产地发展主要依靠遗产自身丰厚资源的魅力、价值、品牌等吸引游客。门票收益完全可以满足遗产地自身保护与开发的需求，收益大于支出，实现自给自足。目前大部分的中国世界文化遗产均可以做到这一点。通过遗产地的门票收益解决遗产地的日常维护费用及基本保护，不少遗产地还拥有大量的资金结余，满足保护与发展的需要。例如，从模式结构上来看，曲阜属于兼备资源和政府支持两种特征的遗产地之一，但是门票收入是整体收入的主体，远高于自身日常维护支出及政府的资金支持，属于资源依赖型的遗产地。

（二）政府支撑型

该模式的突出特点就是依赖于政府财政资金维持保护与发展。由于遗产地自身资源的匮乏，依赖自身的门票等经营性收益难以维持其自身的保护与发展，但遗产本体往往又具有重要历史或时代价值意义，所以需要依靠各级政府给予资金支撑，且支撑度取决于遗产地需求缺口的大小。目前中国有少数遗产地处于这种情况，需要各级政府的支持。

（三）开发补充型

该模式的主要特点是除了门票收入外，还依赖遗产地内的房屋出租收入、餐饮收入、授权经营收入、

衍生产品收入、财税收入等经营性开发来推动自身的保护与可持续发展，遗产自身的增值开发能力较强，最典型的是杭州西湖。西湖申遗成功后成立了杭州西湖风景名胜区管理委员会准一级政府单位，主要负责整个遗产地范围内的经营管理工作，西湖每年收益中的 50% 来自于景区范围内的开发性收入，如房租、税收等，其开发程度较高。

另外，值得一提的是，本课题所指的开发补充型模式，是有利于遗产本体保护、遗产品牌推广，及扩大遗产社会影响力的开发收益及活动，而非导致遗产本体价值破坏的过度性开发，这类开发是应该得到有效控制的。

六、对中国世界文化遗产地可持续发展的几点建议

现阶段，我国世界文化遗产的保护与发展整体良好，文化遗产与区域经济社会发展的互动作用凸显，特别是世界文化遗产对区域经济发展与结构调整、社会就业、生态环境保护、旅游发展等方面起到了有效的带动作用，所以，本课题组一致认为，国家、地方政府及遗产地运营主体在世界文化遗产的保护与发展中应各司其职，充分履行各自的责任与义务，为进一步完善对世界文化遗产保护，推动世界文化遗产可持续发展担当好自己的角色。

从国家的角度讲，国家是世界文化遗产的第一责任人，应承担文化遗产的第一保护责任，负责全国文化遗产规划与管理的全局工作。对于文化遗产事故的出现，除了追究相应的经营管理主体之外，政府的责任重大。为此，"十二五"发展将是我国世界文化遗产事业发展的关键时期，夯实基础、科学规划、加快发展应是我国世界文化遗产事业发展的主题。本课题组建议，1. 国家应理顺管理体制，强化中央统一管理，打造中央、地方、运营主体等多方参与而统一的立体式管理机制。2. 加大经费投入，设立专项资金。一方面通过立法途径规定中央政府拿出 GDP 的相应比例用于遗产保护，另一方面制定符合世界文化遗产地实际需要的优惠政策，鼓励用多渠道的方式筹集社会资金，并将其用于世界文化遗产的保护工作。3. 完善世界文化遗产监督管理制度，利用可持续发展评估体系定期对世界遗产地进行评估指导。

从地方政府的角度看，地方政府应严格执行国家制定的相关法律法规、规划，同时将遗产地保护纳入政府发展规划中，按照国家政策配套拿出 GDP 的相应比例，采取事业预算制，直接用于文化遗产的保护与发展。

从运营主体的角度来看，遗产运营机构应加强专业技术人员的吸收与培养，逐步提高专业人员占就业人员总数的比例，并实行文化遗产保护人员持证上岗等，不断提高遗产保护的相关技术研发能力；同时，在文化遗产保护的基础上，鼓励探索产业化经营发展模式，可建立或委托企业进行遗产地相关产业的经营及产品开发。

经过一年来的调研、思考、数据分析，专家讨论，我们课题组对于中国世界文化遗产地的基本情况、管理运营情况、遗产保护情况、开发情况有了初步的理解。由此设计了可持续发展的评估体系，提炼了若干种发展模式。但是由于时间紧张及资料来源的有限，没有穷尽中国 33 个遗产地的全面情况，目前还只是指导性、总则性的评估体系。课题组认为，此课题的研究可以随着进一步的调研而不断深化，总结出既符合世界遗产组织要求，又符合中国国情的一套切实可行的世界文化遗产可持续发展评估模型，为中国世界文化遗产管理作出我们的贡献。

（执笔人：向勇、邓丽丽，北京大学文化产业研究院）

On the Sustainable Development Model and Evaluation System of China's World Cultural Heritage Sites

Peking University

Abstract

This research centers on the China's world cultural heritage sites in accordance with the general guidelines of sustainable development. Perspectives of economic development, standard of living, consumption structure and capacity, and evaluation of governmental policies are studied to prove China's capacity of the world cultural heritage preservation. The protective, operational and managerial status quo has been overviewed to reveal the overall annual demands for China's world cultural heritage sites. Moreover, the evaluation indexes and comprehensive contributions of China's world cultural heritage sites to the region are also elaborated to establish the sustainable development model and evaluation system of the China's world cultural heritage sites.

Key words: world cultural heritage; demand and supply; sustainable development; model; evaluation system

I Introduction

(I) Objects, Background, Significance, and Goals

1. Objects

The objects are the 33 world cultural heritages, natural, cultural and mixed heritages in China, which entered into the list of UNESCO World Cultural Heritage sites since the 35th World Heritage Committee Convention in June, 2011. According to different characteristics and forms, China's world cultural heritages may be classified into seven categories, namely ancient cultural sites, ancient architectural complex, gardens, tombs, grottos, historic cities or villages and mountains, mainly scattering in the densely populated regions like the Yellow River valleys and middle – lower reaches of the Yangtze River.

2. Background

At present, China's world cultural heritages are distributed in 21 provinces or regions. As this number is increasing, China will rank first in term of country of world cultural heritages As a result, overall protection of the world cultural heritages should become a national strategy and responsibility. That is why our research group aims at this research on sustainable development model and evaluation system of China's world cultural heritage sites. Hopefully this research will help to probe into a mechanism of sustainable development model.

3. Significance

(1) For the central government (State Administration of Cultural Heritage)

To provide the scientific basis for the governmental policies, development plans, sufficient investments and monitoring directions by analyzing the operations and administrations of the heritage sites, indicating assessing index system and abstracting essence of management of China's world cultural heritages.

(2) For municipal administrative bureaus

To reveal contributions of world cultural heritages to local economic and social development and advocate importance of sustainable development of world cultural heritages for integration of local economy and culture.

(3) For operational institutions

To clarify responsibilities and directions of taking protection measures, key performance index and treats in daily operations.

(4) For researchers

To set an example of development model with index system and promote further studies.

4. The Major Research Questions

The first and uttermost question is to decide proper methods to preserve world cultural heritages.

(II) Definitions

1. World Cultural Heritage

World cultural heritage is the product of developments, values and needs of the contemporary society. It is defined as the following points in the *Convention Concerning the Protection of the World Cultural and Natural Heritage* by the USENCO.

(1) Monuments: architectural works, works of monumental sculpture and painting, elements or structures of an archaeological nature, inscriptions, cave dwellings and combinations of features, which are of outstanding universal value from the point of view of history, art or science;

(2) Groups of buildings: groups of separate or connected buildings which, because of their architecture, their homogeneity or their place in the landscape, are of outstanding universal value from the point of view of history, art or science;

(3) Sites: works of man or the combined works of nature and man, and areas including archaeological sites which are of outstanding universal value from the historical, aesthetic, ethnological or anthropological point of view (USENCO, 1972).

Heritage sites act as the material and spatial carriers. This research refers to the protection areas in the bidding text of world cultural heritage, mainly including central and buffering areas.

2. Sustainable Development

World Commission on Environment and Development defines the sustainable development as " meeting the needs of the present without compromising the ability of future generations to meet their needs" (WCED, 1987). The sustainable development embodies the following principles:

(1) Justice Principle: Including intra – generational equity, inter – generational equity and equitable distribution of limited resources.

(2) Sustainability Principle: The economic and social development of human beings cannot exceed the capacity of resources and environment.

(3) Universality Principle: Because of the integrity and interdependency of the globe, sustainable development is a general goal rather than a self – governed one.

The core of sustainable development is to develop economy, society and environment altogether to achieve the conditioned development that is of sustainability.

As the common wealth of human beings, world cultural heritage development should be implemented with intra – generational. equity Namely, the descendants have the same right to enjoy and inherit the authentic and integral heritages as the older generations do. The related administrations, national and local governments should not only protect the valuable heritage resources, but also coordinate in the protection and exploitation on basis of beneficial relationships among differout parties. Make sure not to sacrifice the rights of one party (especially local inhabitants) for the rights of another or others against the principle of the inter – generational equivalence.

(III) Research Routes and Methods

1. Technical Routes

First of all, the research defines the problems. After doing so, related documents could be searched out , researching routes could be designed and outlines conld be clarified for further study of evaluation systems and modes. Then through field surveys, case studies and experts' demonstrations, the final practical evaluation system could be worked out.

2. Research Methods

According to the basic requirements, the research has adopted a methed conbining macro and micro studies, typical investigation and general argumentation, national demonstration and international contrast, qualitative and quantitative research methods. Then, the data analysis should be performed with field investigations, evaluation and monitoring systems. The investigation figures are mainly composed of leaders in charge, chief managers, tourists, local inhabitants and research staffs.

(IV) Main Innovative Points

1. New Analysis Framework

Based on the general requirements, this research has summarized the needs and characteristics of sustainable development of world cultural heritage by surveys of current protection, development status and combination of Chinese conditions with local characteristics. It covers resources, managements, talents, funds and infrastructure capabilities and formulates complete frameworks and modes, which provide theoretical basis for the protection and development of world cultural heritage.

2. New Monitoring Data

Absorbing achievements of latest practice and studies on world cultural heritage sites, this study pioneers on employing first – hand data and implementing qualitative and quantitative analysis, which lays a solid foundation for further researches.

3. Innovative Evaluation Index System

On the basis of modes and data analysis, this research has designed relatively comprehensive evaluation index system for the origins, basic volume, investment proportion, growth rate, continuity and comprehensive effects of sustainable development. It is innovative and practical with meeting the requirements of world cultural heritage protection and further reflecting the special needs of social development and management in China.

(V) Structure

This research mainly aims at three aspects: the relationships between management of world cultural heritage and government, the contributions to economic growth and the impacts of interactive relationship between heritage sites and appellations to the protection. By analyzing rapid economy growth, household consumption and structure changes, China' supplying capacity and policies evaluations can be certificated. By analyzing management, operation, exploitation and summing up the annual demands, the sustainable developmental evaluation systems can be finally worked out.

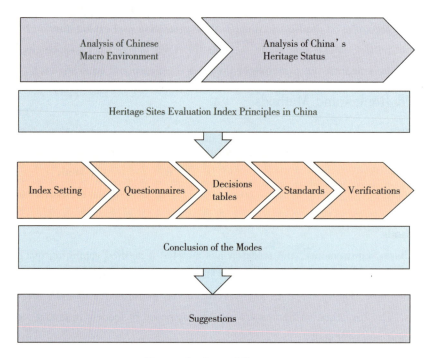

Diagram 1   Integral Structure

II The Sustainable Development Environment of China's World Cultural Heritage Sites

(Ⅰ) Economic Situation

In the period of the Eleventh – Five – Year Plan, China has made great achievements in economic and social developments. The gross domestic product has amounted to 39798.3 billion *yuan*. After adjusting for inflation, it grows by 69.9 percent compared with that of 2005. Annual GDP growth has amounted to 11.2 percent, far exceeding the average rate of the world level. China has become the second largest economy after the United States. According to the statistics, 27 China's world cultural heritage sites (including county – level cities) develop rapidly, among which 25 regions' GDP growth rates are above the national average level. Good economic environment is helpful for the protection and development of regional world cultural heritages. Meanwhile, the increasing of annual budget revenue proves the governmental capability to meet objective needs. In addition, from the perspective of economic structures, 12 regions (proportioned by 44.4 percent) are industrially developed; 11 regions (proportioned by 40.7 percent) have balanced development in three major industries, forming a virtuous circle with solid industry base as well as developed service industry; 4 regions (proportioned by 14.81 percent) lead in service industry with favorable development environment. All these ensure sustainable development of China's world cultural heritage sites with optimized industry structure.

Table 2 Development Conditions of China's World Cultural Heritage Sites in the Period of the Eleventh – Five – Year Plan

In the Period of the Eleventh – Five – Year Plan

Number	Names of the Heritage Sites	City Syntax	Economic Development						The livelihood of the people				Resources and Environment	
			Regional GDP		Regional Average Budget Revenue		Final Retail Sales of Consumer Goods (100 million yuan)	Three Major Industrial Structure	Urban and Rural Residents Income				Forest Coverage Rate (%)	Urban Greening Rate (%) / per capita area (m²)
			Final GDP (100 million yuan)	Annual Growth Rate (%)	Final GDP (100 million yuan)	Annual Growth Rate (%)			Urban Disposable Income (yuan)	Annual Growth Rate (%)	Net Rural Income (yuan)	Annual Growth Rate (%)		
1	Zhoukoudian Peking Man Site	Beijing	13777.9	11.4	2353.9		4470	0.9 : 24.1 : 75	29073	9.2	13262	9	37	45
2	The Summer Palace	Beijing												
3	The Temple of Heaven	Beijing												
4	Imperial Palace of the Ming and Qing Dynasties (Forbidden City, Beijing)	Beijing												
5	The Great Wall (Beijing)	Beijing												
6	Imperial Tombs of the Ming and Qing Dynasties (Beijing the Ming Tombs)	Beijing												
7	Mausoleum of the First Qin Emperor	Xi'an	3241.49	14.5	241.8	27	1611	4.3 : 43.5 : 52.2	22244	17.3	7750	23.5	45	31.97
8	Dazu Rock Carvings	Chongqing	7800	14.9	1018.39	30	2880.1	8.7 : 55.2 : 36.1	17532	11.3	5200	13.1	37	39.80/11.69 m²
9	The West Lake	Hangzhou	5945.82	12.4	671.34	21.8	2146.08	3.5 : 47.8 : 48.7	30035	12.6	13186	11.5	64.56	
10	The Classical Gardens of Suzhou	Suzhou	9168.9	13.9	900.55	20.9		1.7 : 57.7 : 40.6	29219	12.4	14657	11.8	23.5	
11	Historic Monuments in "the Centre of Heaven and Earth" in Dengfeng, Henan	Zhengzhou	4000	13	386.8	28.1	1678	3.1 : 56.7 : 40.2	18897	10.4	9225	13.6	25.68	10.5 m²
12	The Longmen Grottoes	Luoyang	2321.2	14.6	142	18.1	808.8	8.1 : 60.1 : 31.8	17639		5680		45	
13	Temple, Mansion, and Cemetery of Confucius	Qufu	235.29	13.4	10.77	13.1	92.23	10.3 : 40.5 : 49.2	14011		7402			24.2
14	The Potala Palace (Jokhang Temple, Norbulingka)	Lhasa	182	16	15	36	88.8	4.9 : 30.3 : 64.8	16323	11.61	5000	15.79	18.3	
15	Kaiping Diaolou and Villages	Jiangmen	1570.42	13	104.29		655.86	7.5 : 55.5 : 37	21153	10.4	8589	9.98		11 m²
16	Mount Lu	Jiujiang	1032	13.7	116.7	24	284.1	9.5 : 56.2 : 34.3	15764	12.6	5588	11.3	54.7	

续表

In the Period of the Eleventh – Five – Year Plan

Number	Names of the Heritage Sites	City Syntax	Economic Development						The livelihood of the people				Resources and Environment	
			Regional GDP		Regional Average Budget Revenue		Final Retail Sales of Consumer Goods (100 million yuan)	Three Major Industrial Structure	Urban and Rural Residents Income				Forest Coverage Rate (%)	Urban Greening Rate (%) / per capita area (m²)
			Final GDP (100 million yuan)	Annual Growth Rate (%)	Final GDP (100 million yuan)	Annual Growth Rate (%)			Urban Disposable Income (yuan)	Annual Growth Rate (%)	Net Rural Income (yuan)	Annual Growth Rate (%)		
17	Mount Tai	Tai' an	2000	14.5	116.9	23.5	687.4	9.5 : 53.5 : 37	19800	13.9	7592	13	36.9	
18	Mountain Resort and its Outlying Temples, Chengde	Chengde	880.5	14	54.84			15.8 : 51.0 : 33.2	13212	12.2	4382	11.2	55.8	42.6
19	Yungang Grottoes	Datong	694.3	10	2.0615	8.1	303.02	5.1 : 48.8 : 46.1	16103	13.2	4063	14.6	20.11	37.46/7.72 m²
20	Anyang Yin Xu	Anyang	1311.3	14.3	65	17.5	345.3	12.1 : 61.7 : 26.2	16394	13.2	6359	10	29.1	
21	Mogao Grottoes in Dunhuang	Jiuquan	405	14.6	16.68	30.9	87.6	13.4 : 51.9 : 34.7	5852	10	2715	11.3	30.24	10.3 m²
22	Ancient Building Complex in the Wudang Mountains	Shiyan	630	12.5	30	21	375	12.1 : 46.2 : 41.7	12400	12.1	3400	13.3	53	
23	The Old Town Of Lijiang	Lijiang	143.59	13.6	16.46	32.3	45.5	18.1 : 38.3 : 43.6	15521	8.6	3410	13.3	66.2	
24	The Ancient City of Ping Yao	Jinzhong	636.8	12	64.8	27.5		8.5 : 54.9 : 36.6	14628		5194	12.3	37.98	9.84 m²
25	Wutai Mountain	Yizhou	435.4	13.2	42.34	26.2	169.8	10.8 : 44.8 : 44.4	13683	14.3	3445.7	16.3	14.3	
26	Ancient Villages in Southern Anhui – Xidi and Hongcun	Huangshan	309.3	11.8	43.3	28.5	126	12.7 : 44.1 : 43.2	15834	13.2	6710		77.4	
27	The Mount Huang shan													
28	Mount Qingcheng and the Dujiangyan Irrigation System	Dujiangyan	143.5	11.3	55.6	40.8		12.1 : 34.7 : 53.2					57.23	
29	Capital Cities and Tombs of the Ancient Koguryo Kingdom	Ji' an	72	28.2	5.3	29.4	22	8.7 : 52.8 : 38.5	14000		6095	14	78.3	
30	Fujian Tulou	Longyan	991.5	14.6	66.75	22.8		13 : 53.3 : 33.7		11.7		10.9	77.9	
31	Mount Wuyi	Nanping	728.73	13.3	38.58	20.7	254.08	21.9 : 41.9 : 36.2	17332	11.9	6759	10.7	75.7	93.1
32	Mount Emei Scenic Area, including Leshan Giant Buddha Scenic area	Leshan	743.92	15.2	45.77	27.8		13.4 : 59.5 : 27.1	15237	15.2	5613	11.6	54.4	9.3 m²
33	Historic Centre of Macao	Macao	1870.04				437.71		305621.5					

Note: Interregional World Cultural Heritages in this table including Imperial Palace of the Ming and Qing Dynasties, the Great Wall and Imperial Tombs of the Ming and Qing Dynasties are mainly refered to those parts in Beijing; The GDP statistics of Macao is accounted by 82. 65 % of the year – end exchange rate in 2010.

Table 3 Populations and Consumption Conditions of China's World Cultural Heritage Sites in the Period of the Eleventh – Five – Year Plan

Number	Names of the Heritage Sites	Region Syntax	Demographic Factor					Consumption Index			
			Permanent Resident Population (ten thousand)	Urban Population		Rural Population		Urban per Capita Consumption		Rural per Capita Consumption	
				Amount (ten thousand)	Proportion (%)	Amount (ten thousand)	Proportion (%)	Consumption (yuan)	Growth Proportion (%)	Consumption (yuan)	Growth Proportion (%)
1	Zhoukoudian Peking Man Site	Beijing	1961.2	1685.9	86	275.3	14	21984	10.3	11078	
2	The Summer Palace										
3	The Temple of Heaven										
4	Imperial Palace of the Ming and Qing Dynasties (Forbidden City, Beijing)										
5	The Great Wall (Beijing)										
6	Imperial Tombs of the Ming and Qing Dynasties (the Ming Tombs, Beijing)										
7	Mausoleum of the First Qin Emperor	Xi'an	851.34	596.79	70.1	254.55	29.9			6705	19
8	Dazu Rock Carvings	Chongqing	2919	1605.96	55.02	1313.04	44.98	14974.49	12.3	4502.06	24.2
9	The West Lack	Hangzhou	870.04	637.27	73.25	232.77	26.75	18,595	11.2	14995	20.7
10	The Classical Gardens of Suzhou	Suzhou	1046.6					21046	17.7		
11	Historic Monuments in "the Centre of Heaven and Earth" in Dengfeng, Henan	ZhengZhou	862.65	551	63.87	311.65	36.13	14605.48	16		

续表

Number	Names of the Heritage Sites	Region Syntax	Permanent Resident Population (ten thousand)	Demographic Factor				Consumption Index			
				Urban Population		Rural Population		Urban per Capita Consumption		Rural per Capita Consumption	
				Amount (ten thousand)	Proportion (%)	Amount (ten thousand)	Proportion (%)	Consumption (yuan)	Growth Proportion (%)	Consumption (yuan)	Growth Proportion (%)
12	The Longmen Grottoes	Luoyang	654.95					13884	1815 元		
13	Temple, Mansion, and Cemetery of Confucius	Qufu	64.05								
14	The Potala Palace (Jokhang Temple, Norbulingka)	Lhasa	55.94					14500	5.8		
15	Kaiping Diaolou and Villages	Jiang men	446.55	280.43	62.8	166.12	37.2	15561			
16	Mount Lu	Jiujiang	472.88	201.05	42.52	271.83	57.48	10823	15.5		
17	Mount Tai	Tai'an	551.4	283.5	51.41	267.9	48.59	14888	10.9	4855	13.6
18	Mountain Resort and its Outlying Temples, Chengde	Chengde	347.32					10902.6	14.9	4984	35.7
19	Yungang Grottoes	Datong	333.97	188.66	56.49	145.31	43.51	12243	20.7	3740	51.3
20	Anyang Yin Xu	Anyang	515	208.52	40.49	306.48	59.51	11863	12.4	4304	15.5
21	Mogao Grottoes in Dunhuang	Jiuquan	110.07	56.23	51.09	53.84	48.91	14238	17.3	6462.48	14.04
22	Ancient Building Complex in the Wudang Mountains	Shiyan	334.08	136.97	41	197.12	59	3674.2	17.8		
23	The Old Town Of Lijiang	Lijiang	124.48					5056	8.9		
24	The Ancient City of Ping Yao	Jinzhong	327	149.57	45.74	177.43	54.26	11207	10.9	5351.8	40.8
25	Wutai Mountain	Yizhou	308.5	122.8	39.8	185.7	60.2	9064.9	1.8	3793	24.72

续表

Number	Names of the Heritage Sites	Region Syntax	Demographic Factor					Consumption Index			
			Permanent Resident Population (ten thousand)	Urban Population		Rural Population		Urban per Capita Consumption		Rural per Capita Consumption	
				Amount (ten thousand)	Proportion (%)	Amount (ten thousand)	Proportion (%)	Consumption (yuan)	Growth Proportion (%)	Consumption (yuan)	Growth Proportion (%)
26	Ancient Villages in Southern Anhui – Xidi and Hongcun	Huangshan	148.05	36.38	24.57	111.67	75.43	11069	0.6	4163	2.9
27	The Mount Huangshan										
28	Mount Qingcheng and the Dujiangyan Irrigation System	Dujiangyan	60.95	17.27	28.33	43.68	71.67	9715	18.6		
29	Capital Cities and Tombs of the Ancient Koguryo Kingdom	Ji' an	23.24	10.92	47	12.31	53	3844	9.3		
30	Fujian *Tulou*	Longyan	255.95	115.22	45.02	140.73	54.98	14483	9.2	4815	7.3
31	Mount Wuyi	Nanping	313.9	134.23	50.74	130.32	49.26	11284	9.3	4991	9.3
32	Mount Emei Scenic Area, including Leshan Giant Buddha Scenic Area	Leshan	323.58	127.73	39.48	195.84	60.52	4394	3.7		
33	Historic Centre of Macao	Macao	552,503								

Note: Interregional World Cultural Heritages in this table including Imperial Palace of the Ming and Qing Dynasties, the Great Wall and Imperial Tombs of the Ming and Qing Dynasties mainly refers to the parts located in Beijing; The GDP statistics of Macao is accounted by 82. 65% of the year – end exchange rate in 2010.

(II) Consumption Capacity

According to Table 3, there are two trends of the consumption capacity in China's world cultural heritage sites. One is the relatively high urbanization rate and strong consumption capacity of the first class cities. They are capable enough to support the sustainable development and to some extent own less heritage – dependent regional economic and social development. The other is the relatively low urbanization rate and limited consumption capacity of the third and below – third class cities. In these areas, the world cultural heritages have made great contributions to regional economic and social development.

(III) Regional Cultural Resources and Tourism Industry

1. Abundance in Traditional Culture Resources, and its Modernization and Industrialization

Generally speaking, China's world cultural heritage sites are rich in resources. All kinds of ancient capital cities, gardens, immovable cultural relics, museums provide natural basis for the development of cultural industry, especially tourism industry. Developing modern tourism industry is gradually becoming a common measure for every region. Take Xi'an as an example, it is a civilized city which harmoniously mixes historic features with modernization. Xi'an not only makes full use of its historical and cultural resources, but also develops new ecotourism and sightseeing tourism. Take another example, Chongqing develops cultural tourism relying on regional culture resources and boosts performing arts based on rich folk dance. Meanwhile, it develops video and film industry by the support of folk legends and literary stories. Chongqing has already made its abundant traditional culture modernized and industrialized.

2. Rapid Tourism Industry Development

Relying on rich heritage resources, regional tourism industry develops rapidly. Judging from the development conditions in 2011, modern tourism grew drastically. The annual gross income of every region increases fast by the percentage of over 10%, greatly exploiting regional cultural tourism resources.

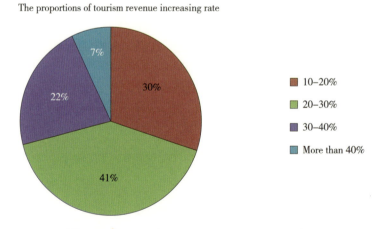

The proportions of tourism revenue increasing rate

- 10–20%
- 20–30%
- 30–40%
- More than 40%

Diagram 4   The Proportions of Tourism Revenue Increasing Rate of China's World Cultural Heritage Sites in 2011

In conclusion, the fast development of China's national power creates favorable environment. Besides, rapid regional development strongly supports fund, management, talents and others for healthy growth of world cultural heritages, which in turn effectively stimulates world heritage sites' development.

III   The Status Quo of China's World Cultural Heritage

(I) Protection Policies

Since the 30 years of reform and opening up, especially in the period of the Eleventh-Five-Year Plan, China's cultural heritage undertakings have made remarkable achievements periodically. China increases economic investment as well as enacts and completes laws for the protection of world cultural heritage. Legislation building has made great success both in the central and local areas. In the period of the Eleventh – Five – Year Plan, China is continuously developing protection and management legislations of world cultural heritage. Legal construction of cultural relics is accelerated and protection system is improved. Based on *Heritage Protection Act* and *World Heritage Convention*, China has enacted a series of laws, regulations and documents, such as *The Rules on Great Wall Protection*, *Historical and Cultural Cities and Towns Protection Ordinance*, *Protection Regulations for World Cultural Heritage*, *China's World Cultural Heritage Management Approach*, *China's World Cultural Heritage Consult and Management Approach*, *Inbound and Outbound Means of Cultural Relics Audit Management Measures*, *Administration of Cultural Relics Identification Interim Measures* and important normative documents like *Field Archaeology Work Regulations*, *National Archaeological Park Management Measures (Trial)*, *Interim Regulations of Inbound Cultural Relic Exhibitions* and *World Cultural Heritage Declaration Management Rules*. Meanwhile, the local people's congress and government are also strengthening the legislation construction of world cultural heritage protection and management with enacting and reformulating a series of laws and regulations based on local conditions. For example, *Mount Sanqing Scenic Spot Management Regulations in Jiangxi province* (2006), *Implementations of the World Natural Heritage Protection Regulations in Sichuan Province of Aba Tibetan and Qiang Autonomous Prefecture* (2008), *Hangzhou West Lake Cultural Heritage Landscape Protection Management Approach* (2008), *Protection Measures of China's Danxia Natural Heritage in Fujian Province* (2009), *Protection and Management Measures of The Potala Palace* (2009). What is more, *The Museum Regulations*, *Natural Heritage Protection Law*, *Intangible Cultural Heritage Law* and *Tourism Law*, are ready to be carried out. These laws, regulations and documents make China's cultural heritage career increasingly complete in management, operation and monitoring. Meanwhile, they provide legal support for cultural heritage and further standardize the daily work.

(II) Management System

1. National Government Management

Since the accession to World Heritage Convention, China has made improvements in the management of world culture heritage. According to the fourth article of the *World Cultural Heritage Protection Management Approach*, State Administration of Cultural Heritage is in charge of national world cultural heritage and responsible for solving vital problems and supervising the work. Local governments above the county level and cultural relics departments in the scope of administrative region should abide by the laws to formulate rules and implement measures.

From the national government's perspective, State Administration of Cultural Heritage is mainly in charge of China's world cultural heritage. The Cultural Relics Preservation and Archaeology Department (World Cultural Heritage Department) is set up to manage and direct the bides, protection, renovations, annual projects, budgets of world cultural heritage (including the cultural heritage part in the mixture of cultural and natural heritages). However, the Construction, Culture, Tourism, Forestry, Environment Protection, even Water Conservancy Department have its own management range in heritage sites. As 5A scenic spots, most world cultural heritages are not only managed by State Administration of Cultural Heritage, but also by National Tourism Administration which has organized secret investigations in the late October of 2011.

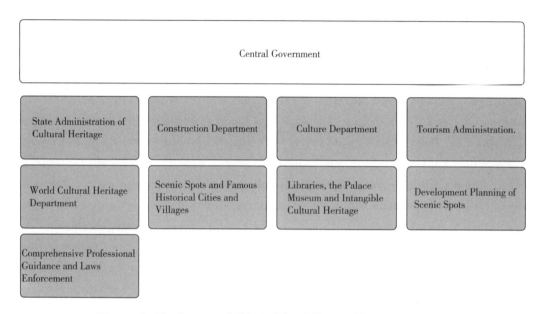

Diagram 5   The Structure of China's Cultural Heritage Management System

2. Local Government Management

China's world cultural heritages are mostly managed by the local governments, which generally adopt direct management, and instruct the corresponding institutions with diverse characteristics. There are three kinds of management mode in all. The first one is the institutional management system. Under this system, the cultural heritages are often covered in a relative larger area which may include ancient buildings, religious sites, natural landscape, and even the township and rural residents. The second one is that the local government has set up administrations or committees with the function of government to implement the unified management to the whole area, and coordinates the relationship with peripheral. For instance, Hangzhou exclusively established the West Lake Scenic Area Management Committee in order to protect and develop the West Lake heritage. Tai'an Municipal Government founded the Taishan Committee, as the agency, to carry out the unified management for Taishan cultural and natural heritage. There is a town government in Qingchengshan scenic area of Dujiangyan City. The administration and town government are equipped with the similar institutions which conduct the management and protection in an orderly way. And the director of the administration also serves as the mayor of the town. The Third one is enterprise management. Some world cultural heritages in whole or in part are operated by the company as assets in a few areas. Take Mount Huangshan as an example, part of its development function is granted to Mount Huangshan Tourism Development Corporation, which is in charge of the operation and management of scenic area development, as well as related tourism works, such ashotel, ropeway, travel agency, etc.

Table 6　An Overview of Administrative Ownership and Operation Management on China's World Cultural Heritages

Number	Name	Location	Administrative ownership	Management and operational institution
1	Zhoukoudian Peking Man Site	Beijing	The Government of Fangshan District	Zhoukoudian Peking Man Site Management Office
2	The Great Wall	Beijing	Badaling Yanqing County Government	Badaling Special Zone Office
		Gansu	Jiayuguan Bureau of Culture Radio and Television	Jiayuguan Heritage Area Management Committee
		Hebei	Shanhaiguan Qinhuangdao City government	Shanhaiguan Bureau of Cultural Relics
		Hebei	Jishanling Luanping County Government	jinshanling Great Wall Management Office
3	The Summer Palace	Beijing	Beijing Park Management Center	Beijing Municipal Gardens Bureau and The Summer Palace Management Office
4	The Temple of Heaven	Beijing	Beijing Park Management Center	Beijing Tiantan Park Management Office
5	Imperial Palaces of the Ming and Qing Dynasties (Forbidden City in Beijing, Imperial Palace in Shenyang)	Beijing / Shenyang in Liaoning Province	The Ministry of Culture / Shenyang Bureau of Culture (Shenyang Bureau of Cultural Relics)	The Palace Museum in Beijing / Museum of Shenyang Imperial Palace
6	Mogao Grottoes in Dunhuang	Dunhuang	The Government of Gansu Province	Dunhuang Research Institute
7	Mausoleum of the First Qin Emperor	Lintong District of Xi'an in Shaanxi province	Cultural Relics Bureau of Xi'an	Qinshihuang Mausoleum Museum
8	Mountain Resort and its Outlying Temples, Chengde	Chengde in Hebei Province	Chengde Bureau of Cultural Relics	Chengde Administration of Landscaping
9	Temple, Mansion, and Cemetery of Confucius	Qufu in Shandong Province	Qufu City government	Qufu Municipal Bureau of Cultural Relics
10	Ancient Building Complex in the Mount Wudang	Shiyan in Hubei province	Shiyan City government	Mount Wudang Committee of Tourism and Special Economic Zone
11	Potala Palace (Jokhang Temple, The Norbulingka)	Tibet (Lhasa)	Tibet Bureau of Cultural Relics	Potala Palace Management Office / Jokhang Temple Management Committee / The Norbulingka Garden Management Office
12	Old Town of Lijiang	Yunnan (Lijiang)	Lijiang Naxi Autonomous County Bureau of Culture of Yunnan Province	Protection Administration of theOld Town of Lijiang
13	Ancient City of Pingyao	Shanxi (Gutao Town)	Pingyao Government	The Pingyao County Management Committee of Protection
14	Yungang Grottoes	Shanxi (Datong)	Datong City Government	Yungang Grottoes Research Institute
15	Mount Wutai	Shanxi (Fanshi County, Wutai County)	Mount Wutai Scenic Area Government	Mount Wutai Administration of Shanxi Province

续表

Number	Name	Location	Administrative ownership	Management and operational institution
16	The Classical Gardens of Suzhou	Jiangsu (Suzhou)	Suzhou City Government	Suzhou Bureau of Landscaping
17	Dazu Rock Carvings	Chongqing (Dazu County)	Dazu County Government of Chongqing	Dazu Rock Carvings Art Museum of Chongqing
18	Ancient Villages in Southern Anhui Province (represented by Xidi and Hongcun)	Anhui (Mount Huangshan Scenic Area in Yixian County)	The city government of the scenic area	
19	Longmen Grottoes	Henan (Luoyang)	Luoyang Government	Longmen Grottoes Park Committee
20	Yin Xu in Anyang	Henan (Anyang Xiaotun village and its surrounding area)	Anyang Government	Yin Xu Management Center
21	Historic Monuments in "the Centre of Heaven and Earth" of Dengfeng	Henan (Dengfeng)	Cultural Relics Bureau of Henan Province / Dengfeng Bureau of Cultural Relics	Dengfeng Bureau of Cultural Relics
22	Mount Qingcheng and the Dujiangyan Irrigation System	Sichuan (Dujiangyan)	Dujiangyan City Government	Administration of Mount Qingcheng and the Dujiangyan Scenic Area
23	Capital Cities and Tombs of the Ancient Koguryo Kingdom	Jilin (Ji'an)	Ji'an City Government	Ji'an Bureau of Cultural Relics
24	The Historic Centre of Macao	Macao	SAR Government	Macao Bureau of Culture
25	Kaiping Diaolou and Villages	Guangdong (Jiangmen)	Kaiping City Government	Kaiping Bureau of Cultural Relics
26	Fujian *Tulou*	Fujian	Culture and Sports Bureau of Yongding County	Office of Tulou Protection
27	Mount Lu	Jiangxi (Jiujiang)	Planning Bureau of Lushan District	Mount Lu Scenic Area Committee
28	The West Lake	Zhejiang (Hangzhou)	Hangzhou Bureau of Landscape and Cultural Relics	West Lake Scenic Area Committee

续表

Number	Name	Location	Administrative ownership	Management and operational institution
			Imperial Tombs of the Ming and Qing Dynasties	
29	Xianling Tomb of Ming Dynasty	Hubei (Zhongxiang County)	Zhongxiang County Bureau of Culture	Management Office of Xianling tomb
	Eastern Imperial Tombs of the Qing Dynasty	Hebei (Zunhua)	Zunhua City Government	Management Office of Eastern Imperial Tombs of the Qing Dynasty
	Western Imperial Tombs of the Qing Dynasty	Hebei (Yixian County)	Yixian County Government	Management Office of Western Imperial Tombs of the Qing Dynasty
	Tomb of Emperor Zhu Yuanzhang	Jiangsu (Nanjing)	Nanjing City Government	Administration of Sun Yatsen Mausoleum
	Ming Tombs	Beijing (Changping District)	The Government of Changping District	Special Zone Office of Ming Tombs
	Three Tombs in Shengjing	Liaoning (Shenyang, Fushun)	Fuling City Government and Zhaoling City Government	Fuling Urban Construction Bureau, Zhaoling Urban Construction Bureau
			The Yongling Xinbin Man Autonomous County Government	Yongling Office of Cultural Relics
30	Mount Tai	Shandong (Tai'an)	Tai'an Bureau of Planning	Mount Tai Scenic Area Committee
31	Mount Huangshan	Anhui (Huangshan)	Huangshan City Government	Mount Huangshan Scenic Area Committee
32	MountEmei—Mount Le	Sichuan (Emeishan)	Emeishan City Government	Mount Emei Scenic Area Committee
33	Mount Wuyi	Fujian	Wuyishan City Government	Mount Wuyi Scenic Area Committee

Resource: data from research group

3. The Internal Management of Heritage Sites

China's world cultural heritages are various and complex, such as the Imperial Palace, Mogao Grottoes, Jokhang Temple, Suzhou Gardens and so on which are the State – level key units of cultural relics protection. Their major bodies are relatively closed, and boundaries are clear. Other heritages are related to community management, so the management of heritage sites varies from each other. Overall, most heritage sites are implemented direct management mechanism by governments or institutions, with the corresponding administrative organizations which set up management departments with different function, according to different features. Those organizations classify and grade the management of heritage monitoring, protection, development, comprehensive management and other affairs in terms of relevant regulations. From the functional point of view, heritage administrative organizations can be divided into two major categories: heritage protection and heritage development.

Take Suzhou Gardens as an example, the Gardening and Greening Management Bureau in Suzhou is responsible for the management of the major body of Suzhou Gardens, which operates the Humble Administrator's Garden Management Office (Zhuozheng Garden) , the Lion Forest Management Office, the Lingering Garden Management Office (Liuyuan Garden) , the Garden of the Master of the Nets Management Office, the East Garden Management Office, World Cultural Heritage Protection and Supervision Center of Classical Gardens and other professional organizations. There are corresponding departments for the main function. The Garden Management Branch, Gardening Branch, Security Branch, and Archives Branch also take charge of protection function other than the World Cultural Heritage Protection and Supervision Center of Classical Gardens. And the Comprehensive Business Department is responsible for the operation, ticket marketing, infrastructure management, and implementation of the ticket checking, guiding, service, and comprehensive repair management.

4. Human Resource Management

The sustainable development of world cultural heritages lies in the talents training and development. According to general conclusion by the research group, the new professional and technical personnel and the training on heritages attract a great attention of administrative organizations which begin to focus on absorbing professional and technical personnel. The number of staff with rich experience and professional knowledge is increasing. At the same time, the world heritage training and research institutions are founded in every heritage area. They are active in extensive cooperation with universities and scientific research units to enhance the staff training and upgrading. Take Dunhuang as an example. From 2006 to 2011, Dunhuang Research Institute positively hired a large number of talents with master, doctor and post – doctoral degrees which have professional knowledge that meet the demands for the Dunhuang heritage protection, utilization, management, and researches. The intellectual staffs account for 70% of the total number of employees in this institute. Meanwhile, Dunhuang Institute has continuously strengthened the professional training to all the staffs, and a team with the ability of comprehensive heritage protection and management, experience and professional knowledge has been basically organized.

(III) Protection Measures

World Cultural Heritage is a kind of precious but non – renewable resource and cultural wealth of human beings. After some heritages succeed in bidding for World Cultural Heritage in recent years, their reputation is raised tremendously with the remarkable economic and social benefits. China has involved in an unprecedented "heritage fever" in which local governments are is actively involved. Much attention has been given to the heritage protection by the central and local governments. Ever since then, the polices and measures regarding the world cultural heritage protection, are further strengthened. According to statistics, 33 world cultural heritage sites have set up the appropriate monitoring organizations, hired monitoring professionals, utilized and developed the advanced technical monitoring means and tools, and established the special funds for the protection monitoring to cooperate with state reinforcement. The protection of cultural heritages has been paid more attention than ever before.

Take West Lake as an example, the process of cultural heritage bidding not only embodies the principle of protection but also is regarded as the process of protection, which is fully in line with the concept of world cultural heritage protection. The West Lake comprehensive protection project implemented in 2002 and the West Lake landscape regulation project launched in 2008 speak for the biggest scale of West Lake protection since the foundation of new China and have significantly improved West Lake's protection. After the successful bid for the Hangzhou world cultural heritage, West Lake adheres to the "six don'ts": First, do not change the target of "returning the lake to citizens"; Second, do not raise the ticket fee; Third, do not administer charge to the museums; Fourth, do not sale the land; Fifth, do not permit damage to cultural relics; Sixth, do not permit occupation of public resources. Establishing and improving the system of resources protection and management of West Lake can realize the maximal and optimal profits of the public resources. All new projects in the heritage community should satisfy the environmental evaluation of the cultural heritages to prevent the West Lake scenic area from creeping of the city development. In order to cooperate with the state to make the monitoring protection of the world cultural heritages, "Monitoring and Management Center of Hangzhou West Lake World Cultural Heritage" was formally established on July 15, 2011, with branches of West Lake landscape Real – time Monitoring and Management Center and World Cultural Heritage Monitoring and Management Center. The cultural landscape of West Lake can always be guaranteed in a good protection status by constructing and implementing the monitoring and warning system.

(IV) Demands and Supplies

The expense demanded to maintain the world cultural heritages in the normal operation generally covers maintenance, personnel costs, administrative expenditure, R&D expenditure, and the major projects expenditure. Whether the demand of heritage protection funds can be met timely is a basic premise to measure the sustainable development of heritage sites. At present, the origin of protection funds of China's world cultural heritages mainly relies on three aspects: ticket incomes, development (business) incomes, and governmental financial support. According to different operating conditions of the heritage sites, the three financial resources are in different proportions for protection needs. On the basis of statistics, 90% of the heritage sites have enough income to meet the financial demand of the heritage protection.

In sum, Chances for sustainable development of China's world heritage sites go with challenges. On the one hand, the domestic economic development is strong in China. With the domestic residents' disposable income increasing, the consumption level of domestic tourism will boost continuously, which provides possibility for the increase of ticket income in heritage sites. In terms of heritage protection policy, the national and municipal governments attach great importance to the protection of world cultural heritages. All kinds of policies, measures, capital investments are constantly added, which has laid a solid foundation for sustainable development of the heritage sites. On the other hand, some adverse aspects exist in the internal part of the heritage sites, such as the low development and indeterminate management system. From the external part, the hot consumption of domestic tourism also probably puts great pressure on the protection of heritage sites. All of these are not favorable to the sustainable development of the world cultural heritages in China. In short, if we want to realize sustainable development of the heritage sites, we must take the above into consideration. Therefore, it is imperative to devise the standards to measure the sustainable development of heritage sites, and promote the sustainable and healthy development.

IV Evaluation System of Sustainable Development of China's World Cultural Heritage Sites

China ranks the third throughout the world in the aspect of the quantity of cultural heritages. It stretches across vast area with a large number of populations and a long history, in which different cultures gather, melt and influence each other. In this background, the characteristics of world heritages, especially the world cultural heritages are diversified. It has been more than 2, 500 years from the prehistoric Peking man to the Tang, Song and Qing dynasties. Across the land of 9, 600, 000 square kilometers in China, there stand many world cultural heritages which are unparalleled by those in Spain, Italy and other European countries no matter from value, culture or complexity. Therefore, the current theory of sustainable development in the world cannot be directly applied to the examination on the issue of China's world cultural heritages. The research group considers that, during the process of studying the evaluation system of sustainable development of world cultural heritages, we should take China's current social situation, natural condition, economic level, culture level and other factors into consideration, and learn the successful experiences on world cultural heritage protection from other countries to establish an evaluation system that accords with Chinese characteristics.

After the description and analysis of comprehensive environment and status on China's heritage sites, this chapter is concerned with the construction and instruction for the sustainable development evaluation system of China's cultural heritages. The whole system is constructed through the qualitative and quantitative studies as a supplement. This system mainly depends on the grading and ranking for evaluation, which aims at a frame and model for the sustainable development evaluation.

The whole evaluation system consists of three major value subjects and four levels of information structure. The three value subjects, including heritage value, protection ability and development level, divide the features of sustainable development into three levels: heritage value foundation, maintenance, innovation and development. They completely cover the development and protection needs of the institutions and the public.

At the same time, in order to evaluate, manage and guide the local and operational institutions of various heritage sites more effectively, and ensure the correct direction of sustainable development, in terms of implementation, the evaluation system makes the value subjects a four – level information structure including: index requirement information, index data information, index judgment information and comprehensive evaluation information. The system covers the entire evaluation workflow from goal setting, information collection to information analysis and makes information specification correspond to the index decom position table, questionnaire, index judgment table, comprehensive evaluation table respectively. The index decomposition table clarifies the requirements and the data of evaluation objects can be acquired by questionnaires. According to the corresponding index, the collected data can be analyzed by the methods of document evaluation and scene verification for preliminary evaluation. Finally, the sustainable development can be evaluated on the basis of the comprehensive information.

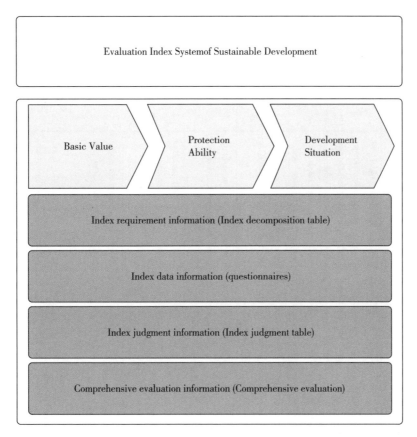

Diagram 7   The Evaluation Index System of Sustainable Development of China's World Heritage Sites

(I) Establishment of the Evaluation System

1. Index Table

The index table of the sustainable development divides the whole heritage sites into some units in accordance with basic informiation, protection ability, and development situation. These units show the properties, characteristics, and comprehensive information of the heritage sites. The first unit mainly includes basic information, value types and the environment, which describe the heritage sites through information collections. The second unit describes the internal situation to investigate the self – protection ability of heritage sites through five modules: the institutions, management documents, technical supports, research and development, and funding. The third unit consists of the number of visitors, service types, institutions, management and investment of development, income, and profit, these blocks are used to investigate the development situation and sustainable development ability on the basis of protection.

Index table includes the category of index, objects of evaluation index and description of index selections and completely forms the internal, external and regional situation, which lays the foundation for information collections, questionnaire setting, and provides evidence for the index judgment and evaluation.

Table 8 The Evaluation Index List of Sustainable Development of China's World Cultural Heritages

Index Category	Index Name	Index Factor	Index Description	Index Function	Data Source
(Ⅰ) The information of heritage sites	1. Basic Information	Names of heritage sites	Official appellations of heritage sites	The official names ensure the uniformity and consistency to the relevant systems of heritage sites	The official websites of World Heritage Sites
		Types of heritage sites	The classification referring to the national law on the protection of Cultural Relics and the heritage features and devided them into ancient tombs, ancient buildings, and so on.	The classification of the heritage sites according to the different features benefits the comparison study of the law of value, and establishment of applied evaluation criteria and development strategy	The National Law on the Protection of Cultural Relics
		The time of being selected into the World Cultural Heritage list	The bidding and selected time for World Cultural Heritage	After formally being listed into World Cultural Heritage, the heritage is put into the special protection area. And the related protection, development requirements become the practical reference and criteria	The official website of World Heritage Sites
		The area of heritage sites	The scope of bidding for the world cultural heritage includes central and buffer area.	The area of heritage sites has a certain effect on the protection measures, protection costs and personnel scales	
		The locations of heritage sites	Heritage sites are directly affiliated with administrative areas with financial relationship, such as province, city, and county	The city size and the social economic development of heritage sites support and interact the sustainable development	Provided by heritage sites
		The names of operational institutions	The institutions directly responsible for the daily operation	The daily operations of heritage sites lay an essential foundation for evaluating the management and operation	
		The types of operational institutions	The nature of the operational units, such as administrative agencies, institutions, enterprises and social groups	It helps to know the basic nature of daily operation and management of heritage sites and the characteristic as well as the influence to the sustainable development for heritage sites.	The websites of China's Heritage Sites
		Ownership of operational institutions	The higher administrative departments to which operational institutions directly belong	It contributes to learn the related management system and mode as well as the influence to the sustainable development	
	2. Forms of Values	Cultural values	The inherent culture, emotions and spiritual values carried by the heritage sites include times, tradition, continuity, legend, miracle, emotion, spirit, religion, politics, symbol, patriotism, people, etc.	The inherent cultural value has a certain influence on the local cultural life, public good and so on but also determines the importance of content level and development potential of the protection	The websites of China's Heritage Sites-The official website of World Heritage Sites
		Professional values	The technical or professional apparent worth of heritage sites includes the importance in the aspects of design, technique, structure, function, technology and rarity, representative and uniqueness related to type, style, builder, period and community	The apparent worth of heritage sites has economic and technical influence on the protection and development of heritage sites	

续表

Index Category	Index Name	Index Factor	Index Description	Index Function	Data Source
（Ⅰ）The information of heritage sites	2. Forms of Values	Protection level of cultural relics	The relics grade, type, category, quantity that heritage involves	The grade and quantity of relics in the heritage sits relate to the degree and cost of protection, which can be regarded as an important constituent to investigate the protection work	The websites of China's Heritage Sites
		Natural environment	Regional plant coverage	Green coverage rate has impact on the local environment, and is also one of the factors influencing the heritage protection	Gardens Bureau of Heritage Sites
			Regional rainfall	Rainfall influences the local air humidity and natural disaster, such as debris flow, flood	Meteorological Bureau of Heritage Sites
			Regional water system, such as rivers, lakes, waterfalls, coastal, etc	Regional water system has influence on the air humidity. There might be flood where water system is rich	Water Conservancy Bureau of Heritage Sites
			Regional environmental quality regarding air, water	The Pollution will seriously affect the change of heritage sites, relating to the analysis of protection.	Environmental Protection Bureau of Heritage Sites
			Regional factors of force – major, such as earthquakes, floods, storms, infectious diseases, disasters	Disasters will affect the heritage protection.	Ministry of Environmental Protection of PRC
	3. Regional Environ – ment	Tourism environment	The quantity of hotels in the region	The number of hotels can influences the development of local economy and the reception capacity. The reasonable grade of the hotel is related to the consumption of local economy	Statistical yearbook
			The quantity of restaurants in the region	The number of restaurants can represent the richness of local special food as one of tourism resources, which can attract more tourists. If there are more high – end restaurants and moderately priced restaurants, there will be more travel groups, and the sizes of restaurants are larger with the higher reception capability	
			The quantityof other resorts in the region	The high – ranking resorts can attract more tourists. If there are many advanced resorts in the surroundings, the attraction of world cultural heritage sites will decline and reduce the pressure of excessive visitors reception	Heritage Area Tourism Bureau
			The conditions of transport facilities in the region	Transport conditions directly impact the number of tourists, which shows whether the heritage site is easy to reach or not	

续表

Index Category	Index Name	Index Factor	Index Description	Index Function	Data Source
	3. Regional Environment		Regional GNP (five years)	Economic gross indicates overall level of economic development by comparing that of different world heritage sites	
			The quantity of population in the region, including the number of household registration, permanent and temporary population	The population scale decides staff of heritage protection and social environment foundation and also decided development space and potentiality of the heritage sites	
			Regional fiscal revenues (five years)	It embodies basic scale of controllable capital of local government, and reflects the capability of support and execution to the protection and development of the heritage sites	
		Social economy	Tertiary industry value in the region (five years)	According to that, the proportion of output value in tertiary industry can be worked out, which directly reflects the degree to which local economy relies on the tertiary industry, including financial, transportation, tourism, culture	Statistical yearbook
			Tourism value in the region (five years)	According to that, the proportion of tourism output value in tertiary industry can be worked out, which indirectly reflects the degree to which service industry relies on the heritage sites	
			Regional residents' disposable income including urban and rural residents (five years)	The living standard and consumption standard of local residents is one of the basic indexes to investigate the development potentiality of heritage sites	
			The Engel coefficients of residents in the region (five years)	The Engel coefficient has relationship with the wealthy degree of the residents in the region, and determines the potential demand of cultural consumption, and is one of the basic indexes to investigate the development potentiality of heritage sites	
(I) The information of heritage sites		Heritage gathering	The development situation of the surrounding buildings and commercial facilities	It aims to investigate the influence that city construction and the commercial real estate have on the protection and development of heritage sites	Provided by operational institution of heritage sites
			Number of other relevant heritages gathered in the region	The number of the heritages in the region is helpful to analyze the interaction of the different heritages	Provided by operational institution of heritage sites

Index Category	Index Name	Index Factor	Index Description	Index Function	Data Source
Ⅱ. Protection ability index	1. Organiza – tions	Internal organization struc- tures and staffing	It refers to the internal department setup and staffing related to the daily operation and ma- intenance of heritage sites. Generally, inclu- ding the tourist management, environmental protection, security, monitoring, mainte- nance, rear – service. Make Sure names of departments, functions and staffing number, etc. should be clarified in detail.	The organization establishment and staffing directly reflects the management levels, protection ability of heritage sites, and the matching degree with the re- quirements of the protection of heritage sites	Provided by the annual reports of the operational institutions of heritage sites
		External administrative in- stitutions	The administrative organizations and depart- ments related to the protection and develop- ment of heritage sites, and department config- urations, including names of organizations, levels, management responsibility, and con- tents, etc.	The government administrative organizations, line or- ganizations, and configurations of the related organi- zations that are related to the protection of the herit- age sites reflect the general management mode and management efficiency of the heritage sites, and the overall support levels	
		External cooperative institu- tions	The external cooperative institutions related to the protection of the heritage sites, including institution names, character, function, and cooperation contents, etc.	The complement of the cooperative institutions and heritage sites on resources and abilities can enhance the overall quality and level of the protection of the heritage sites	
	2. Manage – ment documents	Documentation	The documentation and allocation of the policy and management papers related to the daily op- eration and maintenance work of heritage sites, generally, including planning, regulations, standards, management records, matching de- gree of daily management and job positions should also be considered	Management documents are the important guarantee to regulate, control and coordinate the daily operation and maintenance work of the heritage sites and the important foundation to determine the quality of the protection of them	
		Document management	The management situations related to the is- sue, transferring and updating, including the management requirements, delivery quantity, serviceability and number of updating, etc.	The integrity, applicability and effectiveness of the management documents is the precondition for guar- anteeing the effective implementation of relevant man- agement requirements	
		Document implementation	It refers to the implementation status of the related management documents, including the measures of supervision, inspection, and im- plementation, etc.	Implementation is the ultimate goal to make the man- agement documents, and effective supervision and management measures are the important guarantee for the quality of operation and management	

续表

Index Category	Index Name	Index Factor	Index Description	Index Function	Data Source
II. Protection ability index	3. Technical Support	Allocaction of Supportive Systems or equipments	It refers to the system supportive related to the safety protection, monitoring, maintenance, and environment management, including the category, specification and quantity, cycle and tenure of use Systemsor equipment control	The protection of the heritage sites is a relatively professional system engineering which needs the support of the professional system devices. Professional devices, system configuration, and management ability is the technological base of the sustainable development of heritage sites.	Provided by the annual reports of the operational institutions of heritage sites
		Management of Supportive Systems or equipments	Maintenance and integrity of relavent systems and equipments		
	4. Researchand develop - ment	Research and development ability	It includes the setup of the R&D departments, the number of the R&D staffing, the formation of the R&D staffing, and the R&D devices	The planned and guaranteed technology R&D and application will provide practically basic supportability for the sustainable development	
		Research and development plans	It includes R&D project plans, research budgets, and safeguard mechanism		
		Research and development implementation	It includes annual investment of the R&D funding, the implementation of the R&D projects, and the application of the R&D projects, with investigation of names and influence of key projects		
	5. Social publicity	Projects	It refers to the social publicity, education and projects	In order to investigate the protection of the operational agencies and improve the public awareness of protection	
	6. Funds	Operation costs (demands)	The capital number (5 years) for the good running of the daily operation maintenance work and the R&D work. Generally including repairs, personnel costs, administrative expenses, R&D costs as well as the major items expenditure. List the names, catagories, costs and use respectively by the sources	It aims to analyze capital requirement quantities, implementation conditions, variation trend, and formation characters for the maintenance of the operation and the preservation of cultural relics, and from the respect of finance, to analyze the levels of protection ability and operation conditions.	
		Capital resource (supplies)	The implementation conditions (5 years) of the operation funds, generally including the financial appropriation, administrative appropriation, enterprises donation or sponsor, income redistribution and other funding channels. List the names, costs and use respectively by the sources		

续表

Index Category	Index Name	Index Factor	Index Description	Index Function	Data Source
	1. Number of tourists	Tourist number in regions	It includes (five years) the total tourist number of the region that the heritage site lies and the statistical data of the local, other cities (domestic or overseas) tourist number	It aims to analyze the potentialities and key points for the heritage sites exploitation by grasping the passenger flow volume, component proportion ratio and variation tendency of the regions that the heritage site lies	Area Travel Statistical yearbook
		Tourist number of heritage sites	It includes (five years) the total tourist number of the heritage site and the statistical data of the local, and other cities (domestic or overseas) tourist number	It aims to analyze the law of development of the heritage site itself and the relativity of the local tourism development by grasping the passenger flow volume, component proportion ratio and variation tendency of the heritage site	Annual report of the heritage sites
Ⅲ. Development index		Direct products	Taking the heritage sites ontology as the products to provide direct service, generally including visiting, touring and other auxiliary service, etc	Direct products based on the tourism are the main source of income to provide the basic income guarantee, and acting as the important index to evaluate the operation power of the heritage site itself	
		Derived services	Using the value or contents of the heritage site as facsimiles to exploit other forms of products and services, generally including the souvenirs, and content products (AV, books, films)	The development of the derived and authorized products represents the ability of the operational institutions to exploit the added value and innovate.	
		Franchised services	The authorized service products based on the brand, image, or related theme elements, including patent rights, trademark rights, copyrights and other related intangible asset authorization		
	2. Service types	Adequate and systematic service	It includes the museums, catering services, venue rental (disposable, long－term), retail services and other service products matched with the main business of the heritage sites.	Generally, it is used to measure the ability of the internal and external resource consolidation or exploitation of the heritage sites, meanwhile, with the considerations of the value of the heritage site ontology and affection degree	Provided by the annual reports of operational institutions of heritage sites
		Projects development	Other service items or events carried out for the purpose of serving society and cultural transmission, including science and education projects, cultural projects and public welfare projects, etc.	It is the extension and development of the noumenon value on culture and education level, representing the contribution degree of the heritage site itself to social culture or ideological progress	
		New facilities	Develop new facilities within the heritage sites and produce added products and service income by functional supplement with original heritage site	New facilities, as a necessary complement or a natural extension to the heritage site ontology, to some extent, can expand value coverage of the heritage site or enhance its functionality, but also can weaken the heritage value and even cause some destructive dangers by the overexploitation	

续表

Index Category	Index Name	Index Factor	Index Description	Index Function	Data Source
Ⅲ. Development index	3. Institutions	Department setup and staffing	The department setup and staffing related to the product development, promotion, sales service, including department names, department functions and staffing number	It aims to investigate the attention that the operational institutions pay to the product development, market management and their practical execution ability	Provided by the annual reports of operational institutions of heritage sites
	4. Development management	Operational plans	It refers to the plans and making conditions related to the development and management work, including the product development, promotion, sales, customer service, etc.		
		Implementation situations	It refers to the implementation of the related programs, performance, and corresponding effects		
		Intellectual property right protection	It refers to the protection of intellectual property right related to the heritage sites, including property names, property types, protection measures and registration, protection status		
	5. Developmental investments	Propertyright protection expenditures	Expenditures that related to the intellectual property rights or the protection of intangible assets .	It aims to judge the development input degree by the physical input scale and component proportion ratio that the operational institutions used into the product development and operations	
		Product development expenditures	Expenditures that related to the new products development and maintenance, including labor costs, installation costs, space expenses and administrative expenses, etc.		
		Promotional expenditure	Expenditures that related to the product and service publicity		
		Product sales expenditure	Expenditures in the product sales and customer services, including labor and administrative costs		
		Other operational expenditure	The taxes directly related to operational income and other service expenditure.		
	6. Incomes	Undertaking revenue	Including the ticket income, other additional revenue (guide, tourist cars and boats)	It aims to reflect the value transformation ability, development mode and development level from the other side by investigating the product and market development, actual operational effect and structure of the operational institutions.	
		Operating income	Including derived products income, authorize products income, adequate and systematic service income, and project development income.		

续表

Index Category	Index Name	Index Factor	Index Description	Index Function	Data Source
Ⅲ. Development index	6. Incomes	State revenue	The normal fund of the public institutions provided by local public finance.	It aims to reflect the value transformation ability, development mode and development level from the other side by investigating the product and market development, actual operational effect and structure of the operational institutions.	Provided by the annual reports of operational institutions of heritage sites
		Financial add income	Special funds, and major special funds provided by the central and local government.		
		Grants from the higher authority	It refers to the extra – budgetary funds source		
		Other incomes	It refers to outbound investment, interest, rental, other units subsidies, miscellaneous income, and financing from the relevant international organizations and domestic enterprises, charitable organizations and other NGOs.		
	7. Balance	Institutional balance	Except for the operating income and expense, it is the balance after we make both ends meet within a certain period. Institution balance = financial aid income + grant from the higher authority + Institution revenue + subsidiary unit payment + other income – Institution expenditure – allowance for subsidiary unit – appropriation of money – payment for the higher authority – self – financing forward – sales taxes	It aims to investigate the comprehensive profitability and managerial ability of the operation agencies of heritage sites	
		Operational balance	It is the balance after we make both ends meet within a certain period. Operating balance = operating income – operating expenditure – operating taxes		
	8. Social benefits	Social contributions of the heritage sites to the related regions	It refers to the induced effects of the sustainable development of the heritage site on the region's society, economy, culture and life.	It aims to investigate the induced effects and contribution capacity the heritage site owns to the local society, economy, culture, and life	

Table 9 Index Decision Table of the Sustainable Development Evaluation on the China's World Cultural Heritages

Index types	Index names	Index elements	Decision conclusions	Decision reports (questionnaire, scene)	Standards
(I) Information of the heritage sites (benchmark)	1. Basic information	Names of the heritage sites			☐ accurate ☐ basically accurate ☐ not accurate
		Types of the heritage sites			☐ single ☐ centralized ☐ decentralized
		The time of being selected into The world cultural heritage list			A well-prepared step B preliminary step C preparing step
		Area of heritage sites			Protection scope: A large B medium C small
		Size of regions			Urban size: A large B medium B small
		Operational institutions of heritage sites			A standard B restricted C conditioned
	2. Value types	Cultural value			A comprehensive B physical C spiritual
		Professional value			
		Protection level of relics			A high B medium C low
	3. Regional environment	Natural environment			A positive B no effect C negative
		Tourism environment			A good B ordinary C poor
		Social economy			A develop rapidly B develop steadily C develop slowly / A consumption exuberance B general consumption C under consumption / A reasonable structure B balanced structure C imbalanced structure
		Neighboring regions development			A appropriate exploitation B less exploitation C over exploitation
		Heritage gathering			A dense B less dense C none
		General characteristics			A solid foundation B less solid foundation C weak foundation
(II) Protection ability index (Hedge)	1. Institutions	Internal organization structures and staffing			A sound organization B qualified organization C unsound organization
		External relevant administrations			A centralized management B separated management C multi-management
		External cooperative institutions			A closed cooperation B loose cooperation C no cooperation

续表

Index types	Index names	Index elements	Decision conclusions	Decision reports (questionnaire, scene)	Standards
(II) Protection ability index (Hedge)	2. Management documents	Documentation			A sufficient documents B passably documents C insufficient documents
		Document management			A well – managed B passably managed C ill – managed
		Document implementation			A well implemented B ordinarily implemented C poorly implemented
	3. Technical support	Systems or devices			A sufficient B meet the needs C insufficient
		System or device management			A well – managed B passably managed C ill – managed
	4. R&D	R&D ability			A capable B common C poor
		R&D plans			A good B common C poor
		R&D implementation			A well implemented B ordinarily implemented C poorly – implemented
	5. Social publicity	Publicity			A often B sometimes C never
	6. Capital support	Operation costs (demands)			A reasonable structure B ordinary C unreasonable structure
		Capital sources (supplies)			A sufficient B ordinary C insufficient
(III) Development Index (Increment)	1. Tourist number	General characteristics			A well – protected B ordinarily – protected C ill – protected or over – protected
		Tourist number in regions			□ increase □ stable □ decrease ☐ mainly local □ mainly other cities □ local and others balance
		Tourist number of heritage sites			A steadily increase B stable C steadily decrease ☐ mainly local □ mainly other cities □ balanced
	2. Product forms	Direct products			A sufficient B single C under developed or over developed
		Derived products			
		Authorized products			
		Adequate and systematic service			
		Project development			
		New facilities			

续表

Index types	Index names	Index elements	Decision conclusions	Decision reports (questionnaire, scene)	Standards
(Ⅲ) Development Index (Increment)	3. Institutions	Department setup and staffing			A good B common C poor
		Operational plans			A good B common C poor
	4. Development and management	Implementation situations			A well implemented B ordinarily implemented C poorly implemented
		Intellectual property right protection			A well – protected B partially protected C ill – protected
	5. Development investment	property protection right expenditure			A sufficient B ordinary C insufficient
		Product development expenditure			
		Promotional expenditure			
		Product sales expenditure			
		Other operational expenditure			
	6. Incomes	Undertaking revenue			A development independent B resource independent C government independent
		Operational income			
		State revenue			
		Financial aid income			
		Grant from the high authority			
		Other income			
	7. Operational Balance	Undertaking balance			A profit B balance C deficit
		Operating balance			
	8. Social benefits	Social contributions of heritage sites			A great B common C less
	General characteristics				A well – developed B less developed C underdeveloped or overdeveloped

Table 10　Comprehensive Evaluation Table of the Sustainable Development of the World Heritage in China

Marking items			Marking reports / Marking scheme		
			A good foundations	B Common foundations	C Poor foundations
Basic conditions	Heritage sites ontology and environmental characteristics (not assessment items)				
	Operational and maintenance institutions	Institutions	With integrated organization and clear functional distribution	With basic organizations or related functional distribution	Lack of key organization components
		Staffing	With all ready positions and adequate staffing	Staffing basically meet the needs	Inadequate staffing of key components
		Management documents	With complete management documents and strong systematicness	With necessary basic management documents	Lack of key management documents (log files, etc)
		Technical supports	With complete technical means, well-managed	With basic technical support capability	Lack of support means or cannot meet the needs
		Innovation development	With complete innovation development capabilities and quantitative development input per year	With certain development capabilities, but input general	Lack of development capabilities
Operational ability		Cooperative in-stitutions (options)	With two-way cooperative relations	With certain cooperative relations	
	Operational organization	Institutions	With integrated organization and clear functional distribution	With basic organizations	Lack of key organization components
		Staffing	With all ready positions and adequate staffing	With basic organizations or related functional distribution	Inadequate staffing of key components
		Development plans and control measures	With all ready planning and control measures documents and complete implementation record	With basic planning and control measures	Lack of planning, without effective control measures
Comprehensive ability level			If all the options score A, the capability meets the needs and gives A rating	If at least one of all the options scores B, the capability basically meets the needs and gives B rating	If at least one of the affirmatively chosen items scores C, the capability fails to meet the needs and give C rating

续表

Marking items		Marking reports	Marking scheme		
			A	B	C
Capital support	Cost structures		With reasonable structure and prominent key points	Basically meet the daily expenditure needs	Structure irrational and waste seriously
	Capital channels		Capital source meets expenditure needs (no financial gap)	Capital source basically meets operation and maintenance expenditure needs (financial gap less than 10%)	Capital source fails to meet the expenditure needs (financial gap over 10%)
	Tourist number		Tourists increase	Tourist stable	Tourist decrease
	Management development		with plentiful types, prominent key points and strong systematiness	Single type, basically depend on tourism services	No core product, business or over-exploitation
Development level	Revenue structures		With balanced source of income (non – financial and direct business accounted for over 30%)	Mainly direct business (over 50%)	Mainly grant – in – aids (over 50%)
	Social profits		Give a strong boost to the local society, culture, economy and life	Give a boost to the local society, culture, economy and life to a certain extent.	With fewer contributions to the local society, culture, economy and life
Total scores			All A	Over one as B	over one as C
Evaluation conclusions			The heritage site can develop sustainably	The heritage site can basically develop sustainably	The heritage site can not develop sustainably

2. Questionnaire

The questionnaire is the basic document for information collection. It is filled in by the operational institutions and reported to the National Cultural Relics Department, which is used for sustainable development evaluation and the evaluation system of the research group. Due to the limited space, the questionnaire form is excluded here.

3. Index Decision Table

The index decision table is the first step of the evaluation system as the combination of the written answers of the surveys and on-site observation of experts. It is implemented by the professional institutions designated by the government. The decision report is the analysis related to the judgment and information. Decision standards refer to the information of the relevant standards, system, regulations or legal documents. The conclusion is drawn through the records and relevant indexes, records and standards. Fill A, B, or C in the blanks according to the decision standards.

4. Comprehensive Evaluation Form

It is the final evaluation table that investigates whether the development is sustainable or not. The committee of experts designated by the government and the director of committee is in charge of the specific implementation. The sustainable development grade of the world heritage sites will be judged with comprehensive evaluation standards of the monitoring and regular research data.

(II) Case Studies

The research group made index verification to part of the heritage sites based on the evaluation system. According to the investigation and analysis of the Suzhou Classical Gardens, the Zhoukoudian Peking Man Site, Qufu Confucius Mansion, Confucius Temple, Confucian Garden, Ancient City of Pingyao, and Hangzhou West Lake Cultural Landscape, the research group can verify the reasonableness and integrity of the index system, and measure the scientificity of the grades of the sustainable development evaluation system. Due to the limited space, there is an overview on the five features of the world cultural heritages as follows.

Compared with the other heritage sites, the Suzhou Classical Gardens which is located in a second-tier city with strong economic vitality, adopts higher-level management mode with some advantages in terms of equipment and operation. Meanwhile, the Suzhou Classical Gardens have much ornamental and entertaining value so that only the ticket income can be sufficient to meet the its protection demands. With the government support on policies and funds, Suzhou Classical Gardens possess great strength and abilities on the sustainable development as a world heritage site.

As the birthplace of Confucianism, the characteristics of Qufu Confucius Mansion, Confucius Temple, and the Confucius Garden have great educational and memorable meanings. However, they are all in a third-tier city with relatively undeveloped economy as well as the economic level is relatively lower in Qufu, so the industry structure needs to be adjusted. In another aspect, they play a more important role in local economy. Besides, they have more difficulty in maintenance and management and need various high-tech equipments for the ancient tombs and the forest. Therefore, more capital investment for the heritage protection is required.

The Ancient City of Pingyao, as a world heritage site, is also a city itself. Due to the open management, there are no professional institutions in charge of the management and maintenance to the whole city. In such situation, the damage is sorely serious in the Ancient City of Pingyao, for instance, there are cracks on wall, which has threatened the value of the Ancient City extremely. As a world cultural heritage, Pingyao is facing a lot of difficulties in term of sustainable development.

As the new member in the World Heritage Sites, Hangzhou West Lake Cultural Landscape has relatively mature plans with systematic management system and reasonable structure of protection funds. Therefore, Hangzhou West Lake is of great ability for sustainable development.

To sum up, according to the analysis, survey and research on the different types of heritage sites, research group found that China heritage sites involve complicated types and various features. The diversity of heritage sites presents high requirements to the management of heritage sites. This research is aimed at finding out the similarities in differences and summarizing the operation and development modes of different heritage sites for general rules and corresponding development modes of China's heritage sites. It lays a foundation for effective decision of heritage sites for the administrators.

V The Sustainable Development Models of China's World Heritage Sites

Limited by the economy, social effects, brand, management and development capabilities and other relevant elements, the sustainable development of the world cultural heritage sites presents different features. Focused on the operation and development of the heritage sites ontology in this subject, we generalize the development modes of the world cultural heritage sites as the resource – based model, government – supported model and supplementary – development model.

The point to be made, in this subject research, is that the development of some of the world's cultural heritage presents a variety of characteristics with a unity of over two modes. Considering this situation, the subject group, mainly according to the influential degree of a mode, judges what the development tendency of a heritage site is. If tickets profit a lot, it tends to a resource – based mode. If the government supports a lot, it tends to a government – supported mode, etc. The interactions of different modes constitute the overall sustainable development of heritage sites.

(I) Resource – based Model

This mode is characterized by the "heritage economy" that the development of a heritage site relies mainly on its own rich resource, value, and brands to attract tourists. Tickets income can totally meet the needs of the self – protection and development of the heritage site. With the revenue exceeding the expenditure, the heritage site itself achieves self – sufficiency. At present, most of the world heritage in China can reach this height of meeting the needs of the daily protection and maintenance of the heritage sites. What is more, many heritage sites possess capital balance, which could be used as investiment to protection and developments.

For example, from the view of the mode structure, Qufu is one of the heritage sites with both the characteristics of resource – based and government – supported. However, the subject of the whole revenues is ticket sales, which far exceeds the expenditures of daily maintenance and protection. Therefore, the heritage site – Qufu tends to be the resource – based mode.

(II) Government – supported Model

The outstanding characteristic of this mode is the dependence on the government financial capital for the maintenance, protection and development. With the shortage of the resource, the heritage site itself cannot keep its own protection and development only by the operational income like tickets sales. However, for its great historical and era value, the heritage site needs the government aided capital, and the supporting level depends on the size of the demand gap. At present, only a few heritage sites are in this situation of needing the support of governments of all levels.

（III）Supplementary Development Model

The main characteristic of this model is the protection and sustainable development of heritage sites not merely dependent on ticket incomes but mostly on the incomes of rental housing, catering services, authorized operation, derivative products and tax. Heritage itself has value – added development ability. The West Lake in Hangzhou is the most typical example. After the successful application for heritage site, the West Lake Scenic Attraction Area Management Committee has been established. It is mainly responsible for management of heritage site range. Half percent of the annual revenue of the developed incomes West Lake collected from scenic spot business like rental housing and tax.

Furthermore, the exploitation complemented model refers to the developmental revenues and activities beneficial to the protection, brand promotion and popularization of heritage itself rather than the value – destructed over-exploitation which should be effectively controlled.

VI Suggestions for the Sustainable Development of World Heritage Sites

At present, the protection and development of China's world cultural heritage are generally in good conditions. The interactive promotion of cultural heritage and economic development has been highlighted. The world cultural heritage has played a leading role in the development and restructuring of regional economy, social employment, ecology protection, tourism development. The research group has agreed on that the nation, local governments and operative administrations should perform its own functions and fully implement the duties as the role of completing protection and promote sustainable development.

From the national point, China takes the premier responsibility. As a result, it should protect cultural heritage at the first place and undertake the duty of the overall management. In the critical period of the Twelfth – Five – Year Plan, solid foundation, scientific planning and rapid development should be the themes of China's world cultural heritage evolution. The research group has made the following three suggestions. Firstly, the nation should adjust system and strengthen management in order to build the unified system composed of central government, local organizations and operation institutions. Secondly, it is necessary to enlarge financial investment and form a special fund. On one hand, the central government should take out certain percentage of GDP (e. g. 2% of GDP) to be used as the fund of heritage protection by legislation. On the other hand, it has to work out favorable policies to meet the needs and encourage multi – channel way to raise social capital. Thirdly, it must improve the supervision and management system and make use of the sustainable development rating system to assess and guide the world cultural heritage sites regularly.

From local governmental perspective, they should enforce laws, regulations and programs strictly and make heritage protection as a part of government planning. According to the government policies, they should take out corresponding proportion of GDP (e. g. 2% of GDP) to be directly used for the protection and development of cultural heritages in its budget system.

From the operational institutions' perspective, they should reinforce the absorption and training of professional staff and gradually improve the corresponding abilities. Meanwhile, on the basis of cultural heritage protection, industry management model should be encouraged. The industry operation and products exploitation in heritage sites should be built or delegated to enterprises.

Through surveys, reflections, data analysis and seminars for almost one year, the research group have a preliminary understanding of the basic information, operation conditions, heritage protection and development situations. Thus the sustainable development system and several development models have been put forward. However, the conditions of 33 heritage sites have not all been covered due to limited time and resources. The evaluation system is just general and directive. This research can be constantly deepened along with further investigations. Finally, it will bring out a feasible sustainable development evaluation system of world culture heritage suiting to China's national conditions and helpful for managements.

(Written by Xiang Yong, Deng Lili)

传承与共生——中国世界文化遗产与社区发展研究

杭州市园林文物局

摘 要

本次研究从世界文化遗产与社区发展的"概念的解读与界定、问题的剖析与溯源、经验的分析与借鉴、重构的思路与措施"四大方面的分析入手，通过对中国国内遗产与社区关系紧密的多处遗产地的勘察、访谈、问卷调查，在深度剖析遗产与社区关系的基础上，从世界文化遗产可持续发展的角度，制定了"传承共生、和谐发展"的理想目标，并紧扣课题主题与中国国情，从遗产地社区应该承担的保护职责与其应该受到尊重的基本权益两个方面制定了保障其和谐共生的系列规划措施与保障制度。

关键词：社区，世界文化遗产，可持续发展，传承共生，和谐关系

1 研究目的与概念界定——解读研究

1.1 研究目的

（1）剖析中国目前社区发展与世界文化遗产保护间的关系与问题；
（2）总结我国世界文化遗产与社区良性互动的优秀经验；
（3）探讨如何推动社区在我国世界文化遗产可持续发展中的角色作用；
（4）完善我国社区与世界文化遗产地良性互动、可持续发展的共赢体系。

1.2 社区概念解读

社区的一般定义可描述为：聚居在一定空间的人群所组成的社会生活共同体。

中国对社区的定义与国际上有差别。其社区和政区的概念叠加较多，更倾向于把社区理解为有界的相对封闭的实体，强调其作为地域性社会组织类型的群体，而相对弱化其作为社会关系或情感类型的群体特征。

鉴于以上分析，本次研究在中国特有国情下将遗产地社区定义为：由常住在中国世界文化遗产保护区范围内的人群构成的社会基层管理单元，如村庄、乡镇、街道等。

1.3 研究对象

中国的世界文化遗产共有33处，除29处文化遗产和文化景观外，还有4处双重遗产（泰山、黄山、峨眉山—乐山、武夷山）。根据各遗产地与社区的地缘关系以及遗产突出普遍价值与社区的关联程度，将中国的世界文化遗产分类如下表：

表 2-1　中国世界文化遗产分类表

分类	定义	细分类型	案例	遗产类型	研究方式
第一类"原生型"遗产地	遗产区内有社区，且遗产价值由社区居民创造	古民居、古村落型	福建土楼、皖南古村落——西递宏村、开平碉楼及村庄	世界文化遗产	重点研究，现场调研，访谈，管理部门和社区问卷调查
		古城镇型	丽江古城、平遥古城	世界文化遗产	
		历史城区型	澳门历史城区	世界文化遗产	
第二类"共生型"遗产地	遗产区内有社区，且居民与部分遗产价值有关	文化景观型	杭州西湖文化景观、庐山	文化景观	管理部门和社区问卷调查、电话访谈，并选取典型案例进行现场调研
		山岳型	峨眉山—乐山大佛、五台山、武夷山	世界文化遗产、自然与文化双重遗产	
第三类"伴生型"遗产地	遗产区内无居民居住，社区在遗产缓冲区范围内，且对遗产价值有一定影响	景园型	苏州古典园林、曲阜三孔	世界文化遗产	不在研究范围之内
		宫殿型	高句丽王城王陵及贵族墓葬	世界文化遗产	
		宗教庙宇型	武当山古建筑群、登封"天地之中"历史建筑群	世界文化遗产	
		山岳型	青城山—都江堰水利系统、泰山、黄山	世界文化遗产、自然与文化双重遗产	
第四类遗产地	遗产地内无居民居住，且相关社区对遗产价值影响不大	皇家宫殿陵寝型	秦始皇陵、明清皇家陵寝、明清故宫、颐和园	世界文化遗产	不在研究范围之内
		古人类遗址型	周口店北京人遗址、殷墟、长城	世界文化遗产	
		石窟石刻型	大足石刻、龙门石窟、云冈石窟、莫高窟	世界文化遗产	
		宗教庙宇型	承德避暑山庄及周边寺庙、天坛、布达拉宫	世界文化遗产	

注："原生"是指共同生长相互依附的关系；"共生"是指两者彼此互利地存在一起的关系；"伴生"是指两者生存在一起，但相互影响并不大的关系。

　　考虑到研究内容的典型性和代表性，本次研究以第一类与第二类文化遗产为主、第三类文化遗产为辅展开分析，第四类文化遗产不纳入本次研究范围之内。为了加强研究的针对性，从第一类、第二类遗产地中选取福建土楼、皖南古村落——西递宏村、丽江古城、杭州西湖文化景观、峨眉山—乐山大佛五个遗产地为典型案例展开深入重点的分析。

1.4　研究方法

　　本次研究以"社会调查法"、"案例分析法"为主要研究方法，辅以"文献研究法"、"交叉研究法"、"分类研究法"等研究方法。

1.4.1　社会调查法

　　本次研究采用的社会调查方法包括：实地调研、问卷调查、会议访谈等。其中问卷调查分为"社区问卷调查"和"管理部门问卷调查"两类，前者发放对象为遗产地社区内的居民，后者发放对象为遗产管理部门工作人员。"社区问卷调查"针对福建土楼、皖南古村落——西递宏村、丽江古城、杭州西湖文化景观、峨眉山—乐山大佛这五个具有代表性的世界文化遗产地及相关社区，于2011年12月—2012年2月进行了为期3个月的问卷调查。此次调查共发放社区问卷1650份，回收1069份，回收率64.8%，有效问卷 1022 份，有效率 95.6%。"管理部门问卷调查"共发放管理部门问卷 13 份，回收 13 份，回收率 100%，有效问卷 13 份，有效率 100%。本次研究使用"SPSS19.0 软件"进行数据统计及分析。

社区问卷调查对象基本特征分析如下：

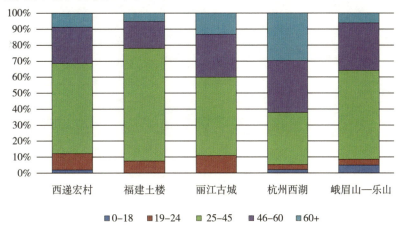

表 2 - 2　受访居民年龄特征

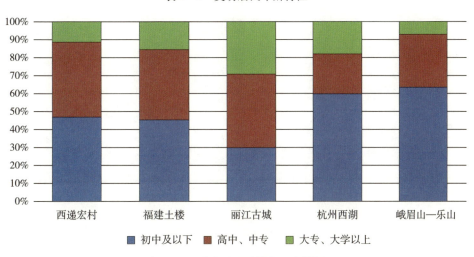

表 2 - 3　受访居民受教育程度特征

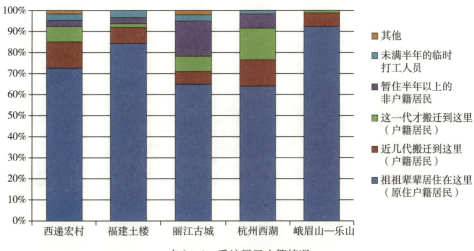

表 2 - 4　受访居民户籍情况

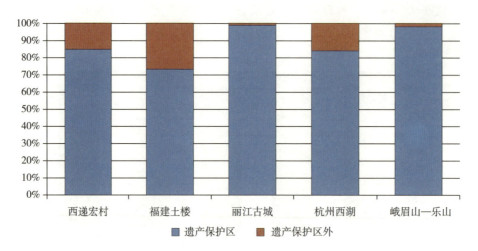

表 2-5 受访居民受是否居住于遗产地内

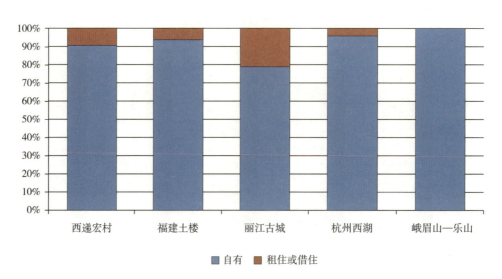

表 2-6 受访居民住房产权属性

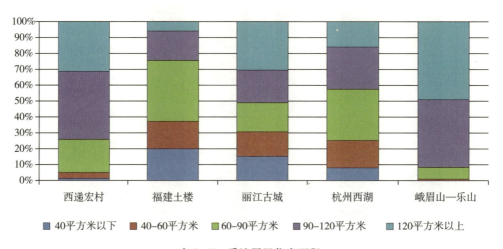

表 2-7 受访居民住房面积

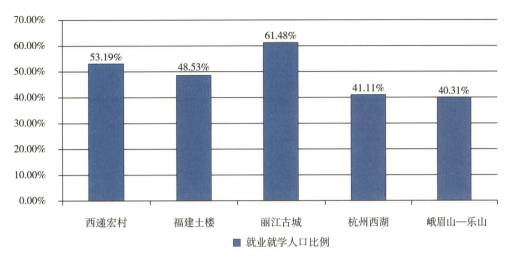

表 2-8 受访居民就学就业人口比例

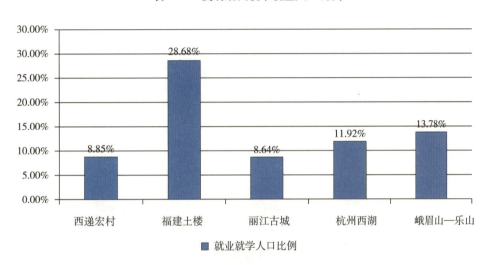

表 2-9 受访居民外出打工人口比例

管理问卷调查对象统计如下：

表 2-10 受访管理部门主要情况一览表

序号	受访部门	所属遗产地	申遗成功年份（年）	行政级别	问卷填写数（份）
1	永定县文物局世遗科	福建土楼	2008	副科级	2
2	安徽省黄山市黟县西递镇人民政府	皖南古村落——西递宏村	2000	副科级	2
3	安徽省黄山市黟县宏村镇宏村村委会	皖南古村落——西递宏村	2000	—	1
4	世界文化遗产丽江古城保护管理局	丽江古城	1997	正处级	1
5	杭州西湖风景名胜区管委会西湖街道	杭州西湖文化景观	2011	正处级	1
6	峨眉山—乐山大佛风景名胜区管理委员会	峨眉山—乐山大佛	1996	正处级	2
7	苏州市园林和绿化管理局	苏州园林	1997	正处级	1
8	武当山旅游经济特区文物局	武当山古建筑群	1994	正科级	1
9	黄山市文物局	黄山	1990	副处级	1
10	北京颐和园管理处	颐和园	1998	正处级	1

1.4.2　案例分析法

一方面，根据所需研究的第一类、第二类遗产地的细分类型特点，选取了福建土楼、杭州西湖文化景观等五个具有代表性和典型性的案例就遗产保护和社区发展的关系进行现状问题剖析、评估和经验总结。研究中针对需要分析的不同方面，灵活选取个案研究法和对比研究法，对所得数据进行深度分析和横向对比，所得的分析结果在同类型遗产地中具有较好的参考价值。另一方面，根据其他遗产地的部门问卷与宣传材料，分析整理了其他遗产地的案例经验作为辅助分析。

1.5　研究框架

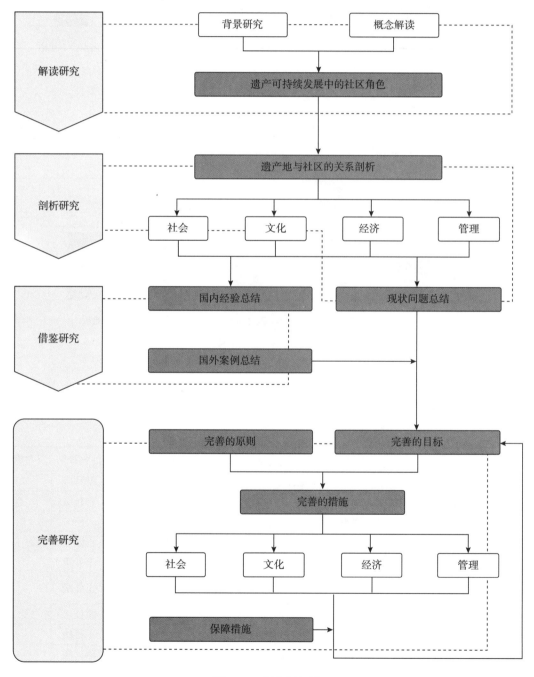

图 2-1　研究框架图

2　现状的剖析与诊断——剖析研究

中国正处于社会转型期，整个社会的经济结构、文化形态、价值观念等都在时刻发生深刻的变化。在世界文化遗产地，其保护与开发并存、古今交融的特性使得这样的改变冲击愈发明显，所带来的矛盾问题也更加复杂尖锐。

本文从社会、文化、经济、管理四个角度共十个方面深入剖析目前中国世界文化遗产地中社区和遗产地的关系，揭示文化遗产保护和社区发展之间的矛盾问题，剖析问题背后的成因。

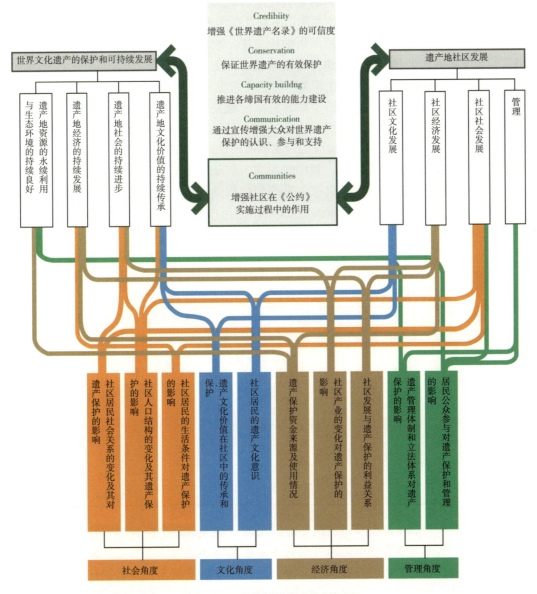

图 3－1　现状剖析的内容框架图

2.1　社会角度

遗产地社区与一般的社区不同，遗产地社区与其所处环境——世界遗产之间特殊的地缘关系、特定的遗产保护环境以及遗产文化价值之间的关联更加微妙，存在的问题也更加独特。

2.1.1 社区居民社会关系的变化及其对遗产保护的影响

从原始社会关系形态到传统社会关系形态，再到现代社会关系形态，人类社会关系的演进始终是一个发展的过程。各遗产地随着申报遗产的成功，各种外来因素的进入急剧加速了原有传承千年的传统乡土社会向现代社会的转变，社会关系构成要素中的业缘关系、地缘关系和血缘关系都发生了巨大的改变。以前的熟人社会变成了现在的半熟人社会；以前血缘社会中奉行的"人情"原则掺进了现代社会的"理性"因素，利益原则成了差序格局中的一个重要维度。

2.1.1.1 血缘关系逐渐淡化的影响

随着遗产地社区社会经济的发展，传统的宗教礼法和风俗习惯逐渐与人们的现代化生活脱节，血缘关系在人们生活中越来越不被重视，其地位和作用不断让位于地缘关系和业缘关系。

在福建土楼、西递宏村这类古村落型遗产地的传统中，浓厚的血缘关系是建立家族纽带及宗教礼法的根本基础，传统文化的产生和传播正是建立在血缘关系之上。因而血缘关系的淡化，使得传统文化在居民生活中的重要性逐渐降低，与传统文化相关联的遗产价值相应的也与居民的日常生产生活渐渐疏远，失去了传承的动力。这在福建土楼这类根植于东方血缘伦理关系和聚族而居民族传统的遗产地中特别突出。目前留驻在土楼内的原住居民越来越少，土楼所特有的一些民俗节庆、祭祖活动，甚至传统的烟草种植产业已很少看见，土楼所特有的基于血缘伦理关系所形成的"天人合一"、人与自然和谐统一的人居环境正被外来人员的商业经营活动所取代。相比较而言，丽江古城这类古城镇型遗产地，因其城镇社区的血缘关系不如乡村社区般紧密，因此，血缘关系的变化程度较小，对传统文化传承和遗产保护的影响也较少，其社会关系更多体现在业缘和地缘关系上的改变。

2.1.1.2 地缘关系日渐开放的影响

地缘关系和血缘关系存在一定的相互关联和区域性。很多地区在未成为世界遗产地，作为旅游资源开发之前，社会分工不发达，人们局限于较小的地缘范围，流动性很小，这时的地缘关系和血缘关系是相互渗透的。申遗成功后旅游业快速发展，遗产地产业分化趋于复杂，人们居住和工作的流动性也随之增强，此时遗产地内居民的地缘关系不再和血缘关系相互渗透，地缘关系由封闭逐渐走向多变开放。遗产地社区的原住民外出务工人口比例与其所在地区平均水平的比较详见表3-1。

表3-1 遗产地原住民外出务工人口占户籍人口比例表

遗产地名称	遗产地原住民外出务工人口比例（%）	所在地区外出务工人口比例（%）
西递宏村	9.37	14.90（黟县）
福建土楼	30.1	6.30（漳州市）
丽江古城	7.89	3.23（丽江市）
杭州西湖	10.20	8.46（杭州市）
峨眉山—乐山	14.17	10.63（四川省）

一方面，按照遗产保护要求需要限制当地经济的常规发展模式，一些规模大且收益高的产业不允许在遗产区范围内发展，大部分遗产地都是通过发展旅游业来增加地方产业收益，而单一的旅游服务产业收益，对某些地区来说，区域经济的带动作用有限，经济压力驱使越来越多的原住民选择季节性外出务工，或干脆搬离遗产地。例如福建土楼的原住民外出务工比例是漳州市域外出务工人口比例近乎5倍。这些原住民流动趋势的加强、生活重心的转移，其经济收入来源和日常生活与古城的关系越来越疏远，从而导致原住民这一重要的遗产价值的传承者和保护实施者对遗产保护的重视程度和参与程度逐渐降低。而另一方面，调查也发现西递宏村的原住民外出务工人口比例远远低于当地平均水平，这与西递宏村基于遗产保护理念指导下发展旅游业、居民较高的门票分成所得，以及居民较好的遗产保护意识不无关系。

因此可以认为，外出务工人口比例低的遗产地其遗产资源的保护和利用适度，对当地居民较为有利，地缘关系较稳定。

2.1.1.3　业缘关系趋于复杂的影响

在越来越重视经济利益的今天，从事不同行业的社区居民的业缘关系由合作关系趋于更加复杂的竞争关系和制约关系。农业社会时期，遗产地居民多数以第一产业为主要经济基础，节奏舒缓的生活使人较少心理的紧张和精神的压抑，伦理型的规范对于抑制一般性的越轨行为有着不可替代的效力。该时期业缘关系以合作关系为主。随着遗产地社区产业结构中第三产业的比重不断增强，经济关系和利益原则开始重新梳理和编织当代社会网络，利益动机、经济标准已无可置疑地成为现代社会生活的准绳。这种变化在多数原为农村社会的遗产地中体现尤为明显。如西递宏村在遗产旅游业发展初期就出现了居民为扩大经营面积而竞相在古民居上破墙开店的现象；土楼也多处出现了家族内部为了旅游分成的收益分配而引发的利益纷争等不和谐事件。

因此，趋于开放的地缘关系以及更加复杂的业缘关系逐渐淡化了血缘关系在遗产地居民社会关系中的主导作用。由于地缘关系和业缘关系对社会群体的凝聚作用均低于血缘关系，这就造成了遗产地居民社区意识的日渐淡薄，居民对于自身所处社区的归属感不如传统农业社会时期那么强烈，以社区为单位的群体活动逐渐减少，这其中也包括一些属于遗产价值组成部分的传统风俗节庆活动，而居民参与也不再积极。

2.1.2　社区人口结构的变化及其遗产保护的影响

2.1.2.1　各遗产地人口结构特点

我们以遗产地社区的户籍人口占常住人口的比例作为判断遗产地内原住民比例的依据，对各遗产地的原住民比例统计如下表：

表3-2　各遗产地常住人口及户籍人口统计表

遗产地名称	2011年常住人口数（人）	2011年户籍人口数（人）	户籍人口占常住人口比例（％）
西递宏村	2868	2568	89.54
丽江古城	24603	6376	25.92
杭州西湖	14287	11723	82.05
峨眉山—乐山	24600	16300	66.26

各遗产地现状人口结构中原住民比例差别较大。其中，西递宏村和杭州西湖的原住民比重较大。丽江古城的原住民比例明显低于其他遗产地。比对网上游客对各遗产地文化氛围的感知结果，户籍人口比例高于80%的遗产地，游客对当地文化氛围的感知程度普遍较高；户籍人口比例高于60%的遗产地，游客对当地文化氛围的感知一般；而户籍人口比例在30%以下的遗产地，则游客明显感觉到当地文化氛围的异化而不满。

2.1.2.2　人口结构的变化和趋势

表3-3　各遗产地申遗前后人口数据比较表

遗产地名称	申遗时常住人口数（人）	申遗时户籍人口数（人）	申遗时原住民比例（％）	2011年常住人口数（人）	2011年户籍人口数（人）	2011年原住民比例（％）	原住民留居率（％）
西递宏村（2000）	2214	2084	94.13	2868	2568	89.54	123.22
丽江古城（1997）	15712	11931	75.93	24603	6376	25.92	53.44
峨眉山—乐山（1996）	21927	18867	86.04	24600	16300	66.26	86.39

　　遗产地社区的人口结构转变主要体现在申遗前后社区中原住民和外来人口的比例变化上。上表中，除西递宏村遗产保护区内的原住居民有所增加外，丽江古城和峨眉山—乐山大佛的原住民比例均发生了不同程度的降低，其中丽江古城的原住民流失率达到46.56%，古城内已充斥了外来经商人员和游客。原住民的流失和外来人口的涌入是国内遗产地社区普遍面临的人口结构变化的严峻问题。

　　导致遗产地社区人口结构变化的主要原因有三点：（1）遗产保护要求下的原住民保护性外迁；（2）原住民的主动外迁；（3）旅游业带来的外来人口。其中原住民保护性外迁是当地管理政策所致，原住民的主动外迁是经济利益下的选择，而旅游业带来的外来人口则是产业结构变化的附加产物。

2.1.2.3　人口结构的改变对遗产保护的影响

　　遗产地社区人口结构的改变不仅使原有的人际关系网络出现断点，社会关系逐渐淡漠，影响到遗产文化价值的传承和遗产保护中的社区参与程度，而且也引起了参与遗产保护的责任主体的变化与责任意识的改变。原社区居民的外迁，使得原有的具有强烈自觉性的遗产保护责任主体越来越少，遗产保护逐渐丧失了民族民间文化保护的载体。较之原住民，外来人口对遗产的情感依赖较低，对遗产价值的认同感也较缺乏，在我国人口素质——尤其是农村人口素质——普遍偏低的情况下，更难以形成自觉的遗产保护行为。由此全国普遍性地出现了遗产本体的老化破损和人为破坏现象。

　　面对人类共同的遗产，外来人员，无论是游客还是经商者，应和原住民的保护责任同等重要。在现今遗产地人口结构的变化形势下，采取强有力的措施留住原住民与进一步强化各类遗产保护主体的责任显得尤为紧迫。

2.1.3　社区居民的生活条件对遗产保护的影响

　　在遗产地社区中，由于种种原因，一些常规的社区居住环境更新措施因受到遗产本体保护要求的制约而无法实现，导致部分遗产地社区的居住环境和公共服务设施配置明显滞后于社区自身的社会经济发展程度，社区居民的许多切身利益得不到保障。

2.1.3.1　居民的居住条件和公共服务设施现状及需求

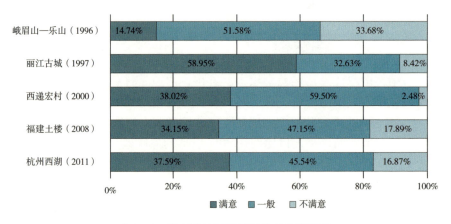

表3-4　遗产地社区居民居住条件满意度

　　根据问卷统计结果分析，居民对居住条件的满意度与当地旅游业发展水平呈正相关。同类型遗产地中，旅游业越发达，当地经济发展水平则越高，居民的居住条件也就越完善。如丽江古城、西递宏村（遗产地），以及杭州西湖（共生型遗产地）三处满意度较高的遗产地，也是旅游业发展与服务水平较高的遗产地。另外还可以看出，遗产价值与社区的原生或共生关系与居民对居住条件的满意度无关。

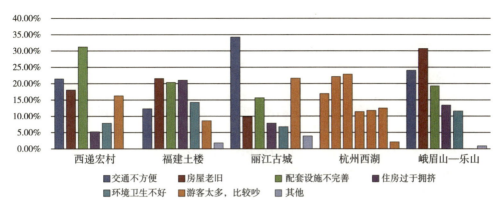

表3-5　遗产地社区居民对居住条件不满意的原因构成

进一步调查居民对居住条件不满意的原因可发现，房屋老旧、配套设施不完善和交通不便利是三个普遍性的问题。房屋老旧的问题普遍存在于遗产地的村庄社区，如峨眉山—乐山大佛内的偏远村庄，既没有遗产保护的修缮帮助又享受不到遗产旅游所带来的经济利益，居民无力承担房屋维护费用；福建土楼对楼内现代卫浴改建有一定限制，目前尚有许多楼内居民无法拥有独立厨卫。配套设施不完善的问题主要存在于保护区内建设控制严格的遗产地，如西递宏村。交通不便利的问题在丽江古城这类经济较为发达，机动车配比较高，但遗产保护区面积较大，又需要保留原有小尺度街巷空间而禁止机动车驶入的古城镇遗产地内表现尤为突出。

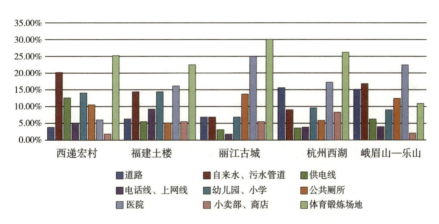

表3-6　遗产地社区缺少的生活服务基础设施

而社区生活服务基础设施的缺失突出体现在社区教育、医疗设施的布点不足，体育锻炼场地的缺乏，以及自来水管、污水管、停车场等现代生活所需的公共设施的缺乏上。由于遗产地的严格保护要求，无法进行大型开挖工程的施工，遗产地内可利用的空间有限，使得以上基础设施缺失成为遗产地社区长期存在又无力解决的顽疾，给社区居民的生活造成极大不便，并成为部分原住民搬离遗产地的重要原因之一。例如，西递宏村和福建土楼长期缺乏完善的污水管网和供电线网，现有的设施已不能满足居民的正常生活需求；丽江古城借鉴文物修复的办法对原石板路面进行编号开挖敷设管线后还原，取得了较好的效果。

2.1.3.2　居民的生活条件对遗产保护的影响

社区居民生活条件对遗产保护的影响主要体现在社区居民日益提升的现代化生活需求与遗产保护所要求的原真性产生的矛盾冲突。在我国快速城市化背景下，这种矛盾冲突普遍存在于遗产地中的古村庄和古民居遗产。社区居民的切身生活需求得不到保障的情况下，也就谈不上居民对遗产保护工作的支持了。如何在保障社区居民的合理生活需求的同时，满足遗产保护的要求，又不对遗产本体产生威胁，需要从遗产保护技术层面和遗产人性化管理角度进行更深入的研究探讨。

2.2　文化角度

文化角度从遗产文化价值在社区环境中的传承保护状况以及社区居民的遗产文化意识出发，分别从客观因素和主观因素分析判断社区对遗产文化价值保护传承的贡献程度、社区居民对待参与遗产文化价值传承的态度，进而研究社区居民参与遗产文化价值传承的潜力。

2.2.1　遗产文化价值在社区中的传承和保护

社区与遗产文化价值的关联程度由遗产地与社区的历史渊源和地缘关系决定。表3-7总结了本次研究选取的五个典型遗产地的文化价值和社区的关联程度：

表3-7　各遗产地社区与遗产文化价值的关联程度总结表

遗产地名称	所属分类	遗产文化价值摘录*	社区与遗产文化价值的关联程度
西递宏村	原生型遗产地	"西递、宏村"是以商业经济为基础，以家族为单位，极具地方特色的传统古村落。……是在深厚的古徽州传统文化影响下，……以商业经济为基础，以家族为社会结构单位的中国传统乡村……真实保存了地方艺术、习俗、饮食等文化生活形态和传统生活方式	紧密
福建土楼	原生型遗产地	福建土楼是在特定的自然地理环境条件下和重大社会变迁和动乱中，根植于东方血缘伦理关系和聚族而居民族传统基础之上的防御型建筑文化传统的独特见证……具有土楼特色的当地传统文化和农耕生活方式、社会关系的传统模式也得以完整地保存	紧密
丽江古城	原生型遗产地	丽江古城集中体现了地方历史文化的交流和民族风俗风情。……独具纳西族特色的建筑、艺术、城镇规划和景观以及社会生活、风俗习惯、工艺美术等人文特征……纳西民居在布局、结构和造型上按照自然条件和传统生活习惯，有机结合汉民族、白族、藏族民居的优秀传统……丽江古城东巴文化、纳西文字、民居建造工艺等非物质文化遗产通过挖掘和梳理，依存于纳西族社会的发展而得以传承和弘扬	紧密
杭州西湖	共生型遗产地	西湖景观是一种独特文化传统的杰出见证，这一传统旨在对景观进行不断的完善，从而创造出系列"题名景观"，用以展现人与自然的完美融合……	一般
峨眉山—乐山	共生型遗产地	峨眉山是佛教的主要圣地之一……峨眉山还以其物种繁多、种类丰富的植物而闻名天下……	较低

＊摘自国家文物局汇编的《中国的世界文化遗产——突出普遍价值》

2.2.1.1 遗产文化价值的自身传承情况

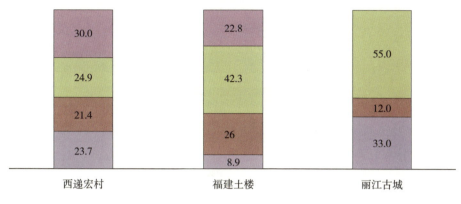

西递宏村: 30.0 / 24.9 / 21.4 / 23.7

福建土楼: 22.8 / 42.3 / 26 / 8.9

丽江古城: 55.0 / 12.0 / 33.0

■ 遗产地特色手工艺　■ 遗产地特色农业　■ 遗产地其他特色生产活动　■ 未参加

表 3-8　遗产地原住民参与传统生产生活方式的比例

这里仅选取社区和遗产文化价值关联紧密的三个原生型遗产地原住民进行横向对比，统计结果显示：丽江古城遗产保护区内虽然拥有较高的原住民流失率，但是古城范围内的居民仍以纳西族为主，因此，许多传统的纳西文化习俗保留较好。相对丽江古城而言，西递宏村和福建土楼受访原住居民中从事传统特色生活生产活动的比例虽然略低，但是其比值仍然高达 70% 以上，在实际调研中依然可以体会到传统民族文化在当地较好的传承状况。

总体看来，原生型遗产地遗产文化价值的自身传承状况较好。传统民风民俗和民族文化在遗产地原住民的日常生产生活中依然占据着重要的地位，传承度较高。

2.2.1.2 外界作用对传统文化的改变

图 3-2　纳西族人合力"竖新房"

外界作用主要包括现代旅游服务业的发展和全球化的影响两方面。随着遗产地现代旅游服务产业的兴起，遗产地的开放度大大增强，异于当地传统文化的外来文化开始涌入遗产地内。部分社区居民在全球化浪潮下摒弃了原有的传统生活方式，逐渐被趋同。在丽江古城，超过 85% 的受访居民认为丽江的传统文化受到了外来文化的影响而被弱化了，体现了当地传统文化面对现代旅游服务业和全球化趋势强大的同化作用时的脆弱。

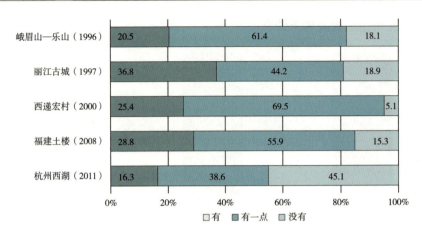

表3－9   遗产地原住民是否因为遗产保护和旅游开发而改变原有的生活方式

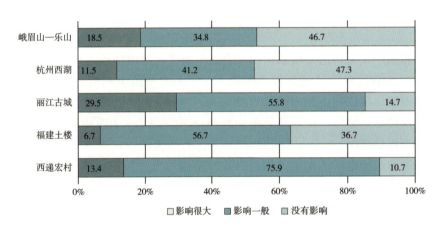

表3－10   在原住民看来，当地传统文化是否受到外界作用的影响而被弱化了

2.2.2   社区居民的遗产文化意识

无论是原住居民还是外来人口，对于其所在遗产地的文化价值是否感到认同和自豪，是否认识到自己有责任和义务保护传承遗产文化价值，以及居民参与传承文化价值相关行动的积极性，综合反映了遗产地社区居民主观意识上参与遗产文化价值保护和传承的潜力。

2.2.2.1   居民对遗产文化价值的认同感和归属感

狭义地来理解遗产地居民的遗产文化意识，即可认为是居民对当地遗产所具有的突出文化价值的认同程度。当人们认同的文化与遗产保护所要保留延续的文化相符合时，人们就会自觉投身于遗产价值的保护行动中。

对比统计数据发现，原生型遗产地居民对遗产特色文化内涵的了解程度均高于共生型遗产地，可以认为，遗产文化价值和社区关联越紧密，其社区居民对当地特色文化的了解程度越高。

我国遗产地居民对遗产价值的认同感普遍较为强烈。其中只有丽江显示超过半数的受访居民拒绝更多人的到访。考虑到丽江古城受到旅游业发展和全球化的影响较大，我们认为丽江古城的居民更多地表达了一种将当地传统文化适当封闭起来以躲避外界不利因素入侵的愿望，是建立在对文化的高度认同感之上的反思。

调查也得知绝大多数居民表示愿意在社区的基础设施完善的前提下，依然居住在此并保留原有生活方式，这说明原住民对所属的社区怀有强烈的归属感，若能加强硬件设施的改善，提升居住品质，将能更好地发挥居民在遗产文化价值的保护和宣传方面的作用。

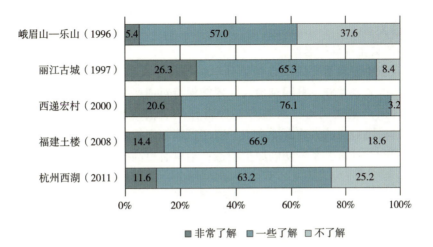

表3-11 原住民对其遗产地特色文化内涵的了解程度

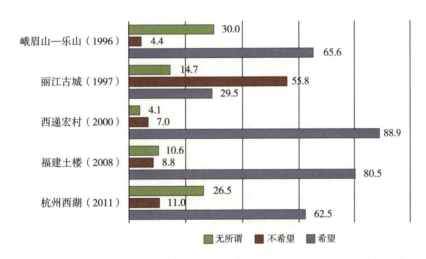

表3-12 原住民是否希望更多的人来到其所在遗产地，并了解当地的传统文化

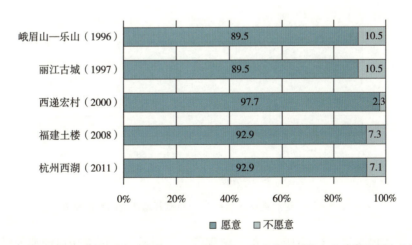

表3-13 如果社区的基础设施完善后，社区居民是否愿意依然居住在此并保留原有生活方式

综合看来，这五个遗产地的居民对遗产价值的认同感和归属感均较为强烈。且这种认同感和归属感会随着遗产与社区和谐关系的构建而增长。

2.2.2.2 居民参与文化传承的态度

社区成员的社区意识中非常重要的一点在于分享参与和主人翁意识。遗产地社区居民也只有在充分认识到自己与遗产保护的紧密关联、共同利益时，才能保持对遗产文化价值保护传承的关注和积极参与。

表3-14显示，各遗产地居民对自身遗产保护责任的觉悟均较高，其中尤以西递宏村最高，达到96.1%，这与西递宏村村民较强的亲族血统意识、遗产管理部门较好的宣传，以及村民较主动的保护意识有关。同时也可看出遗产与社区关系密切的原生型遗产地具有更高的遗产保护意识。

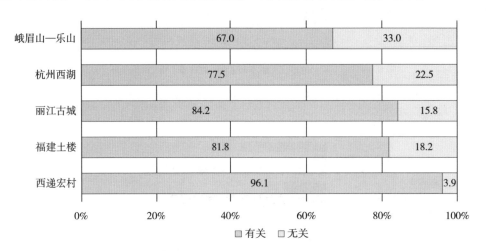

表3-14　遗产地社区居民是否认为自己与遗产保护有关

由表3-15综合看来，西递宏村、丽江古城和福建土楼这三个原生型遗产地的居民对遗产价值的了解程度均高于共生型遗产地。这主要是因为原生型遗产地的遗产价值与当地居民所熟悉的传统文化、民风民俗的关联较大，居民更容易理解其抽象的价值内涵。

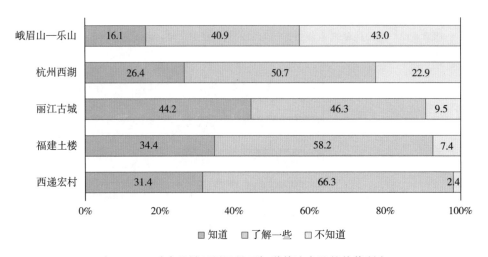

表3-15　遗产地社区居民是否知道其遗产地的价值所在

表3-16显示了居民对遗产地保护要求的了解程度，可以看出目前受访遗产地的居民对遗产保护要求已有一定程度的关注。其中，由于管理部门对遗产保护要求的宣传较重视，宣传期也较长，丽江古城和西递宏村的居民对遗产地保护要求了解程度高于其他遗产地。而居民生产生活对遗产的依存度也影响到

居民对遗产保护要求的关注，如峨眉山—乐山大佛保护区内的大部分村民从事的职业与遗产保护的关系不大，因此受访居民对遗产保护要求的关注度偏低。

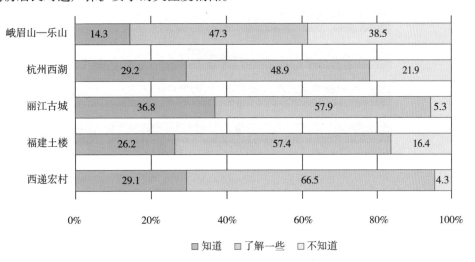

表 3－16　遗产地社区居民是否知道其遗产地的保护要求

在表 3－17 和表 3－18 两项调查中，总体看来，各遗产地受访居民的遗产保护参与积极性普遍较高，丽江古城和西递宏村的受访居民表达了最强烈的意愿来了解和帮助宣传遗产保护相关知识。结合表 3－15 和表 3－16 的调查结果，可以认为，成为遗产地的时间长短、居民生活对遗产的依存度高低以及管理部门的宣传力度大小是影响居民遗产保护参与积极性的主要因素。

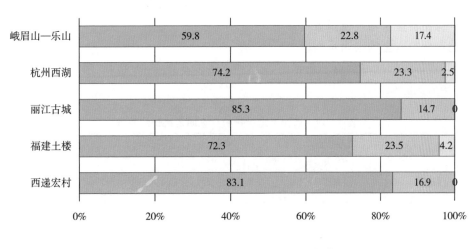

表 3－17　遗产地居民是否愿意了解遗产保护的相关知识

2.2.2.3　居民参与遗产文化价值传承的潜力

从客观因素上来看，遗产地居民参与遗产文化价值的传承保护既有潜力也有威胁。潜力来自于目前原住民自身对与遗产文化价值相关的传统民族文化的较自觉传承，尤其是原生型遗产地中原住民的日常生产生活依然受到传统民族文化的较大影响，一些老传统老风俗被原住民很好地保留下来，使得遗产地文化氛围得到了很好的保护；威胁则来自于不断增强的外界影响因素对传统文化的冲击作用，在现代旅游服务业的大力发展和全球化的必然影响下，遗产地居民容易受到经济利益的驱使而放弃传统生产生活方式，如果遗产文化价值无法为当地居民带去利益的提升，那么威胁的作用将越来越强。

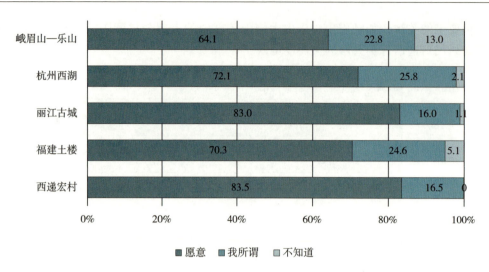

表 3 - 18   遗产地居民是否愿意帮助宣传遗产保护的相关知识和信息

    从主观意识上来看,社区居民参与遗产文化价值传承的意愿较为强烈。这种意愿与居民生活对遗产的依存度,以及成为遗产地的时间成正比,并且可以通过遗产价值及保护要求的宣传来培养。

    综合看来,目前我国实现遗产地社区居民参与遗产文化价值传承的基础较好,潜力较大。

2.3   经济角度

    世界文化遗产因其特殊的社会历史背景和复杂的利益主体关系,其经济方面的研究涉及遗产保护工作自身的经济状况、遗产地社区的经济发展需求,以及这两者之间的利益关系。

2.3.1   遗产保护资金来源及使用情况

2.3.1.1   遗产保护资金的来源及构成

    通过对遗产管理部门的问卷调查、访谈,以及查阅各遗产地申报文件,我们得到了以下各遗产地保护资金的来源和构成比例数据:

表 3 - 19   各遗产地保护资金来源及比例汇总表

遗产所属分类	遗产地名称	国家拨款(%)	地方政府投入(%)	门票收入(%)	捐款(%)	税收(%)	其他(%)
第一类遗产地	西递村	10	30	60	—	—	—
	福建土楼	79.37	15.87	—	2.38	—	2.38
	丽江古城	—	—	100(古城维护费)	—	—	—
第二类共生型遗产地	杭州西湖		35.63	22.64	—	33.27	8.46
	五台山	—	—	78.41	—	19.93	1.66
第三类伴生型遗产地	武当山	70	20	10	—	—	—
	青城山	19.5	27.1	53.4	—	—	—
第四类遗产地	云冈	58.2	25.5	—	—	—	16.2
	殷墟	1.6	73.4	—	25	—	—
	龙门	40	30	—	—	—	30
	大足石刻	19.3	32.3	—	—	—	48.4

遗产保护需要花费大量经费，我国世界文化遗产保护还没有设立专项财政资金，尚未形成一个确保资金来源的渠道和机制。目前我国的遗产地保护与管理所需资金，除一部分由上级部门拨款外，大部分需由各地政府和遗产管理部门自筹。我们在调研中发现部分遗产地资金缺口较大，对于大多数遗产地来说，围绕遗产地开展的旅游开发是创收获得保护与管理资金的主要渠道。

2.3.1.2　遗产保护资金的使用情况

在我国大多数世界文化遗产地旅游产业发展程度较好，门票收入勉强能够满足最基本的保护和管理需求，但在实际操作过程中，保护、维修、研究、管理、消防等方面经费仍显不足。分析其原因，主要有以下几点：

（1）地方财政对门票收入的依赖性较强；

（2）遗产管理机构的保护管理成本较高；

（3）门票收入用于遗产本体保护性修缮的比例偏低；

（4）不少遗产地其他任务（有如接待）较多侵占遗产保护资金。

2.3.2　社区产业的变化对遗产保护的影响

2.3.2.1　社区产业的现状特点

普遍看来，遗产地社区的产业特征明显表现为旅游服务产业的迅速且大规模发展，并伴随着一产二产的衰退。

从遗产保护的角度看来，旅游业为当地注入新的活力的同时，也为遗产本体的保护带来了新的挑战和困难。例如，居民擅自改变遗产本体格局开展经营活动，过多的游客量使得遗产生态环境保护压力巨大等等。这些状况威胁着遗产的原真性和完整性保护，造成遗产价值的降低。

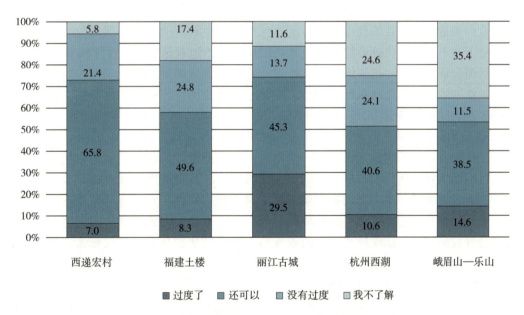

表 3－20　遗产地社区居民其遗产地旅游开发程度的看法

但是，从遗产地居民的角度看来，遗产地社区居民却普遍认可当地旅游开发的适度情况。只有丽江古城的受访居民对当地旅游过度开发表示了明显担忧。可见，居民对遗产旅游服务业发展为遗产保护所带来的负面影响的危机意识还不强。经济利益的重要性在居民的意识中仍然高于遗产保护。

2.3.2.2　社区产业的变化趋势

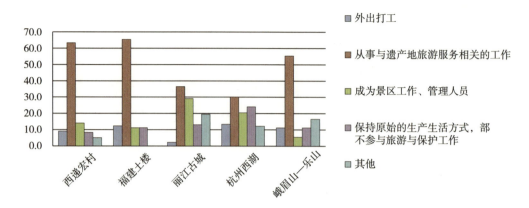

表 3 - 21　遗产地社区居民理想的从业方向

通过受访居民的理想从业方向调查可以预见，旅游服务业在遗产地社区产业中的地位将继续上升，逐渐成为遗产地的主导产业。从事农业的人口比例将进一步下降，社区居民的经济收入来源将越来越脱离一产。而具有遗产文化价值的传统手工业等遗产地社区特色二产将依据不同遗产地的保护政策而呈现不一样的发展趋势。

2.3.2.3　社区产业的变化对遗产保护的影响

遗产地社区产业的变化对遗产保护的影响可以概括为以下两点：

（1）具有遗产价值的传统产业缺乏传承

旅游服务业较偏重经济利益的获得，而传统社区产业产生利润的时间和周期较长、生产方式相对落后、生产效率低下，不符合现代社会的利益追求。因此，遗产地社区普遍发生了偏向旅游服务业为主导的产业转型。然而应认识到，一些传统产业也是遗产地文化价值的重要组成部分，如杭州西湖的龙井茶种植和炒制、丽江古城纳西文化的东巴纸制作、福建土楼周边的传统烟草种植等等。这些古老的传统产业应加以保护传承，使其保持鲜活。

（2）产业过于单一造成遗产资源的非可持续性利用

人们选择经济利益更高的职业无可厚非。但是，由于遗产地社区居民的文化素质普遍不高，在旅游开发中容易盲目跟随，导致居民参与旅游业的形式比较单一。从遗产保护和可持续发展的角度来看，过于单一的第三产业发展冲淡了多产业均衡发展下的遗产文化多样性。从经济学角度看，过多的人力物力投入将使旅游业达到饱和状态，进而引发效率的降低、产生劳动力资源浪费。国内遗产地风景区定位的趋同，旅游产品开发的雷同，已使遗产地旅游业发展呈现亚健康的状态。长久看来，旅游业是否就能成为遗产地社区未来经济可持续发展的主导产业，还需商榷。

2.3.3　社区发展与遗产保护的利益关系

遗产地与社区的利益关系既有限制的一面，也有反哺的一面。

2.3.3.1　利益限制

（1）遗产保护对社区利益的限制

遗产保护区的建立在一定程度上限制了当地居民对自然资源的利用方式，缩小了社区的发展空间，减少了经济发展途径，使遗产地社区经济社会的发展受到一定制约。这样的限制具体可分为两类：对社区居民生产活动的限制，对社区居民日常生活的限制。

遗产保护对居民生产活动的限制主要体现在生产活动的内容和规模的局限上。如山岳型遗产地保护中要求的原住民"退耕还林"政策；旅游发展氛围较浓的遗产地中管理部门对商铺经营活动的较多限制等等。

　　遗产保护对居民生活的限制主要体现在社区人口总量控制和建设控制上。大多数遗产地通过保护规划对遗产范围内的人口总量和建设密度实行控制，遗产范围内的建筑基本无法进行加建和改建行为，可用建设用地很少。遗产区内居民日益增长的建新房和旧屋改善需求较难满足。

（2）遗产开发对社区权益的限制

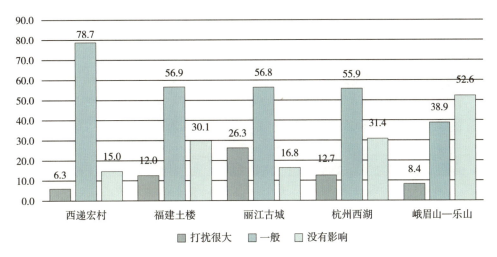

表 3 - 22　旅游开发是否打扰了居民的生活

　　遗产对社区权益的限制还体现在遗产地旅游开发对社区正常生活的影响上。分析反映生活受到旅游开发打扰的比例最高的丽江古城案例可知，物价上涨、噪音和垃圾是丽江古城受访居民认为影响最大的三个方面。这主要是由于丽江古城的商业业态选择，以及过度的旅游开放度造成的。

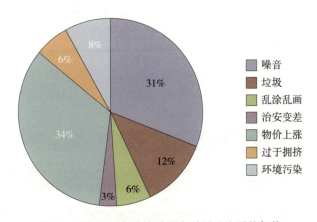

表 3 - 23　丽江古城旅游开发对居民生活的打扰

　　因此，针对社区型遗产地有必要限制遗产地的旅游开放度，且在遗产地旅游开发中选择合适的商业业态，这样既有利于保护居民私密性的生活需求，又有利于旅游服务经济的合理发展，减少对当地居民正常生活的干扰。

（3）多社区受到的不均等限制

　　对遗产地资源的利用为大部分遗产地社区带来很大程度的经济增长，但在某些范围较大且包含有多个社区的遗产地内，社区居民能参与到旅游业发展的机会不均等，相关政策也有不同程度的倾斜：位于主要游线附近的商业发展机会比远离游线的更多；位于重点保护范围内发展旅游商业往往限制比其他区域更多。发展条件的不同直接导致原住民受益的区别，长此以往，社区的经济发展程度出现了较大的差异，呈现出不均衡发展的状态，居民的心态也会出现不平衡。

2.3.3.2 利益反哺

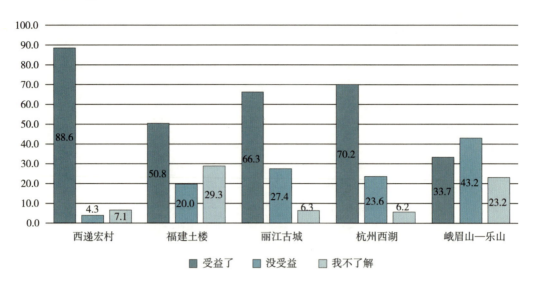

表3-24 遗产地社区居民旅游开发受益程度

尽管遗产旅游业的发展给当地居民带来了种种不便和矛盾，大多数受访的社区群众依然认可旅游开发为当地经济所作出的贡献，认为自己受益于旅游开发。其中，西递宏村的高受益率得益于居民所得的合理的门票收入分成，以及旅游业发展带来的物业升值所增加的租金收益；杭州西湖遗产地所包含的景中村里茶楼、饭馆、农家乐的繁荣发展为茶农们带来了可观的经济收入；而丽江古城较高的居民受益率则主要来自于这几年旅游发展带来的可观租金收入。可见，利益冲突也存在缓和的空间，需要适当的措施来使遗产地居民的生活和旅游业发展转变为互利互惠的利益共同体。

遗产资源的旅游开发利用可以为遗产保护提供一定资金来源，也为遗产地社区经济做出一定的反哺。反哺的形式大致有两种：提高当地居民经济收入，旅游收入的利益分配。

（1）提高当地居民经济收入

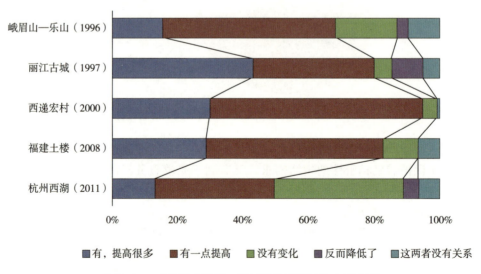

表3-25 成为遗产地后，是否提升了居民的生活水平

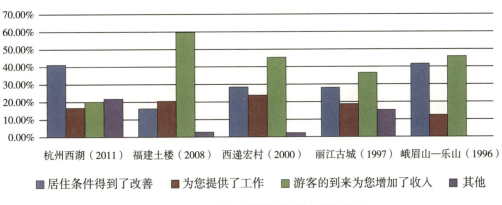

表 3-26　生活水平的提升体现在哪些方面

遗产地旅游业发展带动了当地的经济发展。通过横向对比不同时期申遗成功的五个遗产地，可以看出，随着遗产地保护与利用的时间累积，居民生活水平逐步提升。旅游开发所带来的游客量的提升，是提升居民生活水平的主要原因。对于旅游业发展较好的遗产地居民来说，经济收入的提高是最显著的社区反哺成效。

（2）旅游收入的利益分配

旅游门票收入的分配也是目前国内遗产地社区反哺的重要量化形式之一。

表 3-27　各遗产地 2011 年旅游门票收入分配比例表

遗产地名称	分配所得平均金额（元/人/年）	分配总额占门票总额的比例（%）
福建土楼	20—800 不等	8
西递	3000	14.60
宏村	2000	8
丽江古城	150	1.40

各遗产地的分配比例差异很大。杭州西湖因环西湖公园免费开放，对社区居民没有直接的门票收入分配，政府通过鼓励茶农开农家茶楼等，让遗产区社区居民增加经济收入；峨眉山—乐山大佛因社区所处非核心区域，目前没有实行门票收入分配，政府也是鼓励农民经营"农家乐"。在有分配措施的几个遗产地中，西递宏村的人均所得金额大大高于其他遗产地。这得益于西递宏村较成熟的旅游产业发展、较高的当地政府惠民意识。由于西递村的旅游经营公司属村办企业性质，对村民利益的保护意识更强，对社区的反哺也更合理。不公平的分配机制最容易引起利益集团之间的对立和冲突，因此遗产所在地的人民应能分享利益，是保障遗产管理安全、有效、可持续发展的重要前提。

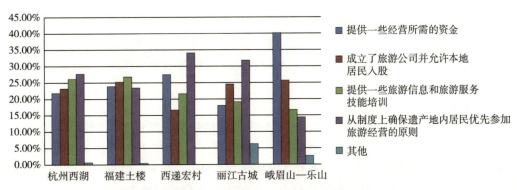

表 3-28　遗产地社区居民希望从遗产管理部门得到的帮助

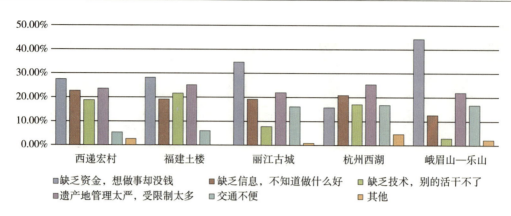

西递宏村　　福建土楼　　丽江古城　　杭州西湖　　峨眉山—乐山

■缺乏资金，想做事却没钱　　■缺乏信息，不知道做什么好　　■缺乏技术，别的活干不了
■遗产地管理太严，受限制太多　　■交通不便　　■其他

表3－29　要提高居民的经济收入，急需解决的问题

通过我们的调查也发现，遗产地居民在为了自身经济收入提高而急需帮助解决的问题上，除了资金以及入股分红的需求外，更希望能首先从制度上确保遗产地内居民优先参与旅游经营的权利，并且，提供旅游信息和服务必备的技能培训。所以，遗产管理部门在实际社区工作中，应认识到"授人以鱼不如授人以渔"，将社区利益反哺的范围从利益分红进一步拓展到策略的合理化和培训的提供上，帮助社区居民"学会"自主创造财富。

2.4　管理角度

2.4.1　遗产管理体制和立法体系对遗产保护的影响

2.4.1.1　行政管理体系

在国家层面，根据国务院确定的部门职责分工，国家文物局为世界文化遗产的业务主管部门，住建部会同国家文物局负责世界文化与自然混合遗产的管理工作。随着世界文化遗产和混合遗产数量不断增多，2002年，国家文物局专门成立了世界遗产处，负责中国世界文化遗产申报、保护、管理等工作，并协助住建部开展世界文化与自然混合遗产的业务管理工作。

在地方层面，世界文化遗产所在地政府基本建立了专门的保护管理机构，负责世界文化遗产的日常保护、管理、监测等工作。目前，已基本形成国家、省、遗产地几个层级的保护管理体系。如四川省为进一步加强四川省世界文化遗产保护管理，加大统筹协调工作力度，于2010年成立了"四川省世界遗产管理委员会"，由副省长挂帅任管委会主任一职，其主要职责是研究制订全省世界文化遗产保护管理相关政策措施，协调解决世界文化遗产申报、保护和管理工作中的重大事项。该机构还综合了省住建厅、省文物局、省旅游局等相关部门的主要负责人，能在更大程度上确保世界文化遗产的保护与管理的力度与广度。

虽说从国家层面到世界文化遗产地的直辖市、县甚至是村镇一级政府一直都在不遗余力地推行世界文化遗产的保护管理工作，并且也取得了不错的成效。但从计划经济时代延续下来的条块分割的管理体制还是对世界文化遗产地的可持续发展带来一定的负面影响。随着市场观念的增强，这种条块分割、多头管理的局面，势必会因缺乏国家层面的综合、统一管理，因利益的纷争而使得遗产间的协调保护变得越来越困难。

2.4.1.2　立法体系

近20年来，中国在世界文化遗产和文物保护管理上取得的进展受到世界的瞩目。但由于遗产保护管理的立法工作在我国起步较晚，相应的全国性法律、法规不完善。目前我国在世界文化遗产保护领域的立法只有文化部在2006年颁布的《世界文化遗产保护管理办法》，属于部门规章，法律效力有限，且内容也不够完善。虽说经过近些年政府及专家的努力，中国历史文化遗产的立法工作已经有了良好的基础，国内世界遗产的保护管理总体上朝着健康有序的方向发展，但目前相关遗产保护的法规性文件多以国务院及其部委或地方政府及其所属部门颁布，制定的"指示"、"办法"、"规定"、"通知"等文件形式出现，由于缺乏正式的立法程序，严格意义上都不能算作国家或地方的行政法规，立法层级较低，并无足够的法律效力。

近年来，国家、地方和有关部门都加快了制定法规、规章保护文化遗产的步伐。详见下表：

表 3-30 世界文化遗产地（已调研）保护管理的相关法律法规

遗产地	批准时间	法律类型	法律法规名称	颁布机构	颁布时间
黄山（双遗产）	1990	地方法规	《黄山市历史文化遗产地保护管理办法》	安徽省黄山市人民政府	2006.8.14
丽江古城	1997	地方法规	《云南省丽江古城保护管理条例》	云南省人民代表大会常务委员会	2006.3.1
皖南古村落（宏村、西递）	2000	地方法规	《安徽省皖南古民居保护条例》	安徽省人民代表大会常务委员会	1998.1.1 颁布；2004.7.1 修订
福建土楼	2008	地方法规	《福建省"福建土楼"世界文化遗产保护条例》	福建省人民代表大会常务委员会	2011.12.1
杭州西湖	2011	地方法规	《西湖文化景观保护管理条例》	浙江省杭州市人民代表大会常务委员会	2012.1.1

在现行的法律、法规中，对管理主体的地位、管理机构的设置、人员结构及资质、遗产地的土地权属、文化遗产的收益及其使用、保护管理项目的申报、保护资金的投入、经济制约、部门协调、发挥民间保护组织作用、鼓励公众参与等具体问题都没有做出明确规定，使得管理部门经常陷于有法不知如何依的尴尬境地。如各个遗产地面临的共同难题是遗产保护资金问题：相关部门对遗产保护的资金并没有形成固定拨付的约定，而是由遗产管理单位根据项目需要提出申请，最终再由国家文物局、地市县两级财政根据需要拨付。这种尺度的把握其实是给政府在决定资金去向时提供了一个很大的空间。世界文化遗产在保护的过程中因资金问题而常常陷入捉襟见肘的境地。由于资金配备体制不健全，一些热门遗产地门票收入虽然可观，但平均用到遗产资源保护上的资金连门票收入的 10% 都不能保证。因此，完善和充实遗产保护法律体系和加强法规的可操作性仍是我国遗产保护立法中的迫切要求。

2.4.1.3 人才建设

由于世界遗产事务进入我国时间不长，相关学科研究开展较晚，尚未形成比较完善的学科体系，制约了整体理论研究水平的提高，也直接影响到相关人员培训的开展，并影响到遗产地保护管理机构的队伍建设。

随着遗产管理的进一步深入，对人才建设的要求显得迫在眉睫。以福建土楼为例，虽然南靖县、永定县都在文物部门下设专门的保护管理科室（行政级别为股级），但专门管理人员只 2—3 人，面对几百甚至上千幢需要管理的土楼，而且各土楼群分布相对分散，"以一敌百"的他们显然是力不从心的。再加上由于历史的原因，从事文物保护的专业人员本身并未接受过系统的文物保护的培训，多以"经验管理"为主，在知识结构上已远远不能满足现代遗产管理的要求。这些问题在峨眉山、丽江等地也不同程度存在。

值得庆幸的是，中国已经认识到这个问题的重要性，并开始致力于培养中国自己的保护世界遗产和传统文化方面的人才。2004 年，联合国教科文组织世界遗产研究教育中心（苏州中心）率先成立；2007、2008 年，"亚太地区世界遗产培训与研究中心"相继在同济大学、北京大学挂牌成立，一套切实可行的遗产管理人员的培训机制正逐步建立。

2.4.1.4　监管体系

2004 年，第 28 届世界遗产大会在苏州召开，中国政府作出庄严承诺：中国将建立高效的世界文化遗产监测预警系统。苏州古典园林在全国率先启动世界文化遗产监测工作，2005 年建立了"苏州市世界文化遗产古典园林保护监管中心"，并于 2006 年在全国范围内率先建立起世界文化遗产动态信息系统和监测预警系统。文化部 2006 年 11 月发布的《世界文化遗产保护管理办法》规定：国家对世界文化遗产保护的重大事项实行专家咨询制度，国家对世界文化遗产保护实行监测巡视制度。2011 年，"苏州经验"正式向中国各遗产地推广，敦煌、丽江、西湖等世界文化遗产地分别建立了遗产监测管理中心。

2.4.2　公众参与对遗产保护和管理的影响

2.4.2.1　公众参与世界文化遗产的保护与监督

2010 年文化遗产日中国政府已明确指出"要加强宣传普及工作，广泛介绍文化遗产知识，增强公民依法保护意识，积极培养文化遗产保护志愿者。营造保护文化遗产人人有责、文化遗产保护成果人人共享的社会环境，形成有利于文化遗产保护的舆论氛围"。国家文物局相继出台《关于进一步发挥文化遗产保护志愿者作用的意见》，鼓励更多的有识之士加入到文化遗产保护、监督的队伍中来。在各遗产地调研过程中发现，越来越多的遗产地管理部门开始通过广泛吸纳志愿者的方式来补充保护管理的力量，通过志愿者自身的优势及专长，开展一系列的宣传活动，达到遗产保护的目的。如丽江、武当山、杭州西湖等遗产地都建立了遗产保护志愿者队伍。

公众淡漠的保护意识造成社会"监督权"的缺失。社会监督实质是公众参与遗产管理和保护事务的一种自觉体现，重视监督就是对公众意见的一种最好的响应。所以，强化社会监督，建立全面、有效、透明的社会监督体制，将世界遗产的管理、保护和利用置于公开的社会监督制度下，汇集各种不同的意见，通过广泛讨论平衡不同的利益，当会减少争议，减少负面问题的出现，更能进一步激发公众参与社会监督的意识。

2.4.2.2　社区参与世界文化遗产管理

由于历史的原因，社区参与政府管理的意识比较单薄，而地方政府对社区主动"参政"也显得很不适应。通过社区参与，可以加强合作、减少冲突，有助于管理者更好地了解社区需要，也有助于社区了解遗产管理的使命及管理者的观点，更有利于解决社区利用与保护及其他利用的冲突等问题，达到保护、管理、利用、开发"多赢"的效果。

从调研情况看，宏村、西递两地已逐步探索出政府主导、部门联动、村民自发、协会参与的切合自身实际的科学保护管理模式。遗产申报成功后，在当地政府的引导下，两个古村落都强化了社区自我管理体系。两村均成立了旅游管委会和遗产保护管理监察大队，以加强遗产地旅游和保护的日常管理、现场管理和日常监控。并成立民间保护协会，制定村规民约，编印遗产保护宣传手册发给村民，同时在两村中小学中开展遗产保护知识宣传教育，培养村民对文化遗产的认同感及荣誉感。2002 年西递村在老年人保护协会的倡议下，全体村民以签名和宣誓的方式承诺"保护世界文化遗产"。列入遗产后的 10 余年间，由于村民的自觉参与，两村没有一幢古建筑损毁或烧毁，世界遗产的保护进入了历史上自我管理最好的时期。

2.5　现状问题总结

综上所述，目前我国社区的社会、经济发展和文化保护，遗产地管理和遗产保护及可持续发展之间的矛盾冲突汇总归纳为以下十点：

（1）遗产地社区居民的社会关系由传统乡土社会的血缘维系向现代社会下的利益维系转变，影响居民在遗产保护中的社区意识；

（2）遗产地社区面临的原住民流失和外来人口涌入这一人口结构变化，带来遗产保护责任主体的变化与遗产文化价值传承责任意识的改变；

（3）遗产地社区居民日益提升的现代化生活需求与遗产保护所要求的原真性产生的矛盾冲突；

（4）现代旅游服务业及全球化对遗产文化价值传承的威胁；

（5）遗产保护资金缺口较大，影响遗产保护的效力；

（6）遗产地社区旅游服务产业的过度发展引起具有遗产价值的传统产业失传危机，以及遗产旅游业的亚健康发展；

（7）遗产保护对社区居民生产活动及日常生活有所限制，造成不便；

（8）旅游收入分配不公以及发展条件不平等引发社区居民对遗产资源利用的争议；

（9）管理体制陈旧、立法体系欠完善、人才缺乏以及监管体制有待成熟制约了政府在遗产保护和社区发展中的作用；

（10）公众参与的轻视造成社区居民在遗产保护中"监督权"缺失，责任和权益模糊。

3 经验的总结与借鉴——借鉴研究

3.1 西湖经验——在惠民理念指导下的遗产保护

西湖申报遗产成功后国家文物局童明康副局长指出，西湖申遗的成功经验非常值得其他地方借鉴，因为西湖申遗过程体现的是保护原则，把申遗过程当做保护过程，而且保护得非常成功。自 2002 年伊始，为解决困扰西湖可持续发展的风景名胜土地资源利用不合理、游览分布不均衡、基础设施不完善等直接影响西湖环境质量的问题，杭州市政府积极有效地实施改善西湖环境、彰显历史文化、惠及社区居民的整治与治理，真正实现了"景区美，百姓富"的目标。

（1）利益相关者参与决策和惠民的利益体现

西湖社区居民中很大一部分是与西湖龙井茶文化传承直接相关的原住民，利益相关者参加决策十分有利于将保护与治理西湖的理念深入人心。允许遗产区内原住民通过各种方式深入参与整治项目的各个环节，为政府决策提供参考，并对调节项目实施者与利益相关者的关系起到积极作用。整治项目实施之前，相关部门将规划设计方案通过各种渠道进行公开展示，在听取和吸纳原住民意见的基础上，最终制订实施方案。

图 4-1　杭州西湖文化景观

自 2002 年 10 月以来，环西湖的公园绿地经整治后均免费开放，以及杭州市所有的博物馆、纪念馆实行免票是杭州市政府惠民政策的充分体现。环西湖公园绿地的免费开放，使杭州市民尤其是居住在西湖周边的社区居民，充分享受西湖丰富的旅游资源。免费西湖使西湖这一公共资源真正了实现经济效益、生态效益、社会效益的最大化和最优化。

（2）茶村整治和茶村经济发展使居民获得实惠

西湖龙井茶是西湖文化景观遗产的重要组成部分，遗产区范围内的茶村和原住民，自宋代以来一直延续着西湖龙井茶种植、采摘、炒制、销售等茶文化的传统。为保护茶村周围的风景资源，又促进茶农发展经济，2003 年伊始杭州市政府投入大量资金用于茶村的基础设施和公共建筑整治，鼓励茶村村民出少量资金用于自己居住的房屋整修，优先整治的茶村村民可获得政府的奖励，这一举措得到了茶农的广泛认可，遗产区范围内涉及的所有茶村村民均积极参与了整治。茶村的环境风貌得到极大的改善，西湖原住民的生活品质得以显著提升。

经过整治的"景中村"根据各自的地理优势，在政府的鼓励和引导下逐步发展以龙井茶为特色的农家茶楼、农家餐饮、自助旅社等不同形式的旅游休闲产业，既扩大了遗产区的游客容量，又使当地茶农找到了持续发展地方经济的有效途径。据统计，2010 年遗产区茶农龙井茶销售收入 6420 万元，比 2002 年增长 100.3%；农家茶楼也从无到有，至 2010 年已有 600 余农户从事与茶和旅游休闲有关的经营，年收入达 5900 万元。2010 年茶农人均收入 12600 元，比 2002 年增长 46.9%。经过以政府为主导的西湖环境综合治理和引导发展与旅游服务相关的第三产业，原住民得到了真正的实惠。

（3）社区的集体经济模式确保社会稳定

杭州市是全国范围内较早实施征地留用地制度的城市之一。所谓"留用地制度"，即政府在征用集体所有土地时，按照征地面积的一定比例核定用地指标，让被征地集体经济组织用于组织发展二、三产业、壮大集体经济、安置失地农民，其实质是一种有效安置方法。

遗产区范围内金沙港村和灵隐村分别在 1999 年和 2002 年实行撤村建居。金沙港村利用留用地自己投资建设了虹桥度假村和百合花饭店、金沙港停车场等设施，通过租赁方式承包给他人经营，集体经济年收入 1200 万元，达到人均 1.5—2 万元。杭州市的留用地政策就是通过村集体经济组织利用留用地增加固定资产、发展二三产业，村民分红收益，获得长期、稳定回报，与农民养老保险收益共同构成杭州市农民收益的"双保险"。

（4）相对共享的利益分配制度体现社会和谐观

自 1999 年开始施行撤村建居以来，西湖景区内各村陆续成立股份合作社。其股份合作社的作用不但在于对资产的经营和管理，更重要的是保障其居民的利益。

以西湖遗产区范围内的茅家埠村为例，2003 年经过综合整治，都锦生故居等景点已成为湖西的游览胜地。整治后的农居先后开出农家茶楼。全村集体收入 2011 年约 1500 万元，除活动、保洁、安全、公务等开销外，余有 900 万元左右全部分红给 420 个股民，村民年均收入都在 2 万元以上。

与其他农村股份合作社以发展为目标的管理经营理念不同，西湖遗产地内的股份合作社将村民的利益放在首位。西湖作为世界文化遗产和国家级风景名胜，建设受到限制，自然资源受到严格保护，而西湖农村股份合作社正是在西湖遗产地内村民发展条件受到限制，不破坏自然资源的情况下，以改善村民生活条件为宗旨而成立的，该机制不仅使村民的幸福感大大提高，更重要的是增强了农民保护西湖遗产的责任意识。

（5）"西湖模式"的社会和文化效应

从社会效应看，一方面，环西湖各景点的免费开放为西湖乃至杭州赢得了良好的声誉，得到了本地社区居民和外地游客的赞誉，取得了社会的普遍认同。另一方面，政府不仅出资为景区原住民改善生活条件，创造就业机会，而且整个过程十分注重公平公正，受到当地居民的好评。从文化效应来看，十分注重对西湖固有历史文化的挖掘、传承和保护，并加大了对各类自然文化资源的整合力度，做到了山水与人文完美结合、自然与人工精致和谐，保持西湖文化序列完整、特色鲜明，使西湖的文化得以延续。

3.2 西递宏村经验——自上而下的保护策略有效激发了自下而上的社区参与

西递、宏村有效运用自上而下的保护策略，使村民充分认识到保护古民居的重要性而自觉投身其中。保护世界文化遗产已经成为西递、宏村村民潜意识中的集体认同。由于西递村村民对原住民文化非常尊重且认同感强烈，村民的遗产价值保护意识普遍较好。

(1)"百村千幢"工程作为遗产保护的后备资源和开发缓冲

为加强后备遗产的保护，黄山市于2009年实施的"百村千幢"古民居保护利用工程，构建了皖南古民居保护体系，分流西递、宏村的游客压力，减缓了旅游开发对遗产的负面影响。

(2) 以遗产保护为导向的利益分配体制增强了遗产保护中的社区参与的意识

西递村的旅游经营公司属村办企业，在西递村的门票利润中，除20%留作村集体公益事业基金之外，其余的80%在村民之间进行分红。西递村利益分配体制的特色是以保护为导向，其分配额度的确定同时考量两方面：人口和房屋建筑面积。按房屋建筑面积分配的资金以古建筑资源保护费的形式发放，是对村民的房产权、公共景物所有权等的有偿使用，供村民作古民居日常维护和修缮之用。

(3) 合理疏导发展压力帮助平衡遗产保护和社区发展的矛盾

宏村通过内部严格管理，外部引导疏解的管理模式，使遗产得到了有效的保护。

宏村尝试在遗产保护、旅游发展和提高居民生活品质中找到一个平衡点：一方面，严格遵守法律法规，禁止拆建、新建、改建等行为；另一方面，在遗产范围外建立旅游工艺品市场，将大部分原遗产保护区内的摊点集中到市场内规范经营，大大缓解了旅游发展对遗产保护的压力。

图4-2 宏村旅游工艺品市场

3.3 丽江经验——遗产旅游与传统文化保护的重新认识

在旅游大潮的冲击下丽江古城曾经历了旅游过度开发所导致的发展失衡，致使一些传统民族文化发生传承危机。近几年来，丽江古城保护管理局和当地政府重新认识、评估丽江古城中旅游发展和传统文化保护的平衡点，积极投入整治，遗产保护取得了较大进展。

（1）《传统商业文化保护规划》扶持传统商业，突出民族特色

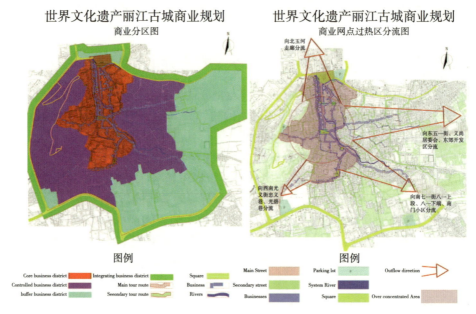

图4-4　丽江古城传统商业文化保护
管理专项规划商业分区图

图4-5　丽江古城传统商业文化保护
管理专项规划商业网点过热区分流图

　　丽江通过《世界文化遗产丽江古城传统商业文化保护管理专项规划》来规范遗产保护区内的商业发展。为淡化现代商业气息、突出民族特色，丽江坚持实行"经营准入制度"，清理整顿与古城风貌不协调的经营项目，规范店铺风格，控制店铺数量。对有民族文化特色的商铺、手工艺加工店、食品店进行挂牌保护。

　　（2）挖掘传统文化，保护遗产环境的完整性

　　2008年起，丽江积极对遗产地内的非物质文化遗产进行保护与挖掘：每年从古城维护费中支出1000万元专项资金，用于古城民族文化的挖掘、整理、传承和展示等工作；进一步加大了对东巴文化、纳西古乐等的保护、传承；在古城五一街打造了具有民族特色的"纳西文化一条街"；组织开展了"丽江古城"楹联征集活动；大力支持丽江纳西文化研究会的活动。

　　（3）"便民、惠民"措施留住原住民

　　旅游的过度发展使古城局部地段的居民发生了较大规模的迁离。古城保护管理局采取了多种"便民、惠民"措施，如：增设户籍居民的生活补助（15元/人/月），增加各种学习、休闲、娱乐活动场所，对修缮房屋有经济困难的家庭给予资金补助等措施。

3.4　澳门——遗产保护在青少年中的教育与推广

　　澳门特区政府自启动申报遗产工作以来就非常重视遗产保护在政府部门、民间社团和学校的教育与推广工作。为配合遗产申报工作，文化局通过举办研讨会和展览、奖励研究、出版刊物、开展学界比赛等一系列活动，宣传推广文物保护。

　　2001年，文化局策划"文物大使培训计划"，招募青少年经过培训担任澳门文化遗产的推广工作。2006年起，民政总署与澳门历史教育学会联合举办"博物馆学生研究员培训计划"。

　　澳门基金会于2007年连同澳门旅游学院、澳门历史教育学会及全澳各中小学校，推出"我们的家园，世界的遗产——澳门历史城区校园推广计划"，旨在向全澳近10万名基础教育的师生宣传推广澳门的文化遗产。除了普及推广教育外，专业教育也是世界遗产教育不可或缺的重要部分。澳门申报世遗期间，澳门旅游学院即着手筹办相关的高等教育课程，2005 年 7 月澳门申报世遗成功，该校于同年 9 月开设四年制的"文化遗产管理"学士学位课程，成为澳门最早，也是至今唯一一家开设这类本科专业的高等教育机构。

4　可持续发展的构建与保障——完善研究

遗产的有效保护与社区的可持续发展是本次研究的理想目标，为了构建这一理想的和谐关系，需要在前期调研的基础上针对我国遗产发展的现状与我国的国情，制定未来发展原则，提出系统的完善思路，并充分发挥自上而下的管理优势制定一套保障管理机制。

4.1　遗产与社区可持续发展应遵循的原则

4.1.1　以人为本

世界文化遗产，归根到底都是由人所创造，包含了人的知识和情感。古村落的建筑和原住民的历史环境和文化氛围，自然风景中蕴含着的宗教或历史名人的思想，其核心即是"人"。因此，在本研究所涉及的世界文化遗产保护工作中坚持以人为本，是在根本上抓住了遗产保护的本源，坚持以人为本是构建遗产与人类和谐关系的重要基础之一。

4.1.2　保护优先

对于遗产保护而言，"保护优先"原则的基本内涵是指在遗产保护活动中应把遗产的保护放在优先位置予以考虑，在遗产保护利益与其他利益冲突时，优先考虑遗产保护利益。在各种遗产的适度利用与保护之间，保护遗产的真实性和完整性是首要的，适度利用必须服从保护要求。

遗产保护工作中的保护优先原则还包括两个方面。一是保障原住民拥有良好生活质量的权利；二是遗产保护利益与经济利益冲突的决策权衡。

4.1.3　和谐共生

"和谐"是指对立事物之间在一定条件下，动态、相对、辩证的统一，是不同事物之间相辅相成、互助合作、互利互惠、互促互补、共同发展的关系。"和谐"的概念自古有之，是中国传统文化的精髓。

"共生"源自生物学中的共生理论。共生既是自然的本质，也是社会的本质。共生关系遍布人类社会的经济、政治、文化、社区、社群、家庭等所有领域。

和谐共生的概念从世界文化遗产保护的角度来看，就是在开展遗产保护工作时，须以民生为根本出发点，努力营造保护世界文化遗产人人有责、世界文化遗产资源人人共享的社会环境，从而形成有利于世界文化遗产保护的舆论氛围，鼓励引导更多社会资金投入世界文化遗产保护事业。

4.2　遗产保护与社区可持续发展的总体思路

4.2.1　传承共生和谐关系的构建目标

遗产与社区传承共生的和谐发展关系，不应仅仅关注可持续发展理论中经济、社会与环境的协调发展，还应特别强调遗产与其相关社区的共同发展问题。简言之，构建社区与遗产传承共生的和谐发展关系就是要在尊重自然规律的前提下维系遗产地生物多样性与文化多样性，并在此基础上推动遗产地社区经济与社会向前发展。

4.3　传承共生和谐关系的构建措施

要实现世界文化遗产和相关社区的传承共生、和谐发展的目标，其涉及的内容十分宽泛，具有特殊性、综合性和社会性的特点。因此，措施的制定应充分考虑与遗产相关的诸如环境目标、经济目标、社会目标和文化目标，坚持以人为本、保护优先、和谐共生原则，使多重目标相互协调，实现统一规划、统一利用、统一管理的"三统一"。

4.2.2 传承共生和谐关系的构建框架

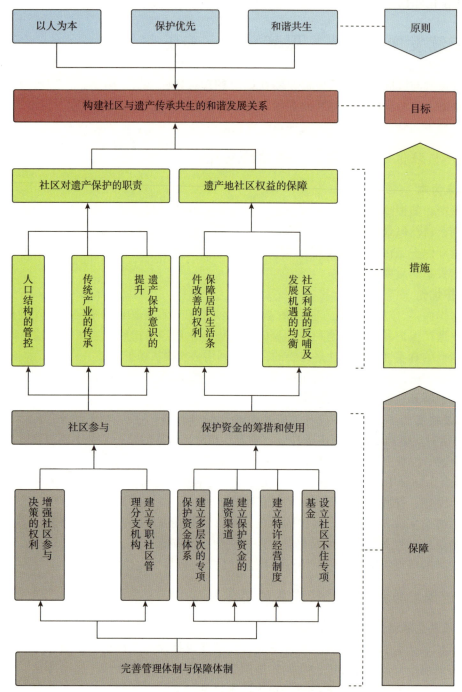

图 5 - 1　传承共生和谐关系的构建框架图

4.3.1　社区对遗产保护的职责

　　在中国目前发展阶段，社会关系普遍存在着"血缘关系逐渐淡化、地缘关系日渐开放、业缘关系趋于复杂"的现象，在遗产地社区，由于旅游开放，原住民的流失和外来人口的涌入，使遗产地面临文化失落的危机。从社会、经济、文化角度究其原因，可知遗产地人口结构的剧变、传统生活与产业的失落、遗产意识的淡薄是其主要原因。因此，目前形势下遗产的可持续发展对社区职责提出了以下要求。

4.3.1.1 人口结构的管控

原生、共生型遗产地最主要的吸引力在于以传统民居为背景的与地方民俗生活融合成一个整体所体现出来的生活气息，并由原住民传承和延续。一旦原住民数量减少，将失去其应有的生活气息。由此，在遗产地的保护管理中：

一要调控原住民比例于合理范围之内。遗产地内原住民和外来人口的比例需要得到有效管控。需根据遗产地的遗产价值，研究确定合理的原住民比例（由以上调研分析可知，原住民80%以上为佳），并采取切实可行的措施加以管控（如经济调控手段），同时，地方政府应当扶持和帮助原住民社区保持传统文化，弱化外来人口带来的文化冲击。帮助维持传统和谐的社会关系，强化遗产文化价值传承所依赖的血缘关系（尤其是村庄型的遗产地）。

二要限制外来人口的比例。对外来人口（特别是外来经商常住人口）的管控是减少外来文化对本地传统文化和习俗的冲击和同化的必要手段。

三要控制游客数量。根据遗产地的旅游环境承载力确定所能容纳的最大游人量，并严格按照限值控制游人总量，保护遗产生态环境。

4.3.1.2 传统产业的传承

针对以上调查中遗产地旅游服务产业成为主导产业、一产二产衰退的产业特征，以及社区居民经济利益的重要性高于遗产保护的思想意识来判断，传统产业的传承正面临严峻的挑战。比较而言，旅游服务业较偏重经济利益的获得，而传统社区产业产生利润的时间和周期较长、生产方式相对落后、生产效率低下，不符合现代社会的利益追求。但长久看来，文化遗产可持续发展的要求是不允许旅游业独自支撑，成为遗产地社区未来经济的主导产业，而必须鼓励支持传统生活与传统产业的可持续发展。

针对目前遗产地普遍存在的传统产业没落的问题，需要提出以下传统产业传承策略：尊重并保持原住民的习俗、风情；支持原住民传承各种特色传统工艺制作。

一要把地方传统文化和工艺作为非物质文化遗产加以传承和振兴，在原住民中鼓励年轻一代成为传统文化和工艺的传人。

二要对传统文化产业的从业人员给予一定的免税或减税的补贴和优惠政策。

三要持续性地提供并逐步加大对传统农业、手工业的财政支持力度，切实树立遗产保护的价值观念，让遗产地社区居民通过维持原有生活与传统产业得到实际的保护收益。

4.3.1.3 遗产保护意识的提升

目前中国遗产地社区居民参与遗产文化价值传承的基础较好，潜力较大，主观意识上参与遗产保护传承的意愿较为强烈，这种意愿与居民生活对遗产的依存度，以及成为遗产地的时间成正比。但是进一步提升遗产保护意识，既有潜力也有威胁。潜力来自于目前原住民自身对与遗产文化价值相关的传统民族文化的较自觉传承，威胁则来自于不断增强的外界影响因素对传统文化的冲击作用。

提升居民遗产保护意识的有效途径是：让居民参与遗产保护、对社区居民进行遗产教育，以及保持原住民与遗产的依存关系。

（1）公众参与保护与管理

一方面，鼓励世界遗产地的原住民传承传统文化；另一方面，鼓励外来人士（外来经商者和游客）参与传统文化的保护与传播。

具体途径可以有：

■ 让公众参与遗产地保护管理规划，增进公众对遗产地的认识；

■ 将遗产地保护及利用状况予以公示，保障公众知情权并获得公众的理解和支持；

■ 组织遗产地传统文化活动，鼓励公众参与，形成互动，增进遗产地传统文化的传播和宣传，展现遗产地的文化活力。

（2）加强社区的保护教育

一是普及世界文化遗产保护理念和知识。树立人人都有保护世界文化遗产的责任的理念，加强宣传教育是关键。原生、共生型的世界文化遗产地，尤其要重视世界遗产文化的宣传和教育，可以通过开展以宣传传统文化为主题的文化活动，让社区居民参与其中，使他们加深对遗产地的文化传统的认同和自豪感，自觉成为遗产保护实践者和宣传者。

二是对社区从业人员进行文化培训。适度发展遗产地的旅游经济，需优先受惠于原住民。对旅游业从业人员进行文化培训，尤其是传统文化的宣传和教育是提高其文化素质的有效途径。对原住民进行教育培训，使其更全面了解遗产地的传统文化，并具有一定的服务技能、掌握一定的专业技术，使原住民真正能够参与到与旅游相关的经营活动中来，并从中受益。

三是增强世界文化遗产的展示宣传。应不断研究世界文化遗产保护和管理工作规律，借鉴国内外的先进经验提高世界文化遗产的宣传展示水平，积极探索具有较强的科学性、趣味性和参与性的世界文化遗产宣传展示方式，满足不同类型、不同层次的人们观赏、学习的需要，增强人们保护世界文化遗产的意识。

（3）保持遗产与社区的依存关系

由调查可知，依存度高的遗产地社区居民的保护意识与意愿更为强烈，因此一方面要加强遗产文化价值、经济价值、社会价值的宣传教育；另一方面要在遗产保护允许的范围内适度发展旅游业，完善基础设施，适当满足居民的生活与经济需求；同时，还需通过财政拨款或社会资金弥补遗产保护对居民的经济损失，加强原生、半生型遗产与社区的遗存关系。

4.3.2 遗产地社区权益的保障

本次研究的世界文化遗产，均由人类所创造，包含了人类的知识和情感。秉持保护优先、以人为本、和谐共生的理念构建遗产与人类可持续发展的关系，除了以上部分所分析的社区应当为遗产保护承担的责任之外，还需尊重社区的基本权利，保障社区的基本利益。

4.3.2.1 保障居民生活条件改善的权利

遗产的可持续发展包含了遗产地社区居民生活条件的提升与完善。

除福建土楼外墙是夯土外，调查走访的大多数遗产地的传统民居多属砖木结构，经过几十年、上百年的风吹雨打，大多都设施陈旧并存有安全隐患，而且在卫生设施等方面不能满足人们现代生活的需要，居民尤其是年轻人多不愿住在古村、古城内，造成原住民数量减少。

因此，一要为满足居民的生活需求，在遗产本体保护许可范围内允许非主体建筑在建筑内部进行适当装修，满足现代生活需求。

二要严格保护遗产建筑，明确不允许内部装修和改变结构，外观的修缮需得到相关部门批准并在相关部门的指导下进行。

三要在利益分配时，给予住户一定的奖励作为房屋修缮资金。并对传统民居保护得较好、传统工艺很好传承的居民给以奖励和鼓励，引导增加社区居民的保护传统的意识，从而实现遗产价值的传承与保护。

四要通过国家或地方立法明确旅游收入的一定比例用以支持遗产地社区基础设施建设，解决居民就医、就业培训、子女就学等实际问题，使遗产地社区居民从遗产保护和可持续发展中获得实惠，增强保护积极性，促进保护和利用良性循环。

4.3.2.2 社区利益的反哺及发展机遇的均衡

遗产保护对社区的生产活动、人口总量和建设项目等方面均有较多的限制。遗产地旅游开发一方面会较大影响社区正常的生活，另一方面会带来发展条件不均等、经济收益不均衡、居民心态不平衡的现象。因此，需要从政府层面给予相应的补偿，并建立一个社区居民公平参与利益分享的机制，使社区居民成为遗产保护的实践者和受益人。

（1）建立一个合理的利益补偿机制

居民作为利益主体之一，承担了民居开发过程中的各项隐性成本，如资源、环境、社会成本等。因此应考虑适当给予其一定经济利益作为对打扰其日常生活的补偿，或让其参与遗产旅游开发活动并参与利益分配，并保证其收益的逐步增长（2011年西递村民分成占总门票收入的14.6%、宏村8%，调研座谈时村干部希望理想的分成比例为20%左右）。

规范旅游企业的经营行为，最小限度地减轻对环境的污染和对当地居民生活质量的副作用（如配备废水及其他污染物质的回收和处理设备），并向居民优惠开放，提高设施利用效率和社会环境质量。

通过遗产保护基金等形式，建立国家补偿机制。对损害社区居民利益的现象进行一定的补偿，如野生动物践踏农田、猛兽猎食牲畜等损害社区利益的现象应有固定的补偿途径，有专门机构评估损失，有正常的申述渠道。

（2）建立一个合理的利益分配机制

因地制宜构建遗产地合理的利益分配机制，规定遗产旅游中社区的合理利益分配比例，并把居民行为直接与其经济利益挂钩，增强其遗产价值的意识。

利益的分配包括：

一是参与遗产旅游的开发、保护，直接获得工资、分成、分红、养老与医疗福利等。如成立社区居民共同参与经营的股份制企业，居民成为股东。

二是社区从与遗产旅游结合建立的服务设施、娱乐项目中获利。如优先支持原住民开设家庭风情旅馆、风情餐饮店，土特色及工艺品商店；优先安排原住民就业，包括参加各种管理与经济实体工作，参与各种演出、礼仪活动、工艺品制作作坊并从中获得合理的经济收益。

三是遗产地旅游业发展对社区的反哺，包括对社区基础设施的建设、文化教育设施的建设等。政府通过提供公共服务，如小额贷款、基础设施建设、直接补贴、培训、扶持民间旅游协会建设等保证遗产旅游业的可持续发展，并确保旅游发展的利益最大化程度留在当地。

四是社区通过设计制作遗产旅游商品出售给游客获得相应的利益。这类旅游商品尽量采用本地原料加工，并优先雇佣原住民参与生产制作。

（3）建立一个有效的利益表达机制

遗产保护和可持续发展的利益相关者都有各自的利益需求，为了实现平等，有必要建立一个能充分表达自身利益的有效的利益表达机制。相对遗产管理部门和旅游开发公司而言，社区居民处于弱势，只有通过参与，结成团体才能表达自身的利益。因此在遗产资源利用所得的分配管理上，应采取让居民代表参与的形式（目前遗产地社区对旅游收益的分配情况了解甚少，影响了对遗产保护的热情与主人翁意识）。

4.4 传承共生和谐关系的保障

4.4.1 社区参与

目前中国遗产地社区居民参与遗产价值传承的基础较好、潜力大，参与遗产保护传承的意愿较为强烈，但总体而言公众参与的水平地区差异较大（经济发达地区参与度较高），很多遗产地仍处于较低的水平。

4.4.1.1 增强社区参与决策的权力

遗产地社区是遗产地真正的主人，他们应对保护、规划、计划、管理规章的制定有知情权，有机会参与讨论、发表意见，并进而参与决策。具体包括：

一是制定规划时要尊重原住民的利益与要求，广泛听取原住民意见，使规划制订具有原住民视角的合理性，或者使原住民的"合理性要求"得到合理的补偿；

二是规划期间建立良好的咨询、建议、反馈机制，既保证规划的科学性，又使规划在执行过程中能得到社区的主动参与而顺利实施；

三是让社区居民参与遗产管理工作中重大决策的制定，并具有表决权。

4.4.1.2 建立专职社区管理分支机构

一是遗产地应加强对遗产地社区的服务，建立专职社区管理分支机构，如社区管理科，其工作职能就是帮助社区经济发展，解决社区居民提出的发展需求和矛盾问题；

二是针对旅游发展，成立社区成员与旅游当局的联席会，定期开会商谈旅游发展相关问题，规范旅游服务的行为，抑制不利的发展方向，谋划合理的发展渠道；

三是针对传统产业的保护与发展，成立当地各行业参加的行业组织，加强交流与沟通协调，提升并保护从事传统产业的社区群体的整体利益。

4.4.2 保护资金的筹措和使用

世界文化遗产是全世界的共同财富，其保护资金的筹集也应多渠道。但是目前中国文化遗产保护资金存在总量不足、缺口较大；保护资金的来源多依赖政府与旅游门票收入，过于单一；将来传统产业的传承与社区反哺的资金需求将日益增大等现实问题。因此，除了国家拨款与门票收入之外，还应当采用创建各种基金、加大政府保护资金投入力度、创办遗产旅游彩票等多渠道的保护资金筹资方式。此外，还可以从加强社区自治、提升社区参与遗产管理、精简政府管理成本的角度出发节省保护资金的管理成本支出。

4.4.2.1 建立多层次的专项保护基金体系

一是可以设立保护我国世界文化遗产的"世界文化遗产基金"，其来源可以是政府财政投入，遗产地经营收入，社会、个人捐赠等。此基金作为国家投入的重要补充，通过多渠道吸纳社会资金来解决世界文化遗产保护资金不足的问题。

二是通过制定有关税收减免的政策鼓励社会投资，用于世界文化遗产的保护与维护。

三是应将世界文化遗产的门票收入交由财政实行专项管理并全部用于世界文化遗产的保护、传统产业的扶持、遗产管理与社区参与，以及社区利益反哺等方面。

四是应将世界文化遗产地内一些特许经营机构（如商店、宾馆、饭店等）的收益，按比例用于世界文化遗产的保护，以及对社区利益的反哺。

4.4.2.2 扩大保护资金的融资渠道

加大世界遗产保护资金的多源融资与社会动员，并借鉴国外的经验，扩大高等级遗产筹措资金的渠道。

一是争取联合国世界遗产委员会，以及国际民族事业、文化事业等机构与团体的支持；

二是因地制宜地争取国务院扶贫办公室、西部开发办公室、国家民族委员会、文化部、文物局及其他相关部委的支持；

三是争取中国民间慈善组织、文化组织等组织的支持与捐助；

四是争取社会、个人的支持，包括多种志愿者、有文化倾向或可以通过合作取得共赢的企业的支持与捐助。

4.4.2.3 建立特许经营制度

目前受国家经济实力所限，世界文化遗产保护区需要自养自足的政策，在相当一段时间内还会继续存在。为了保护文化遗产这一稀缺的宝贵资源，应对世界文化遗产保护区的经营项目和经营权力作出某些限制，即实行特许经营制度，并将有偿出让的收入用于世界文化遗产的保护与社区的反哺。

4.4.2.4 设立社区补助专项基金

应在各级保护资金的专项账户内设立社区补助基金，以激励当地社区保护资源的积极性，并保证遗产周边稳定、和谐的社会环境。

4.4.3 完善管理体制与保障体制

4.4.3.1 完善管理体制

要建立起符合遗产资源良性发展的管理体制，监管分立、责权清晰是解决遗产问题的关键。从市场化和政府管治的有效结合方面来看，世界文化遗产地地方政府为主的世界文化遗产管理体制具备相对合理性，也有许多积极的因素，因此有可能得到进一步完善和强化。

（1）加强国家对世界文化遗产的统一管理

通过健全国家文物保护部际联席会议制度解决职能分工和相互协调的问题，促进文化、建设、财政、国土资源、林业、宗教、旅游等部门加强协作协调解决世界文化遗产保护和管理中的重大问题，在国家层面上形成世界文化遗产保护的合力。

（2）逐步扩大地方的自主权

在坚持法规和世界文化遗产资源保护准则的前提下，完善地方管理为主的遗产资源管理体制，这是符合中国大国国情和经济转型时期社会经济发展要求的现实选择。世界文化遗产所在地省级政府应成立相应的保护管理协调机构加强对世界文化遗产的行业管理，应依照《文物保护法》明确职责，由省级文物行政主管部门负责对世界文化遗产保护工作的行业指导和管理。

（3）提升世界文化遗产地的管理层次

为了提高世界文化遗产的总体管理水平，世界文化遗产地的管理机构原则上应由省级或地市级政府领导，改变目前一些世界文化遗产地由县级或者乡镇进行管理，甚至出现由数个市、县割据管理的局面，逐步解决管理层次过低、多头管理，综合管理水平不到位的问题。

（4）建立科学的社区管理运行机制

世界文化遗产资源作为公益性特征很强的社会资源，其保护主体应该是政府，但是政府在保护管理方面的投入有限。因此，要建立专职社区管理分支机构，如社区管理科。其工作职能就是帮助社区经济发展，解决社区居民提出的具体要求，协调保护与发展的关系，实现社区居民参与遗产保护和遗产旅游经营管理。

4.4.3.2 加强保障措施

（1）加快制定《中国世界文化遗产保护法》

通过立法，明确世界文化遗产的法律地位，明确世界文化遗产保护的基本原则明确世界文化遗产管理机构的职责和任务。

（2）制定或适时修编世界文化遗产地的保护规划

我国大部分世界文化遗产地都在遗产申报时制定有保护规划。当前除了急需制定长城、明清皇家陵寝等涉及多个省市的遗产项目的总体保护规划外，还需适时根据遗产保护的需要修编保护规划。经依法审定的保护规划就是该世界文化遗产地必须严格遵循的保护管理法规，任何更改都要依照相应的法律程序，在保护范围和缓冲区内不能随意拆旧建新，坚决杜绝乱修乱建乱迁现象。

（3）建立世界文化遗产保护专家咨询制度

我国应吸收和借鉴国际先进经验和理念，聘请学术精专、执法严格、操行端正的多学科专家组成专家咨询委员会，并建立相应的工作规则和制约机制。凡涉及世界文化遗产申报、监测、保护、管理、利用的重大事宜，都要在决策前充分论证充分发挥专家咨询在世界文化遗产保护管理工作中的重要作用。

（4）建立国家世界文化遗产保护监测与巡视制度

加强对世界文化遗产的监测及其定期或不定期的专业检查、审议和监督检查。对于在世界文化遗产保护和管理中存在的问题和隐患认真进行分析和梳理，及时予以解决。对于出现的违法违规行为特别是因失职、渎职造成世界文化遗产破坏毁坏的，必须严肃追究有关单位和责任人的责任，从而把世界文遗产的保护和管理工作置于社会监督之下。

（5）要完善公众监督参与机制，强化公众舆论监督。

加强公众舆论的监督对世界遗产地保护与管理的作用，建立完善的公众参与监督的机制，将遗产处于一个更为广泛的监督之中。

可以在遗产与社区之间建立多种形式的联合共管委员会，其任务是共同商议确定发展规划、协调遗产和社区的民事或经济纠纷、加强生态环境教育，提高公众的保护意识等；成员可以由社区管理科和村民委员会组成，并吸收族长、宗教领袖、德高望重者参加。通过多种途径的运用，把社区与世界遗产紧密地结合在一起，共同实现社区和遗产传承共生的和谐发展目标。

5   结语

世界文化遗产是全人类共同的财富，它珍贵、脆弱、不可再生，在中国城市化快速发展浪潮中，中国世界文化遗产的保护状况举世瞩目。遗产与社区研究课题组怀着探寻、纪实的心态，历时五个月，深入遗产与社区关系最为紧密的遗产地，针对社会关系、人口构成、经济收入、旅游参与、文化传承、管理制度等系列热点问题，开展了现场的走访、调研、问卷等工作，并运用新技术开展了问卷调查繁复的统计工作，从而揭示了中国目前经济发展条件下遗产与社区最为真实的复杂关系。

在深度剖析遗产与社区关系的基础上，本次研究从世界文化遗产可持续发展的角度，制定了"传承共生、和谐发展"的理想目标，并紧扣课题主题与中国国情，从遗产地社区应该承担的保护职责与其应该受到尊重的基本权益两个方面制定了保障其和谐共生的系列规划措施与保障制度。

自此，本次世界文化遗产与社区发展课题研究的成果具备了现实基础、理论框架与操作抓手。毫无疑问，我们向中国世界文化遗产的可持续发展迈出了坚实的一步。

（执笔人：华芳、杨小茹、张倩，杭州市园林文物局）

Inheritance and Co-existence: A Study of World Cultural Heritage and Community Development in China

Hangzhou Administration of Gardens and Cultural Heritage

Abstract

This research analyses the world cultural heritage and community development within the following four major aspects: the interpretation and definition of the concept, the traceability and resolving of the existing problems, the analysis and utility of the experience, and the planning and measures of the reconstruction. With the investigations by survey, interview, and questionnaire of the Chinese domestic heritage sites which have a close relationship with communities, the ideal objective has been established as "inheritance, co – existence and harmonious development" from the perspective of the world cultural heritage's sustainable development. Combined with the theme of the research and the national condition of China, the local community's protective responsibilities and fundamental rights should be formulated by series of planning and safeguarding mechanism, in order to ensure the harmonious co – existence.

Key words: Community, World Cultural Heritage, Sustainable Development, Inheritance and Co-existence, Harmonious relationship

1. Goals of the Study and Definition of Concepts—Interpretation of the Study

1.1 Goals of the Study

(1) To analyze the present relations and issues between community development and world cultural heritage conservation of China;

(2) To summarize excellent experiences from the positive interaction between China's world cultural heritage sites and communities;

(3) To explore the role of community in the sustainable development of China's world cultural heritage sites;

(4) To improve the win – win system featuring positive interaction and sustainable development between communities and world cultural heritage sites in China.

1.2 Interpretation of the Concept of Community

Community can be generally defined as: a social and living cluster formed by a group of people inhabited within a certain space.

The Chinese definition of community, which usually involves administration area, is different from the international one. It tends to understand community as a relatively closed entity with boundaries, and stresses the character of community as a regional social organization, while the collective feature of community in terms of social relations or sentiments are not much emphasized.

Based on this, community at heritage site involved in this study is defined as follows: a basic social administration unit formed by people ordinarily living within the protected area of China's world cultural heritage sites, such as villages, towns and residential districts.

1.3　Objects of the Study

China has a total of 33 world cultural heritage sites, including 29 cultural heritage and cultural landscapes, and 4 mixed sites (Mount Taishan, Mount Huangshan, Mount Emei – Leshan, Mount Wuyi). Based on the geographical relations between heritage sites and communities, as well as the relations between heritage OUV and communities, China's world cultural heritages sites are classified as follows:

Table 1 – 1　Classification of China's World Cultural Heritage Sites

Classification	Definition	Sub – category	Heritage Sites	World Heritage Type	Research Method
I.　Original heritage sites	There are communities inside the property, and the heritage value is created by community residents	Ancient residences and villages	Fujian Tulou, Ancient Villages in Southern Anhui—Xidi and Hongcun, Kaiping Diaolou and Villages	World Cultural Heritage	Key studies, site research, interviews, questionnaires for management departments and communities
		Ancients towns and cities	Old Town of Lijiang, Ancient City of Pingyao	World Cultural Heritage	
		Historic center	Historic Center of Macao	World Cultural Heritage	
II.　Co – existing heritage sites	There are communities inside the property, and residents are relevant with part of the heritage value	Cultural landscapes	Hangzhou West Lake Cultural Landscape, Lushan National Park	Cultural Landscape	questionnaires for management departments and communities, interviews through telephone, site research on typical cases
		Mountain heritage	Mount Emei and Leshan, Mount Wutai, Mount Wuyi	World Cultural Heritage mixed sites	
III.　Accompanying heritage sites	There are no communities inside the property, but there are communities inside the buffer zone, and they influence the heritage value to some extent	Gardens	Classic Gardens of Suzhou、Temple and Cemetery of Confucius and the Kong Family Mansion in Qufu	World Cultural Heritage	Not in the scope of the study
		Palaces	Capital Cities and Tombs of the Ancient Koguryo Kingdom	World Cultural Heritage	
		Religious Construction	Ancient Building Complex in the Wudang Mountains, Historic Monuments of Dengfeng in "The Centre of Heaven and Earth"	World Cultural Heritage	
		Mountain heritage	Mount Qingcheng and the Dujiangyan Irrigation System, Mount Taishan, Mount Huangshan	World Cultural Heritage and mixed site	

Classification	Definition	Sub – category	Heritage Sites	World Heritage Type	Research Method
IV. Other	There are no communities inside the property, and nearby communities do not influence much on the heritage value	Imperial palaces and mausoleums	Mausoleum of the First Qin Emperor, Imperial Tombs of the Ming and Qing Dynasties, Imperial Palaces of the Ming and Qing Dynasties, Summer Palace	World Cultural Heritage	Not in the scope of the study
		Sites of ancient man	Peking Man Site at Zhoukoudian, Yin Xu, Great Wall	World Cultural Heritage	
		Grottoes	Dazu Rock Carvings, Longmen Grottoes, Yungang Grottoes, Mogao Caves	World Cultural Heritage	
		Temples	Mountain Resort and its Outlying Temples in Chengde, Temple of Heaven, Historic Ensemble of the Potala Palace	World Cultural Heritage	

To ensure the typicality and representativeness of the objects under study, this study focuses on the first and second heritage groups, which is supplemented by the third, and does not bring in the fourth. In order to make the study more specific, five heritage sites, namely Fujian Tulou, Ancient Villages in Southern Anhui—Xidi and Hongcun, Ancient Town of Lijiang, Hangzhou West Lake Cultural Landscape, Mount Emei – Leshan from the first and second groups have been chosen for in – depth analysis.

1. 4　Research Methodologies

The study adopts social survey and case analysis as its main research methodologies, which are complemented by literature research, cross – over research, and classification research, etc.

1. 4. 1　Social Survey

This study employs several tools for social survey, including the field survey, the questionnaire, and the conference interview. There are two types of questionnaires, one sent to residents living in heritage sites and the other to the administrative staff. From December 2011 to February 2012, the questionnaire survey was conducted in five representative world cultural heritage sites and communities concerned, namely Fujian Tulou, Ancient Villages in Southern Anhui-Xidi and Hongcun, Old Town of Lijiang, Hangzhou West Lake Cultural Landscape, and Mount Emei and Leshan Giant Buddha. During the survey, 1, 650 questionnaires were distributed to community residents, 1, 069 collected, accounting for 64. 8 percent of the total. Of them 1, 022 were valid, 95. 6 percent of those collected. A total of 13 questionnaires were sent to administrative departments, and 13 returned, which were 100 percent valid. The software SPSS19. 0 is employed for statistical analysis.

Features of community respondents are as follows:

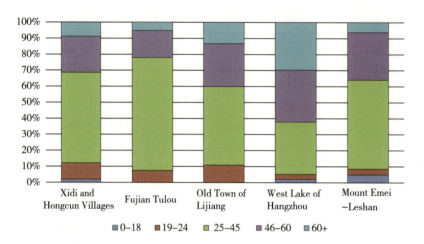

Table 1 – 2   Ages

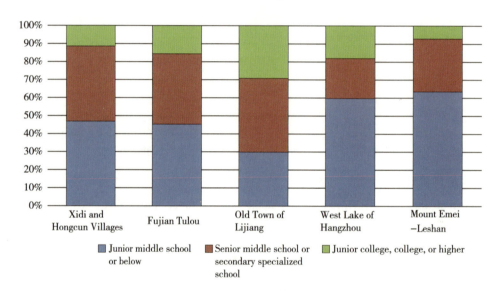

Table 1 – 3   Educational background

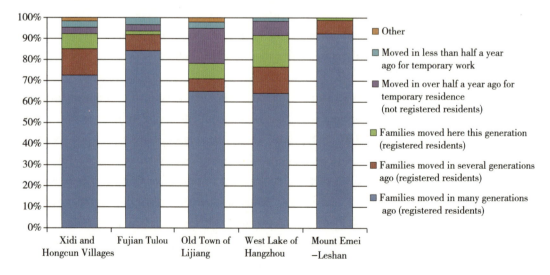

Table 1 – 4   Household registration locations

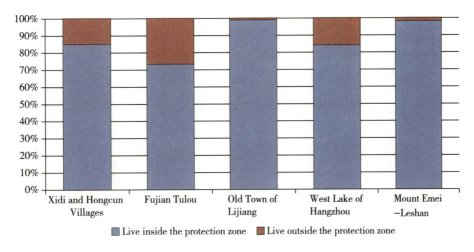

Table 1 −5　Whether or not living in the heritage site

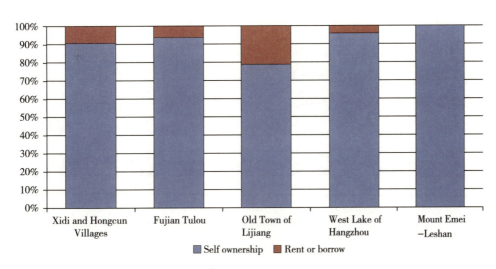

Table 1 −6　Residence ownership

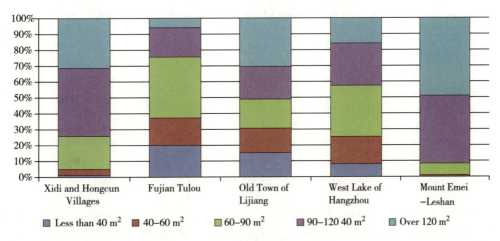

Table 1 −7　Residence size

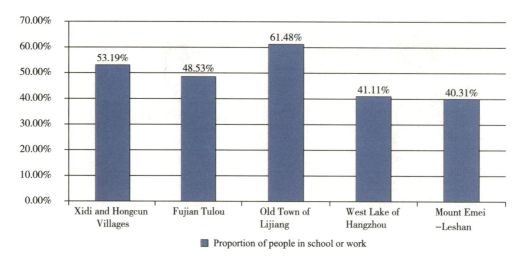

Table 1 – 8   Percentage of students and the employed

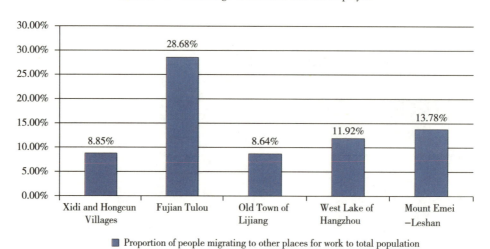

Table 1 – 9   Percentage of migrant workers

Information about administrative departments in the survey are as follows:

Table 1 – 10: Information List of Administrative Respondents

No.	Respondent	Heritage Site	Year of Inscription	Administrative Level	Copies of questionnaires
1	World Heritage Division, Cultural Heritage Bureau of Yongdong County	Fujian Tulou	2008	Vice Division	2
2	Xidi Township Government, Yi County, Huangshan, Anhui Province	Ancient Villages in Southern Anhui: Xidi and Hongcun	2000	Vice Division	2
3	Hongcun Village Committee, Hongcun Town, Yi County, Huangshan, Anhui Province	Ancient Villages in Southern Anhui: Xidi and Hongcun	2000	—	1

No.	Respondent	Heritage Site	Year of Inscription	Administrative Level	Copies of questionnaires
4	The Conservation and Management Bureau of Lijiang Old Town	Old Town of Lijiang	1997	Department	1
5	Xihu Subdistrict of Hangzhou West Lake Scenic Area Administrative Committee	West Lake Cultural Landscape of Hangzhou	2011	Department	1
6	Mount Emei and Leshan Giant Buddha Scenic Area Administrative Committee	Mount Emei and Leshan Giant Buddha	1996	Department	2

1. 4. 2. Case Studies

On the one hand, based on the classified characters of the first and second heritage groups, five representative and typical heritage sites such as the Fujian Tulou and Hangzhou West Lake Cultural Landscape are chosen to analyze, evaluate and summarize the relations between heritage conservation and community development. During the research, according to the different aspects of the analysis, case studies and comparative analysis are flexibly applied, and the acquired data is thoroughly analyzed and horizontally compared to be concluded with results referential for heritage sites of the same category. On the other hand, based on the questionnaires disseminated among management departments of other heritage sites and their publicity materials, their experiences are studied as supplementary analysis.

2 Status quo Analysis and Diagnosis: Analytical Research

China is now in a transitional period and its economic structure, cultural pattern, and social values are experiencing drastic changes. Such changes have brought particularly apparent effects on world heritage sites, which have the demands for both conservation and development and boast both ancient and modern features.

This study gives an in – depth analysis of the relationship between China's world heritage sites and communities located in them in ten aspects from social, cultural, economic and administrative perspectives, reveals contradictory parts between cultural heritage conservation and community development, and analyzes the causes that lead to such contradictions.

2. 1 Social Perspective

Different from ordinary communities, those in the heritage sites have a more delicate connection with the world heritage itself, the specific environment for heritage conservation, and the heritage's cultural value, and so do the problems.

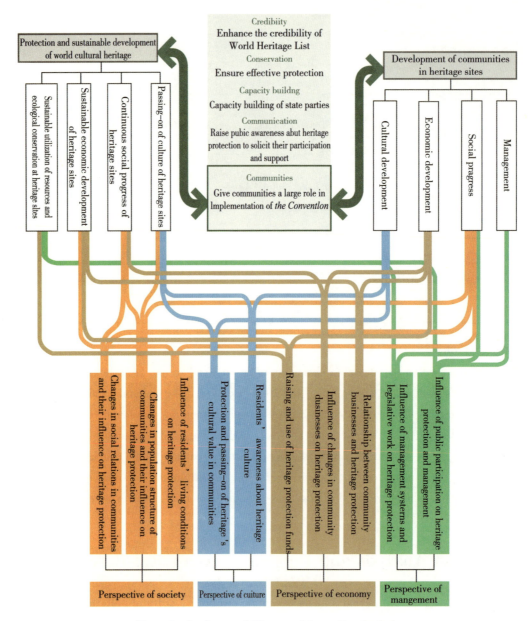

Figure 2 – 1   Structural Diagram of Status Quo Analysis

2. 1. 1   Change in Community Resident's Social Relations and Its Effect on Heritage Conservation

Following successful heritage inscriptions, various external factors have precipitated the transformation of the thousand – year – old traditional agricultural society into modern society, which has brought about dramatic changes to trade and geographic relationship as well as even kinship that constitute social relations. The social circle of acquaintances has changed into a new circle of quasi – acquaintances. The principle of "interpersonal relations" that prevailed in the kinship society has also incorporated the element of rationality, and the principle of interest has become an important dimension in the orderly – diversity pattern.

2. 1. 1. 1   Effect of a gradually weaker kinship

Due to socioeconomic development in communities located in heritage sites, their traditional rituals and customs have gradually drifted away from the modern life. The kinship has become weaker and gradually given way to trade and geographic relations in terms of the status and function in people's life.

At heritage sites of ancient villages such as Fujian Tulou and Anhui's Xidi and Hongcun, the tradition has it that a strong kinship is the fundamental base of the family bond and traditional rituals; it is based on such a kinship that the traditional culture came into being and was disseminated. Therefore, a gradually weaker kinship has made the role of traditional culture less important in local residents' life. And the heritage value in close connection with traditional culture has accordingly drifted away from their daily life and thus lost the force to pass it on. This phenomenon is particularly obvious in heritage sites such as the Tulou rooted in oriental kinship and ethical relations and the ethnic tradition of living together. Fewer and fewer native residents live in the earth buildings, local festivals and ancestor – worshipping rituals peculiar to this heritage site are now rarely seen, and traditional tobacco planting is almost abandoned. The unique harmony between man and nature here based on the kinship is overwhelmed by commercial activities of migrants from other regions. In comparison, heritage sites in the form of ancient towns, such as Lijiang, suffer less. The kinship in towns are traditionally less close than in villages, so it has seen little change and consequently left less effects on passing on traditional culture and conserving heritage sites. The change in social relations in towns are more apparent in trade and geographic ones.

2.1.1.2 Effect of gradually opener geographic relations

Geographic relations and kinship are to some extent connected regionally. Human activities in some regions are usually confined to a smaller scope and the geographic relations and kinship permeate each other. As long as they are inscribed as world heritage sites, local tourism will see rapid development, industrial segmentation becomes more complicated, and local population begins to flow. As a result, the geographic relations and the kinship stop permeating each other, and the formerly closed geographic relations gradually becoming open. Table 2 – 1 shows the comparison between the percentage of emigrant workers in heritage sites and local average percentage.

Table 2 – 1 Percentages of Emigrant Workers in Heritage Sites in Registered Residents

Heritage Sites	Emigrant Workers (%)	Local Average (%)
Xidi and Hongcun	9.37	14.90 (Yi County)
Fujian Tulou	30.1	6.30 (Zhangzhou)
Ancient Town of Lijiang	7.89	3.23 (Lijiang)
West Lake of Hangzhou	10.20	8.46 (Hangzhou)
Mount Emei and Leshan	14.17	10.63 (Sichuan)

Since regular local economic development is usually limited for the sake of heritage conservation, large – scale and profitable industries are banned in the heritage sites and local economic growth is therefore mainly dependent upon tourism. Because this can barely help local economy, more and more native residents seasonally migrate to work or move their homes from the heritage sites, as proved by the phenomenon in Fujian Tulou, whose percentage of migrant workers is five times the average in Zhangzhou. Due to frequent outflows of native residents, the shift of focus in their life, and the change in their income sources, their daily life is less and less connected with ancient hometowns. Because of this distant relationship, those who are perceived to pass on and guard important heritage values are less and less concerned and engaged in heritage conservation. However, it is also found out in the survey that Xidi and Hongcun have a far lower percentage of emigrant workers than the local average. This is closely related with local tourism development based on the concept of heritage conservation, tourism – based dividends for local residents, and their sense of heritage conservation. It therefore can be assumed that in heritage sites that see a relatively low percentage of emigrant workers, heritage resources are properly conserved and used, which are favorable for local residents and stable geographic relations.

2.1.1.3 Effect of gradually sophisticated trade relations

Since economic benefits weigh heavier nowadays, the relations among community residents in different trades have developed from cooperation into competition and restraint. In the agricultural society, most residents in the heritage sites were engaged in the primary industry. However, with a rising percentage of the tertiary industry in local industrial composition, interest and profit has undoubtedly become the yardstick of modern social life. This phenomenon is especially apparent in heritage sites where the agricultural lifestyle prevailed. For instance, many residents in Xidi and Hongcun vied to expand their premises at the cost of ancient buildings. Disputes over tourism interests also caused many cases of family discord in Fujian Tulou.

Therefore, the increasingly open geographic relations and the more and more sophisticated trade relations have gradually weakened the predominant role of kinship in social relations of residents in the heritage sites. Since both geographic and trade relations are less cohesive than the kinship, these residents have a gradually diluted sense of community. Now that they have a weaker sense of belonging than in the traditional agricultural society, group activities based on communities, including traditional festivals that are part of heritage value, start to dwindle, and residents are less enthusiastic about such events.

2.1.2 Structural Change in Community Population and Its Effect on Heritage Conservation

2.1.2.1 Features of heritage sites' population structures

In this survey, the percentage of the registered household population in the permanent population is the indicator to determine the percentage of local residents in the heritage sites. Table 2 – 2 gives a summary of local resident percentages in four heritage sites.

Table 2 – 2 List of permanent populations and registered household populations in heritage sites

Heritage Sites	Permanent Population in 2011	Registered Household Population in 2011	Percentage of Permanent Population in Registered Household Population (%)
Xidi and Hongcun	2868	2568	89.54
Ancient Town of Lijiang	24603	6376	25.92
West Lake of Hangzhou	14287	11723	82.05
Mount Emei and Leshan	24600	16300	66.26

The percentage of local residents in the current population structure varies with the heritage sites. Of them, Xidi and Hongcun in Anhui and the West Lake in Hangzhou have a higher percentage of native residents, but Lijiang has a far lower percentage compared with other heritage sites. According to the online survey of visitors' perception of heritage site's cultural atmosphere, the visitors have a rather good perception in sites that have over 80 percent of native residents, a so – so perception in sites when the percentage is over 60 percent, and a rather dissatisfied perception if it is less than 30 percent.

2.1.2.2 Change and trend of population structure

Table 2 – 3   The population in heritage sites before and after inscription

Heritage Sites	Permanent population before inscription	Registered household population before inscription	Percentage of native residents	Permanent population in 2011	Registered household population in 2011	Percentage of native residents in 2011	Percentage of native residents Stayed
Xidi and Hongcun (2000)	2214	2084	94.13	2868	2568	89.54	123.22
Ancient Town of Lijiang (1997)	15712	11931	75.93	24603	6376	25.92	53.44
Mount Emei and Leshan (1996)	21927	18867	86.04	24600	16300	66.26	86.39

The change in the population structure is mainly reflected in the percentage of local residents and migrants before and after the inscription of heritage sites. As Table 2 – 3 shows, despite the increase in local residents in Xidi and Hongcun, the percentage fell in both Lijiang and Mount Emei and Leshan. In Lijiang, 45.56 percent of local residents have moved out and the ancient town is now crammed with immigrant businessmen and visitors. The outflow of native residents and the influx of migrants are grave problems that China's heritage sites face in their population structure.

Behind such changes are mainly three causes: first, the mandatory moving of native residents for heritage conservation; second, their active moving to other places; and third, migrants brought by the tourism industry. The first cause is the result of local administrative policies, the second is out of the choices of native residents driven by economic benefits, and the third one is a by – product of the change in the industrial structure.

2.1.2.3 Effect of population's structural change on heritage conservation

The change in the population structure in the heritage sites has cut off the former network of interpersonal relations and caused indifference among local residents, which have not only affected the engagement of communities in passing on traditional cultural values and conserving heritage sites but also given rise to the change in responsibility subjects and consciousness of heritage conservation. Due to the outflow of local residents, there are fewer and fewer duty of subjects left who have the acute sense of responsibility in heritage conservation and the carriers of national and folk conservation are gradually lost. Compared with local residents, migrants are less dependent emotionally and have a poor recognition of heritage values. Considering the generally poor population quality, especially in the countryside, it is difficult for voluntary conservation to come into being. This leads to the nationwide phenomenon of heritage sites in disrepair and with manmade damage.

For the heritage of the humanity, migrants, either visitors or businessmen, are expected to shoulder the same responsibility for conservation as the native residents. In consideration of the change in the population structure in heritage sites, it is urgent to retain local residents with effective measures and further strengthen the responsibilities of various subjects for heritage conservation.

2.1.3   Effect of Residents' Living Conditions on Heritage Conservation

The residential environment and facilities in the heritage sites sometimes cannot be improved for the sake of heritage conservation. Due to this fact, the living environment and public facilities in some heritage sites communities obviously lag behind the level of the economic and social development and many vital benefits cannot be ensured for local residents.

2.1.3.1   Residents' living conditions and public facility conditions and demands

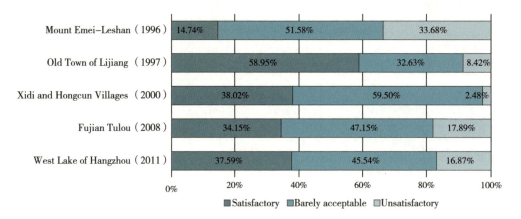

Table 2 – 4   Residents' Degree of Satisfaction with Living Conditions

The analysis of the questionnaires indicates that residents' degree of satisfaction with living conditions is positively correlated with the more development level of local tourism. Among heritage sites in the same category, the more developed the local tourism industry is, the more rapidly the local economy develops, and thus the better the residents' living conditions. For instance, Lijiang, Xidi and Hongcun (heritage site), and the West Lake (a symbiotic heritage site), which boast relatively a higher satisfaction degree, have witnessed better tourism development and service. It is also revealed that the relationship between the heritage value and the community has no connection with resident's degree of satisfaction with the living conditions.

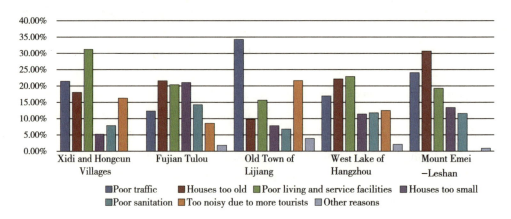

Table 2 – 5   Elements Behind Residents' Dissatisfaction with Living Conditions

A closer look at the causes of residents' dissatisfaction reveals three general problems: old housing, outdated supporting facilities, and inconvenient transport. Old housing is prevalent in villages located in heritage sites. In far – lying villages in the Mount Emei and Leshan Giant Buddha site, local residents have no access to renovation funds or economic benefits from tourism and therefore cannot afford housing repairs. Modern private bathrooms are prohibited to some extent in Fujian Tulou. Outdated supporting facilities are mainly compalined in heritage sites where construction is strictly prohibited, such as Xidi and Hongcun. Inconvenient transport is particularly apparent in ancient towns, such as Lijiang, that boast a rather developed economy, a high vehicle ownership per capita, and a large conserved area but prohibit vehicles in old towns to conserve the original narrow lanes.

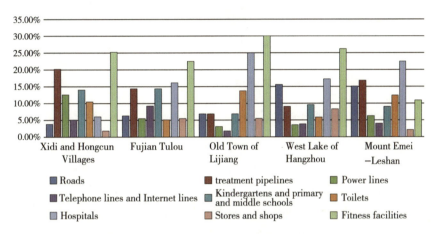

Table 2 – 6   Infrastructure lacked in heritage communities

Infrastructure lacked in the communities mainly includes educational and medical facilities, sporting fields, and public facilities such as water pipes, sewage pipes, and parking lots. Due to the precluded large – scale construction because of strict requirements and the limited available space, the shortage of the above mentioned facilities has been an age – old malady inflicting the communities in heritage sites. The resultant inconvenience is a major cause of some residents' migration. For instance, the outdated sewage pipes and power grids in Anhui's Xidi and Hongcun and Fujian Tulou can no longer meet the living demand of local residents. Lijiang has done a good job in this aspect by adopting the method of cultural relic restoration: it re – paved the road with the previously numbered plates after the pipeline was laid.

2.1.3.2   Effect of residents' living conditions on heritage conservation

The effect of residents' living conditions on heritage conservation is mainly reflected in the contradiction between residents' rising demands for modern life and the condition of authenticity required by heritage conservation. Against the backdrop of rapid urbanization, this contradiction is prevalent in heritage sites of ancient villages or residential buildings. If the residents' demand for basic living cannot be satisfied, it is impossible to enlist their support for heritage conservation. Therefore, a deep analysis of how to meet residents' reasonable living demands without threatening the heritage should be conducted at the technical level of heritage conservation and from the perspective of humanitarian heritage administration.

2.2   Cultural Perspective

Based on the conservation of the heritage sites' cultural value and local residents' awareness of heritage culture, this part analyzes the contribution and attitude of local communities and residents to cultural value's inheritance and conservation and then studies the potential engagement of local residents in this regard.

2. 2. 1. 1   Passing on heritage's cultural value

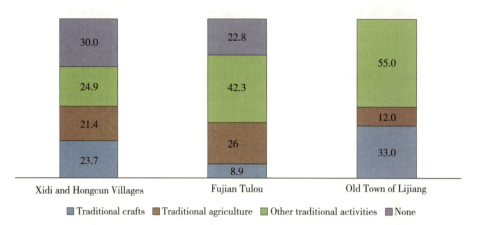

Table 2 – 7   Percentage of Local Residents Engaged in Traditional Lifestyle

Here three heritage sites are selected for comparison in which the heritage values depend on the community. The findings reveal that despite a heavy outflow of native residents from Lijiang, most inhabitants here are of the Naxi ethnic group and therefore many traditional customs are well preserved. In comparision, Anhui's Xidi and Hongcun and Fujian Tulou have fewer residents engaged in the traditional lifestyle, but they account for over 70 percent of the total population in both heritage sites, and the traditional local culture is well passed on.

In general, the cultural value has been well passed on in heritage sites whose values depend on the local communities. Traditional customs and ethnic culture still hold an important position in the daily life of native residents.

Fig. 2 – 1   Naxi people building a new house together

2. 2. 1. 2   Change caused by external influences to traditional culture

External influences mainly refer to the rising modern tourism and service industry and globalization. With the rise of the modern tourism and service industry, the heritage sites have remarkably opened their doors to different, foreign culture. Some residents believe that the wave of globalization has washed away their traditionally distinctive lifestyle. In Lijiang, 85 percent of interviewees said the traditional culture in the ancient town has been weakened by culture from outside. This signifies the weakness of traditional local culture when confronted with the modern tourism and service industry and the rising globalization.

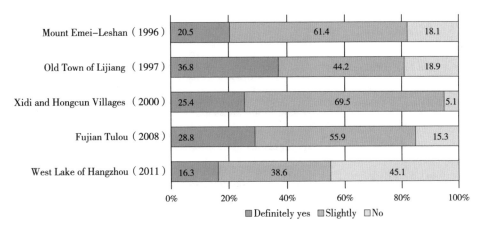

Table 2 – 8   Whether Native Residents Change Their Lifestyle for Heritage Conservation and Tourism Development

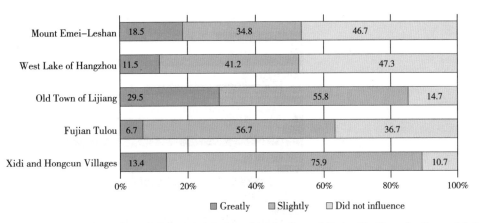

Table 2 – 9   Whether Traditional Local Culture is Weakened in the Eyes of Native Residents by External Influences

2. 2. 2   Community Residents' Sense of Heritage Culture

Whether residents, native and migrant alike, have a sense of identify and take pride in the cultural value in their communities, whether they can recognize their obligations to conserve and pass on the cultural value, and their enthusiasm in activities concerned can comprehensively reflect the potential of community residents to participate in passing on and conserving the heritage's cultural value.

2. 2. 2. 1   Residents' sense of identity and belonging to heritage's cultural value

Strictly speaking, community residents' sense of heritage's cultural value is their identity with the outstanding cultural value of local cultural heritage. When the culture identified by the residents' is in line with the culture conservation efforts tend to protect, then they will be voluntarily engaged in the efforts.

According to table 2 – 10, the statistical comparison shows that residents in heritage sites whose value depend on the local community have a better understanding of their distinctive cultural connotations than sites whose value co – exist with the community. Therefore, it can be assumed that the closer the relationship is between the heritage's cultural value and the community, the higher understanding of local featured culture the residents have.

Residents in China's heritage sites have a generally strong sense of identity with cultural value of their heritage sites. Only among residents interviewed in Lijiang, more than half did not wish there would be more visitors. In consideration of the larger effect of tourism development and globalization on Lijiang, the wish of residents in this old town is interpreted as their hope to protect the traditional culture from unfavorable external influences and contemplation based on their identity with the culture.

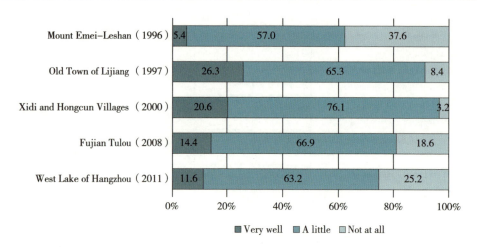

Table 2 – 10　Native Residents' Understanding of Distinctive Culture in Local Heritage Sites

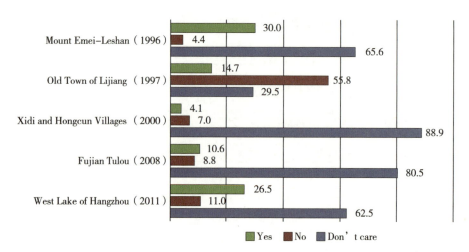

Table 2 – 11　Whether Native Residents Welcome more People to Live in the Heritage Sites and Understand Local Culture

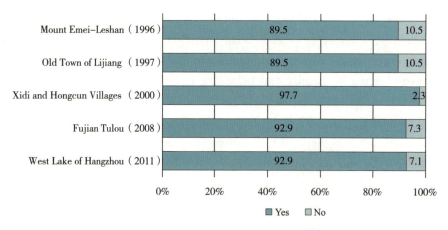

Table 2 – 12　Whether Residents will Stay and Live Their Traditional Lifestyle if Sound Infrastructure is Provided

　　The survey indicates that most residents will stay and lead the traditional life if sound infrastructure is provided, proof of their strong sense of belonging to the communities they live in. The improved infrastructure and living conditions will help residents play a bigger role in promoting and protecting the local cultural value.

In summary, native residents in these five heritage sites have a quite strong sense of identity and belonging to the heritage value and this sense is expected to grow stronger with the establishment of a harmonious relationship between the heritage sites and the communities.

2.2.2.2 Residents' attitude to participating in passing on culture

An important part of the residents' sense of community is sharing, participation and master consciousness. Only when residents in the heritage sites come to fully realize their close relationship with and interest in heritage conservation, can they continuously focus on and participate in heritage conservation.

Table 2 – 13 shows that local residents in all these heritage sites have good consciousness of heritage conservation and Xidi and Hongcun tops the chart with 96.1 percent. This is closely related with the kinship among residents in this site, a good publicity job of local heritage authorities, and the residents' active conservation consciousness. It also reveals that residents in heritage sites whose value depending on the community have a closer connection with communities have better consciousness in this regard.

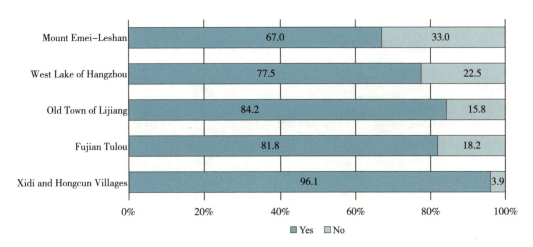

Table 2 – 13 Whether Residents Think They Have Something to do with Heritage Conservation

As is shown in Table 2 – 14, residents in hertiage sites with value depending on the community, namely Xidi and Hongcun, Lijiang, and Fujian Tulou, have a better understanding of heritage value. Since the value of such heritage sites is more concerned with traditional local culture and customs that residents are familiar with, it is easier for them to understand the abstract cultural connotations.

Table 2 – 15 summarizes to what extent local residents know the requirements for heritage conservation. It indicates that residents interviewed were concerned with such requirements to some extent. Due to the long – term publicity efforts of local heritage authorities, residents in Lijiang and Xidi and Hongcun have more knowledge of the requirements. At the same time, residents' dependence on heritage sites also influences their concern with conservation requirements. For instance, most villagers in the Mount Emei and Leshan Giant Buddha Scenic Area are engaged in jobs that have little connection with heritage conservation, so they are less concerned with the requirements.

As Tables 2 – 16 and 2 – 17 show, residents in heritage sites in our survey are generally enthusisatic about participating in their conservation, especially those in Lijiang and Xidi and Hongcun, who expressed the strongest desires to gain and help promote the knowledge of heritage conservation. Combined with the findings in Tables 2 – 14 and 2 – 15, it can be assumed that the length of time since inscription, residents' dependence on heritage, and the heritage authorities' publicty efforts are major influencing factors of local residents' enthusiam about heritage conservation.

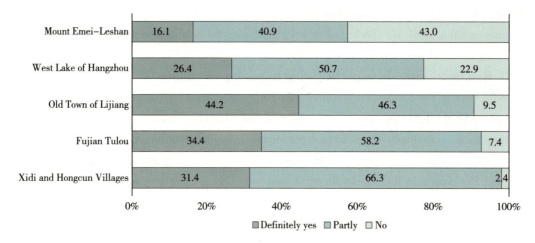

Table 2 – 14　Whether Residents Understand the Value of the Heritage Sites

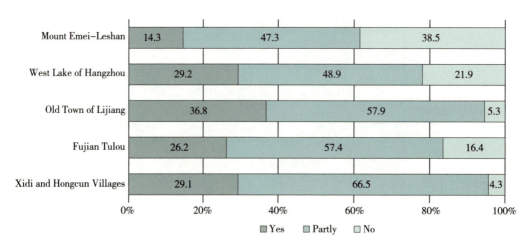

Table 2 – 15　Whether Residents Know Requirements for Heritage Conservation

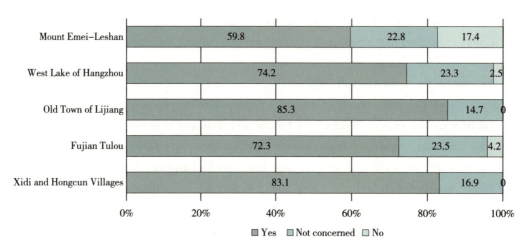

Table 2 – 16　Whether Residents are Willing to Know more about Heritage Conservation

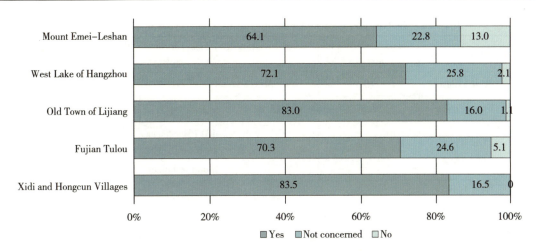

Table 2 – 17   Whether Residents are Willing to Help Promote Knowledge and Information on Heritage Conservation

2. 2. 2. 3   Residents' potential in helping passing on heritage's cultural value

Objectively speaking, local residents are likely to either help or undermine passing on the cultural value. Currently native residents are actively passing on their traditional ethnic culture especially in heritage sites with value depending on the community, because their daily life are permeated with traditional customs, thus contributing to the conservation of the cultural atmosphere. However, increasingly stronger external influences are impacting on traditional culture. Considering the effort to boost local tourism and the inevitable globalization, local residents might be economically allured to give up their traditional lifestyle. If the cultural value of the heritage cannot help benefit the local people, they are more likely to endanger passing on of the cultural value.

However, local residents have strong desires to help passing on the cultural value. Such desires are positively correlated with residents' dependence on heritage and the length of time since inscription and can be cultivated by launching publicity campaigns on heritage value and conservation requirements.

In summary, residents in China's heritage sites are more likely to help pass on the cultural value.

2. 3   Economic Perspective

Due to the special social and historical backgrounds of world heritage sites and complicated relationships between stakeholders, their economic studies are concerned with the economic condition of heritage conservation, the demand of local communities for economic growth, and economic relationship between the two.

2. 3. 1   Sources and Use of Heritage Conservation Funds

2. 3. 1. 1   Sources and compositions of heritage conservation funds

By surveying the heritage authorities and referring to nomination dossiers of heritage sites, we have acquired sources and compositions of heritage conservation funds as shown in Table 2 – 18.

Heritage conservation requires a large amount of funding. China current has no special government funding for world heritage sites, and a definite channel and mechanism is to be established to ensure the sources of funding. In addition to some government subsidies, local governments and heritage authorities have to raise funds to fill the shortfall in the money required for heritage conservation and administration. Our survey reveals that there are severe fund shortages for some heritage sites. For majority of the heritage sites, developing tourism centering on heritage value is a major source of funds for their conservation and management.

表 2 – 18   **Sources and Ratios of Fundings in Deferent Types of Heritage Sites**

Categories	Name	Central government (%)	Local government (%)	Ticket income (%)	Donations (%)	Tax revenue (%)	Other sources (%)
Type I	Xidi Village	10	30	60	–	–	–
	Fujian Tulou	79. 37	15. 87	–	2. 38	–	2. 38
	Old Town of Lijiang	–	–	100 (Maintenance fee for the Old Town of Lijiang)	–	–	–
Type II	West Lake of Hangzhou		35. 63	22. 64	–	33. 27	8. 46
	Mount Wutai	–	–	78. 41	–	19. 93	1. 66
Type II	Mount Wudang	70	20	10	–	–	–
	Mount Qingcheng	19. 5	27. 1	53. 4	–	–	–
Type IV	Yungang Grottoes	58. 2	25. 5	–	–	–	16. 2
	Yin Xu	1. 6	73. 4	–	25	–	–
	Longmen Grottoes	40	30	–	–	–	30
	Dazu Rock Carvings	19. 3	32. 3	–	–	–	48. 4

2. 3. 1. 2   Use of heritage conservation funds

Tourism development at most world cultural heritage sites has generated a ticket income that can just cover the cost of the most fundamental conservation and management. But the practical procedures of conservation, restoration, research, management, and firefighting often suffer fund shortages, which are mainly due to the following causes:

(1) Local authorities are unduly dependent on the ticket income;

(2) Heritage authorities have a relatively high administrative cost;

(3) Too low a percentage of the ticket income is used for renovating the property itself;

(4) Conservation funds are used for other tasks (such as receptions) in heritage sites.

2. 3. 2   Effect of Change in Community Industries on Heritage Conservation

2. 3. 2. 1   Community industries' characteristics

Generally speaking, industries in communities located in heritage sites are characterized by the rapid and large – scale development of tourism and service industry and the recession of the primary and secondary industries.

Tourism, if seen from the perspective of heritage conservation, injects vigor into local economy but meanwhile presents difficulties and challenges to the conservation of the property itself. For example, it may induce the residents to engage in business at the cost of changing the property. And excessive tourists cause too much pressure on the eco – environment in heritage sites. These phenomena endanger the efforts to conserve the heritage's authenticity and integrity and undermine the heritage value.

However, most native residents in heritage sites approve of proper tourism development except those in Lijiang who expressed their obvious worries that local tourism might be overdeveloped. This indicates most residents have not realized the negative effects that local tourism and service industry might produce. In the minds of native residents, economic benefits outweight heritage conservation.

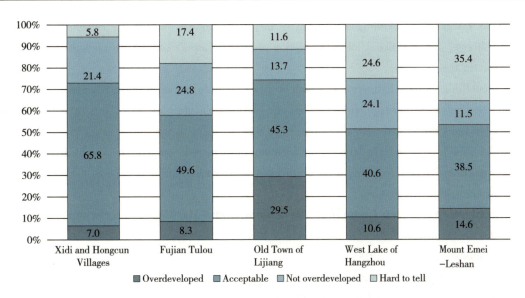

Table 2 – 19　Residents' View of Tourism Development in Heritage Sites

2.3.2.2　Trend of change in community professions

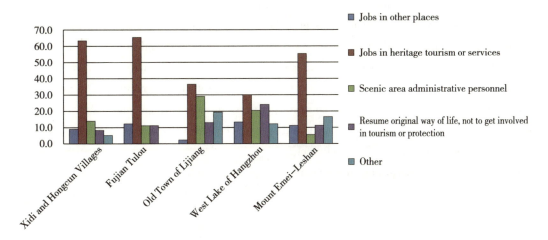

Table 2 – 20　Ideal Professions of Residents in Heritage Sites

It is predictable based on the survey on ideal professions of residents in the heritage sites that the tourism and service industry will gradually predominate. The agricultural population is to drop further and the source of income for local residents is more and more disengaged from the primary industry. And the development of the feature secondary industry such as traditional handicraft business will vary with the conservation policy in different heritage sites.

2.3.2.3　Effect of change in community professions on heritage conservation

The effect of change in community professions on heritage conservation can be summarized in the following two aspects:

(1) Some traditional industries with heritage value face the risk of not being passed on

Traditional community industries, because of the long time required to generate profit, the backward production means, and the low production efficiency, are not in line with the requirement of interest pursuit in the modern society. This has therefore seen the gradual shift to the tourism and service industry in the heritage communities. However, it should be realized that some traditional industries are also important parts of the cultural value in heritage sites, such as Longjing tea planting and frying in the West Lake of Hangzhou, Dongba papermaking in the ancient town of Lijiang, and traditional tobacco planting around Fujian *Tulou*. These ancient industries should be preserved to maintain their vitality.

(2) The monolithic tourism industry may result in unsustainable use of heritage resources

From the perspective of heritage conservation and sustainable development, the overdependence on the tourism has blunted the cultural diversity of heritage sites that prospers in the balanced multi – industrial development. Similar identities of heritage sites and almost identical tourism products have landed local tourism industry in a sub – healthy condition. In the long run, it is controversial whether tourism is to become the predominant industry in the economic pattern of heritage sites.

2.3.3 Relationship Between Community Development and Heritage Conservation

Heritage sites constrain yet contribute to community benefits.

2.3.3.1 Constraints on benefits

(1) Heritage conservation constrains community benefits

The establishment of the protected areas has limited local residents to some extent in their use of natural resources, narrowed the room for community development, and reduced ways to develop local economy, thus imposing certain constraints on economic and social development in communities in heritage sites. Such constraints fall into two categories: those on production activities in communities and on daily life of community residents.

Heritage conservation limits the content and size of local production activities. For instance, the conservation policy for mountainous heritage sites demands that native residents restore farmland to forests; and heritage authorities often put limits on the business activities in heritage sites with a rich atmosphere of tourism, etc.

Heritage conservation limits the population and construction in heritage communities. The total population and the density of buildings are strictly controlled by conservation plans in most heritage sites. Most buildings cannot be expanded or rebuilt and there is little room for new construction. The rising demand of local residents for new housing and improving outdated housing can be barely met.

(2) Heritage development constrains on community rights and benefits

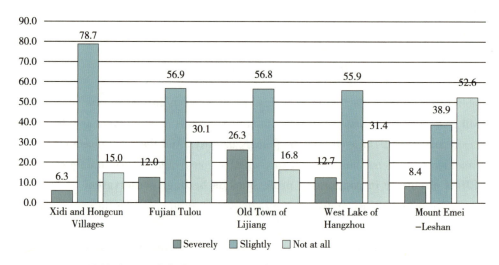

Table 2 – 21   Whether Tourism Development Affects Residential Life

The effect of tourism development in heritage sites on the normal life of communities is another constraint that heritage imposes on community rights and benefits. The study into the case of Lijiang, where residential life suffers the most disturbances, shows that price hikes, noises, and garbage are the most influential factors according to Lijiang residents interviewed. Such disturbances are the result of its specific business form and overexploited tourism.

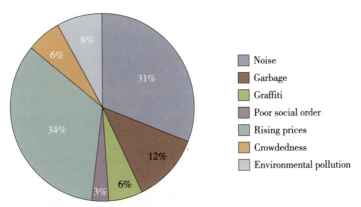

Figure 2 – 22　Tourism Development in Lijiang Affecting Residential life

Therefore, it is necessary to limit the extent of tourism development in communal heritage sites and choose the business form that suits local conditions. This move is expected to protect the privacy of residents' life and is favorable for reasonable development of local tourism economy. Thus, it will cause less disturbances to the life of native residents.

（3）Constraints of inequality among communities

Heritage resources benefit economic development in most of its communities, but native residents have unequal access to tourism development when the heritage site covers more than one community, while policies may also be different for these communities: those located near the main tourism route have more business opportunities and key protective areas face more constraints on tourism development. These have a direct effect on the benefit of native residents in different communities. Now that economic development varies with communities, residents in these communities tend to have different attitudes.

2.3.3.2　Contributions to community benefits

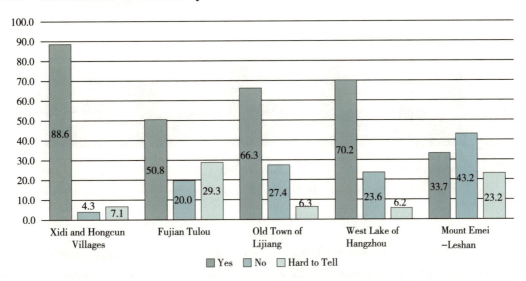

Figure 2 – 23　Opinions of Heritage Community Residents on Their Benefit from Tourism

Despite troubles and problems to their life, most interviewed have admitted that tourism development has done them good as it stimulates local economic growth. Of them, residents in Xidi and Hongcun benefit a lot from local tourism development as they get a proper share of ticket sales and demand higher rents for their houses whose value has increased. Tea growers in the West Lake of Hangzhou earn a considerably higher income as local tea houses, eateries and restaurants to which they sell their tea develop rapidly. Lijiang residents are renting out their houses at much higher rates as the ancient town becomes increasingly popular in recent years. Thus it can be concluded that interest conflicts can be reconciled, and proper measures need to be taken so that tourism development and local people's living can benefit each other.

Development and utilization of heritage resources can finance the conservation efforts and at the same time contribute to local economic development. The contributions are generally to increase the income of local residents and to distribute the tourism revenue.

(1) Development and utilization of heritage resources help increase the income of local residents.

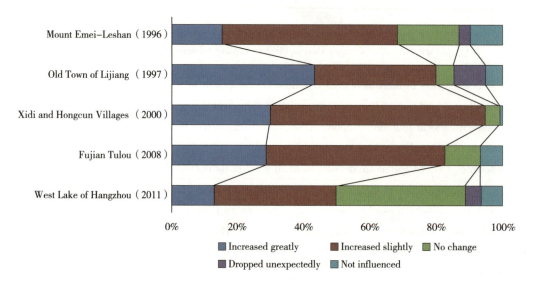

Table 2 – 24　Whether Local Residents have Lived Better Life since World Heritage Inscription

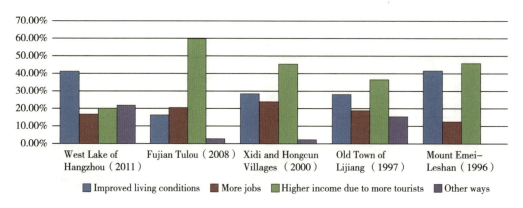

Table 2 – 25　Ways in Which Residents' Lives have Improved

Tourism development in heritage sites stimulates local economic growth. The comparision of changes in the five heritage sites inscribed in different time shows that local residents have enjoyed constantly improved lives as heritage resources were better conserved and utilized. More tourists coming to these sites as a result of tourism development are the main factor driving up their living standards. For residents in heritage sites with more developed tourism, their increased income is a typical example of benefits tourism development has brought.

(2) Development and utilization of heritage resources help distribute tourism revenue

Distributing ticket revenue is a major way to ensure that tourism development benefits local residents.

Table 2 – 26 Proportion of Ticket Revenue in Heritage Sites Going to Local Residents in 2011

Heritage sites	Average amount going to local residents (RMB/person/year)	Proportion to total ticket revenue (%)
Fujian *Tulou*	20 – 800	8
Xidi Village	3, 000	14. 60
Hongcun Village	2, 000	8
Old Town of Lijiang	150	1. 40

The proportion of ticket revenue going to local residents varies greatly among heritage sites. After considering the fact that residents around West Lake of Hangzhou do not have income from tickets as the lake is open to the public for free, the local government has adopted other measures to boost their income, such as encouraging those who grow tea to run tea houses. In the case of Mount Emei – Leshan, since the communities even nearest to the heritage site are outside of the core area, they are not entitled to a share of ticket revenue, but they have been encouraged to run local food – featured restaurants. Among heritage sites where native residents can have a share of ticket revenue, villagers in Xidi and Hongcun receive the biggest amount because tourism here is better promoted and the local government is more aware of the need to conserve their benefits. As a matter of fact, villagers in Xidi run their own agencies to organize tours to the village, so they have the instinct to conserve their own interests. Unfair distribution of benefits could easily cause conflicts between different groups, so the most effective way to ensure the safe and sustainable development of heritage sites is to guarantee the benefits of local residents.

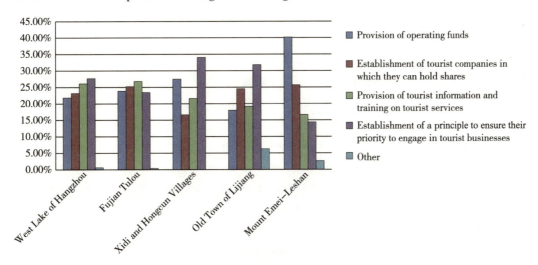

Table 2 – 27   Help that Local Residents Wish to Get from Administrative Authorities

It is found out in our investigation that, in addition to access to funding and the desire to hold shares in tourist companies, residents in heritage sites put more emphasis on a system to conserve their priority to engage in tourism businesses and their access to tourism information and service training. Heritage authorities therefore shall take measures to help them "learn" how to create wealth on their own by providing them with training as needed. In short, it is more important to teach them the skill to make money than to just allocate them money.

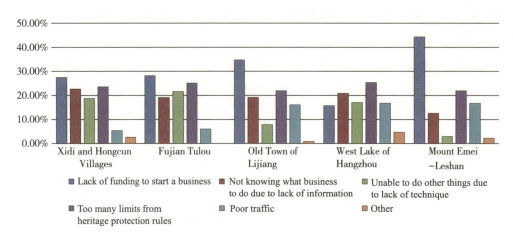

Table 2 – 28   Urgent Problems to be Solved to Increase Local Residents' Income

2. 4   Management Perspective

2. 4. 1   Effect of Management System and Legislation on Heritage Conservation

2. 4. 1. 1   The administrative management system

Nationally, the State Administration of Cultural Heritage is in charge of managing China's world cultural heritage sites and, together with the Ministry of Housing and Urban – Rural Development, manages mixed heritage sites, according to the State Council. The State Administration of Cultural Heritage established the World Heritage Division in 2002, and designated it to be responsible for submitting nomination dossiers for World Heritage inscription and conserving and managing China's heritage sites and to assist the Ministry of Housing and Urban – Rural Development in management of mixed heritage sites.

Locally, governments at all levels have designated special agencies for the day – to – day conservation, management and monitoring of world heritage sites in their jurisdiction. By now a conservation and management system is already in place not only at the national and provincial levels, but also in local governments of places where heritage sites are located. For example, in order to coordinate the efforts of Sichuan province as a whole to better conserve its world heritage sites, the provincial government established the Sichuan Provincial Commission for the Management of World Heritage Sites in 2010 with the Vice Governor acting as Director of the Commission. The commission formulates policy measures for heritage sites conservation and management in the province, and helps solve major issues in the preparation of nomination dossiers and heritage conservation and management. The commission's members include leading officials of the provincial departments of housing and urban – rural development, heritage management, and tourism, so they can make concerted efforts to conserve and manage the province's heritage sites.

At present, both the central government and local authorities (which could be municipalities directly under the central government, or cities, or even towns or villages) are working unremittingly to conserve and manage China's world heritage sites, and remarkable results have been achieved. However, the current management system, which came down from the planned economy and lacks concerted efforts because governments in different places take their own measures to deal with their own problems, shall be improved for the sustainable development of heritage sites.

2. 4. 1. 2   Legislative Work

Since the legislation on world heritage conservation and management was launched relatively late, China does not have a complete national laws and regulations system in this regard. China has made tremendous achievements in the conservation and management of its world heritage sites and cultural heritage in the past 20 years. It has also made noticeable progress in its legislative work in this area as local governments constantly enacted regulations or measures to conserve heritage sites in their jurisdiction, most of which, however, did not produce desirable legal effect because they were enacted by low legislative bodies.

Table 2 – 29 List of Regulations for the Conservation and Management of World Heritage Sites (Those under Investigations)

Heritage Site	Date of inscription	Type	Name	Promulgated by	Promulgation date
Mount Huangshan (mixed heritage site)	1990	Local regulation	Measures of Huangshan City for the Conservation and Management of Historical and Cultural Heritage Sites	Huangshan City People's Government, Anhui Province	Aug. 14, 2006
Old Town of Lijiang	1997	Local regulation	Regulations of Yunnan Province for the Conservation and Management of the Old Town of Lijiang	The Standing Committee of Yunnan Provincial People's Congress	Mar. 1, 2006
Ancient Villages in Southern Anhui-Xidi and Hongcun	2000	Local regulation	Regulations of Anhui Province for the Conservation and Management of Ancient Villages in Southern Anhui	The Standing Committee of Anhui Provincial People's Congress	Jan. 1, 1998, enacted; Jul. 1, 2004, amended
Fujian *Tulou*	2008	Local regulation	Regulations of Fujian Province for the Conservation of World Heritage Site Fujian *Tulou*	The Standing Committee of Fujian Provincial People's Congress	Dec. 1, 2011
West Lake of Hangzhou	2011	Local regulation	Regulations for the Conservation and Management of West Lake Cultural Landscape	The Standing Committee of Hangzhou Municipal People's Congress of Zhejiang Province	Jan. 1, 2012

China's only law on conservation of world cultural heritage up till now-the *Regulations for the Conservation and Management of World Cultural Heritage* promulgated by the Ministry of Culture in 2006-is not producing desirable legal effects because it was enacted by a ministry and fails to cover every aspect of heritage conservation. At the same time, existing regulations in this area fail to clearly define the role of management bodies, the organization of management authorities and the structure and qualification of their staff, land ownership over the heritage site, income from cultural heritage and its use, application for putting a site under conservation, funding for heritage conservation, economic constraint on heritage conservation, coordination between departments, the role of non – governmental conservation organizations, and the participation of the general public in heritage conservation. As a result, management authorities very often cannot fully perform their legal duties. For example, when a heritage authority needs funds for the conservation of heritage sites, it has to submit an application according to its need, then the State Administration of Cultural Heritage and local government (city or county) will consider the application and decide how much to allocate, because there are no detailed rules for the regular fund appropriation.

2.4.1.3 Personnel training

Since world heritage conservation and management has a short history in China and research concerned was initiated rather late, there is yet to be a complete and sound disciplinary system. This has directly influenced personnel training for heritage conservation and management authorities.

As China intensifies its efforts to conserve and manage heritage sites, more qualified personnel are urgently needed. Take the example of Fujian *Tulou*. Although Nanjing and Yongding counties have both established under their cultural heritage departments a special office to take care of the heritage, it is very difficult for such offices of only two or three staff employees to take good care of the hundreds or even thousands of houses scattered across the two counties. Furthermore, many of these personnel have never received any systematic training on heritage conservation and do not have the modern, advanced knowledge of heritage management, and what they rely on is their 'experience.' These problems also exist in Mount Emei, the Old Town of Lijiang and other heritage sites, to different extents.

Faced with the above problems, China has accelerated the work to train more personnel. The UNESCO World Heritage Research and Education Centre was founded in 2004 in Suzhou. Later in 2007 and 2008 the World Heritage Institute of Training and Research for the Asia and the Pacific Region (WHITRAP) was established in Tongji University and Peking University, indicating that a feasible system for training heritage management personnel is being put in place.

2.4.1.4 Monitoring and management system

The World Heritage Committee held its 28th session in 2004 in Suzhou, where the Chinese government faithfully promised to establish an effective monitoring and early warning system for world heritage. Suzhou was the first in China to conduct world heritage monitoring work-it established Suzhou World Heritage 'Classical Gardens' Conservation and Monitoring Centre in 2005 and put in place a dynamic information system and a monitoring and early warning system for world heritage in 2006. It is stipulated in the *Regulations for the Conservation and Management of World Cultural Heritage* promulgated by the Ministry of Culture in November 2006 that China implements an expert advisory system for major issues concerning world cultural heritage conservation and a monitoring and inspection system for the conservation of world cultural heritage. Suzhou's approach was formally introduced to the whole country, and Dunhuang, Lijiang, West Lake and other heritage sites all established their own monitoring centers.

2.4.2 Effect of Public Participation on Heritage Conservation and Management

2.4.2.1 Public participation in conservation and supervision of world cultural heritage

The Chinese government pointed out on 2010's Cultural Heritage Day: "We must redouble our efforts to publicize the importance of conserving cultural heritage and spread knowledge of how to do it so that all our citizens have the instinct to conserve heritage according to law and a large number of them will volunteer to do cultural heritage conservation work. By doing so, we will be able to create public opinion in favor of cultural heritage conservation and an environment in which everyone feels obligated to conserve cultural heritage and all people share in conservation fruits. " By issuing the *Guidelines on Giving Volunteers a Bigger Role to Play in Conservation of Cultural Heritage*, the State Administration of Cultural Heritage encouraged all men of insights to join in the efforts to conserve cultural heritage and exercise supervision. Investigations in heritage sites have indicated that more and more heritage management authorities are recruiting volunteers and pool their strength and wisdom in carrying out activities to conserve cultural heritage. As a matter of fact, Lijiang, Mount Wudang, West Lake of Hangzhou and some other heritage sites have already developed their own contingents of volunteers.

Poor public awareness about heritage conservation could lead to poor public supervision. Exercising good supervision is one of the most important and direct ways for the general public to help conserve and manage heritage sites, and the emphasis of heritage authorities on such supervision is the best response. So, an effective, transparent, and comprehensive system of public supervision should be established and the conservation, management and utilization of world heritage should be put under the supervision of the general public to have the voices of different groups heard and have different interests balanced. This will result in fewer disputes and problems, and at the same time higher enthusiasm of the general people to exercise supervision.

2.4.2.2 Community participation in world cultural heritage management

By participating in heritage management, communities can voice their needs, and at the same time better understand the mission of heritage management and the approaches management authorities have adopted to accomplish that mission. In addition, their participation is conducive to the solution of conflicts such as the one between the conservation and utilization of communities, and helps balance conservation, management, utilization and development.

Investigations indicate that Hongcun and Xidi villages, based on their own conditions, have developed a scientific mechanism for heritage conservation and management, in which the government takes the lead, relevant departments work in concerted efforts, villagers volunteer to help and associations participate in actively. After their inscription to the World Heritage List, the two villages strengthened their self – administration system under the guidance of the local government. Both have established tourism management committees and heritage conservation and management supervisory teams to tighten day – to – day management and monitoring and site management of the heritage site and tourism development. They have also established villagers' conservation associations, drafted regulatory rules, designed and distributed heritage conservation brochures to villagers, carried out activities in primary and middle schools to teach students of the importance of heritage conservation, and motivated all villagers to feel committed and proud to conserve cultural heritage. At the proposal of the Association of the Elderly, all Xidi villagers signed up or vowed to conserve this heritage. Thanks to the villagers' active participation, not a single house in the two villages has been damaged in the past 10 years since the inscription, which shows how good the result could be with villagers' participation in self – management.

2.5 Summary of Current Problems

In conclusion, the conflicts between the social and economic development of communities in heritage sites and culture conservation, heritage site management and the conservation and sustainable development of heritage can be summarized as follows.

(1) As these communities transform from communities where residents are connected by kinship to modern ones in which they are connected more by interests, they sometimes fail to work together in heritage conservation;

(2) As more native residents move out and more migrants move in, the population structure in these communities is changing, and this changing population will have to shoulder the responsibility of heritage conservation and develop their awareness about carrying on the cultural value of the heritage;

(3) A conflict between the ever – growing needs of community residents for a modern life and the need to keep the community unchanged in order to ensure the intactness of heritage is emerging;

(4) Modern tourism and globalization are posing a threat to the efforts to carry forward the cultural value of heritage;

(5) There is a worrying lack of funding to effectively conserve heritage;

(6) The overdevelopment of tourism and services in these communities is putting some traditional businesses of great heritage value in the danger of extinction, and tourism in heritage sites is not developing very healthily;

(7) Heritage conservation is placing some restrictions on community residents' work and life;

(8) The utilization of heritage resources is under harsh dispute due to unfair distribution of tourism revenue and unbalanced development;

(9) The government has yet to play a full role in heritage conservation and community development due to outdated management mechanism, poor legislation, lack of qualified personnel, and immature monitoring and management system; and

(10) The general public's limited participation is leading to poor public supervision, and there are no clear definitions of conservation responsibilities and powers.

3   Summary of Experience and Lessons: Case Studies

3.1   Experience of the West Lake: Heritage Conservation in the Interest of Local Residents

After the inscription of the West Lake of Hangzhou, Tong Mingkang, Deputy Director of the State Administration of Cultural Heritage, pointed out that all heritage sites should learn from the West Lake, because conservation featured the whole process of its nomination. In order to solve problems that impacted West Lake's environment and hindered its sustainable development such as irrational utilization of landscape, unbalanced distribution of tourism resources and poor infrastructure, Hangzhou government has adopted measures since 2002 to effectively improve West Lake's environment, highlight its historical and cultural importance, and manage the landscape in the best interests of community residents, thus realizing the goal of beautiful landscape and rich residents.

Fig 3 – 1   West Lake Cultural Landscape of Hangzhou

(1) Interested parties take part in decision – making to ensure community residents receive real benefits

A large proportion of inhabitants in West Lake communities are native residents who carry on West Lake

Longjing Tea culture, so allowing them to voice their opinions in decision – making is conducive to heightening public awareness to conserve the West Lake and improve its environment. Natives within the heritage site have been allowed to participate in every aspect of the efforts to improve the West Lake's environment, provide helpful reference for government decision – making, and play an active role in reconciling the relationship between those who do the job to improve the lake's environment and those whose interests might be influenced.

Since October 2002, all the parklands surrounding the West Lake and Hangzhou's museums and memorial halls have been opened to the public free of charge. This measure has enabled Hangzhou citizens, especially those living around the West Lake, to enjoy the sceneries for free. A West Lake free of charge is conducive to generating the largest possible economic returns and ecological and social benefits.

(2) Environmental improvement and economic development in tea – growing villages benefit residents

The Longjing Tea is an important component of the West Lake Cultural Landscape. Natives in tea – growing villages have been growing, picking, drying and selling the tea since the Song Dynasty (960 – 1279AD), which is a cultural tradition of heritage value. In order to conserve the sights around theses villages and at the same time develop tea – growing business, Hangzhou government has made large investment since 2003 to build infrastructure for these villages and also encouraged villagers to renovate their own houses by rewarding those who took the lead in doing so. This policy is hailed by all villagers in tea – growing villages within the heritage site. As a result, the environment and landscape of these villages have improved greatly, and so have the lives of West Lake natives.

After environmental improvement, these villages, located within the West Lake Cultural Landscape, have been encouraged and guided by the government to develop their own recreational businesses, such as tea houses featuring Longjing tea, rural food – featured restaurants, and hostels, by making full use of their geographic advantages. These approaches have helped the whole heritage site to accommodate more tourists and tea growers to find a new way for sustainable development. The statistics show that tea growers in the heritage site had a sales revenue of 64.2 million RMB in 2010, 100.3% over in 2002. Tea houses also developed rapidly. There were literally very few tea houses in 2002, but over 600 households were engaged in tea and other related tourist services in 2010, with the annual revenue combined totaling 59 million RMB. The average income of tea growers in 2010 reached 12, 600 RMB, 46.9% over in 2002. The government – led project to comprehensively improve the environment of West Lake and the policy to guide development of tourism and tourism – related services have brought real benefits for natives.

(3) The model of community – owned business ensures social stability

Hangzhou is among the first cities in China to carry out the system of acquisition of collective land, by which village economic organizations use acquired land to increase fixed assets and develop secondary and tertiary industries, while villagers receive long – term, stable returns in the form of bonus. This bonus has always been the second insurance for farmers in Hangzhou, in addition to returns from their old – age insurance.

Jinshagang and Lingyin villages in the heritage site relocated their villagers to multi – story buildings in 1999 and 2002 respectively. Jinshagang Village built the Hongqiao Resort, Baihehua Hotel and Jinshagang Parking Lot on the acquired land and contracted companies to operate them. These village – owned businesses brought the village a yearly income of 12 million RMB, which is 20 – 50 thousand RMB per person.

(4) A system distributing benefits to villagers is good for social harmony

Villages around the West Lake established their own stock cooperatives after they started to relocate their villagers into buildings in 1999. These cooperatives not only operate and manage the villages' assets, but more importantly guarantee the interests of villagers.

Take the example of Maojiabu Village. After a comprehensive environmental improvement campaign in 2003, the former residence of Du Jinsheng and some other sights to the west of the West Lake became very popular, so the village used many houses in good conditions to open tea houses. In 2011, the village's collective income totaled about 15 million RMB, and the net income after deducting business expenses such as those for organizing activities, keeping the village clean and ensuring safety totaled 9 million RMB, which were distributed to 420 stockholding villagers, with each of them receiving over 20, 000 RMB.

Unlike villagers' stock cooperatives in other parts of the country that aim for development, those in the West Lake heritage site always put villagers' interests first. The West Lake is a world cultural heritage site and a national scenic area. There are therefore severe restrictions on development of projects and natural resources are under strict conservation. It was under this context of not causing any damage to the natural environment that these cooperatives were established, and they were established to improve villagers' living conditions. This mechanism makes villagers happier, and more importantly improves their consciousness of conserving the West Lake heritage site.

(5) The impact of the "West Lake Approach" in the sense of society and culture

From the perspective of social effects, the fact that all places of interest around the West Lake are open to the public free of charge has won the lake, and even Hangzhou city, a well – deserved reputation. This is universally recognized and appraised by both Hangzhou citizens and tourists. At the same time, Hangzhou government has won wide support from its citizens because it allocated fund to improve the living conditions of natives and create jobs in a manner of justice and fairness. From the perspective of cultural effects, it can be said that enormous efforts have been made to explore, carry on and conserve the West Lake's history and culture. Natural and cultural resources are integrated to reach harmony between man and nature. As a result, the complete, vast and rich West Lake culture is conserved and carried on.

3. 2. Experience of Xidi and Hongcun: A Top – to – Bottom Conservation Strategy Stimulates the Participation of Communities from Bottom to Top

Xidi and Hongcun villages have adopted a top – to – bottom conservation strategy to help villagers understand the importance of conserving their old houses. Now to conserve this world cultural heritage has become their common aspiration. Xidi villagers are especially willing to do so because they have a deep respect for and recognition of the native culture.

(1) The conservation campaign creates more tourism resources and therefore provides a cushion against overdevelopment

In 2009, Huangshan City launched the conservation campaign to establish a system for conserving old houses in southern Anhui Province. This move is designed to prevent tourists from overwhelming Xidi and Hongcun villages and tourism development from harming the heritage site.

(2) A benefit distribution system oriented to heritage conservation stimulates the participation of communities

Xidi Village has its own tourism companies. Of the ticket revenue, 20% is reserved for public services and 80% is divided among villagers. This mechanism is designed for heritage conservation and two factors are taken into consideration in bonus distribution: the household's population and the building area of its house. The money distributed based on the building area of houses is the subsidy for old building conservation. It is a reward to villagers for their houses' contribution to the village, and can be used for house maintenance and repair.

(3) Take measures to reduce the pressure exerted by tourism development and reconcile the conflict between heritage conservation and community development

Hongcun Village implements the mode of strengthening internal management and alleviating external pressure, which has ensured the effective conservation of the heritage.

Striving to balance heritage conservation, tourism development and improvement in villagers' living standards, it prohibits any attempt to demolish or transform existing houses or build new ones by legal measures and at the same time relieve the pressure exerted by tourism development by relocating stalls inside the protected zone to the market outside the heritage site.

Fig. 3 – 2　Tourist Artware Market in Hongcun

3.3　Experience of Lijiang: A New recognition of Heritage Tourism and Traditional Culture Conservation

The Old Town of Lijiang once suffered overdevelopment in a nationwide wave of tourism development and some traditional ethnic cultures were once endangered with extinction. In recent years, however, the Bureau of Conservation of the Old Town of Lijiang and the local government reviewed their understanding and strived to balance tourism development and traditional culture conservation. Their efforts have resulted in great progress in the conservation of this heritage site.

(1) *The Plan of Protecting Traditional Business Cultures* to support traditional businesses with ethnic features

Lijiang has issued a plan of conserving and managing traditional business cultures in the World Cultural Heritage 'Old Town of Lijiang' to standardize business development within the protected zone. In order to stress ethnic features over modern business, a system for licensing businesses has been carried out to phase out those that do not accord with the old town's style, regulate shops' appearance, and limit the number of shops. And shops, handicraft workshops and food stores with ethnic features are conserved by licenses.

(2) Explore traditional cultures and conserve the integrity of the heritage environment

Lijiang started to explore and conserve its intangible cultural heritage within the heritage site in 2008. Since then, it has allocated 10 million RMB from the old town maintenance funds every year to explore, sort out, and exhibit its ethnic cultures. Inaddition, it has intensified efforts to conserve and carry on Dongba culture and Naxi ancient music, built Wuyi Street into a street of Naxi culture, organized activities to collect couplets depicting the old town, and given strong support to activities of Lijiang Society of Naxi Culture.

(3) Take various measures for the convenience and benefit of natives to prevent them from moving out

Many residents moved away due to overdevelopment years ago. Since then, the heritage authorities has taken measures to retain local residents, such as raising the living subsidy for registered residents to 15 RMB per person per month, building educational and recreational facilities, and supporting families having difficulties renovating their houses.

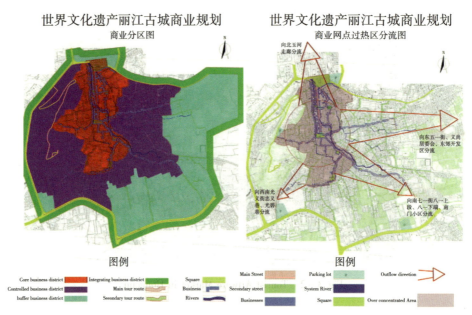

Fig. 3 – 4 Distribution of Businesses, Specific Plan for Conservation and Management of Traditional Business Cultures in the Old Town of Lijiang

Fig. 3 – 5 Outflow of Businesses from Too Concentrated Areas, Specific Plan for Conservation and Management of Traditional Business Cultures in the Old Town of Lijiang

3.4 Macao: Educating the Young About Heritage Conservation

The Macao Special Administrative Region has attached great importance to publicizing heritage conservation in government departments, social organizations and schools since it started the world heritage nomination process.

In 2001, Macao's Cultural Affairs Bureau launched a campaign to train cultural heritage ambassadors, in which young people were recruited and trained to publicize Macao's cultural heritage. In 2006, Macao Civil Affairs Bureau and Macao Association for Historical Education launched a joint program to train museum student researchers.

In 2007, the Macao Foundation, together with the Institute for Tourism Studies of Macao, Macao Association for Historical Education and all primary and middle schools in Macao, launched the campaign "Our Home, World's Heritage-Macao's Historical City Centre" to publicize Macao's historical and cultural heritage among nearly 100, 000 students. After Macao's inscription on the World Heritage List in July 2005, the Institute for Tourism Studies of Macao started to offer a four – year undergraduate program on cultural heritage management in September the same year, becoming the first to do so in Macao.

4　Realizing and Ensuring Sustainable Development: How to Do It

The way to effective heritage conservation and sustainable community development is what this study strives to find out. To realize it, it is necessary to consider the current conservation in China and the country's actual conditions on the basis of early investigations, draft principles for future work with systematic approaches, and put in place a top – to – bottom mechanism to ensure effective management.

4.1　Principles for Heritage Conservation and Sustainable Community Development

4.1.1　Put People First

Every world cultural heritage, in essence, was created by people with their knowledge and emotions. No matter the heritage is about buildings in old villages, or the historical and cultural context of natives, or natural landscape with religious interest or the thought of well – known historical figures, "people" have always been at its core. So only when people are put first in the conservation of world cultural heritage sites discussed herein, the real purpose of heritage conservation is fulfilled. In short, to put people first is an important basis for realizing harmony between heritage and people.

4.1.2　Prioritize Conservation

The basic concept of this principle is that heritage conservation shall always be given top priority. When there is a conflict between the need to conserve heritage and a need to fulfill other interests, the former must be satisfied. When dealing with the relationship between heritage's conservation and proper utilization, to conserve the authenticity and integrity of heritage must always come first, and its proper utilization can only be made on this basis.

There are two other aspects for this principle: first, the rights of natives to live a quality life must be safeguarded; second, how to balance heritage conservation and economic benefits.

4.1.3　Harmonious coexistence

Emerging as early as in ancient time, harmony has always been the very essence of Chinese traditional culture. In harmony, different things complement, help and benefit each other and stimulate each other's development.

To achieve harmony in heritage conservation, it is necessary to make improving the people's wellbeing the starting point of our conservation work, strive to create an environment in which everyone feels obliged to conserve heritage and shares in the fruits of conservation, cultivate public opinion conducive to heritage conservation, and guide more non – governmental investment into this conservation work.

4.2　A General Approach to Heritage Conservation and Sustainable Community Development

4.2.1　The Goal of Harmonious Relationship Between Heritage Sites and Communities

To ensure the harmony between heritage sites and communities, it is necessary to consider the coordinated development of economy, society and the environment and stress the common development of heritage and its communities. In short, in order to achieve this goal, the biodiversity and cultural diversity in the heritage site must be maintained on the basis of following the natural law before the economic and social development of communities are promoted.

4. 2. 2   The Framework for Harmonious Coexistence of Heritage Sites and Communities

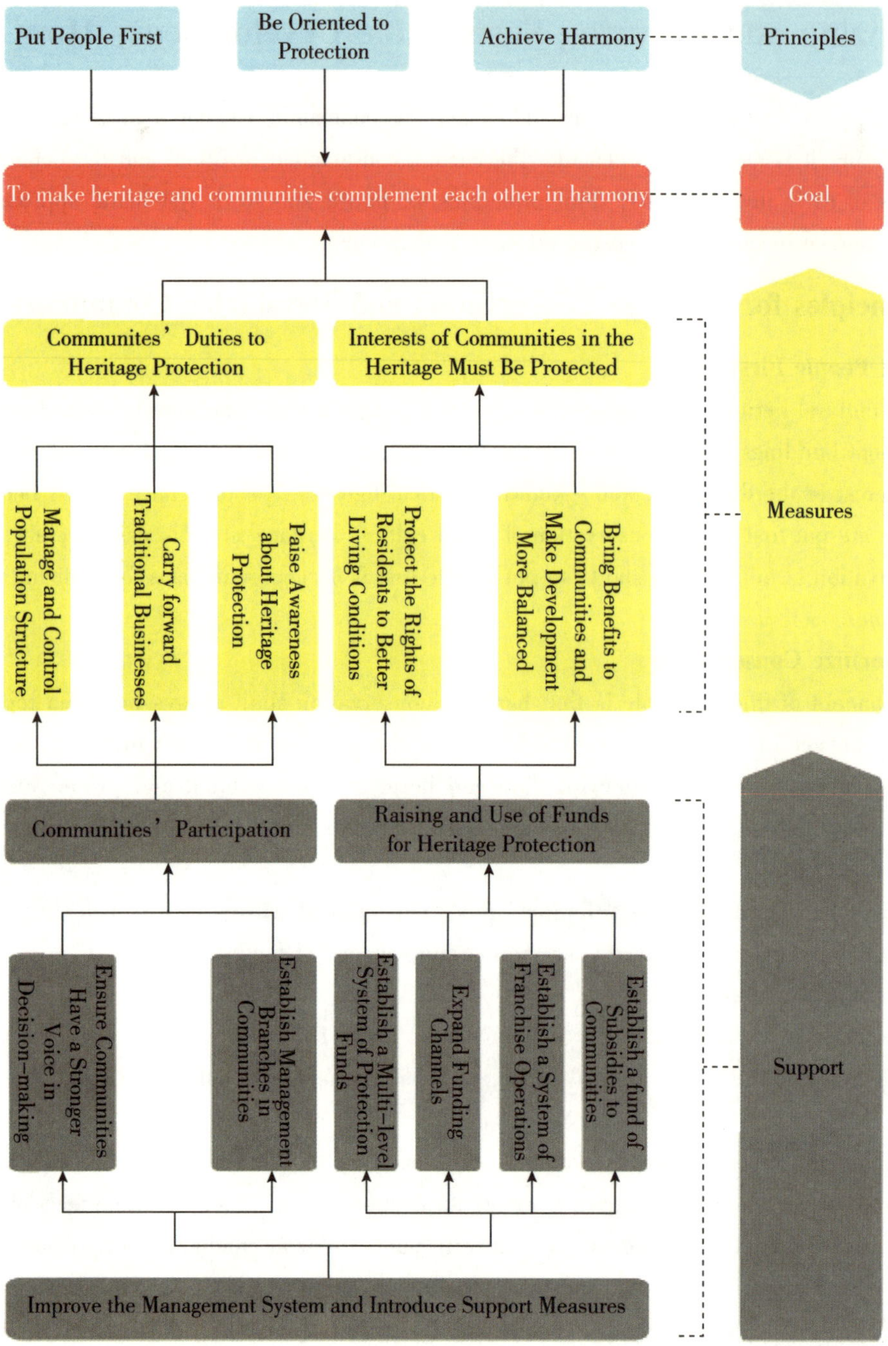

Figure 4 – 1   Framework for Harmonious Coexistence of Heritage Sites and Communities

4. 3   Measures for Harmonious Coexistence of Heritage Sites and Communities

To achieve the goal that heritage and communities complement each other in harmony so that the heritage can be conserved and carried forward and communities can be developed in a sustainable manner, a lot of special, comprehensive and social measures need to be taken. When designing these measures, we need to fully consider heritage – related environmental, economic, social and cultural goals; follow the principles of putting people first, giving top priority to conservation and achieving harmony; set coordinated objectives; and make unified plan and utilization and perform unified management.

4.3.1 Communities' Duties to Heritage Conservation

At the present stage of development in China, people are becoming less connected by blood, moving more frequently, and developing more complicated work relations. This is particularly true in communities around heritage sites as more natives move out and migrants come in, and there is a danger that local cultures could die out. A study from the social, economic and cultural perspectives indicate that reasons for this include the dramatic change in population structure in heritage site, the dying out of traditional businesses and ways of living, and the poor awareness about heritage conservation. As a result, communities need to fulfill the following requirements to ensure the sustainable development of heritage.

4.3.1.1 To manage and control population structure

For a heritage site that features a local ethnic living style in traditional houses, the heritage has to be inherited and carried on by natives. Once the number of natives drop significantly, this very charming living style could die out. So, in the conservation and management of heritage, we must:

First, keep the proportion of natives within a rational range. The proportion of natives to migrants must be under effective control. So, studies shall be carried out to set a proper proportion according to the realities of the heritage site (investigations herein indicate that it's good when natives make 80% or more of the total population), and feasible measures (such as economic measures) must be taken to keep this proportion. In addition, local government needs to help communities of natives maintain their traditional cultures against cultural impact from migrants. Local government also needs to help maintain traditional, harmonious social relations and stress blood relations between people which have a direct bearing on the cultural value of the heritage (especially when the heritage is a village).

Second, restrict proportion of migrants. To control the number of migrants (especially those coming to do business) is a necessary measure to prevent local culture and customs from being impacted or influenced by other cultures.

Third, control number of tourists. The allowed maximum number of tourists shall be determined according to the carrying capacity of the heritage site, and this number must be strictly followed in order to protect the heritage's ecological environment.

4.3.1.2 To carry forward traditional businesses

Judging from the facts we have found out in the above investigations that tourism is becoming dominant and the primary and secondary industries are declining in heritage sites, and that residents in surrounding communities put economic benefits over heritage conservation, there is a severe challenge for the traditional businesses to survive. Comparatively, tourism stresses economic benefits, while communities' traditional businesses fall short of this modern requirement for benefits because they take longer time to produce profits due to their outdated production methods and low efficiency. In the long run, however, a sole development of tourism to make it dominate the economy of a heritage site is not favorable for the sustainable development of the cultural heritage, and traditional ways of living and the sustainable development of traditional businesses must be supported and promoted.

To deal with the general declination of traditional businesses in heritage sites, we need to respect and maintain the customs and living styles of natives and support them in carrying on their traditional crafts. In doing that, the following steps need to be taken:

First, to take the local traditional cultures and crafts as intangible cultural heritage to carry on and revitalize them, and encourage young natives to carry forward these traditional cultures and crafts;

Second, to give proper subsidies or preferential policies such as tax exemption or reduction to employees in the traditional culture sector; and

Third, to provide and constantly increase financial support for traditional agriculture and crafts, foster the value of heritage conservation, and get community residents to believe that they can have real benefits by living in traditional ways and carrying on traditional businesses.

4. 3. 1. 3   To raise awareness about heritage conservation

At present, there is a favorable basis and great potential for residents in communities around heritage sites in China to participate in the efforts to carry on the cultural heritage because they have a comparatively strong willingness to play a role in this work, and this willingness is directly related to their dependency on the heritage and the heritage's date of inscription. However, there is threat as well as potential, with regard to raising public awareness about heritage conservation. There is potential because natives are at present comparatively willing to carry on the heritage – related traditional ethnic cultures, and the threat comes from the ever – growing impact from the outside world on local traditional culture.

The following measures can be taken to effectively raise residents' awareness about heritage conservation: get them to participate in heritage conservation; educate them in it; and maintain the interdependence between them and the heritage.

(1) Involve the public in heritage conservation and management

Natives in the heritage site shall be encouraged to carry on their traditional culture, and at the same time incomers (those who come to do business or travel) shall also be encouraged to play a role in protecting and spreading the traditional culture.

Possible steps include:

■ Let the public play a role in planning on how to conserve and manage the heritage so that they can have a better understanding of it;

■ Keep the public informed of how the heritage is being conserved and utilized in order to win their understanding and support;

■ Encourage the public to participate in activities about the traditional culture of the heritage to show them this culture's vitality so that they will respond by publicizing and spreading it.

(2) Effectively educate communities in heritage conservation

First, promote concepts and knowledge of world heritage conservation. Education in heritage conservation is the key to getting everyone feel obliged to conserve world heritage. In the case of a heritage site that features the living style of natives or the interdependence between natives and the heritage, education and publicity must be given special attention, and community residents must be involved in activities publicizing the heritage's traditional culture so that they will recognize and be proud of this culture and voluntarily do what they can to publicize it.

Second, train tourism employees and residents in the heritage's culture. A proper development of tourism in the heritage site shall first and foremost bring benefits to its natives. For the sake of this tourism development, tourism employees must receive training in the heritage's traditional culture so that they can also publicize it. Training shall also be provided to natives to help them understand their traditional culture more comprehensively and be capable of some service or professional skills so that they can receive real benefits from tourism by engaging in it.

Third, intensify efforts to present and publicize the heritage. We need to conduct constant studies to find out the rules of world heritage conservation and management, publicize the heritage more effectively by learning from advanced domestic and foreign practices, and explore new publicity ways that are more interesting and get more people involved, so that people from all walks of life can appreciate and know more about it and become more voluntary to conserve it.

(3) Maintain the interdependence between the heritage and communities around it

Investigations indicate that the more community residents are dependent on the heritage, the more they feel obliged and the more they are willing to conserve it. Therefore, we must spare no effort to publicize the heritage's value in cultural, economic and social terms, and at the same time properly develop tourism and improve infrastructure to meet the living and financial needs of natives on the basis of not causing any problem to heritage conservation. In addition, government investment needs to be made or non – governmental investment can be solicited to pay natives for the sacrifices they have made to conserve the heritage, and the interdependence between the heritage and communities around it needs to be heightened.

4. 3. 2   The Interests of Communities Around the Heritage must be Protected

All the world cultural heritage sites investigated in this paper were created by people with their knowledge and emotions. In order to make the relationship between the heritage and people a sustainable one following the principles of putting people first, giving top priority to conservation and achieving harmony, communities' basic rights and interests must be safeguarded, although they also need to perform the above conservation duties.

4. 3. 2. 1   To protect the rights of residents to better living conditions

A sustainable development of heritage shall be able to improve the living conditions of residents in communities around it.

Except Fujian *Tulou* whose outer walls were built with rammed earth, the traditional houses in most of the heritage sites investigated were built with bricks and woods, which after tens or hundreds of years of wind and rain are already in poor conditions with safety hazards. Furthermore, these houses do not have the sanitation facilities necessary for a modern life, so many residents, and especially young ones, have moved out from old villages or towns, causing the number of natives to decline. Therefore:

First, in order to meet the needs of residents in daily life, they shall be allowed to properly decorate the inside of their houses to live a modern life if their houses do not constitute the main feature of the heritage and the decoration will not influence the heritage's features.

Second, buildings that constitute the main feature of the heritage must be conserved without allowing any attempt to decorate the inside of these buildings or change their structure, and any repair to their appearance must be made with approval and under guidance.

Third, residents shall be given a reward to maintain their houses in good conditions, and special bonus and award can be given to residents who keep their traditional houses in excellent shape or outstandingly carry on traditional crafts so that all residents become more aware of the need to conserve heritage and the heritage can be genuinely conserved and carried on.

Fourth, there shall be national or local legislation to regulate that a certain proportion of tourism revenue needs to be allocated to build infrastructure in the heritage site and help residents solve problems in medical treatment, finding jobs and receiving training, and their children's education, so that they can become more willing to conserve the heritage as they receive real benefits from its conservation and sustainable development. If this is done, the heritage's conservation and utilization can complement each other.

4. 3. 2. 2   Bring benefits to communities and ensure more balanced development

Heritage conservation will inevitably place many restrictions on communities' production activities, total populations and projects allowed. Heritage tourism has a heavy influence on the daily life of communities, and at the same time could cause residents to have serious complaints as they are offered different development opportunities and receive differentiated economic benefits. Bearing this in mind, local government needs to give proper compensation as needed and put in place a mechanism allowing all residents to share in tourism revenue fairly, so that they benefit from heritage conservation.

(1) Establish a proper mechanism for compensating residents

Residents have swallowed many hidden costs, such as the effects on resources and environment and changes to their social relations, as their houses are developed to be a part of the heritage. So they shall be compensated properly, because after all they are often interrupted in their day – to – day life. Or, they can be allowed to engage in tourism business, so that their income can keep increasing.

Tourist companies need to standardize business conducts to reduce the pollution they cause to the environment and the adverse effects they have on the life of local residents (such as by putting in place equipment for the recycling and treatment of sewage and other pollutants). They shall also offer their equipment and facilities to the use for residents at a discounted charge, and increase efficiency to improve the environment.

A nationwide mechanism for compensating residents shall be put in place by establishing heritage conservation funds. If residents suffer any damage, for example their land is trampled by wild animals or their livestock is eaten by wild animals, they can report the damage to a designated body for assessment and get compensated through proper channels.

(2) Establish a proper mechanism for dividing tourism benefits

Different heritage sites shall establish their own mechanisms for dividing tourism revenue according to the local realities to give a proper proportion to communities so that residents can link economic benefits they receive with the efforts they make and thereby become more determined to conserve heritage.

The following interests of residents shall be protected:

First, when they participate in heritage tourism conservation and development, they earn wages and bonuses, share in profits and receive welfare treatments such as old – age and medical insurance. If a stock company is established in a community for all its residents to manage, they shall all be stockholders.

Second, when communities operate heritage tourism and provide services, natives shall be the first to open styled hotels and food stores, local product shops and artifact stores, and the first to be given properly – paid jobs, such as to work in any offices, performances, publicity activities, or artifact workshops.

Third, a portion of tourism revenue shall be used to build infrastructure as well as culture – related and education facilities for communities. In addition, local government shall take measures, such as providing small loans, direct subsidies, training and other public services, building infrastructure and supporting development of non – governmental tourism organizations, to ensure the sustainable development of heritage tourism, and make sure that tourism benefits are used in the interest of local people.

Fourth, communities can get income by designing and making souvenirs and selling them to tourists. In making these souvenirs, local materials shall be used and natives shall be employed.

(3) Establish an effective mechanism for expressing concern for benefits

All parties involved in the conservation and sustainable development of heritage have their demand for benefits, so there must be a mechanism for them to expressing it. Compared to management authorities and tourist companies, residents have a weaker voice, so they must have a mechanism by which they voice as one. Therefore, in dividing benefits from utilization of heritage resources, residents shall be allowed to have their voice heard through their representatives (at present communities know very little about the division of tourism benefits, which is unfavorable for the enthusiasm of residents to conserve heritage).

4.4 How to Ensure the Harmonious Coexistence of Heritage Sites and Communities

4.4.1 Communities' Participation

Generally speaking, there is a favorable basis and great potential for residents in communities around heritage sites in China to participate in the efforts to carry on the cultural heritage because they have a comparatively strong willingness to play a role in this work, but conditions in different heritage sites are very different (there is a higher percent of participation in areas with more developed economy) -in fact, the conditions in some places are pretty bad.

4.4.1.1 Ensure communities have a stronger voice in decision – making

Heritage communities are the true master of the heritage site, so they shall be informed of all regulations and plans for its conservation and management, and be allowed to voice their opinions in discussions and play a role in making decision. For example:

First, the interests and demand of native residents shall be considered and their voices shall be heard when a conservation and management plan is being formulated, so that the plan can be rational and proper in the eyes of natives and their proper demand can be fulfilled.

Second, a mechanism shall be put in place to receive advice, suggestions and feedback from communities when a plan is being formulated, so as to ensure the plan is well – defined and smoothly implemented with active participation of communities.

Third, community residents shall be allowed to voice their opinions and vote on the making of major decisions concerning heritage management.

4.4.1.2 Establish management branches in communities

First, a heritage site shall improve its services to communities by establishing management branches (which could be a community management office) there, whose duties are to help communities develop economy and solve problems in development.

Second, in order to better manage tourism development, a joint conference system can be established for community residents and tourism authorities to regularly discuss problems in tourism development, standardize tourism services, prevent negative trends, and explore appropriate path for development.

Third, in order to conserve and develop traditional businesses, a trade association involving all local businesses can be established so that they can communicate and exchange ideas on how to conserve the interests of people in traditional businesses.

4.4.2 Fund Raising and Fund Use for Heritage Conservation

At present, there is a worrying shortfall of funds to conserve cultural heritage in China, and most of the currently available money comes from government allocations and ticket revenue. As the money needed to carry on traditional businesses and give more benefits to communities grows bigger, the situation could get worse. So, more funds need to be raised, and solution to this problem can include establishment of more funds, more government investment, and introduction of heritage tourism lottery. In addition, measures can be taken to reduce management costs, such as getting more communities to exercise self – management, increasing their participation in heritage management, and streamlining management setups and personnel.

4.4.2.1 Establish a multi – level system of conservation funds

First, establish a national world heritage fund to conserve China's world heritage sites, and the funds may come from government investment, business income in heritage sites, and donations from organizations and individuals. This organization can seek funds from various channels to cover the shortfall of funds for heritage conservation.

Second, encourage companies and organizations to invest in heritage conservation and maintenance by giving them tax exemption or reduction.

Third, submit all ticket revenues in heritage sites to the government for unified management so that they can be all used to conserve and manage heritage, support traditional businesses, encourage participation of communities, and give benefits to community residents.

Fourth, allocate a proper proportion of business revenues generated by franchised shops, hotels and restaurants within heritage sites to conserve heritage and benefit community residents.

4.4.2.2 Expand sources for heritage conservation funds

Fund sources should be expanded, social organizations be mobilized and, based on experience of foreign countries, advanced fund channels should be expanded.

First, win financial support from the UNESCO World Heritage Committee and other international groups and organizations dedicated to ethnic and cultural affairs;

Second, win financial support from ministries or commissions under the State Council;

Third, solicit financial support and donations from charities, cultural organizations and other social groups;

Fourth, strive to win financial support and donations from social organizations and individuals, such as volunteers, cultural enterprises and other enterprises that are willing to provide some funds in the form of cooperation.

4.4.2.3 Establish a system of franchise operations

In order to better conserve the invaluable heritage resources, a system of franchise operations shall be established to regulate businesses and operations within the heritage conservation zone, with revenue from this used to conserve the heritage and give benefits to communities.

4.4.2.4 Establish a fund to subsidize communities

A fund to subsidize communities shall be established under every conservation fund. This will make communities more willing to protect heritage environment and ensure a stable and harmonious social atmosphere.

4.4.3 Improve the Management System and Safeguarding Mechanism

4.4.3.1 Improve the management system

A management system that has responsibilities and power well defined and separates supervision from management is conducive to sound development of heritage resources. The current system, in which local governments of heritage sites take the lead in management, has quite a few strengths because it has utilized both market forces and government management, and therefore is worth improving。

(1) Strengthen national unified management of world cultural heritage sites

A system of joint conferences for cultural heritage conservation affairs, under which ministries or commissions of culture, construction, finance, land resources, forestry, religious affairs and tourism, each with well – defined duties, work in concerted efforts to solve major issues in the conservation and management of the country's world cultural heritage sites, can be established to pool nationwide strengths to conserve our heritage.

(2) Gradually give local governments more decision – making power

It accords with China's realities and the requirements of economic and social development at the current stage of economic transformation and is feasible to improve the system in which local governments take the lead in management of heritage resources on the basis of observing all the laws, regulations and principles for heritage conservation. Provincial governments can set up bodies to coordinate and guide conservation and management work.

（3）Manage heritage at higher levels

In order to generally improve the management of world heritage sites, the responsible administrative bodies shall be put directly under the provincial or municipal governments. So the current situation, in which many world heritage sites are being managed by bodies under the county or township level, must be changed.

（4）Establish a scientific mechanism for communities to exercise management

Heritage sites are public resources that should be conserved mainly by the government. However, considering the limited government input, management branches (which could be a community management office) should be established in communities to help develop economy, solve problems, balance heritage conservation and community development, and involve resident in heritage conservation and tourism development.

4. 4. 3. 2　Strengthen safeguarding measures

（1）Accelerate to promulgate the law of world heritage conservation in China

This legislation shall be made to define the legal status of world cultural heritage, basic principles for its conservation, and the duties and tasks of bodies responsible for its management.

（2）Formulate and modify as needed plans for the conservation of world cultural heritage sites

There had already been conservation plans for most of China's world cultural heritage sites when they nominated for inscription on the World Heritage List. At present, what is urgently needed is master plans for the conservation of the Great Wall, Imperial Tombs of the Ming and Qing Dynasties and some other heritage sites that are located across several provinces or municipalities, and some plans need to be modified as needed. However, modification to any conservation plans must be made in strict accordance with the law because these plans are protected by the law and are binding rules that must be followed in the management of corresponding heritage sites. No unauthorized demolition or repair of existing buildings or construction of new ones can be allowed in conservation and buffer zones.

（3）Establish a nationwide monitoring and inspection system for the conservation of world cultural heritage

An examining and supervisory system can be established to monitor and inspect regularly or randomly the conservation of world cultural heritage, and an expert advisory system is also helpful. All problems and hazards in heritage conservation and management must be sorted out carefully, analyzed and solved promptly. Any violation of laws or regulations or neglect or dereliction of duty causing damage to the heritage must be investigated, and responsible departments and persons must be held accountable. In addition, the heritage conservation and management work must be put under supervision by the general public.

（4）Establish a sound mechanism for public participation to strengthen public supervision

Public supervision is favorable for the conservation and management of heritage sites, so a sound mechanism shall be established to get more people to supervise the conservation and management work.

Heritage authorities and communities can set up joint management committees in various forms to discuss development plans, handle civil and economic disputes between heritage sites and communities, and educate the general public about the importance of protecting the ecological environment. Committees shall be composed of personnel from the community management office, villagers' committee members, clan chiefs, religious leaders, and other respected residents. Various measures can be taken to integrate heritage sites with communities around it so that they can complement each other in harmony.

（Written by Hua Fang, Yang Xiaoru, Zhang Qian）